*The*
# UNIVERSITY
## OF ILLINOIS
### 1894–1904

*The*
# UNIVERSITY OF ILLINOIS
## 1894–1904

*The Shaping of the University*

WINTON U. SOLBERG

UNIVERSITY OF ILLINOIS PRESS
URBANA AND CHICAGO

Publication of this work has been supported by grants from the
University of Illinois President's Office and from the Oliver M.
Dickerson Fund, which was established by Mr. Dickerson (Ph.D.,
Illinois, 1906) to enable the publication of selected works in
American history, designated by the executive committee of the
Department of History of the University of Illinois at Urbana-
Champaign.

Library of Congress Cataloging-in-Publication Data

Solberg, Winton U., 1922–
    The University of Illinois, 1894–1904 : the shaping of the
    university / Winton U. Solberg.
        p.  cm.
    Includes bibliographical references (p. ) and index.
    ISBN 0-252-02579-2 (cloth : alk. paper)
    1. University of Illinois (Urbana-Champaign campus)--History.
I. Title

LD2379.S64 2000
378.773'66—dc21
                                                    99-054726

C  5  4  3  2  1

*To Robert W. Tomilson*

# CONTENTS

## Part III

## Student Life and Culture

## Part IV

## Poised for Take-off

*Illustrations follow pages 30, 150, and 320*

# PREFACE

The American university is among the nation's most influential intellectual and cultural institutions. To understand our national heritage, we need university histories that tell the stories of of the leading participants in the academic enterprise, drawing on primary sources. The truth is in the details seen in broad perspective and intelligently interpreted.

In a previous volume, *The University of Illinois, 1867–1894: An Intellectual and Cultural History* (Urbana, 1968), I traced the early development of what began as a land-grant institution. The present book carries the story forward during the critical years of educational reconstruction when the college gave way to the university as the paradigm in American higher education.

As related in Part I, in the early 1890s the trustees began a search for a new president in an effort to implement their goal of upgrading the still fledgling establishment. After a long search they chose Andrew S. Draper, a man with no college or university experience, who had earned a reputation as a school administrator. John P. Altgeld, the first Democrat elected governor since the University opened, took office in 1893, and he vigorously supported efforts to make the public institution a complete university worthy of the people of Illinois.

Part II is based on the assumption that what young people study both reflects contemporary ideals and goes far toward shaping society in later years. Accordingly, the composition of the faculty and the courses taught receive considerable attention, along with the four undergraduate colleges, new schools of music and library science, the departments of military science and physical training, a fledgling graduate school, and professional schools in Urbana and Chicago. Draper initiated few if any of these advances. And neither he nor the trustees redeemed their pledge to expand and improve the study of the humanities.

Part III demonstrates that much of what students learn during their collegiate years results from their own efforts. Often, however, the authorities influenced students' choices, as was the case in forging common bonds of union that united the University community and in the ways in which Draper and the faculty cared for and disciplined students. The sections on hazing and on religion deal with topics rarely treated in any detail in university historics. The literary societies and the intercollegiate debate society were testimonials to the inquiring minds of the students. Fraternities soon eclipsed the literary societies, however, and the social life of students revealed a split between Greeks and "barbarians." This inquiry also shows how the presence of fraternities and the rise of intercollegiate football changed the character of the University.

Part IV describes President Draper's sudden resignation, an event that precipitated the final round in the endless struggle between Draper and the deans over who had power to determine University policy. The deans had sought a new course for the institution and believed Draper unfit for office; at his resignation they were free to pursue a new conception of the institution.

By 1904 the school possessed the structure but not the spirit of a university. It was devoted to teaching undergraduates but had not yet assumed a commitment to advancing knowledge by research and the training of graduate students. And yet the University was poised for take-off under a new leader, a promise that would be fulfilled in subsequent administrations and will be explored in the next volume of the University's history.

# ACKNOWLEDGMENTS

A substantial book like the present one is in large measure a collaborative enterprise. Now that it is finished, I am pleased to acknowledge those who have aided me in completing this study.

Over several years the Research Board of the University of Illinois at Champaign-Urbana provided funds that made it possible to employ research assistants. On this volume Michael F. Conlin, James M. Cornelius, and Robert W. Tomilson served faithfully and cheerfully in this capacity.

This history draws on a massive quantity of primary sources in the University of Illinois Archives. At every stage of my research, university archivists Maynard J. Brichford and more recently William J. Maher assisted in unearthing the treasures they manage. I have also relied on Elizabeth R. Cardman, an assistant archivist, and on the ever-ready Robert T. Chapel.

Colleagues to whom I am indebted for reading and commenting on various portions of the manuscript are as follows: James M. Cornelius, Chapters 1–4, 6, parts of 7, 8, and 12, and 19; Bruce H. Mainous, James M. McGlathery, Charles C. Stewart, and Emile J. Talbot, Chapter 3; Elizabeth P. Rogers and Robert L. Switzer, chemistry in Chapter 4; Richard Hay, geology in Chapter 4; Denton E. Alexander, Chapter 5; Michael F. Conlin, Chapter 6; Patricia F. Stenstrom and Elizabeth R. Cardman, the Library School in Chapter 7; Phyllis W. Danner, the School of Music in Chapter 7, and Chapters 11 and 14; John E. Cribbet, the late George T. Frampton, and Victor J. Stone, the College of Law in Chapter 9; Robert L. Adelsperger, Chapter 10; Nicholas Temperley, Chapter 14; and John Straw, Chapter 15.

Elizabeth G. Dulany, associate director emeritus of the University of Illinois Press, continues to brighten all my dealings with the press. Copenhaver Cumpston was especially helpful with the selection of illustrations and the graphic design. Willis G. Regier, who took over as director of the press after I had submitted my manuscript, has happily supported publication of this history. Two outside readers who evaluated my manuscript for the press made valuable comments. One of them was especially helpful in resolving questions as to how much context and detail to include. I am pleased to thank Marjorie Pannell for her careful and intelligent copyediting of my manuscript and Janet Greenwood for her efficient editorial direction.

For a subvention that made possible the publication of this volume, I am deeply grateful to the Department of History and its Dickerson Fund, and to the Office of President James Stukel of the University of Illinois.

# SOURCES AND
# ABBREVIATIONS

This study is based largely on primary sources in the Archives of the University of Illinois, housed in the University Library in Champaign-Urbana. It also draws on a large number of secondary works, which are cited in the notes. The materials used do not lend themselves to a conventional bibliography.

The University of Illinois has attracted relatively little attention from historians. The first history of the institution was Allan Nevins's *Illinois* (New York: Oxford University Press, 1917). Nevins (A.B., 1912, A.M., 1913) was a journalist in New York City when he wrote this book, and he relied heavily on information supplied by faculty and former students. At the instigation of President Edmund J. James, Burt E. Powell published the large *Semi-Centennial History of the University of Illinois*, vol. 1, *The Movement for Industrial Education and the Establishment of the University, 1840–1870* (Urbana: University of Illinois, 1918), which advances the untenable thesis that the Morrill Act resulted from an alliance between two adopted sons of Illinois—Jonathan Baldwin Turner and President Abraham Lincoln. Carl Stephens (A.B., 1912), executive director of the University of Illinois Alumni Association and University Historian (1943–50), wrote "The University of Illinois: A History, 1867–1947" (RS 26/1/21). *Illini Years, 1868–1950: A Picture History of the University of Illinois* (Urbana: University of Illinois Press, 1950), is based on Stephens's manuscript.

In the interest of limiting the documentation in the present book, I do not provide references for biographical information readily available in standard reference works, for courses of study and curricular matters easily found in annual catalogs, and for many items that can be readily found in the official records of the Board of Trustees.

Even so, the documentation is extensive because scholarly obligations require me to furnish evidence for my conclusions, and readers will find the notes helpful in pursuing points of interest. The following abbreviations relate to published works and to frequently cited Records Series in the Archives.

## PUBLICATIONS

*Alumni Record* The *Semi-Centennial Alumni Record of the University of Illinois,* ed. Franklin W. Scott. [Urbana]: University of Illinois, 1918.

*Catalogue* University of Illinois, *Catalogue* (also called the *Catalog;* more rarely, the *Register*). Citations give the title and year. The material discussed can easily be located in these publications.

*00th Report* University of Illinois, *00th Report of the Board of Trustees of the University of Illinois.* Citations give the number of the report in Arabic numerals, the year of publication in parentheses, and page references: e.g., *18th Report* (1896), 281.

Solberg Winton U. Solberg, *The University of Illinois, 1867–1894: An Intellectual and Cultural History.* Urbana: University of Illinois Press, 1968.

## RECORDS SERIES

| | |
|---|---|
| 2/4/1 | Andrew S. Draper General Correspondence |
| 2/4/2 | Andrew S. Draper Faculty Correspondence |
| 2/4/3 | Andrew S. Draper Letterbooks |
| 2/4/4 | Andrew S. Draper Subject File |
| 2/4/5 | Andrew S. Draper Personal Letters |
| 2/4/10 | Andrew S. Draper General Scrapbooks |
| 2/5/1 | Edmund J. James Personal Correspondence |
| 2/5/3 | Edmund J. James General Correspondence |
| 2/5/6 | Edmund J. James Faculty Correspondence |
| 2/5/15 | Staff Appointments File |
| 3/1/1 | Council of Administration Minutes |
| 4/1/1 | Faculty Record |
| 4/2/1 | Senate Minutes |
| 8/1/1 | Eugene Davenport Letterbooks |
| 8/1/5 | Agriculture Administration File |
| 8/1/21 | Eugene Davenport Papers |

| | |
|---|---|
| 11/1/1 | Engineering Dean's Office |
| 15/1/2 | College of Science Letterbooks |
| 15/1/3 | College of Science Correspondence |
| 15/1/4 | College of Literature and Arts Letterbooks |
| 15/1/6 | College of Science and College of Literature and Arts Minute-books, 1878–1913 |
| 15/1/11 | Literature and Arts Annual Reports |
| 15/1/13 | College of Science Annual Reports |
| 15/4/1 | Botany: Departmental Correspondence |
| 26/1/20 | Carl Stephens Papers |
| 26/4/1 | Alumni Morgue |
| 52/1/1 | College of Physicians and Surgeons Faculty Minutes |
| 52/1/2 | College of Physicians and Surgeons Executive Faculty Minutes |

# PART I

# THE SETTING

# CHAPTER 1

# A New Era

The University of Illinois was a product of the 1862 Morrill Land Grant Act, which provided states the means to establish new types of schools of the higher grade. The University was chartered in 1867 and began operations a year later. Under the provisions of the law, the University was obligated to emphasize industrial education without excluding other scientific and classical studies. The institution grew at a time when American higher education was undergoing a radical transformation, and adjusting to the new conditions was difficult. For years the study of engineering flourished, agriculture languished, and the liberal arts and sciences made only a decent showing.

By 1891 the University was at a crucial stage in its development. The first two regents (presidents) had charted dissimilar courses, and for nearly a quarter of a century the school found it difficult to discover its own identity. In 1885, in an attempt to shed the handicap associated with the original name of Illinois Industrial University, which many interpreted to mean either a reformatory or a charitable institution in which compulsory manual labor figured prominently, the name had been changed to University of Illinois. Two years later the Alumni Association spearheaded the enactment of a law that altered the method of choosing members of the Board of Trustees from appointment by the governor to election by the voters, a reform designed to give alumni a large voice in the governing body. Selim H. Peabody, who became regent in 1880, had the misfortune to serve during the troubled years of transition. On 9 June 1891 the trustees divided five to five on his reelection, and the next day Peabody submitted his resignation, to take effect on 1 September.

Thomas J. Burrill, the senior faculty member, served as acting regent for the next three years, during which time the University became open to fresh ideas. Despite substantial changes, the institution still lacked a clear sense of direction and was little understood by the people of Illinois. Meanwhile, the reconstruction that would replace the college with the university as the paradigm of American higher education was proceeding apace. A landmark in that advance was the formation in 1900 of the Association of American Universities (AAU) by several of the nation's leading universities. The AAU's stated objectives were to establish greater uniformity in Ph.D. requirements, achieve foreign recognition of the American doctorate, and bolster the standards of the weaker American universities. One of the latter, Illinois needed substantial reform before it would qualify for membership in the AAU.[1]

## SELECTING A PRESIDENT

Selim Peabody's management had given the University of Illinois a poor reputation. At the time of his resignation, many colleges were looking for a new president, and members of the board were not united on the qualities desired in a candidate. Several thought that the University's technical departments were strong enough to take care of themselves and that the "cultural" side needed emphasis. All agreed in favoring someone with "business capacity" rather than clerical or academic credentials. Their ideal candidate was a man of affairs, a moral guide, an administrator and persuasive orator, an educational leader versed in practical politics, a person with a national reputation for something accomplished, and not too far advanced in years. The trustees hoped to attract this paragon to settle on the flat, treeless, swampy prairie for about $4,000 a year.[2]

On 10 June 1891 the governing board directed its Committee on Instruction and two additional trustees to make a diligent search for a suitable man for the office. The members of the search committee were the three schoolmen on the Committee on Instruction—Francis M. McKay (class of 1881), the principal of Douglas School in Chicago; George R. Shawhan (class of 1875), superintendent of schools in Champaign County; and Henry Raab, state superintendent of public instruction and an ex-officio member of the board—along with Emory Cobb, a banker and farmer from Kankakee, and Nelson W. Graham, a Carbondale businessman and president of the board. The composition of the committee indicates that the trustees thought in terms of the University's relation to the public schools, not of its potential to advance the frontiers of knowledge.

In their hunger for a "big name" the search committee made offers to several disparate types. In 1891 McKay invited John Fiske, a noted historian and popularizer of Darwinism who made his home in the shadow of Harvard University, to take the position, informing him that the trustees would go as high as $10,000 a year. Fiske declined, saying this was much less than he earned by his literary work.[3]

The trustees did not consult the faculty, and they ignored a faculty proposal to consider Andrew Sloan Draper.[4] In the spring of 1892 McKay and Graham undertook an inspection trip in the East to interview prospective candidates, starting with Professor Woodrow Wilson at Princeton. Wilson's letters illuminate the selection process and the aspirations of the board.[5] After meeting with Wilson at Princeton, on 26 April McKay offered to recommend him at a salary of $6,000. With proper management, McKay wrote to Wilson, Illinois could in a few years be made one of the leading state universities in the land. Admitting that the work done so far had been principally technical and agricultural, the trustees wished to develop the literary side generously "under the guidance of some man of Eastern training and traditions."[6]

Wilson seriously considered the offer, but he feared that the position would prevent him from original literary work. So he consulted friends. Cyrus Hall McCormick of Chicago, a Princeton trustee, advised against acceptance. "The University of Illinois has very little standing in this Community," he wrote. "It is regarded as only a high school, and a very ordinary one at that."[7] Wilson's wife urged careful weighing of the offer. But Wilson hesitated: the University depended on legislative grants that had to be renewed every two years, and his fundraising task would never be done. On 12 May Wilson informed McKay that he had initially been strongly inclined to accept, believing that the regency would call forth his best powers. Even the University's dependence on the legislature he managed to place in an attractive light, "for it aroused the latent politician within me." But he declined because his literary plans would always have to be subordinated to executive duties.[8]

Several other professors were suggested for the regency, including John T. Shaw, of Oberlin, Horatio S. White and Jeremiah W. Jenks, of Cornell University, Edmund J. James, of the University of Pennsylvania, and Melvil Dewey, of the New York State Library School in Albany. At least four candidates visited the University, among them Washington Gladden, a Congregational minister from Columbus, Ohio, who enjoyed a national reputation as a spokesman for the Social Gospel. In 1892 Gladden gave the commencement address at the University; shortly thereafter he was notified that he had been elected regent at a salary not exceeding $6,000 a year. He concluded that he would rather remain in Ohio.[9]

The search was still in progress in November, when elections for national and state office were held. The Republican party had dominated Illinois politics for thirty years, but in 1892 an insurgent Democratic party, led by John P. Altgeld, challenged it. Altgeld, a man of foreign birth and humble origins, was elected governor of Illinois not only as a Democrat but as a spokesman for economic and social change. He quickly carried out constructive measures. Viewing public education as the great hope of social democracy and justice, he spared no effort to improve the state's school system. He was instrumental in establishing normal schools at DeKalb and Charleston, and he gave the University heartier support than had any previous governor.[10]

The 1892 elections also returned a majority of Democrats to the Board of Trustees for the first time in the history of the University. On 13 December 1892, even before the new members were seated, the board unanimously resolved "that the University should be placed on a par with the best of the other state universities," and agreed to ask the General Assembly "for ample means to carry its purpose into effect."[11]

With the new board's emphasis on excellence in higher education rather than on the University's relationship to the public schools, the search for a regent took a new turn. Early in 1894 McKay's search committee, which had unsuccessfully sought a candidate for two and one-half years, was replaced by a committee chaired by James E. Armstrong (class of 1881), a Democrat and the principal of Englewood High School in Chicago. Armstrong thought the office demanded organizational and executive ability and a person who could attract legislative and public support for the University. On 26 February he wrote to ask Andrew S. Draper about his interest, adding that Draper's name had been suggested by faculty members earlier but had been dropped because Draper was said to be too much of a politician. Armstrong thought that Draper possessed the ability to make Illinois a great university: "everything seems ready for the master hand."[12]

In mid-March Armstrong, Burrill, and Graham interviewed Draper in Cleveland. On 12 April Draper visited the campus, and the next day he met the full board in Chicago. Toward the end of a special evening session the trustees called in Draper to discuss matters. Draper bargained hard. His salary in his two previous positions had been $5,000, but he insisted on as much as the University of Chicago paid its department heads—$7,000. He then withdrew from the deliberations, and the board unanimously elected him. The next day Graham offered Draper the position at $7,000.[13]

On 10 May Draper accepted. Although he agreed to go to Illinois, his heart remained in New York. "I do not think we shall remain there [in Illinois] more than from five to eight years," he wrote his mother. "It may lead to something in New York State again."[14] Draper viewed the presidency as an interlude in a New York–based career. While at Illinois he regularly spent his summers in New York state.

## "The Master Hand"

Draper was the very model of the self-made man. He was born on 21 June 1848 on a poor farm near Westford in Otsego County, New York, the first of four children. He attended a one-room rural school until 1855, when an accident disabled his father and the family moved to Albany, where they faced economic hardship. The boy continued his education in city schools while carrying a paper route, and with scholarship help he was able to attend Albany Academy for three years. After graduating in 1866 he taught school for more than two years, during which time he also worked as a salesman and collection agent for a large lumber firm. Wanting a better future, Draper and a cousin agreed to become law partners. In 1870 he entered Albany Law School, and upon graduating in 1871 he formed a partnership with his cousin in Albany.[15] The study of law for one year ended his formal education; he had no college or university experience.

Draper's legal practice was never large, but it afforded a modest living while he sought to rise in status by linking his ancestry to the New England Puritans, by assuming the dress and manner of a respectable middle-class professional man, and by becoming a leader in diverse organizations. In 1867 he had become active in the Independent Order of Good Templars, a temperance organization. Speaking to local lodges, he earned money and spread his name. In 1876 he was elected head of the Good Templars in the state, a post he held until 1881.

Draper had a flair for politics, and for years he took an active part in Republican party affairs. From 1879 to 1881 he served on Albany's Board of Public Instruction, and in 1880 he won election to the New York Assembly as a candidate of Roscoe Conkling's political machine; he gained prominence in his term as a state legislator but was defeated for reelection. As chairman from 1880 to 1883 of the Albany County Republican Committee and as a member in 1883 of the Republican State Committee, he enjoyed considerable patronage power. In 1884, as a delegate to the Republican national convention, he supported Chester A. Arthur against James G. Blaine for president. After Blaine was nominated, Draper managed his campaign in New York.

When Blaine lost to Cleveland, Draper damned partisan politics as "treacherous business" and vowed to return to his law practice.[16] But President Arthur rewarded his campaign work by appointing him to the United States Court of Alabama Claims. He took his seat as a federal judge in 1885 and served a year. Having decided to abandon politics, and not eager to return to the law, Draper sought a new profession. He aspired to become the state superintendent of public instruction. The office was to be filled by a joint ballot of the legislature, Republican in both branches. Despite the opposition of New York schoolmen, who objected to his political involvement and lack of experience, Draper obtained the party's backing and won.

The state's jurisdiction over education was divided between the Board of Regents of the University of the State of New York and the Department of Public Instruction. The regents oversaw higher education, whereas the department regulated the state's secondary schools. Both bodies claimed control over the public high schools, but the regents maintained indirect authority over them through their influence on the education of public school teachers. Draper, an aggressive, fearless, and forceful superintendent, turned his back on politics and operated his office on the basis of merit. He advanced the interests of his department by his strong advocacy of greater centralization in public school administration. He strengthened teacher training in normal schools controlled by his department, reorganized teachers' institutes, and assumed new power over the certification and licensing of teachers. Draper gained the support of the New York State Teachers' Association by playing on their desire for status and professional recognition, and his growing reputation led to his election as president (1889–90) of the Department of Superintendence of the National Education Association, in some ways the most influential of that association's departments. In 1892, however, the Democrats gained control of the legislature and replaced Draper with their own man.

By now Draper's heart was in educational work, and he was rescued by events in Cleveland, where a broad municipal reform movement had led to a demand for reform of the public schools. The city established a school organization with an elected school council, an elected school director, who was to be the executive officer of the council and the business manager of the schools, and an appointed school superintendent, who was to have dominant power over school affairs, including the hiring and firing of teachers. The position of superintendent appealed to Draper, and he was confident that he could enhance his reputation by reforming a large public school system. He accepted the post for one year, later agreeing to stay a second year. His success in Cleveland led the National Educational Association to elect him to its Committee of Fifteen on Elementary Education. The Illinois offer came as Draper's work in Cleveland was ending and no position was available in New York to advance his career.

Draper had risen to national prominence largely by force of character. A representative example of the Horatio Alger success story, he was an imposing man who dressed well and carried himself erectly. He was blessed with abundant common sense. Aggressive, outspoken, and gruff, he had strong convictions and was capable of acting decisively on them. When the trustees interviewed Draper, "his big personality and his ideas of how he thought the University should be run, so impressed the old men on the board that they were willing to allow him to set his own terms."[17]

An indomitable will made Draper determined to succeed. He always prepared, and well in advance. He was open and direct, even blunt, and autocratic in the extreme. He had a military attitude toward members of the faculty,
whom he regarded not as associates but as inferiors to command, even in the
details of their own field.[18]

Draper's mind was formed by the time he became president of the University. He had little interest in philosophical speculations or in fine distinctions. Although he wrote clearly and forcefully, his prose could be an odd mixture of grandiloquence and commonplaces. He was not an original thinker,
and educational administration was not conducive to wide reading or deep
learning. His reading was limited to biography and history; he claimed to know
John Fiske's books on American history better than he knew the Bible.

Draper shared the mental outlook of most Protestant, upper-middle-class
white men in the Northeast at the time.[19] He subscribed to the prevalent idea
of Anglo-Saxon supremacy, which held that the American nation, settled largely by people from northwestern Europe and Great Britain, had a unique
capacity for self-government and a civilizing mission in the world. The creed
called for cultural assimilation rather than cultural pluralism. "The area of enlargement of Saxon influence," he said in an address to graduating students, "is
but a part of the plan of the Almighty for breaking down barbarism and for the
uplifting and regeneration of the savage world."[20] His book *The Rescue of Cuba*
(1899) extolled the war with Spain as a campaign for liberty, humanity, justice, and the spread of Protestantism and democracy.

Draper's early years in educational administration came at a time of acute
social crisis generated by the growth of industrialism and urbanism. Draper
feared the social instability arising out of conflict between labor and capital
and out of incipient socialism and anarchism. His remedy for social discontent was double-pronged. First, he proposed that political and other civil institutions adopt the organizational ideas advocated by civil service enthusiasts
and by American corporate business. Second, he urged centralized administration, convinced that government was a powerful force in shaping society.
His exemplar was the Republican party, which offered a strong central government, sound economic policies, and moral leadership.

Within this framework, Draper saw the public school as a near panacea for
the nation's social, political, and economic problems. The public school was the
best agency available for creating a cohesive and stable social order, and professionals who were expert in educational matters, efficient, and ethical were
essential to administer the schools.

Draper viewed centralization as essential to educational administration.
School bureaucrats needed the largest freedom in order to operate effectively.
Thus it was necessary to discriminate between legislative and executive action
in administering schools. Governing boards should be legislative bodies, with

no executive functions. Boards legislate; individuals execute. Teachers may well have a voice in determining educational policies of their institutions, Draper believed, but they did not have to be consulted about, and should have no part in, managing the schools.

Draper was a strong supporter of the state university. Although Draper's knowledge of American education was often faulty and stongly partisan, he made a convincing case for a leadership role of universities in his many writings on the subject. In his view, the American nation, with its democratic purpose, its ideals of freedom and equality, and its mixture of nearly all kinds of people in the world, had necessitated the creation of a distinctively American university. Our universities had to appeal to a wider constituency than European universities, he declared, and they had to devote themselves to public service. The newer western states had responded to the need for change more quickly and thoroughly than had the older eastern states. The state universities, an integral part of the public school system in their states, gave a decisive trend to the future of American education.[21]

Draper's letter of acceptance provided clues to what lay ahead. A state university, the appropriate head of the state school system, "should build for classical culture ... but it should not spend too much time in clearing up the involved subtilities of the dead past or of fathoming the depths of purely philosophical speculation." Public moneys should go into educational work that most directly affected the life of the people. A state university should engage in scientific research to the end that it might "disseminate the latest scientific information upon the employment of the people." The university "should train for manly and womanly character, for intellectual power and versatility, and for influence upon and success in the practical affairs of life." Draper had been selected because he had experience in "organizing and articulating public educational work" and because of the views he subscribed to. The terms of his employment afforded a broad opportunity for marked success or conspicuous failure.[22]


## PRESIDENT DRAPER TAKES CHARGE

Draper assumed his duties on 1 August 1894. The Board of Trustees held a special meeting that day. Governor Altgeld, an ex-officio member, came to meet Draper. These two men took the measure of each other. Altgeld convinced Draper of his interest in the University and that they could work together. He complained about the Republicans' lack of support for and bad management of the University, and spoke of things he wanted done. He wanted more buildings, more teachers, more students, "more carrying of liberal learning to all the people and all of the interests of the State, and much more money to do things with." Finding it "a little surprising to hear a live governor talk like that," Draper said that one had to ignore all political partisanship to make substantial headway in building a real university. Altgeld agreed; he would ask nothing of Draper in the special interest of the Democratic party, and he would personally and officially respond so far as he properly could to all of Draper's requests in the interests of a greater university.[23] At this meeting the board changed Draper's title from regent to president. No head of a university could have had a better first day on the job.

Altgeld was one of the few governors of Illinois to take a sincere interest in higher education. Self-educated, he identified with the less privileged and believed that an active government was needed to advance human welfare. He recognized that several states in the Midwest were ahead of Illinois in developing their universities—he cited Michigan, Wisconsin, Missouri, and Iowa—and that thousands of Illinois youths went to neighboring states or the East for the education they should have been able to get at home. Altgeld was eager to give Illinois an educational institution of which all would feel proud; the many private colleges in Illinois could not do the job.[24]

On 15 November 1894, speaking at Draper's inauguration, Altgeld said that the University was ready to embark on a vigorous manhood. The time had come to enlarge its work and bring it to the attention of the people. The state of Illinois led all others in "material grandeur," or natural wealth, and it had to have an educational institution on the same plane of greatness. The University needed to put in charge of this work a man "who was more than a scholar, more than an educator, more even than a general; a man who, while possessing all of these qualifications, was also thoroughly imbued with the spirit of the age, with a sense of the needs of our people; a man who was not only progressive, but aggressive." In Draper, Altgeld said, "we believe we have found that man."[25]

Draper's inaugural address was a bundle of platitudes. The University, he said, needed to cultivate both the educational forces that go toward the economic side of life and those that go toward the making of men. It needed to increase its facilities and do more in all directions. Illinois, "among the very first of the great states in wealth and energy and earning power," was able to do well whatever it was well to do. The University should fix and enforce the minimum standards of qualifications for admission to the learned professions and for admission to the civil service of state and local governments, it should support the interests of education in the public penal and charitable institutions of the state, it should render public service by scientific examinations of matters closely related to the life of the people, and it should aid the public libraries. The University was bound to "prosecute all lines of research and give to the world the results of its experimentations and investigations." In addition, the University should encourage all other universities, and it should "articulate sharply with the public school system." Illinois, Draper reminded his audience, had lagged behind neighboring states in founding a public university. Now it should forge ahead.[26]

Altgeld was as good as his word. In January 1895, speaking to the General Assembly, he said that the people of Illinois knew scarcely anything about the University. Inasmuch as Illinois was now one of the wealthiest and greatest states on the globe, it should have one of the greatest educational institutions. He proposed building on the solid foundations already laid to erect a complete university, and urged upon lawmakers a liberal policy toward the University.[27]

## DRAPER AND THE BOARD OF TRUSTEES

In Illinois's state university, relations between the president and the Board of Trustees—often contrary, always sensitive—were much influenced by state politics. The president was the agent of the board, and the quality of the board was vital to the welfare of the University. Allegedly, partisan politics rarely intruded into board affairs. But members were chosen by the political process. Nine were elected to the board, and the state's governor, the president of the State Board of Agriculture, and the state superintendent of public instruction were ex-officio members. The elected members were usually swept into office by the victorious political party for a six-year term. The president of the board was elected by board members at the annual March meeting. These contests were often spirited and close. In March 1895, for example, it took a two-to-one Democratic majority twelve ballots to elect a Democrat president of the board. A year later a Democrat was elected president by a five-to-four vote.

Draper served under seven presidents of the board. Nelson W. Graham (b. 1815), a transplanted Virginian and Carbondale businessman, held the office from 1893 to 1896. His successor was James E. Armstrong (b. 1855), class of 1881, a Democrat and principal of a Chicago high school who also dabbled in law and farming. Francis M. McKay (b. 1851), also class of 1881 and a teacher in Chicago, was a Republican. First elected to the board in 1886, he lost a reelection bid in 1894 but won a second term in 1896. He became president by acclamation in 1897 and was elected again in 1898. Alexander McLean (b. 1833), a native of Glasgow, Scotland, was a resident of Macomb, a real estate agent, and secretary of two state fraternal organizations. A Republican active in local politics, he was appointed to the board in 1876 and was later elected to three consecutive terms, serving as a trustee from 1876 to 1901, the longest continuous membership on the board. He served as president from 1899 to 1900. Thomas J. Smith (b. 1836), a Republican lawyer from

Champaign, served as president for one year. Augustus F. Nightingale (b. 1843), a Massachusetts native who held bachelor's and master's degrees from Wesleyan University in Connecticut and a doctorate from Upper Iowa University, was a Republican and an educator. He had taught at the college level and served as superintendent of schools in Omaha before becoming assistant superintendent of public schools in Chicago and later superintendent of Cook County schools. He was elected in 1898. Frederic L. Hatch (b. 1848), a cattle and hog breeder from Spring Grove and a Republican, was first elected a trustee in 1898, then served as president from 1903 to 1905.

Three others were prominent during Draper's presidency. Samuel A. Bullard (b. 1853), of Springfield, who graduated from the University with a degree in architecture in 1878, was a member of the board from 1889 to 1907. A Republican, he served as president of the board from 1891 to 1893. Richard P. Morgan (b. 1828), a native of Massachusetts, a Democrat, and a distinguished civil engineer from Dwight, become a trustee in 1891 and served one term. Napoleon B. Morrison (b. 1824), a Vermont native, was for many years a civil engineer before moving to Illinois in 1862. He settled in Odin, where he engaged in mercantile business, became the owner-operator of a coal mine, and took a strong interest in agriculture and stock raising. In 1892 the Democratic victory catapulted Colonel Morrison into office.

Women were gaining prominence in public affairs in the 1890s, and the first women to hold statewide public office in Illinois were University trustees.[28] Dr. Julia Holmes Smith (b. 1839) was the pioneer. Born in Savannah, Georgia, she was educated by tutors and graduated from the Springler Institute in New York in 1857. After her husband died, in 1864, she became the drama critic of the *New Orleans Picayune*. In 1872 she married Sabin Smith and moved to Boston, where she studied at the Boston University School of Medicine. In 1876 the couple moved to Chicago, and a year later she graduated from the Homeopathic Medical College. As Dr. Holmes and Mrs. Smith, she won distinction in many fields. She conducted a successful medical practice until the age of seventy-two, was active in homeopathic societies, and served for three years as dean of the National Medical College. Her later literary interests focused on medical topics. In 1886 the Illinois Women's Press Association was founded in her home. She played an important part in the Illinois Equal Suffrage Association and the Political Equity League. With the women's club movement sweeping the country, Julia Holmes Smith was a member of the Fortnightly Club, a group of socially prominent Chicago women devoted to self-improvement who organized in 1873. Many of these lightseekers were prominent in forming the Woman's Club in 1876, which stressed practical work related to the interests of women. Mrs. Smith served as president of the Woman's Club from 1879 to 1881. She also served on the board of directors of the Congress of Women of the World's Columbian Exposition. In 1894

Dr. Smith ran unsuccessfully as a candidate for trustee on the Democratic ticket. In February 1895, when John H. Bryant resigned from the board, Governor Altgeld appointed her in his place.

Lucy L. Coues Flower officially became a trustee a month later. An adopted child of a prominent New England family, she was born in 1838, perhaps in Boston; was educated in the Portsmouth, New Hampshire, schools; and attended the Packer Collegiate Institute, in Brooklyn. After working briefly in the U.S. Patent Office, she moved to Madison, Wisconsin, where she embarked on a career in education as a schoolteacher. In 1862 she married James M. Flower, an attorney. The couple had three children by 1873, when they moved to Chicago, where her husband became a successful lawyer and an influential Republican and Mrs. Flower became prominent for her charitable, educational, and welfare work. A member of the Fortnightly Club, she was at heart an activist who threw herself into the activities of philanthropic and reform organizations, and especially the Woman's Club, which she served as president. She helped guide the destinies of the Chicago Nursery and Half-Orphan Asylum, the Lake Geneva Fresh Air Association, and Hull House. She was instrumental in establishing Juvenile Court, the first of its kind in the nation, and during the World's Columbian Exposition was active in the affairs of the World's Congress Auxiliary. Together with Frances Willard she formed the Chicago Women's League, a coalition of women's organizations devoted to social betterment. In 1889 she lobbied to get a woman on the Chicago Board of Education, and two years later she was the second woman appointed to the post.

In 1894 the Democratic mayor refused to reappoint her, allegedly because she was a Republican and a woman. Infuriated by the decision, Republican women made her their candidate for trustee. In Illinois at the time women could vote only in elections to school boards. Flower and Smith were slated by their respective parties. Both women were supremely qualified as trustees, wrote the Democratic *Chicago Herald*, which added that the contest was materially simplified by the fact that there was no such thing as the University of Illinois, never had been, and, with the many private universities in Chicago, it was not likely that there ever would be. "All the duties to be performed consist of looking over the records of a bucolic school in the interior and awarding diplomas of husbandry to graduates thereof at stated intervals." In the general election the Republicans won, with Flower garnering more votes than either McLean or Bullard.[29]

Lucy Flower and Julia Holmes Smith were forerunners of a new era for women in Illinois politics. Exemplars of progressive womanhood, they both cared about gender issues and worked hard to advance women's welfare. By 1896 all the political parties felt obligated to nominate women as trustees, and in that year eleven of eighteen candidates for the board were women.

The Democrats again nominated Julia Holmes Smith; the Republicans nominated Mary Turner Carriel, of Jacksonville. Born in 1845, Carriel earned a bachelor's degree from Jacksonville Presbyterian Academy, married Dr. Henry F. Carriel, the administrator of the Illinois Hospital for the Insane, and had four children. She took a prominent part in the historical society and the suffrage league of Morgan County, the Sorosis chapter in Jacksonville, and other women's organizations but was not active politically. Since she was the daughter of Jonathan Baldwin Turner, a prime mover in founding the University, Republican party leaders hoped to trade on her name. Carriel received the largest vote of the three Republican candidates.

In 1898 the Democrats again nominated Julia Holmes Smith, while Republicans named Alice Asbury Abbott. A native of Quincy, Alice Asbury was educated in a private school. In 1871 she married Abial R. Abbott; the couple had two daughters and lived in Chicago, where Mrs. Abbott edited a science journal and was a member of both the Fortnightly Club and the Woman's Club. In 1892 she gained prominence by publishing an incomplete and unauthorized English translation of Baroness Bertha von Suttner's *Die Waffen Nieder* (Lay Down Your Arms; 1889), a pacifist book that was enormously popular in Europe and was credited with influencing the establishment of the Nobel Peace Price, which the baroness was awarded in 1905. In 1894 Abbott helped organize women to elect Lucy Flower, whom she supported as a Republican, not as a woman. Two years later, after John R. Tanner was elected governor on the Republican ticket, Abbott aligned herself with Tanner, and in 1898 he enlisted the Women's Relief Corps of Illinois to secure her nomination as a trustee. Abbott won an office but trailed the Republican men on the ticket.

In 1900 Lucy Flower richly deserved a second term. She was enormously popular with the women of Chicago and the Illinois Federation of Woman's Clubs, but she had offended the Cook County Women's Republican Club by favoring nonpartisan school boards, and she had earned the enmity of Governor Tanner by criticizing him for dismissing Florence Kelley as state factory inspector and by being an independent-minded woman. So Tanner instructed his lieutenants—Mrs. Abbott was chair of the Illinois Women's Republican Committee—to bring about her defeat, and Republican women enlisted the aid of the Women's Relief Corps, the auxiliary of the Grand Army of the Republic, to rebuff Flower. Meeting in Jacksonville, the state convention of the Women's Relief Corps endorsed Carrie T. Alexander of Belleville, and her nomination was assured before the Republican Women's Convention met in Peoria shortly thereafter. The *Chicago Tribune* reported that Flower would be nominated from the floor of the Republican state convention the next day, but the convention was a riotous affair that buried the Tanner machine, and late at night, after most delegates had left the hall, Alexander was shouted in.

A product of Tanner's machine, Carrie Alexander (née Thomas) lacked many qualifications for the position of trustee. Born in Belleville, she had attended the public schools, graduated from Monticello Seminary, and taught school before marrying Henry A. Alexander. When he died ten months later, she became the owner of the Belleville Citizens Street Railway. She identified herself with charitable and educational projects and in 1898–99 served as state president of the Women's Relief Corps. Since Republicans could not stress Alexander's merits, they argued that she gave the ticket sectional balance. In the election she trailed the male Republican candidates for trustee. The Democrats slated Julia Holmes Smith, who led her defeated ticket in the race.[30]

In 1900 Laura B. Evans (b. 1860) withdrew as a candidate for trustee after the Women's Relief Corps slated Alexander, but two years later she was elected on the Republican ticket.[31] A native of Weston, Missouri, Evans graduated from high school and a seminary in Waynesville, Illinois, married an accountant, and was a mother and homemaker in Taylorville. She was president of the board of the public library and a local leader in educational and cultural life and women's activities. In all likelihood her affiliation with the Women's Relief Corps was instrumental in securing her nomination.

Lucy Flower was the most interesting, most remarkable, and perhaps the most influential trustee during her time on the board. She enjoyed cordial relations with Draper, and on most issues they agreed, though not always to the advantage of the University.

Flower's letters to Draper are valuable for their comments on state politics and their incisive evaluations of trustees. In 1898 she declared, "we have too few strong men." Nightingale was too busy to give time to University matters; he should not have taken a position for which he had no time. "What is the matter with Mr. Hatch?" she inquired. Abbott told Flower that she was writing out a course of reading for Hatch. "He means all right," Flower wrote, "but his vision is extremely limited." Flower was "dreadfully disappointed in Carriel." Appealing to Carriel's regard for her father, Abbott had acquired a very strong influence over Carriel. Flower expected Abbott but not Carriel to act without thinking. Yet Carriel acted from impulse and was not likely "to be of force."[32]

Some evidence indicates that Draper quietly promoted able individuals of both major parties for nomination as trustees. John Farson, a Chicago banker and lawyer who had attended the University from 1874 to 1876, was perhaps one. But he believed that he could be of more service to Draper and the University off rather than on the board. Farson worked behind the scenes to get Chicago newspapers to publicize the University, to obtain strong candidates as trustees—he disliked the idea of another schoolteacher, and thought that two ladies were quite enough—and to secure support for the University in Springfield.[33]

## The Problem of Authority

When Draper took office, he was filled with the idea that he could dictate the policy of the University.[34] His authority as president was large but not clearly defined. He had to work with a governing board and with deans and faculty members who were experts in their own subject areas. Draper failed to understand that in higher education, power is widely dispersed. He had to learn this lesson by painful experience.

As acting regent, Thomas J. Burrill had called on the faculty to assume an active role in the government of the University. In 1891 the general faculty established nine standing committees, elected by the faculty after nomination by the executive committee, to free the regent and the collective faculty from numerous details. The executive committee, consisting of the regent, the vice president, and the deans, was empowered to act for the faculty whenever necessary. Faculty bylaws adopted a year later provided for election by the general faculty of the dean of each college. Burrill also took measures to enhance the dignity and liberty of the faculty. He persuaded the board to rescind the rule that made the term of faculty duty the whole year and that required professors to secure leaves of absence for vacations.[35]

A strong proponent of centralized administration, Draper reorganized the structure of the University. On 10 September, in one of his first official acts, he created the Council of Administration. Its members were the president and the four deans. Although its powers were not clearly delineated, the council initially assumed responsibility for student affairs—that is, athletics, discipline, organizations, and publications—and exercised jurisdiction over large areas of academic activity. The following January the board enhanced the authority of the president. In a revision of their bylaws, the trustees charged the president with supervising the educational facilities and the departments and officers of the University, recommending faculty appointments to the faculty, and making an annual report on work in the departments.[36]

A month later the board endorsed revised faculty bylaws. According to these bylaws, the University faculty consisted of the president and all resident professors and assistant professors, others with independent charge of departments of instruction, and the librarian. The faculty, which had control of the discipline and studies of the University, was to meet once a month during term time and to have six standing committees. Members of the faculty were to elect five of these annually; the sixth was the Council of Administration, whose members now also included the vice president, Thomas J. Burrill. The council was to have all the authority of the faculty itself when necessity or the dispatch of business required, provided that the council not change any action of the faculty without written consent of a majority of the faculty.

The faculty of each of the four colleges consisted of the president and of such professors, instructors, and assistants as the president assigned it. Deans were responsible for the execution of all rules and orders made by the faculty of their colleges, and all official communications from members of a college to higher University authority were to be transmitted through its dean. A college faculty was to meet at the call of its dean and on written request of one-third of the faculty. The duty of the college faculty was to recommend policies to the University faculty. The bylaws listed thirty-two "departments of administration," ranging from agriculture to zoology.[37]

Under these bylaws the University or general faculty was a legislative body with ultimate authority in vital areas, while the administrative powers of the general faculty were transferred to the Council of Administration. This structure enabled the council, which Draper dominated, to have a controlling role in University affairs.

On 12 June 1895 the trustees adopted the Plan of Government of the Instructional Force of the University of Illinois. It clothed the president with all the authority needed to secure efficiency in all departments and the orderly and economical administration of the University, and made him answerable only to the Board of Trustees. The plan distinguished between the general faculty and the faculty of each college. The former included the president, the dean of the general faculty, the deans of the colleges, and all academic ranks except instructors, assistants, and fellows. The dean of the general faculty, who was also the vice president, was given oversight of the instructional departments and supervision of the Graduate School. Members of the Council of Administration were associated with the president in an advisory capacity, and the council was now awarded exclusive jurisdiction over disciplinary matters. The general faculty was to have legislative functions touching educational policy, but under specified circumstances the Council of Administration might act in such matters at its discretion, without being subject to review by the faculty. Members of the faculty were to report to any superior authority upon request, and all communications to superior authorities were to be transmitted "through all intermediary officers, to the end that they may have knowledge thereof and an opportunity to comment thereupon if they think advisable."[38]

Draper operated within this organizational framework for some time. The structure he devised defined responsibility and enabled University officials to deal with problems swiftly and decisively. But a tightly centralized administration coupled with autocratic power created problems.

Although the bylaws defined a chain of command and areas of responsibility, they were silent as to whether deans and faculty members could communicate directly with trustees or only through the president's office. According to Draper's assistant, trouble arose when certain trustees assumed executive functions. This statement is accurate so far as it goes, but the reality was more complex. When the dean of the College of Agriculture felt he was being stonewalled by Draper in his effort to revitalize his college, he turned to the organized farming community. Draper's riposte was heard in the same forum. In an address to the Illinois Farmers' Institute in February 1898, Draper complained that it was almost hopeless to build a great university when there was discord on the board or among the faculty, or between faculty and trustees, or if there was insubordination or lack of confidence on the part of everybody who ought to help.[39]

Finding the situation unacceptable, Draper called for clarification. At a meeting on 30 September 1898, which Draper did not attend, the board unanimously adopted a resolution which declared that circumstances had arisen that made it desirable to define the official relations between the trustees and the president of the University. The functions of the trustees were legislative, while the president was the chief executive and responsible agent of the trustees. The board went on to express high appreciation of President Draper and his "strong, generous, straightforward, and just administration of the affairs of the University." At the December board meeting Draper expressed approval of the board's action. He viewed the principles laid down by the trustees as fundamental to sound administration.[40]

This harmony was short-lived. In February 1899, presumably in an effort to ease tensions, Carriel fulsomely praised Draper at the annual meeting of the Illinois Farmers' Institute. A month later Alice Asbury Abbott joined the board. She became a strong partisan of the dean of agriculture and acquired a strong influence over Carriel. According to Lucy Flower, Abbott readily subscribed to the idea of the board's authority in all matters, and she persuaded Carriel and certain other trustees that the board should be able to communicate directly with the faculty. Abbott inspired a cryptic resolution, which Carriel offered the board that September, "with regard to quarterly reports from the Deans of the several colleges." Flower's substitute resolution was voted down, whereupon the whole question was referred to Carriel and Flower to report upon.[41]

At its meeting on 19 December the board subverted the centralized administrative structure that Draper had erected when it adopted a resolution introduced by Carriel. This resolution, the cryptic item of September, specified that typewritten copies of reports by deans to the president should be sent to each board member five days before their quarterly meetings. These reports were to be confined to internal affairs of the colleges and to their instructional needs. At board meetings the president was to approve or disapprove of any suggestion in these reports, "which shall be considered the first official recognition of their existence." Lucy Flower was absent; no vote was recorded. The issue had probably been settled in September.[42]

Draper should have adamantly opposed this resolution, which weakened his authority by allowing deans to present their cases directly to the trustees rather than through the president. He later explained his inaction by saying that certain elements in the proposal "unintentionally invaded the executive freedom of the President," but that he "did not care to seem to be a stickler for prerogative, unnecessarily, and said little about it."[43] This explanation seems disingenuous. The board's action was hardly unintentional; moreover, Draper was a stickler for prerogative. Draper and Flower had been defeated, and they had to swallow their defeat.

Draper labored under the handicap of this policy for years. In the spring of 1901, when amendments to the 1895 Plan of Government of the Instructional Force were being considered, Draper appealed for advice to Burrill, the grand old man of the campus. Draper's query has to be inferred from Burrill's reply; apparently he wanted to make the dean of undergraduates, Thomas Arkle Clark, also the assistant to the president. Burrill opposed the appointment of any one man who should stand between the president and the heads of departments, excluding the vice president and the deans. The president's most important duty was the selection of department heads, each of whom had to work out his own salvation. The president might advise but should neither direct nor supervise the work of a department. Free relations between the president and department heads were needed; mutual respect and confidence were essential to the best results. "The University is not a machine," Burrill added. "Rigorous law and exacting regulations never can with us take the place of a prevailing spirit of sympathy and of help-giving. There are wheels within wheels but the cogs are not mechanical ones." He advised Draper to improve relations with department heads and to find some means by which to distribute the load. The Council of Administration was a detriment and faculty meetings were almost valueless. With nothing to bring the faculty together in any regular way, misunderstandings were inevitable. As a remedy, Burrill suggested informal fortnightly meetings of the president, deans, and department heads. Burrill spoke truth to power. His letter is significant in illuminating Draper's administrative style. But Draper ignored the advice.[44]

As amended on 11 June 1901, the Plan of Government incorporated some important changes. This document, renamed the University Statutes, defined the general faculty as including the president, the vice president and dean of the Graduate School, the dean of undergraduates and assistant to the president, the deans of the separate colleges, the dean of the Woman's Department, and all professors, associate professors, assistant professors, and instructors. The occupants in the first five offices named were to constitute the Council of Administration. The president, the deans, and the professors or ranking heads of departments were to constitute the University Senate, a new creation. Members of the general faculty associated with each college or school were to constitute the faculty thereof. The dean of undergraduates and assistant to the president was, in his latter capacity, to be available to help the president. The senate rather than the general faculty was empowered to exercise legislative functions touching on the educational policy of the University. These statutes accelerated a centralized administration and the concentration of power.[45]

Questions as to the location and extent of authority within the University were still lively on 6 April 1902, when Draper met with an accident. His horses were startled and ran wildly, overturning his carriage and throwing Draper against a post. His left leg was broken and his right leg, badly bruised, developed a blood clot. Doctors had to amputate the right leg above the knee. On 23 April the board tendered him a year's leave of absence on full pay. Burrill served as acting president while Draper recuperated, much of the time in New York state. On 1 October Draper returned to Urbana.

On 8 June 1903 the board rescinded its decision giving the deans access to the trustees. This dubious experiment had lasted over three years. As Draper explained, the Carriel resolution had led to a lessening of respect for the office of the president and a change in the character of the reports. It enabled deans to introduce recommendations concerning matters for which they had no responsible authority. It permitted confidential information to reach individuals personally interested, in advance of lawful action. The president could not meet his responsible duties unless his executive freedom was kept intact. Draper wanted power restored to the executive office; he asked the board to give the president discretionary power to send to the trustees in advance of meetings such reports as he considered compatible with the best interests of the University. The board approved with eight ayes, Hatch nay, and three absent.[46]

## THE UNIVERSITY AND THE STATE GOVERNMENT

The Board of Trustees bore the responsibility for securing the financial means with which to operate. These funds were derived from various sources: interest on the endowment created with proceeds from the Morrill Land Grant Act, federal moneys from the Hatch Act and the Second Morrill Act, student fees, the biennial state appropriation, and state appropriations for such agencies as the State Laboratory of Natural History. For years the trustees had been timid in their requests for the regular appropriation and the state had been niggardly in its giving. From 1869 through 1893 the General Assembly had provided a paltry annual average appropriation of some $30,000 for everything—buildings, equipment, instruction, and operating expenses. Few states in the Union had made such proportionately small contributions for these purposes.[47]

A new era began when the Democratic party came into power and Governor Altgeld committed himself to strengthening and expanding the University. In 1893, before Draper arrived, the Board of Trustees boldly asked for appropriations aggregating $550,500. This was in excess of anything ever before requested or granted (two years earlier a total of $135,200 had been provided, up to then the largest sum ever voted by the legislature at any one session).

The board's request provoked spirited discussion in the state Senate's appropriations committee, where one of the Republican minority members was Henry M. Dunlap, a fruit-grower and farmer from Savoy. An 1875 graduate of the University, Dunlap had been elected in 1892 from the district that included the University. He served for many years, becoming the leader in shepherding the University's appropriation bills through the General Assembly. In 1893 the Democrats on the committee, eager to make a record for economy, cut out and reduced the proposed amounts until a mere shred of the original bill remained. At this point Altgeld intervened, and at a hearing the next day Democrats were respectful rather than hostile toward the University. The bill that passed provided $295,700, including $160,000 for an engineering building and $120,000 for operating expenses. Altgeld told the committee that he would personally sponsor a tax increase to provide for liberal amounts to the University. The governor had made a difference of $240,000 overnight.[48]

President Draper became the point man in the appropriations process. He thought the time had come for boldness. Late in 1894, Draper and the board requested an appropriation of $621,000. He asked the Alumni Association to mobilize public sentiment on behalf of the appropriation, and he asked faculty members to provide written statements in support of specific items.[49]

On 12 February 1895, Draper and the trustees met with Governor Altgeld, after which Draper read to the General Assembly an address that the trustees had endorsed. The time had come to decide whether the University was to become a first-class or a fifth-class university, Draper declared. He appealed to state pride by demonstrating that Ohio, Michigan, Wisconsin, Missouri, Minnesota, and California surpassed Illinois in support of their state universities. He described the need for buildings and operating expenses, observed that no university was complete without professional schools, and called for the development of humanities and kindred lines of learning to attract more women students to the campus.[50]

Although Governor Altgeld was a declared friend of the University, Republicans controlled both houses. Altgeld chided the board for asking for so much. He told Draper and the trustees that if the bill passed both houses he would have to reduce it by at least half.[51] But the trustees went forward, and Draper lobbied hard, pushing every button and pulling every string to accomplish his purposes. He knew politics and made a good impression. "His charming personality," Dunlap observed, went well with members of the legislature, who soon discovered "that he was not to be 'bluffed', and that he was earnest and sincere in what he said."[52]

Dunlap steered the proposal through the Senate committee, which trimmed other items but retained funds for the library building and the president's house. But the bill hung fire in the House, where members of the appropriations subcommittee, including Thomas B. Needles, its chair, opposed the library building and the president's house. Receiving a telegram at 11 p.m. on 23 April that the full House committee would deal with the matter the next day, Draper and two other University officials rushed to Tolono to get the train for Springfield, arriving at 6 a.m. The president arranged an early appointment with the governor, who told Draper to attend to the Republicans and that he would attend to the Democrats.

The committee met that afternoon, and, as Davenport reported the episode, when Draper was introduced, Needles, "a kind of rough neck who considered himself above the common herd," was smoking with his feet on the table, where he evidently intended to leave them while Draper spoke. Draper declared in his best manner, "I am to address the committee upon the work and needs of the UNIVERSITY OF ILLINOIS, and I will begin when I have the respectful attention of every member of the committee." Down came Needles's feet. On a motion to insert the library building, the item passed the subcommittee by a vote of seventeen to six. The full committee then reported the bill, and it sailed through. In its final form it included $150,000 for a library building and $15,000 for an observatory (no allowance was made for the president's house, which was built with funds raised by sale of a University-owned farm). The total sum granted was $427,000, which placed Illinois second only to Pennsylvania in total state appropriations to universities that year.[53]

By 1897 the University could claim even greater state support. New buildings, increased enrollments, and curricular expansion all required proportionately larger operating expenses. In addition, plans were underway to add a law school, a medical school, a women's department, and a state chemical water survey. Funds were also needed to replace the loss by fire of the chemical laboratory. For the biennium the trustees sought an appropriation of $621,000. Dunlap asked Draper to prepare the appropriation bills for him, making the requests for a women's building and a chemical laboratory independent of each other. The Illinois Federation of Women's Clubs, which strongly supported expansion of opportunities for women at the University, sent a delegation to Springfield to press for a women's building, and Trustee Flower spoke to the Senate and House appropriations committees on the subject. Draper himself went to Springfield to lobby for the University bill with Republican Governor John R. Tanner and the Republican majority in the General Assembly. After shaving a bit from most requests and eliminating funds for new buildings, legislators provided a total of $449,164.[54]

On 5 April, with the appropriation bill still under discussion, the Globe Savings Bank in Chicago failed, and with its collapse the Board of Trustees learned that Charles W. Spalding, the board's treasurer, had misappropriated nearly $93,000 from University operating funds and embezzled $456,713 from the endowment fund. The board had first elected Spalding treasurer in July 1893 on the recommendation of Napoleon B. Morrison, and that August the board's finance committee, on the advice of Governor Altgeld, had approved his bond, after which the board's executive committee had done likewise. In June 1895, when Spalding came up for reappointment, Morrison had presented the bond submitted by Spalding and moved approval, and the board had been given the general impression that the person responsible for Spalding was Governor Altgeld. Lucy Flower, who had just come on the board, had disapproved as soon as she learned who Spalding's bondsmen were. She had objected so strenuously that the vote was recorded—seven ayes and two nays. Only Richard P. Morgan had joined Flower in opposition.

The board had allowed Spalding too much rope. He had deposited the University's cash funds to his personal account rather than to the account of treasurer of the University, and he had sold University securities that could not have been sold had he been properly supervised. Spalding was unable to return the bonds, having pledged many of them to secure loans to purchase property in several states. Since his defalcation appeared to leave the University without means to pay ordinary expenses to the end of the fiscal year, John Farson offered to be one of ten men to advance the University $50,000, or as much thereof as might be necessary to carry the University through the crisis.

Draper quickly devised a plan to deal with the emergency, enlisting Senator Dunlap to help implement it. On Dunlap's motion the Senate appointed a committee to investigate the matter, locate the wrong, and exonerate the "educational administration" of the University from all blame. After the committee reported, the General Assembly passed a law that established a commission to handle all claims growing out of the affair and to pay all moneys recovered into the state treasury, and the state agreed to pay the University 5 percent annually on the endowment fund forever. In addition, the state appropriated sums to make good all losses to operating funds.[55]

In 1899 the board asked for an appropriation of $805,400, with this sum divided about evenly between operating expenses and plant additions. Davenport mobilized the Farmers' Institute to lobby for an agricultural building. Draper opposed this part of the request. According to Davenport, when Draper threw his weight against an agricultural building in Springfield, members of the legislature informed him as to when the next train to Champaign departed.[56] A group of women led by Nora Dunlap, the wife of Senator Dunlap, lobbied for the women's building. After the usual legislative jockeying, the General Assembly approved an appropriation of $593,000, including $150,000 for an agricultural building and $40,000 for a women's building.

At this point Draper informed the board that he opposed use of the funds granted to erect an agricultural building. Since there were few students in the College of Agriculture, he argued, the money should be used instead to establish an agricultural high school. The trustees rejected his proposal. Then Governor Tanner dealt a sudden and unexpected blow. He reduced the amount appropriated by $99,000 and eliminated funds for the women's building, leaving the University with a total of $494,400.

Tanner knew little of the University and cared less, Lucy Flower observed, but politics rather than ignorance explains his action. Trustee Alice Abbott, an ally of Tanner who thought the requests were "perfectly outrageous," may have influenced the governor. Above all, Tanner hated Dunlap because Dunlap carried weight and could not be used. Thus he cut the appropriation to humble Dunlap and to pose as a defender of the state treasury.[57]

Tanner's blow aroused strong local opposition, and on 24 April students reportedly burned the governor in effigy on the campus. Such accounts aroused considerable anti-University feeling in Springfield. But after investigating the matter the board declared that no students were identified with an event that had occurred in Champaign's West Side Park.[58]

By 1900 the University was beginning to bask in the glow of a growing reputation. "It was no longer a poor relation given grudging support," observed Dunlap, "but a live institution in which the people of the state were beginning to feel a just pride."[59] In 1901 the board asked for $953,400 for the biennium, including $521,400 for salaries and operating expenses and $432,000 for the physical plant. The latter included $150,000 for a chemical laboratory and $100,000 for a women's building. Since his colleagues suspected Dunlap of partiality to the University, they left him off the appropriations committee. The House agreed to grant only one building instead of two, and asked Dunlap to decide between them. Although Dunlap's wife wanted the women's building, he believed that the chemical building was needed more, and the bill provided $100,000 for that purpose. The appropriation of $804,330 exceeded that of previous years.

In 1903 the trustees were emboldened to request large state support. They sought a regular appropriation of over a million dollars ($1,153,920)— $801,400 for operating expenses and $352,520 for plant additions, of which $175,000 was for an auditorium and music building and $100,000 for a women's building. The Senate struck out the proposed women's building, with two senators saying they would rather give $100,000 more for engineering than $80,000 for a "fad," but under pressure from Mrs. Dunlap and the household science clubs of the state, the House restored the item. Strenuous efforts

TABLE 1

BIENNIAL STATE APPROPRIATIONS FOR THE
UNIVERSITY OF ILLINOIS, 1893–1905

| Biennium | Appropriation |
|----------|---------------|
| 1893–95 | $295,700 |
| 1895–97 | 427,000 |
| 1897–99 | 449,164 |
| 1899–01 | 494,400 |
| 1901–03 | 804,330 |
| 1903–05 | 1,152,400 |

were made to reduce the total of the state's appropriations by at least a million dollars. The women's building was a good target. But Governor Richard Yates, who succeeded Tanner in 1901, keeping his promise to Mrs. Dunlap, did not sacrifice it. The total appropriation was $1,152,400.[60] During his administration Draper dealt with the biennial appropriation five times, consistently winning increases in state support for the University (Table 1).[61]

An 1895 law provided for annual inspection of state educational institutions. The first of these occurred that spring, when a Senate committee made an inspection. In later years the University invited all members of the General Assembly to visit the campus. Faculty members, students, and townspeople joined in making these visits a gala occasion.

Draper's election to the presidency in 1894 was ripe with promise. His force of character and decisive nature served the developing institution well. His relations with the state government in Springfield were good, and he won increasingly larger state appropriations. Within the University Draper battled to protect the integrity of his office. But his centralized administration and autocratic style bred resistance. Could Draper lead in creating a complete and genuine university?

## NOTES

1. Roger L. Geiger, *To Advance Knowledge: The Growth of American Research Universities, 1900–1940* (New York: Oxford University Press, 1986), 18–19.
2. Thomas J. Burrill, "In Quest of a President," *Illio 1903*, 37–38. At the time professors in Columbia College (later University) in New York City were paid $5,000 a year.
3. Ibid.; Milton Berman, *John Fiske: The Evolution of a Popularizer* (Cambridge, Mass.: Harvard University Press, 1961), 223 (drawing on McKay to Fiske, 5 April and 10 July 1891).

4. 4/1/1, 3:125; Burrill, "In Quest of a President," 38.
5. *The Papers of Woodrow Wilson,* ed. Arthur S. Link, vol. 7 (Princeton: Princeton University Press, 1969), 594–623 passim.
6. Ibid., 609.
7. Ibid., 613.
8. Ibid., 632–33.
9. Burrill, "In Quest of a President," 37; *16th Report* (1892), 251; Washington Gladden, *Recollections* (Boston: Houghton Mifflin Co., 1909), 414. Gladden errs in placing his address in 1893.
10. Ernest L. Bogart and Charles M. Thompson, *The Centennial History of Illinois,* vol. 4, *The Industrial State, 1870–1893* (Chicago: A. C. McClurg & Co., 1922), 182–87; Neil Thorburn, "John P. Altgeld: Promoter of Higher Education in Illinois," in *Essays in Illinois History,* ed. Donald F. Tingley (Carbondale: Southern Illinois University Press for Eastern Illinois University, 1968), 37–51.
11. *17th Report* (1894), 76.
12. Armstrong to Draper, 26 February 1894, 2/4/5, B:1.
13. The highest faculty salary at the time went to Thomas J. Burrill, who received $2,700 from University funds and $300 from the Agricultural Experiment Station. Most senior professors were paid $2,000 a year.
14. As quoted in Harlan H. Horner, *The Life and Work of Andrew Sloan Draper* ([Urbana]: University of Illinois Press, 1934), 100.
15. This account draws on Horner, *Andrew Sloan Draper,* an admiring biography; on Ronald M. Johnson, "Captain of Education: An Intellectual Biography of Andrew S. Draper, 1848–1913" (Ph.D. diss., University of Illinois, 1970), a critical analysis; and idem, "Schoolman among Scholars: Andrew S. Draper at the University of Illinois, 1894–1904," *Illinois Historical Journal,* 78 (Winter 1985), 257–72.
16. Johnson, "Captain of Education," 17.
17. Armstrong to Stewart S. Howe, 13 January 1929, 26/4/1.
18. Eugene Davenport, "Notable People I Have Known," 2, 8/1/21, B:4; Draper to Ellen H. Richards, 23 October 1902, 2/4/4, B:1, F:Miscellaneous Papers, 1902–3.
19. Johnson, "Captain of Education," 37, 69–70, 81, 88, 108, 121, 169, and passim. Johnson provides a bibliography of Draper's publications.
20. Andrew Sloan Draper, "The Point of View" (baccalaureate address), *Illini,* 21 June 1899.
21. Andrew S. Draper, "American Universities and the National Life," in National Education Association, *Journal of Proceedings and Addresses,* 37 (1898), 103–22; idem, "The American Type of University," in New York State Education Department, *Addresses and Papers by Andrew S. Draper, 1907* (Albany, 1907), 62–75; idem, "The Democratic Advance in American Universities," in New York State Education Department, *Addresses and Papers by Andrew S. Draper, 1908–1909* (Albany, 1909), pt. 3, ch. 1–3.
22. *17th Report* (1894), 263–65.
23. Andrew Sloan Draper, "Governor Altgeld and the University of Illinois," *Alumni Quarterly,* 7 (April 1913), 78–79.
24. Thorburn, "John P. Altgeld: Promoter of Higher Education in Illinois," 37–51; John P. Altgeld, "On Need of Great State University," in *Live Questions* (Chicago: Geo. S. Bowen & Son, 1899), 463–64.

25. *Proceedings and Addresses at the Inauguration of Andrew Sloan Draper . . . as President of the University of Illinois* (Urbana: University [of Illinois], 1895), 21–24 (quotation at 24).

26. Ibid., 29–50 (quotations at 43, 46, 47).

27. "Biennial Message of John P. Altgeld . . . to the 39th General Assembly," in *Reports to the General Assembly of Illinois, 1895*, vol. 1 (Springfield, 1898), 19–20.

28. Jean C. Tello's "The Devoted Dozen: Women Trustees of the University of Illinois, 1894–1930," a 1989 seminar paper prepared for the author and in his possession, provides useful information and valuable insights on the women trustees. See also Mrs. J. C. Croly, *The History of the Woman's Club Movement in America* (New York, 1898), ix–xi, 60–73, 376, 394; and Muriel Beadle, *The Fortnightly of Chicago: The City and Its Women: 1873–1973* (Chicago: Henry Regnery, 1973).

29. *Chicago Herald,* 9 September 1894, a clipping in Flower and Coues Family Scrapbooks, B:1, Scrapbook 4, Chicago Historical Society; *Election Returns, Petitions, and Papers*, RS 103.32, Illinois State Archives, Springfield. The election returns for 1896, 1898, and 1900 are also from this source.

30. Flower to Draper, 6 November 1899; n.d. [early May 1900] with undated clippings from the *Chicago Evening Post* and the *Chicago Daily Tribune;* 2, 28 May 1900, 2/4/1, B:4, F:Flower, 1896–1900; *Chicago Daily Tribune,* 8, 9, 10 May 1900, Flower and Coues Family Scrapbooks, B:1, Scrapbook 4, pp. 83–84, Chicago Historical Society; *Daily Advocate,* 23 October 1906.

31. *Chicago Daily Tribune,* 8 May 1900.

32. Flower to Draper: strong men, 20 March [1898]; Nightingale, n.d. [fall 1899?]; Hatch, n.d. [fall 1899?], n.d. [?]; disappointed in Carriel, 14 March [1900?]; Abbott's influence, n.d. [fall 1899?]; Abbott and Carriel act impulsively, n.d. [fall 1899?]; not of force (4 December [1902]; 2/4/1, B:4, F:Flower, 1894–96 (first reference), 1896–1900 (other references). Flower's handwriting is very hard to read; letters are undated or give month and date but no year.

33. Richard P. Morgan to Draper, 9 November 1896; James R. Mann (a Congressman) to Draper, 14 March 1898; Farson to Draper, 9 November 1894; 14 June 1897, 2/4/1, B:10, F:Morgan; B:9, F:Mann; B:4, F:Farson.

34. Davenport, "Notable People," 3, 8/1/21, B:4.

35. Solberg, 331–33.

36. *18th Report* (1896), 58. Draper's reports to the board are in the minutes of the trustees. He also submitted a biennial report to the state superintendent of public instruction.

37. Ibid., 68–70.

38. Ibid., 103–4.

39. Horner, *Andrew Sloan Draper,* 117; Illinois Farmers' Institute, *Annual Report* (1898), 30–31.

40. *20th Report* (1901), 20–22, 31–32.

41. IFI, *Annual Report* (1899), 225–26; Flower to Draper, 13 September [1899], 2/4/1, B:4, F:Flower, 1896–1900; *20th Report* (1901), 214.

42. *20th Report* (1901), 239.

43. *22nd Report* (1904), 97.

44. Burrill to Draper, 28 May 1901, 2/4/2, B:7, F:Burrill.

45. *21st Report* (1902), 86. For the "Plan of Government," see *18th Report* (1896), 103–4. The Senate first met on 13 September 1901.

46. *22nd Report* (1904), 97–98.

47. J[ames] E. Armstrong to Frank W. Scott, 12 November 1918, 26/1/20, B:10, F:Early Days. Figures on the biennial state appropriation are readily available in official reports of the Board of Trustees (where the requested appropriation appears in the December meeting before the legislative session of odd years), in *Sixteen Years at the University of Illinois: A Statistical Study of the Administration of President Edmund J. James* (Urbana: University of Illinois Press, 1920), 15, and in Henry M. Dunlap, "A History of the Illinois Industrial University," 2 vol. typescript known hereafter as "Legislative History" [1937], 153–284, 2/9/10, B:1. Dunlap describes the appropriations process starting in 1892. The figures in these sources often disagree, and Dunlap is not always reliable. On the University's requests, I draw mainly on the board's reports; on appropriations I cite *Sixteen Years*. As for the average annual appropriation in the years noted, Dunlap makes it $33,432 and *Sixteen Years* gives $30,208. See also Thomas J. Burrill, "Report of the University of Illinois," Superintendent of Public Instruction, *Twentieth Biennial Report, 1892–1894* (1894), 8–9.

48. Dunlap, "Legislative History," 156–63; T. J. Burrill, "Governor Altgeld's Methods," *Alumni Quarterly*, 7 (April 1913), 83–84. Dunlap's and Burrill's figures are slightly discrepant.

49. *18th Report* (1896), 33, 59, 60, 61–66. The request included $250,000 for a library building, $80,000 for an addition to Natural History Hall, $80,000 to extend the equipment of the College of Engineering, $40,000 for a dairy building, $20,000 for a president's house, and $15,000 for an observatory. Draper's role in the appropriations process may be followed in 2/4/3. For a detailed account, see John Franch, "Pushing Every Button, Pulling Every String: The University of Illinois, the 1895 Legislature, and the Struggle over Appropriations," *Illinois Historical Journal*, 87 (Summer 1994), 74–94.

50. *18th Report* (1896), 61–66.

51. Draper to Alexander McLean, 31 January 1895, 2/4/3; see also Morrison to Draper, 28 January 1895, 2/4/1, B:10, F:Morrison.

52. Dunlap, "Legislative History," 175.

53. Draper to James E. Armstrong, 25 April 1895, 2/4/3; *Reports to the General Assembly of the State of Illinois* (1895), 1:19; *18th Report* (1896), 51; Draper, "Governor Altgeld and the University of Illinois," 79–80; Dunlap, "Legislative History," 163–76; Davenport, "Notable People," 4; St. George L. Sioussat, "Statistics on State Aid to Higher Education," in *State Aid to Higher Education*, vol. 18 in *Johns Hopkins University Studies in Historical and Political Science*, ed. Herbert B. Adams (Baltimore: Johns Hopkins University Press, 1898), 28; *18th Report* (1896), 125.

54. Draper to James E. Armstrong, 28 December 1896, Draper to Caroline C. Lutz, 19 January, 1 February 1897, 2/4/3; Flower to Draper, 27 November [1896], 2/4/1, B:4, F:Flower, 1894–96; Dunlap, "Legislative History," 197.

55. On 10 March 1897 the finance committee of the board had examined Spalding's report for the quarter ending 31 December 1896 and found it correct: 1/1/3, Trustees Secretary, Documents, B:5, F:9 March 1897. On Spalding's appointment and the crisis, see *17th Report* (1894), 77, 135; *18th Report* (1896), 101–2; *19th Report* (1898), 94–95, 97–101, 102, 106, 107, 124, 139–40; unidentified and undated newspaper clippings in the Flower and Coues Family Scrapbook, B:1, Scrapbook 3, Chicago Historical Society; Dunlap, "Legislative History," 181–88; Farson to

Draper, 14 April 1897, 2/4/1, B:4, F: Farson; and Horner, *Andrew Sloan Draper*, 156–57.

56. Davenport, "Notable People," 2–3.
57. Dunlap, "Legislative History," 199–215; Flower to Draper, 6 January [1899], n.d. [Winter 1899], Sunday morning [April 1899], 6 May [1899], 2/4/1, B:4, F:Flower, 1896–1900.
58. *20th Report* (1901), 80–81.
59. Dunlap, "Legislative History," 251.
60. William L. Pillsbury to Draper, 22, 28 April 1903, 2/4/2, B:9, F:Pillsbury; Dunlap, "Legislative History," 264–66, 268–69, 281.
61. For the figures, see *Sixteen Years*, 15. Acting President Burrill gives somewhat larger figures for each biennium in his report on the University of Illinois for 1902–4 in *Twenty-Fifth Biennial Report of the Superintendent of Public Instruction of the State of Illinois, 1902–1904* (Springfield, 1904), 54.

John P. Altgeld, the first Democrat elected governor of Illinois after the University opened, was an ex-officio member of the Board of Trustees during his term of office, from 1893 to 1897. Self-educated, he identified with the less privileged and supported efforts to erect a complete university, an educational institution of which all would be proud. Courtesy of the University of Illinois Archives.

At a time when Illinois women could vote only in elections to school boards, the first women to hold statewide public office in Illinois were University trustees. Lucy L. Flower, a Republican who became known for her charitable, educational, and welfare work in Chicago, was elected to the board in 1894. The first woman elected as a trustee, Flower allied herself closely with President Draper. She cared about gender issues and worked hard to advance the welfare of women students. In 1900 Republican Governor John R. Tanner successfully denied her reelection to the board. Courtesy of the University of Illinois Archives.

Andrew S. Draper served as president of the University from 1894 to 1904. This photo was published in the *Illio '98*.

The deans of the four undergraduate colleges were Nathan C. Ricker, Engineering; Stephen A. Forbes, Science; David Kinley, Literature and Arts; and Eugene Davenport, Agriculture. James B. Scott was dean of the law school. Violet Jayne was dean of women, and Thomas A. Clark was dean of men. This composite photo was published in the *Illio '03.*

A botanist who gained wide recognition for his scientific achievements, Thomas J. Burrill was a member of the faculty from the time the University opened in 1868. He served as acting regent (or president) on three occasions between 1879 and 1890, and again from 1891 to 1894. From 1894 to 1901 he was dean of the general faculty, from 1894 to 1905 he was dean of the Graduate School, and from 1879 to 1912 he was vice president of the University. Courtesy of the University of Illinois Archives.

Starting in 1897, Katharine L. Sharp was head librarian, professor of library economy, and director of the Library School. A graduate of Melvil Dewey's New York State Library School in Albany, and Dewey's favorite pupil, Sharp was, according to Dewey, "the best woman librarian in America." Sharp pushed herself hard to fulfill her varied duties. Working beyond the limits of her natural strength, Sharp paid a high price in nervous exhaustion. Courtesy of the University of Illinois Archives.

After Daniel H. Burnham of Chicago resigned as architect of the new Library Building, the commission went to Nathan C. Ricker and James M. White of the University's architecture department. They prepared four designs, and the responsible parties selected a modern Romanesque design influenced by Henry Hobson Richardson. The building, which was made of pink sandstone with a cherry-red clay tile roof, became available in the fall of 1897 and was later named Altgeld Hall. Courtesy of the University of Illinois Archives.

The Engineering Building, a commodious structure on the north side of Green Street, was designed by George W. Bullard, an 1882 architecture graduate of the University, and dedicated on 15 November 1894. Courtesy of the University of Illinois Archives.

In his effort to rejuvenate the College of Agriculture, Dean Davenport found it necessary to circumvent President Draper and take his case to the Illinois Farmers's Institute to realize his goal. Despite opposition from Draper, Davenport emphasized the need for a new building to house the agricultural operations. The Agricultural Building (later Davenport Hall), described as the largest single edifice in the world devoted to agriculture, was formally dedicated on 21 May 1901. Courtesy of the University of Illinois Archives.

# CHAPTER 2

# THE ACADEMIC ENTERPRISE

During Andrew Sloan Draper's administration, the creation of new schools and colleges gave the University of Illinois the structure if not the spirit of a true university. But the University continued to emphasize undergraduate instruction rather than the expansion of knowledge. The main purpose of the school was to educate students. This chapter looks at the institution as academic enterprise.

## THE UNIVERSITY IN CONTEXT

The University was part of a national and state system of education. Although small by present standards, in 1894–95 the University ranked fourteenth among the nation's universities and colleges in the number of undergraduates enrolled. The University was the capstone of the state's public school system. In 1890 the population of Illinois was 3,826,000, including 57,000 African Americans, with over half of the state's population (2,107,000) living in rural areas. The state then had 793,000 people of high school and college age (fifteen to twenty-four years old). By 1900 the state had 4,822,000 people, including 85,000 African Americans. More than half (2,616,000) now lived in urban areas, and there were 915,000 youths of high school and college age. In these years the total population had grown by over 26 percent, the black population by 49 percent, the urban population by more than

24 percent, and youths of high school and college age by more than 15 percent.[1]

In 1894 the state had 239 high schools with a total enrollment of 23,673 pupils. Nearly twice as many women (15,165) as men (8,508) attended high school. In most schools the course of study ran three or four years and the school year lasted eight or nine months. In 1894, 3,073 Illinois students graduated from high school, with women graduates outnumbering men (2,183 to 890). The schools did not produce many young people prepared to enter college, and Illinois sent more students to colleges in other states than these states sent to Illinois.[2]

The University was located in the heart of the great prairie district of east central Illinois. Heavy rains often converted the treeless, swampy plain into an undrained, mosquito-ridden swamp. Although within the corporate limits of Urbana, the University was physically situated between Urbana and Champaign. Only a few streets were brick-paved. An electric street railway ran between the two cities, which in 1894 had a combined population of about 11,000, a number of schools and churches, and many saloons. The towns were inhabited mainly by strait-laced Methodists and Baptists.

In 1894–95 the University was organized into four colleges and a few other units. The campus included five main buildings: University Hall or Old Main (which dated from 1873); the Chemical Laboratory (1878); the Mechanical Building and Drill Hall, also known as the Wood Shop and Testing Laboratory (1871); Military Hall, later called the Old Armory (1890); and Natural History Hall (1893). The official names of these structures were not always consistent, and popular usage went its own way. On the evening of Draper's inauguration, on 15 November 1894, Engineering Hall, a commodious building on the north side of Green Street, was dedicated. All told, the University occupied nearly seven hundred acres of the richest farmland in the world.

Draper systematized the operations and modernized the physical plant of the University. He prompted the board to institute business methods and to establish the office of the superintendent of buildings and grounds. During his tenure the University installed a central heating, lighting, and power plant, a system of clocks and bells, and a telephone system.

In 1894 the faculty consisted of thirty-four individuals with the rank of assistant professor or higher and thirty-seven instructors or assistants, for a total of seventy-one.[3] The enrollment was 751—627 men and 124 women. Since the University had no dormitory or dining hall, students had to find room and board in Urbana or Champaign.

The University relied primarily on two sources to ensure a supply of qualified students. One was its Preparatory School. The minimum age for admission to the school was sixteen, but in 1894–95 the average age was nearly nineteen. To be admitted, a student had to pass entrance examinations in arithmetic, English, geography, and history or present a first- or second-grade teacher's certificate. Students could prepare for university work by pursuing one of three general courses—science and mathematics, English-Latin, or the classical course. In 1894–95 the school (later, the Academy) enrolled 147 pupils; up until 1903–4 the number ranged from 129 to 315 a year. About 60 percent entered after taking entrance examinations, while 40 percent were conditioned University students who were not ready for more advanced studies. Students could progress at their own pace and enter the University as soon as they were prepared.[4]

Another means of recruiting students was the system of accredited high schools. Upon request the University sent a visitor to evaluate high schools and report to the general faculty, which was empowered to place schools on an accredited list. Graduates of such schools were admitted without examination to any University course for which their studies prepared them.

Students admitted to the University were to be at least sixteen years old, had to pass an entrance examination, and paid a matriculation fee of $10. One entrance examination was given for the College of Literature and Arts, another for the other three colleges, and a third without a college designation. "Specials," or nondegree students over age twenty-one, were admitted without examination. Students paid $7.50 for each of three terms for incidentals, but tuition was free. About $250 a year was needed to cover all expenses.[5]

Electivism was a distinguishing feature of the modern university. Although the technical departments mandated much prescribed work, students in all scientific and literary branches chose their own course of study for a degree, with certain restrictions. A complete course of study in various programs took four years to complete. The academic year was divided into three terms. Forty full-term credits together with an acceptable thesis were required for graduation (the chemistry department required forty-one) until 1899–1900. Thereafter the academic year was divided into two semesters, and 130 semester hours were required for graduation.

In 1894 the University library was woefully inadequate. The collection, some 26,000 volumes housed in a room on the second floor of University Hall, was augmented by the libraries of the Agricultural Experiment Station and the State Laboratory of Natural History. From 1873 to 1894 a faculty member doubled as librarian. Students had done the cataloging without rules, and the card catalog was kept at the librarian's desk. To find a book, patrons had to search the entire collection.

On 1 August 1894 the trustees appointed Percy F. Bicknell (b. 1860) as librarian at a salary of $1,500 a year. Bicknell had earned an A.B. (1884) at Williams College and had been the assistant librarian of the Library Company of Philadelphia. The University's first full-time librarian, Bicknell sought to remedy the defects of the library. He proposed to recatalog the books according to the Dewey Decimal System, hire a skilled cataloger, and develop the collection. With student assistants he soon made a dictionary card catalog of 6,240 volumes and asked for funds to continue this work and hire a permanent assistant. Despite these improvements, the library was far from what it should be. In 1896, for example, Illinois, with 29,100 volumes, ranked not only behind Harvard (460,000), Yale (210,000), and Princeton (102,000), but also behind Michigan (98,707), California (62,323), Minnesota (39,909), Wisconsin (36,800), and Nebraska (32,000).[6]

On 3 May 1897, with no warning, Draper informed Bicknell that plans to appoint a new librarian required his retirement. Embittered, Bicknell published in a national journal a scathing criticism, without naming his targets, of Draper and the trustees for stressing sports over scholarship in bidding for institutional recognition.[7]

Meanwhile, plans to construct a new library building were proceeding. After the legislature appropriated $150,000 for the purpose, Daniel H. Burnham of Chicago was named as architect. But when problems arose over the two designs he submitted he resigned, and the commission then went to Nathan C. Ricker and James M. White of the University's architecture department. They prepared four designs, and the responsible parties selected a modern Romanesque design influenced by Henry Hobson Richardson. The building was made of pink sandstone from the Kettle River area of Minnesota, with a cherry-red clay tile roof. The Library (later Altgeld Hall), a fireproof structure 113 by 167 feet with a tower of 132 feet to support a chime of bells, was dedicated on 8 June 1897. The stack room had a capacity for ninety thousand volumes that could be enlarged to one hundred fifty thousand volumes.[8]

The new librarian was Katharine L. Sharp. Born in 1865 in Elgin, Illinois, and rooted in the Puritan tradition, Sharp had attended Northwestern University. An excellent student, active in the affairs of her class, and a leader in the Kappa Kappa Gamma sorority, she graduated in 1885 with a Ph.B. and received a Ph.M. in 1887. In October 1888, after teaching briefly, she became the head librarian of the new Scoville Institute in Oak Park (later the Oak Park Public Library). Attracted to librarianship as a profession, she applied to the New York State Library School at Albany, the only library school then in existence. Entering with the second class, she graduated in 1892 with a Bachelor of Library Science (B.L.S.) degree.[9]

In the summers of 1891 and 1892 Sharp organized libraries in two midwestern towns, and in the fall of 1892 she prepared a comparative library exhibit for the World's Columbian Exposition in Chicago. Her work commanded attention, and in January 1893 she was appointed head of the Department of Library Science at the newly founded Armour Institute in Chicago. Sharp directed this department until 1897, when she accepted the appointment at the University of Illinois as head librarian, professor of library economy, and director of the library school.

Sharp brought a new level of professional expertise to the library. To master the collection, she undertook remedial work in accessioning, cataloging, and classification. Sharp stressed reference work, and the staff made lists of books and periodicals designed to promote good reading. She extended the hours of operation and permitted students to borrow books for home use without a professor's request. During her tenure the University became one of the original depository libraries for all catalog cards printed by the Library of Congress. Under Sharp the holdings more than doubled, but in 1903–4 the library still ranked behind the leading private universities as well as the universities of Michigan, California, Minnesota, and Wisconsin. Sharp contributed more to the standardization of procedures than to collection development.[10]

## THE PRESIDENT AND THE FACULTY

The Board of Trustees exercised ultimate authority in the University, but President Draper expected to act with unfettered freedom within the lines of general policy laid down by the board. A "captain of erudition" (as Thorstein Veblen described the university presidents of the time), Draper devoted his entire energy to advancing the institution's welfare. Presidents of other state universities looked to him as a model, and in 1902 Columbia University conferred on Draper an honorary LL.D.[11]

Draper espoused strong views on the educational mission of a university, regarding mere scholarship as one of the narrowest phases of human development. To him, the purpose of the American university was "the making of men even more than the making of scholars." Admittedly, America lagged behind Germany in the pursuit of serious scholarship, but American universities, Draper believed, trained not for study alone but for life. "The lines in American universities," he observed, "are setting for character quite as much as for scholarship."[12] His views showed Draper looking to a past model of educational function and placed him somewhat out of step with his contemporaries, for the emerging universities valued scholarship.

Draper's strong views extended to relations with the faculty as well. A schoolman, he failed to understand that collegiality was the norm in higher education. Deans and faculty members had to secure his approval for any absence from the University, to take classes on field trips, and to invite lecturers to the campus. A rigid disciplinarian, Draper censured others of various ranks, whom he viewed as subordinates, for minor infractions. Nothing was too trivial to escape his notice.

Draper's blunt and autocratic style bred resistance, as a dispute over attendance at public lectures revealed. On 26 January 1898 Draper wrote the faculty
expressing "extreme regret" that while many gathered for social affairs, not
10 percent had attended a series of evening lectures on a subject of public interest. The younger faculty were the chief offenders. It was the duty of the
faculty to support general University enterprises. "Teachers cannot show so
little eagerness for intellectual advancement," Draper warned, "and expect to
reach or maintain themselves in the most advanced positions."[13]

Evarts B. Greene, who had taken his doctorate in American history at Harvard and studied in Berlin for a year before joining the Illinois faculty in 1894,
was "very much hurt" by Draper's letter. Greene devoted his days to teaching
and wanted his evenings for research and writing. "There exists in the Faculty at this time," he protested to Draper, "a state of feeling which if continued
will prove seriously detrimental to the higher interests of the University." It
was unfair to ask men to attend four evening lectures in a single week and to
consider regular attendance at such meetings a test of fidelity to University
interests or of intellectual energy, he said. Moreover, Draper's position was
inconsistent with a reasonable degree of personal liberty. Finally, Draper's
threat that failure to appear at University events might hamper advancement
aroused strong feelings. Some faculty members, Greene noted, might be willing to make a show of interest. Others were intensely irritated and bitter.
Draper, Greene pointed out, was estranging many who might easily be made
enthusiastic servants of the University.[14]

Draper's reply to Greene is a study in intransigent self-righteousness. He
was trying to correct a manifest evil about which he knew more than Greene,
he said. Greene had most of the qualities needed to remain in the University's
service, but he had been "at variance with the overwhelming weight of numbers and experience upon many subjects of University policy since you have
been here, especially what you conceive to be a lack of effort for a higher plane
of scholarship." And now, Draper charged, "you assume to criticize the President of the University. . . . If the liberty of anyone is being assailed, it seems to
me that it is the liberty of the President."

Draper then resorted to personal attack. He did not doubt Greene's good
intentions, but "the extent to which you have been in conflict with the opinions
of the President and of the more experienced persons associated with the University administration ought to suggest to you that youth and good intentions
cannot be a sufficient explanation of the same for an indefinite period of time."
Draper trusted that Greene would now realize that a professor would be "more
happy and efficient in prosecuting his work by falling in with the trend of University life and in supporting the efforts of the administration for the common advancement, rather than by dwelling upon the extreme of personal prerogatives and imagining that some one is against him and disposed to limit

his freedom." Draper hoped "that you and I may be in perfect sympathy and accord, and that you may render the University the great service for which some of your qualities eminently fit you."[15]

Underlying Draper's response to Greene was not only Draper's autocratic style, but also his emphasis on teaching, not research, as the main business of faculty members. The search for new truth quickened the pulse of a university, and where the discovery of knowledge seemed possible, ample time must be given for it. Yet Draper disliked protracted investigations of fine points, and he charged that the term "research" was used in universities "with a flippancy and a presumption that are often absurd." Too many teachers lacked the capacity for research, he believed, and those who engaged in it should be held accountable for results. People turned to the University to solve practical problems. Draper approved of scientific research designed to benefit the multitude by making healthier homes, richer farms, safer railways, thriftier cities, and the like.[16]

Draper harbored a basically negative view of university teachers. They had great fun legislating, but "it is not quite certain that, outside of their specialties, they will ever come to conclusions, or that, if they do, their conclusions will stand." Yet such activity gave relaxation to teachers, who "are given to disorderliness and argumentation beyond any other class who stands so thoroughly for doing things in regular order." Teachers have a "passionate fondness . . . for that irrelevant discussion which seems to destroy all sense of educational perspective." Whatever the cause, "they will keep it [irrelevant discussion] going by the hour with apparently more pleasure than they can find in any other pastime unless they are menaced by the apparition of coming to an agreement."[17]

Because of the great power vested in his position, Draper was able to make his views felt. He had full responsibility for the instructional work and all but final authority in faculty recruitment. He asked the age, marital status, church membership, life history, and educational career of applicants, in that order, and for a photograph. His ideal candidate was a person with teaching ability, demonstrated qualities of leadership, and a capacity to extend the influence of the University by applying his or her knowledge to the solution of pressing practical problems.

Competition for the best faculty members was keen, and the supply limited. American graduate schools were still in their infancy, and study in a German university was costly. Graduates of leading universities were often reluctant to take jobs in "freshwater" midwestern schools. In addition, Illinois was known for low salaries and heavy teaching loads. Location complicated recruitment. Sometimes Draper used teachers' agencies to identify candidates. Many appointees were recent University graduates.

Draper assured candidates that they would find an agreeable home and plenty of opportunities at the University, but he made no promises as to the future. If faculty members were upright, energetic, cooperative, and their work flourished, they would be rewarded according to their desserts. Draper insisted that an agreement was a legal contract binding upon both parties. Unlike President Charles W. Eliot of Harvard, he bitterly denounced those who broke a contract to accept a better job elsewhere.[18]

Draper bore the main responsibility for the nurture of the faculty. He was a hard taskmaster. Under rules he persuaded the board to adopt in the fall of 1895, employment of teachers was either continuous or for a period of ten months. Instructors were to hold themselves in readiness for service at any time during the period of their employment. Absence from ordinary service in the University for any cause other than sickness needed the president's approval if for less than ten days, and the trustees' approval if for a longer time. Instructors were to be in attendance up to 1 July and after 1 September unless leave had been granted by the president; in July and August they were to keep the president notified of their whereabouts and to respond quickly to any call for service. The board reserved the right to terminate service at any time for any reason that might be deemed sufficient. No summary dismissal would be made except for conduct prejudicial to the University, nor would faculty be dismissed without opportunity for a hearing, if the facts were disputed. For any failure to comply with all the conditions of loyal and interested service, the board would feel free to withhold salary so far as the interests of the University might seem to demand.[19]

Faculty salaries were low. In 1883 the standard salary for senior faculty members at Columbia University was $5,000, but in 1894 the trustees set the Illinois scale as follows: deans, $2,000, rising by annual increases to $2,500; professors, $1,800, rising to $2,250; associate professors, $1,600 to $2,000; assistant professors, $1,200 to $1,800; instructors, $800 to $1,200; assistants, $600 to $800; and fellows, $400. Most faculty members were paid less than top of the scale for their rank. The University, Draper admitted in 1896, could not offer salaries that would enable it to hire topnotch professors. In 1900, however, a committee of the trustees reported that the average faculty salary at Illinois compared "very favorably" with that at other state universities, and an independent study of salaries at eight midwestern state universities found that Illinois compared at least favorably with the others. Still to be addressed was the salary differential within rank. Most midwestern state universities had a "normal" salary for full professors, but at Illinois appreciable inequities existed in salaries of faculty of the same rank in different colleges. In August 1904, shortly after Draper had departed, five professors asked that some method of equalizing salaries be considered. Their request was referred to the authorities for investigation. On 17 January 1905, the board's Committee on Instruction reported that it had found the salary list extending over the last ten years "full of incongruities and inconsistencies." In other words, Draper had played favorites. The committee recommended that the whole subject of salaries be referred to the president of the University with a request that he investigate the entire matter and report to the board as soon as practicable.[20]

Salaries seemed especially low in relation to the work required. Teaching loads were heavy. Some faculty members, especially in chemistry, taught nearly forty hours a week. As late as 1904 deans taught five or six hours a week, professors who were heads of departments from six or eight to fifteen hours a week, full professors with no administrative responsibilities from six to fifteen hours a week, and assistant professors from eight or nine to sixteen or eighteen hours a week.[21]

In distinction to its somewhat laggardly response in improving faculty salaries, however, the University was a leader in enacting a sabbatical-leave policy. In 1895, confronted with two requests for a year's leave of absence for study in Europe, the board declared that it was the purpose of the University to encourage study by its teachers in the leading institutions of the world. So it approved the requests and pledged to try to provide positions for the two men when they returned. Two years later the board recommended that three professors, each of whom had served for twenty-five years, be given a year's leave of absence at half pay, to be taken consecutively in such order as they might arrange among themselves and with the president.[22]

In 1900 the Board of Trustees devised a policy on the subject. The board decided that an Illinois professor who had served seven consecutive years might be given a furlough for one year at half pay, providing that such leaves did not hamper the work of the University and that a professor taking such a sabbatical pledge to remain at the University for three years after returning at the salary of his grade. In turn, the University would agree to retain him in its service during his leave and for one year thereafter.[23] In December 1902 Draper extended the privilege to associate and assistant professors who had served for seven consecutive years, making it clear that such leaves were granted for the purpose of foreign study, not for relief from regular work.[24]

Both Draper's support of sabbatical leaves and his authoritarian restrictions on faculty in other matters can be understood in light of his strong convictions on academic freedom—a concept not yet well understood in American higher education. Academic freedom rested on certain principles, he asserted, especially "the subordination of self to the atmosphere of the place and the common good." Academic freedom was not for the teacher as much as for the unlocking of scientific truth, and it had to be balanced with accountability. Individuality must be made to respect organization. Accordingly, self-seeking and sensationalism were repugnant to the freedom of a university. "Everything which lacks complete intellectual sanity and sincerity is . . . a menace to academic freedom." In the mental and philosophical sciences, which involved matters of opinion, the right of individual expression was free, but "the right of

place, and of association, and of time, and of opportunity, is not without its
very decisive limitations." Such limitations also applied to teaching with respect to the Christian religion and democratic political institutions. In teaching topics that were subjects of party warfare, "live questions," the teacher
must not be an advocate but a judge, hearing contending views and determining only what he has a right to decide. A professor's quest must be within the domain of his own professorship. The ultimate means of dealing with
those who violated these norms was to submit the matter to the discretion
of the board.[25]

A university had to give free play to teaching that was scholarly, free, and
aggressive, but it also had to stand for character as well as for scholarship.
Draper saw "more danger to the future of some American universities through
the fettering of administrative, rather than of academic, freedom." The forces
essential to the representative character of the American university had to be
held in rational equilibrium. Each of these forces—the public, the donors, the
trustees, the president, the teachers, the students, and the alumni—was to have
its independence; none was to trench upon the independence of the others.
As for a teacher, Draper accepted no rule concerning his treatment "which
does not make him a well rounded, independent, manly, attractive character,
who asks no special privilege and avoids no ordinary obligation."[26]

Many of Draper's views on academic freedom were valid, but his main ideas
were bound to have a chilling effect on the intellectual climate of the campus.
He valued the conventional teacher, one who was not likely to challenge the
orthodoxies of the day. He would be the judge of "intellectual sanity." He
wanted teachers to have "capital," the chief elements of which were "content-
ment, enthusiasm, loyalty, [and] efficiency."[27]

Draper set the tone for the campus. He was the dominant figure in the
University Club, which was open to all faculty members and designed to promote collegiality. The club met each month during the college year for games,
conversation, dancing, and a supper. Near the end of the academic year members celebrated with a banquet and a guest speaker. Here as elsewhere Draper's
heavy hand strained relations.

## The Student Body

Since students learn from each other, the nature of the student body influences the educational process. In 1894–95 the University enrolled a total of 751
students. Of this number 525 were undergraduates. This group included 465
men (87 percent) and 60 women (13 percent); 335 (64 percent) were in their
freshman or sophomore year, and 190 (36 percent) were in their junior or senior year. Thus the student body was predominantly male, and the academic

### TABLE 2
### UNDERGRADUATE ENROLLMENT, 1894–1904

| Year | Undergraduate Enrollment (No.) | Women (%) | Freshmen-Sophomores (%) |
|------|------|------|------|
| 1894–95 | 525 | 13 | 64 |
| 1895–96 | 571 | 15 | 64 |
| 1896–97 | 535 | 15 | 62 |
| 1897–98 | 571 | 18 | 60 |
| 1898–99 | 665 | 23 | 62 |
| 1899–00 | 755 | 28 | 57 |
| 1900–01 | 886 | 27 | 60 |
| 1901–02 | 1,026 | 29 | 62 |
| 1902–03 | 1,264 | 30 | 62 |
| 1903–04 | 1,480 | 26 | 64 |

work was mainly at the introductory level. Indeed, although undergraduate enrollments increased fairly steadily from 1894 to 1904 (Table 2), nearly two-thirds of undergraduates did not continue their studies beyond two years. Table 2 also shows that the proportion of women undergraduate students increased slowly, to 30 percent in 1902–3, after which it temporarily regressed.

In the years 1894–1904 the undergraduate students came largely from Champaign County and the counties in the central part of the state. The next largest contingent came from Cook County and other counties in northern Illinois. The southern counties of the state supplied few students. The number of out-of-state students was relatively small at first. Foreign nations sent few students. These trends are illustrated for three different years in Table 3.[28]

In 1894–95, 27 of the 102 counties in the state sent not one student. Of the 49 students from out of state, 13 came from Iowa, 6 from Indiana, 5 from Pennsylvania, 4 each from Wisconsin and Ohio, 3 from Nebraska, and 2 each from Kansas, Kentucky, and Missouri. Arizona, Colorado, Louisiana, Massachusetts, Michigan, New Jersey, New York, and South Dakota each sent 1. One student came from Japan.

An analysis of enrollments in 1898–99 shows that the source of the 668 undergraduates in attendance had widened. Champaign County again supplied more than any other county, and over half of the students came from central Illinois. Several counties in southern Illinois sent 1 or more students, but 13 southern counties sent no students. Seventy out-of-state students, from 18 states, were enrolled in 1898–99. Iowa (14) and Indiana (13) sent the largest number, Michigan and Ohio each sent 6, and other states sent from 1 to 4 each. In addition, Japan and Spain each sent one student.

TABLE 3
GEOGRAPHIC ORIGIN OF UNDERGRADUATE STUDENTS,
1894–1904

| Locality | 1894–95 | 1898–99 | 1903–04 |
|---|---|---|---|
| Middle counties | 295 | 365 | 732 |
| (Champaign) | (128) | (157) | (239) |
| Northern counties | 151 | 185 | 456 |
| (Cook) | (42) | (59) | (188) |
| Southern counties | 28 | 46 | 97 |
| Out of state | 49 | 70 | 183 |
| Foreign | 1 | 2 | 12 |
| Total | 524 | 668 | 1,480 |

In 1903–4 the geographic source of the in-state students followed the same pattern as in earlier years. Roughly half of the total came from the midstate counties. A preponderance of the others came from the northern part of the state. Eight southern counties sent no student to the University. A total of 183 students from 26 other states and the District of Columbia were enrolled. The states contributing the largest numbers were Iowa (34), Indiana (23), Ohio (21), Michigan (17), Missouri (16), and New York (13). Wisconsin supplied 8, and other states from 1 to 5. Of the 12 undergraduates from abroad or the territories, 6 were from Mexico, 2 from Japan, and 1 each from Norway, Russia, the Hawaiian Islands, and the Philippine Islands.

A statistical profile of the class of 1896, which numbered 110, including 18 women, illustrates the composition of one cohort. The average age was 21 years and 18 days. The oldest graduating senior was 33, the youngest 18. The average height was 5 feet, 8.1 inches; the average weight was 145.2 pounds. The nationality of the parents was American, 69.5 percent; German, 11.5; English, 6.0; Irish, 3.5; Welsh, 1.5; French, 1.5; and Dutch, 0.5, leaving 6 percent unaccounted for.[29]

Most undergraduates were white and of European descent, but ten African Americans attended the University in the period 1894–1904 (Jonathan A. Rogan, an African American from Decatur, had been a freshman in civil engineering in 1887–88). Among them was George Washington Riley, of Champaign, a "special" student of art and design from 1895 to 1897.[30] Six African Americans were registered in the College of Literature and Arts: William W. Smith, of Broadlands (Champaign County), completed four years of study in 1900, becoming the first black graduate of the University. Albert R. Lee, of Champaign, was a freshman in 1897–98; Myrtle L. Moss, of Champaign, who was a freshman in 1901–2, studied for a total of three years; Bertha Owens, of

Mound City (on the Ohio River in Pulaski County), was a "special" student in 1901–2; and Ripley M. Young, from Levings, in Pulaski County, was a freshman in 1901–2. Maudelle T. Brown, of St. Louis, who was a freshman in 1903–4, graduated in 1906 with honors in mathematics. She was the first female black graduate of the University. In 1901–2 Fred E. Spellman, of Quincy, was a freshman in electrical engineering; in 1903–4 Roy M. Young, from Springfield, was a freshman in civil engineering; and in 1904 Walter T. Bailey graduated with a degree in architecture.[31]

Geographic origins help explain the characteristic and distinguishing attitudes and habits of the campus. In the years from 1894 to 1904 most students came from farms or villages and from families with little in the way of material resources or intellectual culture. They saw the University as the vestibule to a brighter future.

In proportion to population, in 1896 the people of Illinois sent more students to college than did several neighboring states, but Illinois sent twice as many students to the colleges of Indiana, Ohio, and Wisconsin as it received into its colleges, and many times more to Michigan. Two years later Indiana, Ohio, Iowa, Kansas, Nebraska, and California all had more of their sons and daughters pursuing college courses at their state universities than Illinois had.[32]

## TOWN-GOWN CONFLICT AND POLITICAL ACTIVITY

Town-gown conflicts have persisted since the rise of universities in the Middle Ages, and a university's involvement in politics always risks exposing it to entanglement in issues unrelated to academic purposes. In December 1890 the Board of Trustees prohibited the use of University buildings and grounds for political purposes.[33] A few years later the flag-law controversy plunged the University into a political dispute. This conflict erupted in March 1896, when the Champaign County state's attorney persuaded a grand jury to indict the governor and the trustees for breach of a law requiring display of the U.S. flag over every public building in Illinois. This absurd indictment—University officials believed they had complied with the law by flying one flag from a 150-foot flagstaff over Military Hall rather than one on each University building—was apparently designed to discredit Governor Altgeld, a Democrat and an ex-officio board member. One Chicago newspaper labeled grand jury members "the biggest asses with the longest ears that ever stood on terra firma since Noah liberated the animals from the ark."[34]

Draper believed that the flag-law episode resulted from a disposition in the community to manage the affairs of the University. On 2 April, viewing the affair as pretty well over, he wrote that he was trying to get what advertising he could out of it, and that he was also trying "to make people in the surrounding neighborhood learn the lesson that it is well for them to keep their hands off the University." The court was eager to have a motion made to quash the indictment, but it might be good if the trustees were brought into court, although Draper saw not the "remotest danger" of such an event.[35]

When the state's attorney offered to quash the indictment provided the board put a flag on one of the University buildings, the trustees refused on the grounds that they were already complying with the spirit of the law. On 26 June an indictment that seemed silly turned serious when the county sheriff interrupted a board meeting to arrest seven trustees for violating the flag law and accompanied them to the courthouse, where they were released after posting bond. The judge who tried their case would not grant a change of venue, but he ended the matter by finding the flag law unconstitutional.[36]

At a board meeting on 22 April, with the flag-law dispute unresolved, Samuel M. Inglis, an ex-officio trustee elected in 1894 on the Republican ticket, noted complaints that University people had been unduly active in local political contests. He persuaded the board to recognize that University teachers who resided in either Champaign or Urbana were citizens who had a right to vote, but the status of students was uncertain, and no one should vote whose right to do so was unclear. Also, the University should never be involved in any political or partisan issue, and it should not be made the basis of political operations. To avoid even the appearance of such a result, everyone connected with the University should refrain from political activity. Political parties should refrain from sending carriages to the University to take students to polling places, Inglis said, and such carriages should be denied the privileges of the campus. Students who had a right to vote should exercise their own judgment, not respond to a solicitation made for one candidate or another at the doors of the University.[37]

The insistence that the University should not be involved in any political or partisan issue enunciated a principle that later became known as institutional neutrality. First formulated in 1869 by Charles W. Eliot in his inaugural address as president of Harvard University, the idea was that no part of a university in its corporate capacity should take an official stand on disputed philosophical, political, or ideological issues. In due time the principle became recognized as a safeguard of academic freedom. But the warning that individuals connected with the University should refrain from political activity tended to discourage discussion of politics, thereby limiting academic freedom and promoting insularity.

Student political activity on campus generally was manifested in the activities of clubs. The liquor question was much to the fore in the late nineteenth century, and "dry" forces organized the national Prohibition party to plead their cause. In 1894 a Prohibition Club existed on the campus. Early the following, year, when the American Republican College League called for a meeting of delegates in Missouri and Illinois, the editor of the *Illini* declared that political clubs in colleges, rightly conducted, were an excellent thing. Students should study the questions of the day so that they would know about them when they left the University. But except for reporting progress on the University's appropriations bill in the legislature, the paper gave little coverage to politics.

In February 1895 a group of students met on campus and formed the Republican Club. The purpose of the club was to hold debates, lectures, and discussions and to present papers on political topics. The emergence of political clubs led the faculty to appoint a committee to deal with the recognition of these groups. The student yearbook usually listed political clubs among the organizations of the University.[38]

In September 1896, as the McKinley-Bryan presidential campaign began, about four hundred Republican students went about Champaign one evening calling for speeches from representative Republicans. The student newspaper hardly noticed the election, but it reported that many students went home to vote. In a student convocation on election day, President Draper discussed the "import and importance" of the election.[39]

During the heated 1896 campaign Democratic students were apparently inactive, but in February 1898 forty of them met at the Imperial Building in Champaign, where they heard an address by the chairman of the Democratic Central Committee of Champaign and formed the William Jennings Bryan Club. The members' request to use Military Hall for a lecture by Bryan in May was rebuffed by the trustees on the grounds that such usage was contrary to University policy.[40]

By the fall of 1899 the Spanish-American War and the Second Boer War had made imperialism a lively issue. That November, the William Jennings Bryan Club held a meeting at the office of a law firm in Champaign to discuss the subject. Around the same time two professors lectured on South Africa and recent events in the Transvaal to a large audience on campus. So a fine line was drawn: faculty members could discuss a political issue on campus without sponsorship by a political club, but a political club dealing with a similar topic had to meet off campus.[41]

Early in 1900 the *Illini* announced that the best policy for the University as an organization was not to participate in politics, but persons connected with the University need not give up the rights of suffrage. They should see that individuals favorably inclined toward the University be chosen to represent the local district in both houses of the state's General Assembly. Professors and students should not only vote in elections but also take an active part in the city primaries. The *Illini* urged all students "who feel they are justified in doing so" to aid a fellow student who was a candidate for the lower house in the Urbana primary election.[42]

In 1900 Richard Yates, a Republican, and Samuel Alschuler, a Democrat, vied to be governor. According to the *Illini*, between 75 and 80 percent of the Illinois students were Republicans. The officers of the Republican Club worked with both the state and county committees of the party to provide transportation for students to return home and vote.[43]

The University community apparently accepted the principle of institutional neutrality. In the fall of 1900 the *Student Democrat* scored University authorities because, it alleged, the University Band had taken part in a parade for candidate Richard Yates. The authorities did not send the band to participate, the *Illini* responded; President Draper had merely permitted the parade managers to negotiate with the band for its services.[44]

In 1902 a number of University graduates ran for office, and several students participated in the primary campaign. The number of votes cast by students at this time was reportedly larger than ever before in Champaign and Urbana. In the fall the Republican Club again offered to provide transportation for students from closely contested districts to go home to vote, while the college newspaper advised students who did not go home to vote to register in their wards and vote locally. The *Illini* took no sides in political matters, it declared, adding that bona fide student residents were entitled to vote and should use their weapon to strike for good government.[45]

But what constituted taking sides was open to question. On 16 April 1903 the *Illini* ran photographs and descriptions of the two candidates for city attorney. In a letter printed in the *Illini* the next day, President Draper criticized the publication of portraits and commendatory notices of candidates for office. The fact that this was done for opposing candidates did not change his opinion. Draper also took the opportunity to denounce the practice of students voting in local elections.[46]

The prohibition of politics from the campus remained in force for half a century. The benefits of insulating the University from divisive political issues become clear by comparison with the situation at foreign universities, where rival parties have used student affiliates as pawns, often transforming universities into bloody battlegrounds. But the ban also discouraged students from involvement in national and state politics and helped keep them in a state of arrested political development.

The University was called into being to educate the youth of Illinois. Officials took their duties seriously, knowing that what students studied in college went far toward determining the shape of society in the future. In the next section we turn to the ways in which the University cultivated the minds of the young.

# NOTES

1. On the number of the nation's universities and colleges, see *Report of the Commissioner of Education for the Year 1894–95* (Washington, D.C.: GPO, 1896), vol. 1, 149–51. On the size of these institutions see House of Representatives, 54th Cong., 1st sess., doc. 5, *Report of the Secretary of the Interior,* 5 vols. Vol. 5, pt. 1 (Washington, D.C., 1896), 2116–31. On Illinois population data, see U.S. Bureau of the Census, *Historical Statistics of the United States: Colonial Times to 1970* (Washington, D.C.: GPO, 1975), pt. 1, 27.

2. Superintendent of Public Instruction of the State of Illinois, *Twentieth Biennial Report, 1892–1894* (Springfield, 1894), xxix; *Historical Statistics,* pt. 1, 379; William T. Harris (U.S. Commissioner of Education) to Draper, 15 January 1897, 2/4/1, B:7, F:Harris.

3. These figures are compiled from the University catalog. The complete faculty roll is given as thirty-two in 4/1/1, 3:254 (14 September 1894).

4. *17th Report* (1894), 220–21; Edward G. Howe to Draper, 5 March 1895, 2/4/2, B:1, F:Howe; *Register* (1903–4), 319.

5. *21st Report* (1902), 31–32, 46; Draper to George E. Lake, 6 August 1894, 2/4/3.

6. *17th Report* (1894), 268; *18th Report* (1896), 21–22, 29; Bicknell, "Report on the Cataloging of the Library . . . ," n.d., and idem, "To the Board of Trustees of the University of Illinois," 3 June 1896, 2/4/2, B:2, F:Bicknell; U.S. Bureau of Education, *Statistics of Libraries and Library Legislation in the United States* (Washington, D.C., 1897), passim.

7. Draper to Bicknell, 3 May 1897, 2/4/3; Percy F. Bicknell, "The University Ideal," *Education,* 18 (October 1897), 108–11; Draper to Frank H. Kasson (editor of *Education*), 23 October 1897, 2/4/3.

8. *18th Report* (1896), passim; Nelson W. Graham to Draper, 20 December 1895, Richard P. Morgan to Draper, 16 October 1895, 2/4/1, B:5, F:Graham; B:10, F:Morgan, 1894–99; Neil Thorburn, "John P. Altgeld: Promoter of Higher Education in Illinois," in *Essays in Illinois History,* ed. Donald F. Tingley (Carbondale: Southern Illinois University Press for Eastern Illinois University, 1968), 50–51.

9. Laurel A. Grotzinger, *The Power and the Dignity: Librarianship and Katharine Sharp* (New York: Scarecrow Press, 1966).

10. [Katharine Sharp], "Report of the Head Librarian," 1 June 1898, 2/4/2, B:4, F:Sharp; [idem], "Report of the Head Librarian," 1 June 1899, ibid., B:5, F:Sharp; Sharp, "Annual Report of the Head Librarian," 1903, and "University Library Statistics, Mar. 1902," 2/4/4, B:2, F:Department Reports, 1903. On library growth, see Harlan H. Horner, *The Life and Work of Andrew Sloan Draper* ([Urbana]: University of Illinois Press, 1934), 127.

11. Andrew Sloan Draper, "Government in American Universities," *Educational Review,* 28 (October 1904), 230–33; idem, *American Education* (Boston: Houghton Mifflin, 1909), 223–35.

12. Andrew Sloan Draper, "The College Graduate in Affairs," *Illini,* 13 June 1895; idem, "University Questions Concerning the Common Schools," *Educational Review,* 27 (February 1904), 128 (first quotation); idem, "Government in American Universities," 236 (second quotation); idem, "The University Presidency," in

*Addresses by Andrew S. Draper* (Albany: New York State Education Department, 1906), 39.

13. Draper to Members of the Corps of Instruction, 26 January 1898, 2/4/10, B:1, vol. 1.

14. Greene to Draper, 28 January 1898, 2/4/2, B:4, F:1897–98, E–J.

15. Draper to Greene, 31 January 1898, 2/4/3.

16. Draper, "Government in American Universities," 228, 233–34 (quotation); idem, "Weaknesses in American Universities," in *Addresses and Papers by Andrew S. Draper, 1911–1912* (Albany: New York State Department of Education, [1912]), 149; idem, *American Education*, 198–99.

17. Draper, *American Education*, 225 (first two quotations); idem, "Weaknesses in American Universities," 147 (last two quotations).

18. Draper, "The Ethics of Getting Teachers and of Getting Positions," *Educational Review*, 20 (June 1900), 30–43; Charles W. Eliot to Draper, 31 March 1899, 2/4/1, B:3, F:Eliot. For an example of a "broken contract," see William H. Browne to Draper, 31 July 1902, 10 August 1902, 2/4/2, B:8, F:Brooks.

19. *18th Report* (1896), 175–76, 186.

20. *20th Report* (1901), 39, 270, 305; *18th Report*(1896), 110–11; Draper to President R. H. Jesse (University of Missouri), 11 September 1896, 2/4/3; C. W. Foulk and R. F. Earhart, "State University Salaries," *Popular Science Monthly*, 67 (December 1905), 423–34; *22nd Report* (1904), 330; *23rd Report* (1906), 39.

21. Draper to Chancellor Frank Strong (University of Kansas), 16 January 1904, 2/4/3.

22. *18th Report* (1896), 237; *19th Report* (1898), 125; Burrill to James E. Armstrong, 2 April 1898, 15/4/1, Botany: Departmental Correspondence, B:1.

23. *20th Report* (1901), 260, 305.

24. *21st Report* (1902), 208.

25. Draper, "The Rational Limits of Academic Freedom," *University [of Chicago] Record*, 12 (April 1908), 134–46; reprinted in *Addresses and Papers by Andrew S. Draper, 1908–1909* (Albany: New York State Education Department, [1909]), 3–20 (quotations at 9, 12, 13, and 14 respectively).

26. Ibid., 17 (first quotation), 19 (second quotation).

27. Draper, "The Ethics of Getting Teachers and of Getting Positions," 41.

28. University catalogs of the period list the home town and the collegiate status of all students. The description that follows is based on this information. As used here, the southern part of the state contains thirty counties and is defined as including, on the north, Madison, Bond, Marion, Clay, Richland, and Lawrence, and all the counties to the south. The northern part of the state contains twenty-two counties and includes, on the south, Rock Island, Henry, Bureau, La Salle, Grundy, and Kankakee, and all the counties to the north. The middle part of the state contains the other forty-six counties. Some biennial reports of the president give attendance data for the entire University, including attendance by counties, states, and countries. See the *Biennial Report of the Superintendent of Public Instruction* as follows: *22nd Report*(1896–98), 14–16; *23rd Report* (1898–1900), 74–76; *24th Report* (1900–2), 47–48; *25th Report* (1902–4), 49–51.

29. *Illio '96*, 167.

30. Finishing his course in 1897, Riley went to Nashville, Tennessee, where he caught "typhoid malaria" and died on 17 June. *Illini*, 24 September 1897.

31. Information on the enrollment of African Americans from 1894 to 1904 is teased out of many records, especially catalogs, contemporary publications, 2/9/16 (a Negro matriculants list), and 2/6/21 (the Albert Lee Papers).

32. *Twenty-First Biennial Report of the Superintendent of Public Instruction of the State of Illinois* (1894–96), 147; *Twenty-Second Biennial Report of the Superintendent of Public Instruction of the State of Illinois* (1896–98), 23.

33. *16th Report* (1892), 47.

34. Newspaper clipping from unidentified Chicago newspaper, Flower and Coues Family Scrapbooks, pp. 17–19 (quotation at 18), B:1, Scrapbook 3, Chicago Historical Society.

35. Draper to (Trustee) Richard P. Morgan, 2 April 1896, 2/4/3.

36. Draper to James E. Armstrong, 30 June 1896, 2/4/3; *18th Report* (1896), 254, 262, 263.

37. *18th Report* (1896), 237.

38. *Illini*, 17, 31 January, 7, 14 February 1895; 4/1/1, 3:278; *Illio '95*, 79; *Illio '96*, 100.

39. *Illini*, 25 September, 6 November 1896.

40. Ibid., 4 February, 7, 14 October 1898; *19th Report* (1898), 249.

41. *Illini*, 9 October, 1 November 1899.

42. Ibid., 23 February, 16 March 1900.

43. Ibid., 24 September, 8 October 1900.

44. Ibid., 29 October 1900.

45. Ibid., 3 March, 30 September 1902; 4 February 1903.

46. Ibid., 16, 17 April 1903.

# PART II

---

# CULTIVATING THE MIND

# CHAPTER 3

# "A Set of 'Cheap Men'"

## Literature and Arts

The Morrill Act of 1862 required land-grant institutions to teach "such branches of learning as are related to agriculture and the mechanic arts" without excluding other scientific and classical studies, and from its beginning the University taught the liberal arts. The College of Literature and Arts, which included two schools—Ancient Languages and Literature, and English and Modern Languages—was established to promote classical and literary studies. In the early years about 40 percent of the student body took liberal arts courses.[1]

In 1891 the trustees acknowledged that the "cultural side" of the University needed emphasis, and after Draper became president they restated their intent to invigorate the liberal arts. President Draper expressed no enthusiasm for "classical culture," but he acknowledged that the liberal arts college had enjoyed less nourishment than any of the other colleges and that the state needed to provide the youth of Illinois with "the best literary culture."[2]

### David Kinley's College

In 1894 the Board of Trustees named David Kinley dean of the College of Literature and Arts. Born in 1861 in Dundee, Scotland, as a boy Kinley emigrated with his mother and one sibling to Massachusetts to join his father, who had left a year earlier to find work. After three years in the Andover high school, Kinley spent two years at Phillips Academy, graduating in 1878. Kinley entered Yale on a scholarship, and in 1884, having taken two years out because of ill health, and having studied with William Graham Sumner, he graduated with an A.B. For six years Kinley served as principal of a high school in North Andover, after which he studied for two years at Johns Hopkins University with Richard T. Ely, a leading spokesman for the "new economics." Johns Hopkins made Kinley familiar with a research-oriented university. When Ely left for the University of Wisconsin he invited Kinley to accompany him. Kinley published his doctoral dissertation as *The Independent Treasury of the United States* (1893), and that fall he joined the Illinois faculty as an assistant professor of political economy and social science with the understanding that he was to start a department of economics. He also hoped to create a school of political science.[3]

When Kinley became dean, the college was little known by the people of Illinois, and within the University it was overshadowed by the College of Engineering, which enrolled 320 students, compared to 176 in the College of Literature and Arts. Although both the College of Science and the College of Agriculture had fewer students (99 and 9 respectively) than Literature and Arts, they dealt with tangible things that the public could understand, whereas the liberal arts had a hard time demonstrating what George Santayana once called "the utility of useless knowledge."[4] The college contained twelve of the twenty-nine departments of administration in the University.[5]

The ninety-one courses offered were structured into four groups—Ancient Languages and Literature, Modern Languages and Literature, Philosophical Studies, and History and the Political Sciences. Students chose one group for their principal study. The work of the first year and part of the second was prescribed; that of the last two years was elective. Initially the college awarded both the bachelor of literature (B.L.) degree and the bachelor of arts (A.B.) degree; after 1894 it awarded only the A.B.[6]

Kinley wished to promote the humanities as well as the social sciences. He followed advances in higher education closely and was determined to create a college of liberal arts equal to the best in the nation. He believed that any successful academic enterprise had to operate on two important business principles—supply must precede and stimulate demand, and the quality of its offerings must be as good as the quality of the competition's. Accordingly, Illinois had to compete with such universities as Chicago, Wisconsin, and Michigan.[7]

In March 1895 Kinley recommended redirection of the college. He wanted to expand the scope of the college, strengthening it in general philosophy and the arts and establishing a school of political science, economics, and history similar to those found at Columbia, Michigan, and Wisconsin. He suggested offering courses in administrative and constitutional history and law, historical and comparative jurisprudence, international law, and kindred branches, subjects that were part of a liberal education. In addition, Kinley urged the promotion of graduate study. No institution could gain a place among the great universities unless it offered ample facilities for advanced study and research, he wrote to Draper. The college must have ample library facilities and free its chief instructors from the drudgery of elementary work. In both respects Illinois was behind the times.[8]

In the fall of 1895 the reorganization became effective. Under the new arrangements, which resembled those in other universities, students could choose between two systems of instruction. The general course system required less than three years of work in any one line for graduation, and no thesis. Much of the work of the first two years was required, the remainder elective. This route permitted a smattering of many types of learning. The specialized or group course system required at least two years of work in a single subject before the senior year, followed by a final year in that subject and the writing of a thesis. This route encouraged concentration in a single study. The groups were the Classical, English and Modern Languages, Philosophical, and Political Science. The courses available were classed as prescribed and elective. The former included mathematics, English, rhetoric, a foreign language, history, logic, military science, and natural science. The electives were subdivided into List A (major courses), and List B (other courses in the college), not all of which were in one of the four groups.[9]

Kinley encountered many obstacles in his effort to revitalize the liberal arts. Perhaps the most formidable was President Draper, who demonstrated little willingness to support "liberal culture" and little sympathy for advanced study of a nonutilitarian nature. Kinley sought the best instructors available, and the faculty he assembled was young. Some of the people he hired had German doctorates (although Kinley was not a fan of German universities), but many lacked even a master's degree.

Kinley fought hard for a proportionate share of the available resources. In 1895 he informed Draper that $2,000 was too low for the annual salary of a full professor. State universities in Wisconsin, Michigan, Minnesota, Texas, and Virginia all paid considerably more. Kinley often pleaded with Draper for small increments for individual faculty members.[10]

Kinley objected to the favored treatment of the College of Engineering. Enrollment in the liberal arts had increased at a much faster rate than in engineering, he noted in an annual report, but the liberal arts college was behind the engineering college in many important ways. The average salary of a full professor in the liberal arts was $1,780, compared to $2,233 in engineering. These and other inequities—in faculty rank, in heads of department, and in material equipment—created the impression that the faculty of the college was "a set of 'cheap men.'" Moreover, students of the college felt that less was done to promote literary work than technical work. Some graduates said that had they realized this fact as fully before they matriculated at Illinois as they did afterward, they would have gone elsewhere to college.[11]

Kinley pressed his case relentlessly. In 1899 he concluded that the college was at a turning point, and if it could not be started on an enlarged course, he preferred to resign the deanship and return to his own department. The College of Literature and Arts had to become "the center of culture in the University to balance the severely practical spirit of the technical departments."[12] But he remained in office, continuing his hardscrabble efforts. In 1900, for example, he compared the College of Literature and Arts at Illinois with corresponding divisions at California, Cornell, Michigan, Wisconsin, Minnesota, Nebraska, and Stanford. "Our College," he reported, "is not only the lowest in the number of instructors, but the lowest by a very great deal." In history, political science, and economics, Illinois had five instructors, in the other departments an average of ten.[13]

Despite the obstacles, Kinley made some progress. He instituted college assemblies to promote unity of feeling among liberal arts students, to develop the aesthetic side of education, and to arouse interest in topics beyond class work. The assemblies ideally met once a month. At the first assembly each year, Kinley emphasized liberal culture. The programs included lectures on such topics as the novel, art, and the New England college; songs of Shakespeare; and scenes from Homer's *Iliad*—presented in costume. Kinley once secured $25 to conduct these gatherings, but usually Draper denied funds for the purpose, although he persuaded the Board of Trustees to appropriate $250 for the purpose of domesticating squirrels on the campus.[14]

TABLE 4

TOTAL ENROLLMENTS AND NUMBER OF B.A. DEGREES AWARDED,
COLLEGE OF LITERATURE AND ARTS, 1894–1904

|  | 94–95 | 95–96 | 96–97 | 97–98 | 98–99 | 99–00 | 00–01 | 01–02 | 02–03 | 03–04 |
|---|---|---|---|---|---|---|---|---|---|---|
| Men | 102 | 105 | 125 | 145 | 159 | 162 | 198 | 201 | 202 | NA |
| Women | 74 | 104 | 120 | 115 | 118 | 176 | 185 | 223 | 262 | NA |
| Total | 176 | 209 | 245 | 260 | 277 | 338 | 383 | 424 | 464 | 541 |
| B.A.s awarded | 16 | 26 | 19 | 27 | 36 | 37 | 60 | 64 | 57 | 81 |

NA: Not available.

*Source:* The information in this table is drawn from the dean's annual reports for the College of Literature and Arts in the years noted (RS 15.1.11).

TABLE 5

## STUDENT ENROLLMENTS BY DEPARTMENT, COLLEGE OF LITERATURE AND ARTS, 1894–1904

| | 94–95 | 95–96 | 96–97 | 97–98 | 98–99 | 99–00 | 00–01 | 01–02 | 02–03 | 03–04 |
|---|---|---|---|---|---|---|---|---|---|---|
| Art and Design | 117 | 160 | 300 | 256 | 317 | 315 | 362 | 333 | 369 | 454 |
| Economics | 73 | 115 | 180 | 180 | 253 | 250 | 249 | 253 | 309 | 735 |
| English | 241 | 375 | 380 | 418 | 553 | 357 | 511 | 535 | 710 | 773 |
| French | 392 | 261 | 272 | 313 | 507 | 443 | 452 | 496 | 552 | 510 |
| German | 397 | 512 | 492 | 705 | 760 | 616 | 727 | 585 | 880 | 1,055 |
| Greek | 44 | 38 | 48 | 29 | 43 | 33 | 55 | 41 | 37 | 53 |
| History | 160 | 257 | 266 | 304 | 419 | 439 | 532 | 529 | 561 | 531 |
| Italian and Spanish* | 16 | 8 | | | | | | | | |
| Latin | 109 | 116 | 125 | 128 | 130 | 111 | 114 | 112 | 124 | 154 |
| Pedagogy† | 41 | 45 | 119 | 131 | 124 | 17 | 115 | 80 | 162 | 97 |
| Philosophy | 52 | 58 | 86 | 119 | 132 | 122 | 111 | 129 | 136 | 177 |
| Political Science‡ | — | 76 | 146 | 172 | 206 | 170 | 211 | 68 | — | 33 |
| Psychology | 52 | 92 | 110 | 37 | 24 | 9 | 34 | 63 | — | 71 |
| Rhetoric | 450 | 594 | 617 | 666 | 691 | 684 | 719 | 942 | 1,131 | 1,393 |

*The figures for Italian and Spanish are combined with French department enrollments after 1895–96.

†The Department of Pedagogy became the Department of Education in 1901.

‡Political Science was known first as Public Law and Administration and later as Government.

*Source:* The information in this table is drawn from the dean's annual reports for the College of Literature and Arts in the years noted (RS 15.1.11).

Another measure of achievement was attendance. From 1894 to 1904 enrollments in the liberal arts tripled, a rate of growth faster than that of any of the other undergraduate colleges. In many years a roughly equal number of men and women were enrolled in the college, but the number of women grew faster than the number of men—which reinforced the perception that the college was a feminine preserve. Most departments, including English, history, pedagogy, philosophy, and rhetoric, kept pace with the rate of growth in the college. Some departments, among them French, Greek, Latin, psychology, and political science, lagged behind the pace. The economics department grew at an exceptional rate over the decade, mainly because of an enrollment spike in 1903–4. Few students took advanced courses, but from 1895 to 1904 the number of B.A.s awarded quintupled. Tables 4 and 5 illustrate the advances in liberal arts in the four groups, to which we now turn.

## THE CLASSICAL GROUP

The languages and literature of ancient Greece and Rome had been the core of the liberal arts curriculum for centuries, and American colleges had insisted that the study of Greek and Latin disciplined the mind and cultivated the taste. In 1894–95 Latin was required for admission to the college, and some Greek was required of students desiring to pursue Greek.

Charles M. Moss (b. 1853), who held a doctorate from Syracuse University, was the professor of Greek. He served as head of the department from 1891 to 1918. In 1894–95 the department offered nine undergraduate courses, but the subject did not attract "our constituency," and the Greek department was the smallest in the college. It enrolled from twenty-nine to fifty-five students a year from 1894 to 1904, with an annual average of forty-two. With a view to arousing larger interest, in 1900 the department introduced a beginning course in Greek. It was a qualified success. Nevertheless, Kinley thought that Moss lacked the enthusiasm needed to attract students to a discipline that in itself had little appeal.[15]

The Latin department advanced in these same years under Herbert J. Barton (b. 1853), whose highest degree was a master of arts from Dartmouth. "While [Barton] is not a great Latin scholar," Kinley reported, "he is a good Latin teacher." In 1894–95 the department offered ten courses. During the following decade enrollments ranged from 109 to 154 students a year, with an average of 122. Barton was an excellent drillmaster, but he lacked the training and background in research necessary to develop graduate work in most lines of his specialty.[16]

A disproportionately large number of the senior theses written between 1894 and 1904 were in the classics. Four were on Greek topics and eleven on Latin topics. Two theses compared Greek and Latin authors or works, and one was titled "Plautus's Menaechmi as the Basis for Shakespeare's *Comedy of Errors*."[17]

The classics professors apparently took a philological approach, but Kinley, who disliked the emphasis on syntax and etymology, urged the introduction of a course on the life of the Romans and the addition of an archeologist to the faculty. In 1900–1 Moss was teaching twenty hours a week, which justified the addition of another staff member, and that fall Kenneth P. R. Neville (b. 1876), who held an A.B. from Harvard and had been a graduate student in classics at Cornell and Illinois, joined the faculty as an instructor in Latin and Greek. In 1901, Kinley suggested offering courses in Latin and Greek literature in translation the next year. By 1903–4 a total of sixteen courses were offered in the Greek department and fifteen in the Latin department. A year later the two units were incorporated into a newly created Department of Classics.[18]

## THE ENGLISH AND MODERN LANGUAGES GROUP

In American colleges the classics had been valued as the best means of transmitting the cultural tradition. In the late nineteenth century, however, the classics were eclipsed and academic literary studies began to find their home in English and modern language departments. Because English was regarded as a subject for women and sissies, teachers trained in the German philological tradition often taught as the classicists had, emphasizing grammar rather than literature and making their subject hard in order to be taken seriously.

By the 1890s the ranks of literature professors had split into two camps, neatly fitting Gerald Graff's distinction of investigators versus generalists. The investigators, devoted to the scientific study of literature (often from the perspective of philology), stressed research and facts. The generalists assigned literature the mission of transmitting the cultural tradition, and they sought from it moral values rather than facts. Exemplars of the two camps were found at Illinois.[19]

### English

The English department was headed by Daniel K. Dodge (b. 1863), who had joined the faculty in 1892 with a doctorate from Columbia. An authority on philology and Scandinavian literature whose training had been on the critical side, Dodge nevertheless defended the generalist position in an article in *The Dial* that was later reprinted in *English in American Universities* (1895). As Dodge related, the aim of the department was the development of general culture rather than preparation for scientific research. In 1894 the department listed fourteen courses, all of which were devoted to English (not American) literature. The first-year course surveyed the entire field of literature; the other offerings were divided between language (philology) and literature, with most students choosing the latter. A course in Old English (Anglo-Saxon) was available, and Shakespeare received considerable attention.[20]

English was one of the largest departments in the college. Its enrollments ranged from 241 to 773 a year between 1894 and 1904, with an average of 365. It had a preponderance of women students and a large number of women instructors. Enrollments increased markedly beginning in 1900, the year in which American literature was reintroduced.[21] Despite large enrollments, only six senior theses in English are recorded.

Dodge published many articles on educational and Scandinavian subjects as well as a monograph, *Abraham Lincoln: The Evolution of His Literary Style* (1900). Although students valued his work, Kinley thought that Dodge lacked originality and force. Kinley wanted to stimulate study of the creative and aesthetic side of literature.

Edward C. Baldwin (b. 1870), a Connecticut Yankee with bachelor's and doctoral degrees from Yale, joined the faculty in 1899. Kinley regarded him as the best scholar in the department and likely to be productive. Baldwin experienced some difficulty in adjusting to his new environment, but he introduced literary study of the Bible, and the course enrollment doubled the second year it was offered. Knowing that his tenure was uncertain, Baldwin labored under great nervous strain. Kinley wanted to relieve the strain, believing that Baldwin's courses would then become even more attractive to students. By 1903–4 Dodge, Baldwin, and two colleagues were offering twenty-six undergraduate and three postgraduate courses, but the English department was not yet strong enough in personnel and influence to satisfy Kinley.[22]

The arrival of Neville in classics enabled faculty in five departments—Greek, Latin, English, French, and German—to introduce in 1902–3 a program in comparative literature and philology, perhaps one of the earliest of its type in the nation. The offerings were Greek Literature, Latin Literature, Development of the Drama, General Introduction to the Science of Language, Historical Latin Grammar, and History of Classical Philology. Neville taught the last three of these courses.

Rhetoric, the art or science of effective speaking and writing, had been an educational staple since antiquity. For some years the English department at Illinois had taught a required course in writing, and the rhetoric and oratory department had taught elocution. But in 1894 the latter department was divided into two—rhetoric, and oratory and oral rhetoric.[23]

Because rhetoric was required of all University students, the department grew at the same pace as the student body. In the decade starting in 1894, annual enrollments ranged from a low of 450 to a high of 1,393, with an average of 789 a year, making rhetoric the largest department in the college.

Thomas Arkle Clark headed this department (his early life is discussed in a later chapter). In 1894 he was put in charge of rhetoric. That summer he attended the University of Chicago, a year later he became an assistant professor of rhetoric, and in 1898–99 he studied at Harvard but fell short of degree requirements (so his highest degree was a B.L. from Illinois). On returning to Urbana he was made professor of rhetoric at a salary of $1,700. Clark cherished literature because it transmitted the cultural tradition. He published elementary texts, including *Elements of English* (1890) and *Composition in the High Schools of Illinois* (1896), as well as *Biographies of Great American Authors* (1900–1) and *Biographies of Great English Authors* (1901–2), each of which contained sketches of literary figures, followed by selections from their works. Clark cared about students and was skillful at advancing both his own and his department's interests. Kinley praised him, and in 1900–1 Draper made Clark acting dean of the college.

Clark's department required a course in Rhetoric and Themes of all students, with one class for those in Literature and Arts and another for students in the colleges of Agriculture, Engineering, and Science. The advanced courses were Daily Themes and Philosophy of Rhetoric.

The study of oratory and elocution was waning in American culture in the late nineteenth century, but it hung on at Illinois for some time. The Department of Oratory and Oral Rhetoric offered five courses, all taught by Anita M. Kellogg, who held a bachelor of elocution (B.E.) degree. In addition to basic courses, Kellogg taught both Expression and Interpretive Reading. The former included instruction in "public addresses, bible and hymn reading, reading of church service, delivery of sermons, conduct of meetings."[24]

In 1895 the Department of Oratory and Oral Rhetoric disappeared. Some officials and students lamented its loss. Although Kinley disliked ordinary teachers of elocution because they stressed "dramatic arts," he wanted more work in public speaking and someone to prepare students for intercollegiate debates and oratorical contests.[25]

In 1898 the Department of Rhetoric became the Department of Rhetoric and Oratory, with Clark as its head. By 1903–4 this department was offering fifteen courses that complemented the work of the English department. The subjects taught laid the foundations for what would later become programs in speech communication, journalism, and business writing. Between 1894 and 1904 at least eleven men and seven women taught in the department. Most of them held only a bachelor's degree and were burdened with reading compositions. However little Clark's department may have contributed to the intellectual life of the campus, it generated large enrollments and was well regarded by the administration.

## German

Edward Snyder had long been the mainstay of the German department, and when he went on leave in 1894–95 his duties were assumed by Elizabeth C. Bruner, an assistant professor with an A.B. She resigned at the end of the academic year, and the department got a fresh start with the appointment of Lewis A. Rhoades (b. 1860) as an assistant professor. Rhoades had taken bachelor's and master's degrees at the University of Michigan in 1884 and 1886 respectively, and a doctorate at the University of Göttingen in 1892. He had taught at Michigan for two years and at Cornell for three years before coming to Illinois. A respected scholar, he provided effective leadership, although he chafed because Illinois allowed departments much less liberty of action than either Michigan or Cornell. He encountered some adversity because of his tendency to speak too freely of free speech, and at times he created the impression of being somewhat pompous and dogmatic.[26]

In 1897 George H. Meyer (b. 1865), who held bachelor's and master's degrees from Colgate University, arrived as an instructor. Kinley rated him highly and promoted him to assistant professor. In 1903, when Rhoades resigned to take a position at Ohio State, Meyer became head of the department. He managed it well. In 1904 he went on leave at half pay and for the next two years studied at the universities of Berlin and Jena.

In 1898 Neil C. Brooks (b. 1869), a native of Kansas City, became an instructor in the department. After taking a bachelor's degree at the University of Kansas, Brooks had studied at the University of Berlin for two years. In 1898 he earned a doctorate at Harvard University, thus becoming the first member of the German faculty with an American doctorate.

The German department sought to give students a reading knowledge of the language and to introduce them to German literature. The emphasis was on grammar and translation. From 1894 to 1896 the department offered the same six courses, two of which were in scientific and technical German. Rhoades wanted to deemphasize the purely linguistic work. In 1896–97 the offerings numbered nine, including three in scientific and technical German, one on Goethe, and one on the history of German literature. A year later a course on either Lessing or Schiller was added, and for the next three years the catalog listed thirteen courses. Now two literature courses—one on Lessing or Schiller and one on Goethe—were available, along with one or two courses for students in the colleges of Engineering and Science. The new possibilities were a course on Heine and the Romantic poets and a teachers' seminary. In 1900, courses in Middle High German, Old High German, and advanced prose composition were introduced, making a total of fifteen courses. Much of the work was designed to aid students in technical fields, but serious students could study Goethe, Lessing, and Schiller, and advanced work in the history of the German language and philology was available. In 1902–3 the curriculum was enlarged and reoriented. The catalog listed twenty-two courses for undergraduates and three for graduates.

Six senior theses in the German department are readily identifiable, fewer than in Latin. A thesis on Schiller's *Jungfrau von Orleans* treated a subject on which Rhoades later published a book. Kinley wanted the department to place more stress on conversation and writing than on literary treatments.

After rhetoric and oratory, the German department was the largest in the college. Its annual enrollments ranged from 397 to 1,055 in the ten years after 1894, for an average enrollment of 627 a year, including the Preparatory School. Women students were more heavily represented in German than in any other department in Literature and Arts. Many men studied German for technical and scientific purposes, but the courses designed to teach German to students of engineering and science caused continuing controversy. Such students were little interested in German philology or literature, and their instructors were unwilling to teach by using pages full of terms from chemistry, geology, or physiology. Draper, who wanted science students to have the language, wrote to other university presidents seeking advice on how to teach it. Rhoades once balked at teaching a German course for scientists and engineers, but the Council of Administration overruled him.[27]

For many years Rhoades, Meyer, and Brooks carried much of the teaching load in German, aided briefly by three other men and one woman. Dean Kinley commended the German department, and pleaded for additional instructors. In 1900 Daisy L. Blaisdell (b. 1866), who held bachelor's and master's degrees from Smith College, joined the faculty as an instructor. She had "certain mannerisms" that Kinley found disagreeable, but her spirit and general attitude were good. Blaisdell did graduate work at the University from 1906 to 1909, rose to the rank of assistant professor, and taught until her retirement in 1931.[28]

### French/Romance Languages

In 1894 the Department of Romance Languages included French, Italian, and Spanish, but only French could be chosen as a major subject.[29] French, the fourth most popular field in the college (history was third), lagged behind German because of the demand for scientific and technical German.

In the years from 1894 to 1904 the curriculum in Romance languages went through three stages. In the first stage, the academic year 1894–95, three instructors made available seven courses, five in French and one each in Italian and Spanish. James D. Bruner, who had joined the faculty as an assistant professor in 1893, headed the work. He became a professor in 1894 (the catalog listed him as a Ph.D., a degree he received in 1904 from Johns Hopkins University), and despite his eccentricities, Kinley wanted to keep him. But Bruner and his wife left at the end of the year. He became an assistant professor at the University of Chicago.[30]

In the second stage, which lasted from 1895 to 1903, the department marked time. The mainstays of the faculty were now Herman S. Piatt and George D. Fairfield. Piatt (b. 1869), from Lincoln, Illinois, came from the family after which Piatt County was named. After graduating from the University in 1892 he went on for a master's degree, and in 1894 he joined the faculty as an instructor. In 1896–97 he studied at the University of Strassburg, earning a doctorate with a dissertation on the origin of the neuter *il* in French. Fairfield (b. 1866), a former vice-consul of the United States in Lyons, France, studied at the University of Chicago in 1893–94; the catalog listed him as holding an M.A. degree. He taught at DePauw University before his appointment in 1895 as an assistant professor.

Kinley regarded neither man as an obvious head of the department, but in 1899 he appointed Fairfield.[31] The instructional staff lacked stability. Fairfield's married life while he was a resident of Urbana caused gossip. His wife, who accused him of being too friendly with several women in his classes, sued for divorce on a charge of extreme and repeated cruelty. He fought the case and won, later allowing her to secure a divorce on a charge of desertion. When Piatt went on leave in 1896–97, David H. Carnahan, class of 1896, was appointed assistant professor (he earned a doctorate at Yale in 1905). Kinley pleaded for more instructors. One man and two women with bachelor's degrees served as fellows or assistants to meet the needs. In 1901 Piatt resigned, spending most of his later career as a public school principal in New York City. Fairfield departed in 1903, taught elsewhere for several years, and then managed buildings in Chicago.[32]

The departures of Piatt and then of Fairfield opened up faculty positions, and beginning with the academic year 1903–4 the French department was entirely reconstructed. In 1903 Thomas E. Oliver (b. 1871) was appointed professor of Romance languages. A Harvard A.B. (1893), he attended Harvard Medical School the following year, then studied at the universities of Leipzig (1894–95) and Heidelberg (1895–97); went to Paris, where he studied at both the Sorbonne and the École des Hautes Études, Collège de France (1897–98); and returned to Heidelberg, where in 1899 he received an A.M. and a Ph.D. He taught at the University of Michigan for one year and at the College for Women of Western Reserve University for three years before casting his lot with Illinois. When he arrived, one of his colleagues was Florence Nightingale Jones, an Oberlin A.B. with a master's degree from Nebraska who had studied at the Sorbonne in 1896–97. She joined the faculty in 1900 as an instructor, and in 1903 earned a doctorate at the University of Chicago. Quiet in her ways and a good teacher, her influence made for ideals that were said to be "high and good."[33]

Under Oliver, the curriculum of the department expanded. While listing no course in Italian and only one in Spanish, the catalog announced thirteen undergraduate courses in French plus special courses for graduate students. Oliver seemingly revitalized the Romanic languages at Illinois, but Kinley was not impressed. The department, he wrote in 1904, was not as strong as it had been in past years. Oliver was not strong in scholarship or executive ability, although he appeared to teach well. Yet "Tommy" Oliver, as he came to be known, served on the faculty for thirty-seven years, retiring in 1940.

## THE PHILOSOPHICAL GROUP

The Philosophical Group comprised three studies that reflected contemporary ideas about intellectual affinities among them: pedagogy, philosophy, and psychology. They were closely linked, and a student could take any one as a major subject.

## Pedagogy

Pedagogy was considered vital to national welfare because it involved the transmission of the cultural heritage to the next generation. Although many normal schools existed—by the end of the century Illinois had four—they were engaged primarily in teacher training rather than in the science of pedagogy. The first permanent university chair in pedagogy was established at the University of Michigan in 1879; by 1890 such chairs existed in over a hundred institutions. At the time the curriculum of the schools needed attention because knowledge had expanded rapidly but in a disorderly way. Expert opinion on curriculum-making was unavailable in the United States, which lacked a distinctive philosophy of education.[34]

In the 1890s pedagogy at Illinois developed under various influences. A number of able and well-trained men joined and left the department in rapid succession. Charles DeGarmo, the first of these, had published two books based on Herbartian educational theories before he was appointed professor of psychology in December 1890. He served only one semester.[35]

William O. Krohn, who arrived in 1892 as an assistant professor of psychology and pedagogy, offered six courses in pedagogy that year, after which he confined himself to psychology. Krohn's course in the philosophy of education used selections from Rosenkranz and Bain as well as Herbert Spencer's *Education: Intellectual, Moral, and Physical.*

In 1893 Frank M. McMurry (b. 1862) replaced Krohn as professor of pedagogy. He began his instruction with seven students, using Bain and Spencer in his philosophy of education course. In 1893 McMurry established a model school to test pedagogical theory; his was probably the first practice-teaching experiment in any American university. McMurry believed that he was probably the only professor of elementary education in the United States at the time. "I was advised by good authority not to let it be known that my chief interest was in the primary school, for fear I might lose my position," he later wrote. "It was then beneath the dignity of any university to identify itself with training for the instruction of young children. It was bad enough to train for instruction in the high school."[36]

DeGarmo left Illinois to become president of Swarthmore College; subsequently he served as a professor at Cornell University. McMurry spent most of his later career as a professor at Teachers College, Columbia University. Both men were on the executive council of the National Herbart Society for the Scientific Study of Education at its inception in 1895, and by virtue of their positions, speeches, and publications they exerted a strong influence on American education. The reasons for their departure from the University cannot be ascertained. Some problem—it may have been his effort to found a model school—apparently derailed McMurry. We know only that after one year the trustees felt justified in terminating him.[37]

In 1894 William J. Eckoff came to fill the pedagogy post. Born in Germany, Eckoff had been president of a college in Nicaragua. He took a doctorate at New York University and taught briefly at Columbia University and the University of Colorado. A strong Herbartian who also drew on the antithetical educational ideas of Herbert Spencer, he introduced and taught a slate of seven courses that attracted forty-one students. Yet Kinley found him undesirable—"so erratic in his views, and so averse to adapting himself to the existing situation here," he told Draper, "that his continuance will ... be a drawback. Few, if any, of his colleagues respect him or have confidence in his discretion and judgment. His irreconcilability to the existing order and his refusal to be directed by the suggestions, or even orders, of his official superiors, are a standing bar to his usefulness." At the end of the year Eckoff resigned.[38]

Draper wanted a professor of pedagogy who knew what a good high school was and how to make one, who was a good listener and a good public speaker, and who would attend state educational conventions. In 1895 the department finally gained such a person and a measure of stability with Arnold Tompkins. Born in 1849 near Paris, Illinois, Tompkins had studied at Indiana University (1868) and Butler University (1870) before graduating from Indiana State Normal School in 1880. He received an A.B. (1889) and an M.A. (1891) from Indiana University and pursued graduate study at the University of Chicago and Ohio University in Athens. Meanwhile, he had taught in public schools and been a school superintendent, gaining a reputation as one of the most popular lecturers at teachers' institutes in the United States. In addition, he had served as professor of English at both DePauw University and Indiana State Normal School, and as dean of the Normal School at DePauw. Appointed with glowing recommendations, Tompkins completed his doctorate at Ohio University the year after joining the University.[39]

Tompkins was metaphysical in his thinking. He saw universal laws in the minutest details and wanted to build a school of pedagogy as the concrete realization of the best philosophy of education. Neither he nor Draper was interested in the model school, which was dissolved after McMurry left. Tompkins described the point of view taken by his department as "the highest known in the pedagogical field—the Herbartian," but he had imbibed a heady Hegelianism at Indiana State Normal School, and it was reflected in his desire to "bring all phases of professional life into the unity of a great controlling principle." He introduced a new slate of courses. His course, The Universal Form of Method in Education ("as determined by the nature of life"), dealt with the subject in its subjective aspect, its objective aspect, and the three forms of the relation of the former two, "giving rise to the logic, ethics, and esthetics of education—the fundamental educational categories." In 1897 he introduced a new course, The Beautiful as a Factor in Education.[40]

Tompkins, a teacher of magnetic power and breezy humor, was popular with students. A brilliant speaker who could "read" and then captivate an audience, he was in great demand beyond the campus. His engagements threatened to interfere with his University duties, so much so that Draper once considered cutting Tompkins's salary because he was away so often.[41]

Relations between the University and the high schools of the state were an ongoing problem. Tompkins questioned the system of accreditation. To visit a high school only to accredit it for admission drew an arbitrary distinction and generated friction between the schools and the University. Accordingly, Tompkins suggested considering the admission of all students in a probationary mode, which would free the visitor to help the school meet University requirements and have a unifying effect. Accreditation cut into faculty time, so in 1896 the University created a new position to conduct the work. John E. McGilvrey (b. 1867), who had an A.B. from Indiana University, was appointed high school visitor and made an assistant professor of pedagogy.[42]

Tompkins gave new life to the Department of Pedagogy. Its enrollments increased dramatically, with an annual average of 105 students during his tenure. But after four years he left the University. In October 1897, after declining an offer as regent at Southern Illinois University, he reiterated his desire to build a school rather than a department of pedagogy. The Council of Administration rejected the proposal, although it favored development of the philosophical pedagogical work.

By March 1899, however, Tompkins was frustrated. Pedagogy was subordinated to the other departments, he felt, and he could not afford to stay at the University unless it was advanced. He proposed that it be taught only in a graduate program during the summer. Burrill urged Draper to speak to the trustees about upgrading pedagogy, and at a meeting on 13 June the board's Committee on Instruction recommended establishing a teachers' college with Tompkins as dean. Action was deferred in order to hear from the deans, and after they had been heard, one board member moved to give Tompkins "the assurance that he shall have every opportunity to make his department all that is necessary for the interests of the teachers of the State of Illinois" and a raise in salary. On 21 June, however, Tompkins resigned to become president of Illinois State Normal University.[43]

Draper's first choice to replace Tompkins was Elmer E. Brown of the University of California. Tompkins had been paid $2,000. The University was willing to pay Brown $2,250, but he was already earning $3,000 at California and declined, later becoming the U.S. Commissioner of Education. With Draper in Europe, Burrill and the Committee on Instruction took over the search. The candidate they identified, Louis H. Galbreath, suddenly fell ill and died.[44]

In September the board authorized Draper to fill the vacancy. He cast a wide net, receiving recommendations from Nicholas Murray Butler,

John Dewey, and William T. Harris, along with many who nominated themselves. He could move slowly, since not more than six students had manifested any real demand for the subject. His correspondence lays bare his ideas about the field. He wanted the highest kind of pedagogical work, but he wanted more than a philosophical thinker on pedagogical questions. He wanted a professor who recognized that the public school system was the crucial area, a person who would make the public schools his laboratory and welcome the opportunity to help them. And he wanted harmony with all the educational forces of the state. The University should not parallel or rival the work of the normal schools, and it should not operate a practice or model school. Draper sent tentative offers to four or five men in September and went east to pursue the search, but those he met were either unavailable or unsuitable. The trouble was, he wanted for $2,000 a man who could command $4,000 to $5,000.[45]

In November the dean of Teachers College at Columbia University recommended Edwin Grant Dexter (b. 1868), who had taken bachelor's and master's degrees at Brown University, a diploma at Teachers College, and a Ph.D. in education, psychology, and philosophy at Columbia in 1899. At the time Dexter was a professor of psychology at Colorado State Normal School in Greeley. Dexter received some strong recommendations and some lukewarm ones: President Nicholas Murray Butler of Columbia called him "a good man, but not, I think, a first class man," and J. McKeen Cattell of Columbia described him as acceptable as an instructor or assistant professor. Draper met Dexter in Omaha, and in December he hired him as professor of pedagogy at $2,000 a year on the understanding that Dexter would arrive in 1900. Dexter proposed to make the University "the recognized source of supply for the best fitted high school teachers in the market."[46]

Since McGilvrey had resigned because he felt underpaid, Draper also had to find a new person to be assistant in pedagogy and high school visitor. He insisted that the appointee be familiar with the Illinois scene. Stratton D. Brooks (b. 1869), principal of La Salle–Peru Township High School, came highly recommended. He was well educated, having earned bachelor's and master's degrees in pedagogy from the normal school at Ypsilanti, Michigan, an A.B. from Michigan, and an A.M. from Harvard. He had been a high school principal for years and active in state educational circles. The board offered him $1,300; he wanted $2,000 but agreed to come for $1,600.[47]

In 1899–1900 Brooks offered a course that attracted seventeen students, and a year later Dexter gave a new impulse to the work in pedagogy. Since an appointment had not been made in psychology, Dexter proposed a marriage of convenience between pedagogy and psychology under his direction. This arrangement lasted for two years, during which time Dexter entirely reoriented the Department of Pedagogy. Its aim was to meet the needs of secondary school teachers and to supplement the work of the normal schools (whose task was to train elementary school teachers). His proposed "school" of education would award an A.B. or B.S. He wanted his classes restricted to juniors, seniors, and graduate students, and he offered a slate of courses geared to the training of teachers, a practical program that must have delighted Draper. Dexter announced his readiness to direct "experimental and statistical problems in education and child study."[48]

In 1901 the pedagogy department was renamed the Department of Education, and Dexter adjusted the program of studies. He and Brooks shared the teaching of ten courses. From 1900–1 to 1903–4 enrollments rode a roller coaster: 115, 80, 162, and 97. The Department of Education, said Kinley in 1904, was by no means as good as it should be. It needed at least one more instructor, someone of more scientific exactness than Dexter. Dexter was a good teacher who published a great deal, and a good department head. Kinley did not want to lose him. But his work needed to be "more thorough and searching, scientifically."[49]

## Philosophy

Philosophy was a one-man operation headed by Arthur Hill Daniels. Born in Massachusetts in 1865, Daniels had taken a divinity degree at Yale in 1890 and a Ph.D. at Clark University in 1893, after which he joined the Illinois faculty as an instructor. In 1894 Daniels announced eight courses, all in philosophy, logic, and ethics. He later added variations on these subjects, including courses in esthetics, the philosophy of religion, the philosophy of nature, the philosophy of Herbert Spencer, and a graduate course in the philosophy of Kant. He also taught courses in anthropology, ethnography, and ethnology.

Kinley called philosophy a "mongrel" department because Daniels taught so many different subjects. The department was small, and it seemed unimportant in the life of the University. From 1894 to 1904 enrollments ranged from a low of 52 to a high of 177 annually, with an average of 112. Logic, required of all students in the group, turned them against philosophy, and the elective work did not grow. With the omission of logic from the prescribed list Kinley hoped the department would prosper, but "our environment and constituency are such that philosophy does not attract the large run of students," he admitted. "It is not practical enough." Yet Kinley thought that no department of the college exercised a better influence on students, intellectually and ethically, than philosophy. Draper found Daniels "thoroughly pleasing, but not very strong." Kinley found him "serviceable" in many ways outside his class work; he bore responsibilities well and had possibilities for larger usefulness. "Prof. Daniels is not a genius, but he is a good worker, has good judgment, and is a thorough scholar in his tastes and habits of work."[50]

*Psychology*

A new era in American psychology began with publication of William James's *Principles of Psychology* (1890), and psychology first found a place in the University in 1892, when William O. Krohn (b. 1868) joined the faculty as an assistant professor. After earning a doctorate in philosophy at Yale in 1889, Krohn had headed a department of philosophy, psychology, and ethics in colleges affiliated with Western Reserve University for two years, had studied medicine and laboratory psychology at Freiburg, Germany, for one year, and had been a fellow at Clark University for several months. The work in psychology at Clark under G. Stanley Hall was then among the best available in the nation.[51]

During his first year Krohn carried responsibility for both psychology (five courses) and pedagogy (six courses). In 1893, when McMurry took over pedagogy, Krohn focused on psychology. His aim was to acquaint students with the nature of the mind in both its normal and abnormal phases, with special attention given to scientific methods of studying children. Krohn devised a curriculum of eight courses, including Laboratory Psychology, Comparative Psychology, Psychology of Crime, Psychology of the Abnormal Types, and Advanced Experimental Psychology. This program remained largely fixed for several years.

Krohn's professional preparation was excellent, and he kept abreast of his field. In 1892 he used a brief version of James's *Principles of Psychology* (1890) as a text in his introductory course, while in the comparative psychology course he drew on George J. Romanes and C. Lloyd Morgan, pioneers in the evolutionary understanding of animal behavior and intelligence who had published significant works in the 1880s and '90s. In 1894 Krohn published *Practical Lessons in Psychology*, a book that grew out of lectures to schoolteachers that the author characterized as having "a practical ring rather than a scholastic rattle." The University had a psychological laboratory in Natural History Hall with apparatus, and Krohn had students in his laboratory psychology course perform experiments.[52]

Kinley nevertheless viewed Krohn as undesirable. He "does us good service in lecturing about the state," Kinley wrote in 1895, "for he creates a good impression on his first few appearances, everywhere. But his character for veracity and his general unreliability are a standing reproach to the University and a pernicious example to students." So Draper recommended that Krohn be dropped at the end of the year.[53]

But Krohn weathered this crisis and remained in Urbana two more years. As a teacher he attracted an average of eighty-four students a year between 1894 and 1897. He was active in the Illinois Society for Child Study, organized in 1894, and became the editor of the *Child-Study Monthly*, founded a year later. By 1897, however, Draper wanted the services of both Krohn in psychology and Summers in physiology terminated. Draper thought that a strong man in laboratory psychology with a good instructor in physiology would produce better results. Krohn went to the Eastern Hospital for the Insane in Kankakee.[54]

Krohn's replacement was John P. Hylan (b. 1870), a native of New Hampshire who had prepared at Phillips Exeter Academy, attended Harvard for four years without taking a degree, and studied for two years under Hall at Clark University. He simplified the curriculum while proceeding along lines similar to those set by Krohn. He offered six courses for undergraduates plus a research course. In 1897–98 Hylan attracted thirty-seven students, and in 1898–99 twenty-four.[55]

When Hylan left, in 1899, Draper was "about disgusted with the psychology business." Krohn's interest in abnormal psychology had attracted students out of morbid curiosity, Draper observed, while Krohn and Hylan, both holders of a Ph.D. from Clark University, had "insisted upon projecting a lot of work which had no relation to anything in the heavens above or the earth beneath, and accordingly they have made a failure of it." The course of study was wholly elective, Draper pointed out, and during 1898–99 only two or three students had studied psychology (Kinley's figures showed twenty-four). Draper wanted closer integration of psychology with pedagogy and philosophy, but he considered pedagogy more important than psychology. Although convinced that psychology could be improved, he bluntly told G. Stanley Hall that he had little use for Clark University men.[56]

In 1899 Draper chose Robert H. Kelley of the University of Chicago as Hylan's replacement, but the board refused approval on the grounds that Kelley's work had not been sufficiently in physiological and experimental psychology and that Tompkins's resignation had changed the picture. Daniels gave a course in psychology that year in which nine students enrolled.[57]

By the summer of 1899 Thaddeus L. Bolton had become the leading candidate for the position. Then the appointment was held in abeyance pending selection of a professor of pedagogy. After Dexter was named to the pedagogical post in the spring of 1900, Draper recommended Bolton as an instructor in psychology. A thirty-five-year-old native of Illinois, Bolton had taken his Ph.D. in psychology at Clark, had studied three months each at the universities of Berlin, Leipzig, and Heidelberg, and had taught for several years before taking a position at the University of Nebraska. Draper recommended Bolton, describing him as "scholarly, but perhaps not brilliant, thoroughly honest and right spirited, although he may lack in aggressiveness." Only a trial would tell how he would adapt to Illinois. "Men in experimental psychology who are scholarly and forceful, and yet sane and safe," Draper added, "are very rare. There are no men with established reputations in this work who are available." Bolton assured Draper that he would come for $1,000 for ten months, but when the offer arrived he turned it down because Nebraska raised his salary. Draper called his behavior "highly dishonorable."[58]

From 1900 to 1902 Dexter assumed responsibility for both departments. For 1900–1 the catalog listed five undergraduate courses and one graduate course in psychology, all repeats. In fact, only one course was offered, during one semester, and it enrolled thirty-four students.

Dexter nominated Stephen S. Colvin (b. 1869) to be an assistant in psychology. Colvin had taken undergraduate and master's degrees and had then studied English and philosophy for another year at Brown University. He went on to spend two years in Germany, studying philosophy at Berlin and Strassburg, after which he taught English for four years at the Worcester, Massachusetts, high school while studying psychology and education at Clark University. Since Colvin had specialized in the philosophical and pedagogical aspects of psychology rather than in laboratory work, Dexter assured Draper, there was no danger that he would stress the pathological and morbid in psychology, as some of his predecessors had.[59]

Expecting an instructorship, Colvin was appointed an assistant professor in 1901 (Draper must have viewed him as "safe"), and for three years he carried most of the teaching load in the department. Colvin was the instructor of record for seven of the eight undergraduate courses available. For a time Dexter and Colvin shared a course entitled Experimental Psychology. In addition, the department offered a research course for graduates. In 1901–2 sixty-three students enrolled in psychology courses. In 1904 Kinley urged that the Department of Psychology be separated from the Department of Education, for two reasons. One was that only part of the vast field of psychology was of direct use in the Department of Education. The other reason was that Dexter did not know enough about psychology to make him a good manager of that department. In June 1904 psychology was made a separate department, with Colvin, promoted to associate professor, as head. After a decade of erratic development, the Department of Psychology had at last gained a solid footing.[60]

## THE POLITICAL SCIENCE GROUP

The Political Science Group included economics, history, and political science, each of which was beginning to go its own way in the late nineteenth century. The oldest organization in the country devoted to inquiry in the social sciences was the American Social Science Association (ASSA). Founded in 1865, this "mother of associations" gave rise to numerous progeny. In 1884 the American Historical Association (AHA) came into being; a year later the American Economic Association (AEA) was organized. In 1904 the American Political Science Association broke away from the ASSA, and in 1905 the American Sociological Society was organized.

The maturing of academic disciplines was not lost on Kinley. In 1895 he had pushed for a school of political science, and in 1898 he asked Draper to urge this matter on the trustees. Meanwhile, the departments developed independently.[61]

## Economics

Economics enjoyed steady growth. In 1894 the catalog listed twelve courses in this department, nine in economics and three in sociology. Kinley was the instructor for everything listed, but the advanced courses were offered only in alternate years. In 1894–95 the departmental enrollment was seventy-three.

Many courses added in later years addressed contemporary problems, and men with appropriate specialties were recruited for the faculty. In 1897 Matthew B. Hammond (b. 1868), who graduated from the University of Michigan and then studied economics, history, sociology, and political science at the universities of Wisconsin, Tübingen, and Berlin, became an assistant. In 1898 he received a Ph.D. from Columbia.

Hammond took over much of the basic work in economics and sociology as well as three new courses, freeing Kinley to focus on his own interests, money and banking and the financial history of the United States, and to introduce new courses on the money market, the labor problem, the monopoly problem, theories of production and consumption, and distribution (later called The Distribution of Wealth). For graduate students Kinley offered The Theory of Value and The Theory of Distribution.

In 1898 the economics offerings were amplified with two new undergraduate courses—Problems of Pauperism and Crime, and Social Institutions—and a graduate course on the history of economic thought.

In 1900 Nathan A. Weston (b. 1868), who had earned a B.L. from Illinois in 1889, taught in the Preparatory School, and pursued graduate studies at Wisconsin and Cornell, was named an instructor. A year later, when Weston received a Ph.D. from Cornell, he assumed responsibility for both English Economic History and Principles of Economics. He shared the economic seminary with Kinley and introduced two new courses—Socialism and Social Reform, and Modern Industrial Organization. Another new course, Charities and Correction, fell to Hammond to teach.

Kinley was heavily burdened. At one point he taught nineteen to twenty hours each week, had seven graduate students, was dean of the college and secretary of the Council of Administration, and had no clerical help. During 1900–1 he went on leave, and while he was in Europe his plans for a school of political science began to materialize. In 1901 the trustees secured $12,000 to extend the college by establishing a school of social and political science and commerce. Since the appropriation was for two years, the board agreed to let the funds accumulate a year while they ripened their plans.

Meanwhile, Kinley's ideas on a school had changed. The University still needed to offer work in the political sciences, he believed, but other institutions had preempted this area, and educational opinion now favored training for business. The faculty senate, having debated the most desirable form of organization and the appropriate grade of work for the commercial courses, proposed establishing a department in the college rather than a separate school, with undergraduate work leading to the bachelor's degree rather than a graduate program. To augment the existing staff, Kinley wanted four more faculty members. He searched diligently for the best people at the salary he could offer, and in 1902–3 the economics department began to offer a program of training for business.[62]

George M. Fisk (b. 1864) joined the faculty as professor of commerce. After earning a Ph.D. from the University of Munich in 1896, Fisk had served as second secretary in the American Embassy in Berlin and as professor of commerce at Tome Institute in Port Deposit, Maryland. The catalog listed him as offering nine courses, but in his first semester he actually taught only two, Commercial Geography (twelve students) and Commercial Politics (three).

Maurice H. Robinson (b. 1865), who had taken two degrees at Dartmouth before earning a Ph.D. at Yale in 1902, was named professor of industry and transportation. The catalog listed him as offering ten courses, but in his first semester he taught Railway Administration (six students) and Corporation Finance (thirteen). In the second semester Fisk had twenty-two students and Robinson had eighty-six.

Kinley wanted businessmen to advise him on developing academic programs, and in 1902–3 he brought seven of them to the University to lecture. The visitors included the chairman of the Interstate Commerce Commission, a railroad president, two bankers, and the superintendent of the U.S. Census.

By the end of the academic year, Kinley believed that in transportation, in commerce and finance, and in certain social questions, Illinois had facilities as good as those of any university in the country (with four or five exceptions); and in regard to the teaching ability and scholarly standing of the staff, only two institutions in the country could be fairly regarded as stronger than Illinois. He boasted about having one of the best library holdings in his field in the West, while acknowledging that Illinois needed to develop accounting and statistics, especially the statistics of insurance.[63]

By 1903–4 the Department of Economics had earned a respectable standing. That year it offered ten courses in general economics, two in economic history, five in finance, nine in commerce, five in industry and transportation, four in statistics, and two in sociology. Course enrollments, which had been 73 in 1894–95, reached 735, a tenfold increase, with an average of 260 a year over the ten-year period. Most of the students were men. Training in business attracted some who might otherwise have gone into law or teaching. Kinley viewed economics as a liberal subject—the two exceptions were courses in commercial geography and railroad administration—that had grown in attractiveness owing to the trend of the times.[64]

## History

History is society's collective memory and an essential element of a liberal education. As Santayana observed, "those who are ignorant of the past are condemned to repeat it." But as a scientific discipline and an organized profession history came of age only in the 1880s, and for all practical purposes the history department at the University dates from 1894, when Evarts B. Greene, the first person with a doctorate in the subject, joined the faculty as an assistant professor.[65]

Greene was born in Japan in 1870 of missionary parents. He returned to the United States for his higher education, earning bachelor's, master's, and doctoral degrees from Harvard. Upon receiving his Ph.D., in 1893, Greene studied at the University of Berlin for a year. When he arrived on the Urbana campus the catalog listed eight courses in history, all with Greene as instructor. The offerings emphasized medieval and modern European history. Greene's main interest was American history, but there was only one course in this area for undergraduates.

Greene was a splendid addition to the faculty. Kinley praised him highly, adding that the history department did excellent work and was well liked by students. Enrollments were 160 in 1894–95, a comparatively high figure, and 531 in 1903–4, yielding an average of 441 a year. Over the decade the history department was the third largest in the college, following rhetoric and oratory and German. Since rhetoric was required and many students in engineering and science took German out of necessity, history may be described as the most popular department in the college. The subject tended to be equally attractive to both male and female students. Yet the department labored under severe handicaps. One was a shortage of books and maps, another was a short-age of faculty.[66]

In June 1895 the trustees appointed Frank Zinkeisen assistant professor of history and established a department of medieval history. Zinkeisen, a native of Milwaukee, had taken bachelor's and master's degrees at Harvard and a doc-torate at the University of Berlin in 1893. He had been an assistant at Harvard and had published two articles. When he arrived in September, however, he had a severe case of stage fright and immediately resigned because of "ill health." He soon regretted his error and confessed that he had temporar-ily lost sight of "broader lines" through "excessive specialization." Draper warmly encouraged him, but Zinkeisen ended his life by throwing himself under a train in Chicago. He was twenty-eight.[67]

George D. Hammond (b. 1864) was quickly engaged. He had graduated summa cum laude from Harvard in 1893, studied for a year at the University of Berlin, and served as a professor of history at St. Lawrence University. Greene had known him as a fellow student. Hammond's work was to be main-ly in ancient and medieval history. In 1896–97, with Hammond absent owing to illness, George H. Alden (b. 1866), who had an A.B. from Harvard and had done graduate work at Chicago and Wisconsin, replaced him.

On Hammond's final withdrawal (he died in 1899), the post went to Arthur C. Howland (b. 1869), a Cornell A.B. who had pursued graduate study at Göt-tingen, Leipzig, and Cornell and had completed his Ph.D. at the University of Pennsylvania in 1897. He took over teaching English Constitutional History and introduced courses in ancient and medieval European history.

Greene valued Howland as an excellent teacher and respected scholar, adding that the opening of the School of Law suggested the desirability of strengthening the history department on the side of institutional history and of correlating studies in history and law in the medieval period. Greene recom-mended promotion. Kinley thought that Howland possessed "the quality of adaptability necessary to success here." But apparently Howland displeased Draper, for he lasted only one year. He became professor of medieval history at the University of Pennsylvania.[68]

The history department gained a measure of stability with two new ap-pointments. One was Henry L. Schoolcraft (b. 1868), who arrived in 1898 and earned a Ph.D. from the University of Chicago the following year. He as-sumed responsibility for most of the work in ancient and medieval history. In 1899–1900 the demand for his course in Roman history was so great that a graduate student was used to help teach the subject. Schoolcraft did good work and remained on the faculty for ten years.

Another new arrival was Clarence W. Alvord (b. 1868), who had prepared at Phillips Andover Academy, graduated from Williams College, and pursued advanced study in Berlin and at the University of Chicago. In 1897 he became an instructor in the Preparatory School, and in 1901 Greene secured his appointment in the history department. He rose in rank, earned a Ph.D. at Illinois in 1908, and achieved prominence as a scholar of early American history and editor of the leading journal in American history.

An enlarged staff enriched the history offerings. Alvord taught ancient and European history for years and in 1901 introduced a course on the Italian Renaissance. A year later Schoolcraft offered a course on early modern German history. These advances enable Greene to concentrate on American history. Greene was inclined to be more severe a teacher than Kinley thought best, but Kinley held him in high regard in scholarship, teaching ability, and willingness to bear responsibility.[69]

A teacher and a scholar, Greene was also a man of courage who dared to challenge President Draper over the obligation of faculty members to attend general lectures. This conflict revealed the tension over rival claims in the University. Draper valued institutional loyalty; Greene valued professional freedom. Greene's conduct in this matter may have justified an assessment Kinley rendered in 1904. "I sometimes feel," Kinley wrote, "that he [Greene] has the scholar's lack of a just appreciation of the relative importance of things." Time, Kinley added, was rapidly curing the fault. Draper's conduct in this matter sprang from a need to dominate, a malady for which there was no known cure.[70]

Greene's qualities eminently fitted him for service to the University. For a quarter of a century he was one of the most admired and influential members of the faculty. He gave the history department able and far-sighted leadership, won respect for it in and beyond the University, and from 1905 to 1913 served as dean of the College of Literature and Arts.

## Political Science

Kinley entertained high hopes for the field of political science. In 1894 he had drawn up a scheme for such a school, including a law school. Draper and others considered the plans that September, students petitioned for courses in political science and jurisprudence the following spring, and in May Draper hired Charles W. Tooke as the first step toward developing a strong department of political science and public law. Tooke (b. 1870) had earned bachelor's and master's degrees at Syracuse University and studied history and politics at Cornell in 1893–94 before going to Columbia University as a fellow in administrative law in 1894–95. In 1895 he joined the faculty as an assistant professor of political science.[71]

Tooke devised a program designed to train students for citizenship and prepare them for politics or law by emphasizing the theory of the state, the development of political ideas, and the growth of national institutions. His curriculum contained nine courses, and in 1896 the department was renamed public law and administration and Tooke was made an assistant professor.

Tooke proposed to teach the elementary course every year and the advanced courses in alternate years. Apart from two slight changes in 1897, the curriculum remained as originally devised for some time. Tooke attracted students. After his first year, enrollments in public law and administration doubled, and Kinley recommended a promotion in salary and rank. Draper praised Tooke's leadership. In 1899 Tooke became a full professor.[72]

Since the department emphasized legal subjects, Kinley resumed his effort to establish a school of political science like the one at the University of Wisconsin. But Draper remained unreceptive. In June 1899, perhaps as a palliative, the trustees assigned $500 for lectures in political science.[73]

At this juncture a dispute arose over three courses offered by Tooke's department—International Law, Constitutional Law, and Roman Law. The School of Law had opened in 1897, two years after Tooke joined the faculty. He taught there as well as in his own department. Catalogs listed him as an assistant professor of public law in the college and as an instructor in the School (or College) of Law. From 1897 to 1899 Tooke offered Constitutional Law, International Law, and Roman Law in both the liberal arts college and the law school.[74]

In May 1899, when he was hired as dean of the law school, James B. Scott expressed an interest in teaching International Law and Constitutional Law, and "it was intended" to let him do so. He was well qualified for the purpose, having earned a doctorate of civil and canon law at the University of Heidelberg in 1894. In the fall, when Scott arrived in Urbana, he asked to teach Roman Law also. Kinley demurred, arguing that the three courses belonged in the liberal arts college and that their loss would be a serious blow to the establishment of a political science department. Draper acceded to Kinley's wishes.[75]

By November, however, "it had been decided" that Scott rather than Tooke would teach the three courses in the law school to law students. Scott refused to discuss the matter with Tooke. Kinley proposed that Scott teach the subjects in the law school and Tooke teach them in the college. Scott declared that the law school would not give credit for the courses to a law student who had taken them in the college. Kinley then proposed that Tooke be made a member of the law faculty and that his department be transferred to the law school, leaving Tooke also a member of the college faculty for the year, on condition that the college faculty be strengthened in political science so as not to weaken its representation in the general faculty and that the subjects still be open to college students. Scott apparently opposed this arrangement. Kinley objected to the plan to take the subjects in question from Tooke, whether Tooke agreed or not, and give them to Scott. Draper's role in these matters cannot be clearly discerned. He liked Scott and had not supported Kinley's plans for political science. So Kinley availed himself of the privilege of submitting a report on the subject to Draper with the request that it be sent to the Board of Trustees.[76]

After discussing the matter with Draper on 4 December 1899, Kinley put his reasons for objecting to the transfer in writing, buttressing them with responses solicited from eminent lawyers, justices, and law school deans throughout the nation. First, he noted, the three subjects were elements of a liberal education. Second, on this point leading legal practitioners and heads of the nation's best law schools agreed with Kinley. "I think that to add the study of Roman law to the required work of a law student is empty humbug," Chief Justice Oliver Wendell Holmes of Massachusetts wrote. "International law, of course, has little to do in any sense, with the practice of the profession. I should almost as soon require chemistry. Constitutional law, I think, should be required by all means." Third, American law schools were schools for technical training. The leading ones did not view the three subjects as primarily law subjects. Fourth, the proposal to transfer the subjects to another college was not in conformity with practice at the University of Illinois. And fifth, the proposal to transfer could not be justified on the ground that the courses were poorly or improperly taught by Tooke. The evidence showed that Tooke was well trained and a good instructor. Scott nevertheless insisted that the three subjects were law subjects and refused to discuss the matter with Tooke.[77]

Draper, Kinley, and Scott met on 5 December to resolve the dispute. They agreed that the School of Law was to offer the three subjects, with the work to be divided between Scott and Tooke as they saw fit. The law school could announce Tooke as a member of its faculty, and the college could continue to offer courses that were considered of value to general scholarship. Thus, Draper sided with Scott and dealt Kinley a grievous blow.[78]

Tooke steered his own course through these troubled waters. During 1899–1900 the catalog listed him in the College of Law in two capacities—as an instructor of three courses and as a third-year student. In 1900 he received a law degree from the University and became a professor of law.

Tooke's transfer was to take place in June 1900. But owing to unsettled conditions in the law school faculty it did not occur at that time. Meanwhile, Tooke continued to teach in the college and to carry practically full law work in addition. On 28 September 1901 Tooke was officially transferred from Literature and Arts to Law on the understanding that he was to teach in both colleges "according to the character of the different courses."[79]

Justifiably, Kinley was unhappy with this entire affair—Scott's discourteous behavior, the wrong done Tooke, Tooke's going to the law school, and his taking along the three courses. Kinley found it odd that the dean of the law school was teaching at least one class composed entirely of literature students (while affirming that he needed more law faculty) and that he taught the literature students and the law students in separate classes.[80] And by 1904, as Kinley had anticipated, the law people had dropped International Law, Roman Law, and Elementary Jurisprudence.[81]

Tooke's transfer destroyed public law and administration as a department. Enrollments reached a high of 211 in 1900–1, then plummeted. Kinley confessed that he had had "no greater disappointment" in his connection with the University than the breaking down of this department.[82] In 1901–2 a Department of Government was created, but of the eight courses listed in the catalog only one was actually available that year, a course in political ethics taught by Daniels, and it had to be taken in the philosophy department. The department enrolled sixty-eight students that year and none in 1902–3. In 1903–4, when Weston taught the introductory course, thirty-three students took government classes. But Weston was needed in economics. As a result, the University of Illinois had "no proper facilities for taking care of a student in political science."[83]

In June 1900, after Tooke's transfer had been settled in principle, Draper acknowledged the need to develop the political sciences. So the board asked for $16,000 and the legislature granted $12,000 for the purpose. In April 1904, after Draper announced his resignation, the board agreed that it was desirable to establish a full professorship in political science.[84]

Kinley, taking the initiative in recruiting, sought outstanding scholars. He made unofficial offers to Charles E. Merriam and Westel W. Willoughby. Obviously Kinley wanted an excellent scholar more than a particular specialty. Since neither man was available, Kinley turned to his third choice, John A. Fairlie, a Columbia Ph.D. and an assistant professor of administrative law at the University of Michigan. In the event, however, he recommended James W. Garner (b. 1871), a native of Mississippi who had taken a doctorate at Columbia and served as an instructor there and at the University of Pennsylvania.

The Department of Political Science became operative in 1904 with Garner as assistant professor and head. He introduced a new and distinctly political science orientation. His curriculum consisted of eight undergraduate courses and two "seminaries" for advanced students. Garner's arrival was partial fulfillment of Kinley's vision. Garner placed the study of political science on a sound foundation. He was head of the department until he retired in 1939, during which time he published many works on political science and international law, earned a reputation in the latter field, and won many honors, including the presidency of the American Political Science Association.

In sum, Literature and Arts embraced studies at the core of a true university. Kinley advanced the enterprise, with little help from the board or Draper. In 1904 the college was not on a par with similar colleges at the leading universities. Draper proposed that a "literary man" head the college (apparently wishing to name Thomas A. Clark as dean). Kinley appealed to a trustee to delay the proposal.[85]

## NOTES

1. On the origins of the college, see Solberg, 104. In 1894–1895 official records used the names College of Liberal Arts, College of Arts and Letters, and College of Literature and Arts interchangeably. The last was the most common (15/1/6, 81, 87, 88).
2. *17th Report* (1894), 263–65; Draper to William H. Hinrichsen, 17 October 1894, 2/4/3; Draper, "Report of the University of Illinois," in *Twenty-First Biennial Report of the Superintendent of Public Instruction of the State of Illinois* (1894–96), 143.
3. David Kinley, *The Autobiography of David Kinley* (Urbana: University of Illinois Press, 1949), 12–29; Kinley to Draper, 5 March 1898, 15/1/4.
4. The figures, which include enrollment in the Preparatory School, are drawn from reports of the Board of Trustees, catalogs, and the dean's annual reports, 15/1/11.
5. 4/1/1, 3:262 (22 October 1894). The record lists twenty-eight departments, not including rhetoric.
6. 15/1/6, 74.
7. The point is well stated in Kinley to Draper, 1 November 1902, 2/4/2, B:9, F:Kinley.
8. Kinley to Draper, 6 March 1895, 2/4/2, B:1, F:Kinley.
9. 15/1/6, 26 September (p. 96); 13 December 1895 (p. 102); *Catalogue* (1895–96), 48–52.
10. Kinley to Draper, 6 March 1895, 2/4/2, B:1, F:Kinley.
11. Kinley emphasized the points made in this paragraph in several annual reports (15/1/11), especially 1898–99 and 1899–1900, from which the figures and quotations are taken.
12. 15/1/11, 1898–99.
13. Ibid., 1899–1900.
14. *21st Report* (1902), 107.
15. Kinley to High School Principals, 19 March 1900, 15/1/4; 15/1/11, 1900–1, 28 May 1901; Kinley to Draper, 2 February 1904, 15/1/4.
16. 15/1/11, 1903–4; Kinley to Draper, 2 February 1904, 15/1/4.
17. For the titles of senior theses from various departments from November 1897 to October 1903, see 15/1/6, 146, 157, 166, 169, 170, 177–78, 203, 206.
18. 15/1/11, 1901–2, 1902–3; Kinley to Moss, 12 December 1901, Kinley to Barton, 12 December 1901, 15/1/4.
19. Gerald Graff, *Professing Literature: An Institutional History* (Chicago: University of Chicago Press, 1987), chaps. 1–7 passim.

20. Daniel K. Dodge, "English at the University of Illinois," *The Dial*, 16 (1 May 1894), 261–62. Dodge writes that the introductory course included American literature, but the catalogs do not support him. In earlier colleges students had taken up American literature in their literary societies. On American literature at Illinois, see the *Register* (1867–68), (1880–81), (1889–90), and Dodge to Draper, 28 March 1899, 2/4/2, B:5, F:B–G.

21. *Catalog* (1901), 227.

22. Kinley to Draper, 2 February 1904, 15/1/4; 15/1/11, 1903–4.

23. Official documents often reverse the order, calling the unit the Department of Oral Rhetoric and Oratory.

24. *Catalogue* (1894–95), 160.

25. Kinley to Draper, 4 October, 1 December 1898, 2/4/2, B:5, F:Kinley; Kinley to Clark, 28 December 1898, 15/1/4; 15/1/11, 1897–98.

26. Draper to Dr. Herman Kiefer, 8 September 1899, 2/4/3; Kinley to President W. O. Thompson (of Ohio State University), 13 May 1903; Kinley to President James B. Angell (of the University of Michigan), 11 September 1899, 15/1/4. On this department, see James M. McGlathery, *German and Scandinavian at Illinois: A History* (Urbana: University of Illinois, Department of Germanic Language and Literature, 1990).

27. Draper to the presidents of Ohio State, Wisconsin, Minnesota, and Cornell, October 1898, 2/4/3; Kinley to Rhoades, 21 September 1899, 15/1/4.

28. Kinley to Draper, 2 February 1904, 15/1/4.

29. The department was officially known as Romance Languages until 1899, when the name was changed to Romanic Languages to parallel the name Germanic Languages.

30. Kinley to Draper, 6 March 1895, 2/4/2, B:1, F:Kinley.

31. 15/1/11, 1895–96, 1898–99; Kinley to Draper, 16 February 1899, 2/4/2, B:5, F:Kinley; Fairfield to Draper, 8 May 1899, 2/4/2, B:5, F:B–G; Burrill to Draper, 5 June 1899, 2/4/2, B:5, F:Burrill.

32. Clipping of 3 August 1921 from unidentified newspaper, 26/4/1, George D. Fairfield Folder.

33. Kinley to Draper, 2 February 1904, 15/1/4.

34. Edmund J. James, *Chairs of Pedagogics in Our Universities* (Philadelphia: Philadelphia Social Science Association, 1887); Mary L. Seguel, *The Curriculum Field: Its Formative Years* (New York: Teachers College Press, 1966), 7–16; Henry C. Johnson, Jr., and Erwin V. Johanningmeier, *Teachers for the Prairie: the University and the Schools, 1868–1945* (Urbana: University of Illinois Press, 1972).

35. *16th Report* (1892), 37.

36. *17th Report* (1894), 128; Frank McMurry, "Some Reflections of the Past Forty Years of Education," *Peabody Journal of Education*, 4 (May 1927), 332.

37. Draper to Edmund Palmer, 16 January 1895, 2/4/3. See also W. C. Bagley, "History of the Department and School of Education," [1916], 1–3, 10/1/10, History of the Department and School of Education.

38. Kinley to Draper, 6 March 1895, 2/4/2, B:1, F:Kinley; Draper to Eckoff, 28 May 1895, 2/4/3; Eckoff to Draper, 29 May 1895, 2/4/2, B:1. F:Eckoff.

39. Draper to Lewis H. Jones, 27 May 1895; Draper to Tompkins, 1 June 1895, 2/4/3; Tompkins to Draper, 28 May 1895, 2/4/2, B:2, F:Arnold Tompkins.

40. Tompkins to Draper, 28 May, 3 June 1895, 4 November 1896 (second quotation, in an enclosure), 2/4/2, B:2, 3, F:Tompkins; Draper to Tompkins, 1 June 1895, 2/4/3; *Catalogue* (1895–96), 59, 196 (first, third, and fourth quotations).
41. Draper to H. M. Slauson, 12 May 1896, 2/4/3.
42. Tompkins to Draper, 9 December 1895, 2/4/2, B:2, F:Tompkins; Draper to H. M. Slauson, 12 May 1896, 2/4/3; Tompkins to Draper, 7 January 1896, 2/4/2, B:2, F:Tompkins.
43. Tompkins to Draper, 2 August 1897, 2/4/2, B:3, F:Tompkins; 3/1/1/, 1:75–76; Kinley to Tompkins, 14 October 1897, 15/1/4; Tompkins to Draper, 7 March 1899, 2/4/2, B:5, F:Tompkins; Burrill to Draper, 14 March 1899, 2/4/2, B:5. F:Burrill; Draper to Lucy Flower, 25 May 1899, 2/4/3; Tompkins to Draper, 21 June 1899, 2/4/2, B:5, F:Tompkins; *20th Report* (1901), 94, 95, 100–1, 120.
44. Draper to Lucy Flower, 22 June 1899; Burrill to Galbreath, 8 August 1899, 2/4/3.
45. Draper to Lucy L. Flower, 25 September 1899; Draper to Professor Earl Barnes, 6 September 1899; Draper to Professor Howard Sandison, 18 September 1899; Draper to Lucy Flower, 19 September 1899, 2/4/3. On the search, see 2/4/3 for September through November.
46. James E. Russell to Draper, 9 November; Butler to Draper, 27 November; Cattell to Draper, 27 November 1899, 2/4/2, B:6, F:Dexter; *20th Report* (1901), 223; Dexter to Draper, 31 December 1899, 2/4/2, B:6, F:Dexter.
47. 2/5/15, Stratton D. Brooks Folder; Brooks to Draper, 6 October 1899, 2/4/2, B:6, F:Brooks; *20th Report* (1901), 235.
48. Dexter to Draper, 13 March, 14 November, 19 January 1900, 2/4/2, B:6, F:Dexter; *Catalog* (1899–1900), 249 (the quotation).
49. Kinley to Draper, 2 February 1904; Kinley to Professor John M. Burnam, 24 May 1904, 15/1/4.
50. Kinley to Draper, 30 April 1902, 2/4/4, B:2, F:Department Reports, 1903 *[sic]* (first quotation); Kinley to Draper, 31 May 1902, ibid., B:2, F:Department Reports, 1902 (second quotation); Kinley to Draper, 1 November 1902, 2/4/2, B:9, F:Kinley (third quotation); Draper to G. Stanley Hall, 26 June 1897, 2/4/3 (fourth quotation); Kinley to Draper, 2 February 1904, 15/1/4 (last quotation). In his 2 February 1904 letter Kinley added that he did not regard Daniels "as a man who could successfully manage a department in which there were several other strong men," though Daniels had taken care of his own work in "very good shape." In 1933–34, however, Daniels served as acting president of the University.
51. A. A. Roback, *A History of American Psychology*, rev. ed. (New York: Collier Books, 1964), 137–79.
52. Krohn to the Board of Trustees, 8 June 1895, 2/4/2, B:1, F:Krohn.
53. Kinley to Draper, 6 March 1895, 2/4/2, B:1, F:Kinley; *18th Report* (1896), 71–72, 77; Draper to O. T. Bright, 13 March 1895, 2/4/3; William O. Krohn, *Practical Lessons in Psychology* (Chicago: Werner Co., 1894), 4.
54. *19th Report* (1898), 113.
55. Hylan studied in Germany after leaving Urbana and in 1901 obtained his doctorate at Clark. The *Catalogue* (1897–98) erroneously lists him as having a Ph.D. degree.
56. Draper to G. Van Ness Dearborn, 15 March 1899; Draper to Nicholas Murray Butler, 23 March 1899; Draper to Lucy L. Flower, 22 June 1899; Draper to T. L.

Bolton, 2 August 1899; Draper to J. M. K. Cattell, 22 March 1899; Draper to G. Stanley Hall, 26 June 1897, 2/4/3.

57. *20th Report* (1901), 86; Draper to Kelly, 15 June 1899, 2/4/3; 15/1/11, 1899–1900.

58. *20th Report* (1901), 259, 275.

59. Dexter to Draper, 13 March 1900, 2/4/2, B:6, F:Dexter; Dexter to Draper, [Spring 1901], 2/5/15, Steven S. Colvin Folder.

60. Kinley to Draper, 2 February 1904, 15/1/4; *22nd Report* (1904), 292.

61. See Herbert B. Adams, *The Study of History in American Colleges and Universities* (Washington, D.C., 1887); Anna Haddow, *Political Science in American Colleges and Universities, 1636–1900* (New York: D. Appleton-Century Co., 1939); Howard W. Odum, *American Sociology: The Story of Sociology in the United States through 1950* (New York: Longmans, Green, 1951); Bernard Crick *The American Science of Politics: Its Origins and Conditions* (Berkeley: University of California Press, 1964); John Higham, *History: Professional Scholarship in America* (Baltimore: Johns Hopkins University Press, 1983; originally published with Leonard Krieger and Felix Gilbert as part of *History* [Englewood Cliffs, N.J.: Prentice-Hall, 1965]); Albert Somit and Joseph Tanenhaus, *The Development of American Political Science from Burgess to Behavioralism* (Boston: Allyn & Bacon, 1967); Thomas L. Haskell, *The Emergence of Professional Social Science: The American Social Science Association and the Nineteenth-Century Crisis of Authority* (Urbana: University of Illinois Press, 1977); Dorothy Ross, *The Origins of American Social Science* (New York: Cambridge University Press, 1991).

62. Kinley to Francis McKay, 26 March 1900, 15/1/4; *21st Report* (1902), 31, 86, 208, 226; Kinley to Draper, 30 April, 25 May, 3 December 1901, 3 March 1902, 2/4/2, B:7, 8, F:Kinley; 4/2/1, 7 November 1901.

63. 15/1/11, 1902–3; Kinley to Thomas F. Kane, 17 December 1902, 15/1/4.

64. Kinley to Draper, 22 February 1904, 15/1/4.

65. Jack R. Kirby, "Evarts Boutell Greene: The Career of a Professional Historian" (Ph.D. diss., University of Illinois, 1969), provides an overview.

66. 15/1/11, 1895–96.

67. *18th Report* (1896), 95, 102, 179; Zinkeisen to Draper, various April dates, 17 October 1895, 2/4/2, B:2, F:Zinkeisen; Draper to Zinkeisen, 23 September 1895, 2/4/3.

68. Greene to Draper, 25 February 1898, Kinley to Draper, 5 March 1898, 2/4/2, B:4, F:Greene, Kinley.

69. Kinley to Draper, 2 February 1904, 15/1/4.

70. Ibid.

71. Kinley to Draper, 5 March, 20 April 1898, 15/1/4; *18th Report* (1896), 26, 73, 95, 102; Draper to Tooke, 22 May 1895, 2/4/3.

72. 15/1/11, 1895–96; Kinley to Munro Smith, 27 October 1899, 15/1/4; *20th Report* (1901), 92; Kinley to J. W. Jenks, 27 October 1899, 15/1/4.

73. Kinley to Draper, 5 March, 20 April 1898, 15/1/4; 15/1/11, 1897–98; Kinley to Draper, 17 January, 11 May 1899, 15/1/4; 15/1/11, 1899–1900.

74. Kinley to E. R. A. Seligman, 1 November 1899, 15/1/4.

75. Kinley to Draper, 5 June 1899, 15/1/4.

76. Kinley to Draper, 1, 16, 23 November 1899, 15/1/4.

77. Kinley to Draper, 4 December 1899, 2/4/2, B:6, F:Kinley. The Holmes quotation is in Exhibit D.
78. Draper to Kinley and Scott, 6 December 1899, 2/4/3.
79. 15/1/11, 1899–1900, 1900–1; Kinley to S. N. Patten, 18 June 1900; Kinley to Draper, 27 September 1901, 15/1/4; *21st Report* (1902), 204.
80. Kinley to Evarts B. Greene, 9 October 1901; Kinley to Greene, 26 November 1901, 15/1/4. In 1902 Tooke left the University. For a time he practiced law in Syracuse; later he served on the law faculties at Georgetown and New York universities.
81. Kinley to Tooke, 1 April 1904, 15/1/4.
82. Kinley to Draper, 1 November 1902, 2/4/2, B:9, F:Kinley.
83. 15/1/11, 1899–1900; Kinley to Burrill, 13 November 1903, 15/1/4.
84. Kinley to S. N. Patten, 18 June 1900; Kinley to Mrs. [Mary Turner] Carriel, 23 June 1903, 15/1/4; *21st Report* (1902), 31; *22nd Report* (1904), 277.
85. Draper to Kinley, 17 February 1904, 2/4/3; Kinley to J. E. Armstrong, 4 March 1904, 15/1/4.

CHAPTER **4**

# SCIENCE FOR THE COMMON GOOD

In the late nineteenth century science was transforming the world and enabling people to apply the powers of nature to their own uses. Thus science was claiming the place in education formerly held by classical studies. In 1894 the College of Science at the University was reorganized. The studies in the college were arranged into the Chemical, Natural Science, Mathematical, and Philosophical groups, each of which was to serve educational rather than administrative purposes.[1]

Stephen A. Forbes served as dean of the college from 1888 to 1905. Born in 1844 in a log house in Silver Creek, Stephenson County, Illinois, near the Wisconsin border, he was left fatherless and in relative poverty at ten. His formal education was incomplete and fragmentary. He attended district school until he was fourteen, studied at home for two years under the tutelage of his older brother, attended Beloit Academy for a year, and continued his education in the Civil War. He gained knowledge of the world and of men during combat and in Confederate prisons, and through all the blasts and storms he "kept the solitary flame of his separate intellectual life steadily burning."[2]

Returning to civilian life in 1865, Forbes spent a year at Rush Medical College in Chicago, later resuming the study of medicine under a preceptor at Makanda, Illinois. From 1868 to 1871 he taught school in southern Illinois and studied natural history as an avocation. As a naturalist Forbes was almost entirely self-taught, but he was influenced by dedicated Illinois naturalists, especially Major John Wesley Powell and George W. Vasey. In 1870 Forbes published his first scientific article, "Botanical Notes," in *American Entomologist and Botanist.* In 1871 he studied briefly at Illinois State Normal University, and in June 1872 he replaced Powell as curator of the Illinois Museum of Natural History of the Illinois Natural History Society, which was housed at Illinois State Normal University in Normal, Illinois. Forbes developed the museum as a teaching unit within the school, he supplied specimens to public schools, he formed a network of scientific collaborators by correspondence, and he founded a bulletin as an outlet for scientific research.[3] From 1875 to 1878, while retaining his curatorship, Forbes was an instructor in zoology at Illinois State Normal University.

In 1877 the General Assembly established a state museum at Springfield under the name of the Illinois State Historical Library and Natural History Museum and converted the museum at Normal into the State Laboratory of Natural History. The museum was created to house the collections of the Illinois Natural History Museum at Normal and the collections of the Illinois Geological Survey, then in the basement of the capitol.[4]

In 1882 Forbes became the fourth person to hold the office of state entomologist. At the time only two other states, New York and Missouri, employed such an official. It was understood that the the state entomologist's office and that of the State Laboratory of Natural History were to be merged and managed as one. In 1884 Indiana University conferred on Forbes his first academic degree, a Ph.D. Professor David Starr Jordan, head of the Department of Natural Science at Indiana, arranged for the degree in recognition of Forbes's scientific work. Forbes satisfied the thesis requirement with a paper titled "The Regulative Action of Birds Upon Insect Oscillations."[5]

Appointed to the University of Illinois effective 1 September 1884, Forbes joined the faculty on 1 January 1885, bringing the State Laboratory of Natural History and the state entomologist's office with him. The laboratory was nominally controlled by the trustees of the University but was practically independent in its management. Its principal function was to make a natural history survey of the state. It was also charged with supplying natural history specimens to the state museum, to state educational institutions, and to the public schools, and with publishing reports on the zoology and botany of Illinois. The work of the survey was essentially ecological at a time when the word *ecological* had not yet become current in America.[6]

An accomplished research scientist with a wide network of scientific correspondents, Forbes was pulled in many directions by his diverse duties. With long absences from the campus he could not always give the college the degree of direction it needed.[7] He nevertheless insisted that the College of Science occupy a central place in the University. Its aims were to provide a liberal education of a scientific character, to prepare people for work as scientists, to train

TABLE 6
ENROLLMENTS IN THE COLLEGE OF SCIENCE, 1894–1904

| Year | Men | Women | Total |
|------|-----|-------|-------|
| 1894–95 | NA | NA | 99 |
| 1895–96 | NA | NA | 119 |
| 1896–97 | NA | NA | 123 |
| 1897–98 | NA | NA | 141 |
| 1898–99 | NA | NA | 159 |
| 1899–00 | 128 | 29 | 157 |
| 1900–01 | 126 | 25 | 151 |
| 1901–02 | 108 | 29 | 137 |
| 1902–03 | 106 | 32 | 139 |
| 1903–04 | 99 | 34 | 133 |

NA: Not available.

teachers of science, and to offer premedical study. To Forbes, most of the college's courses were equally well adapted to men and women.[8]

The College of Science was housed in Natural History Hall. The building contained the Natural History Museum, whose geological and zoological collections were intended to illustrate courses of study in natural history. The nearby herbarium contained specimens of flowering plants indigenous to Illinois and beyond, along with specimens of the flora of foreign species and of fungi and wood.

In 1894–95, 99 of the 525 undergraduates were enrolled in courses in the College of Science. During the preceding twelve years enrollment in courses offered by the college had increased in proportion to the enrollment overall at the University, but around 1900 the science enrollment fell off sharply, a reversal Forbes attributed both to students' "reactionary" inclination to pursue purely literary and linguistic studies and to the better equipment and "more immediate pecuniary value" of engineering courses. Forbes constantly battled the notion that courses in the College of Literature and Arts were more liberal in character than those in the College of Science,[9] and he wanted the College of Science to develop at a pace even with that of the other colleges within the University. Although he did not systematically report enrollments in the college or its departments, we know that the number of students registered in the college increased gradually until 1900–1, and then declined (Table 6).

Freshmen often accounted for the largest part of the enrollment—reflecting, Forbes thought, the election of science by women. In 1898–99 about two-thirds of the undergraduates were in the Natural Science Group (zoology and botany) and a little more than a fourth were in the Chemical Group. The number in geology was usually low. The college taught large numbers from other colleges, but other colleges received relatively few students from Science.[10]

When President Draper arrived, Forbes pointed out to him three general deficiencies in the college. First, certain courses essential to the scheme of the college, especially those dealing with the cosmos, the earth, and individual development, were not offered or were imperfectly developed. Forbes wanted astronomy taught for its own value, not as ancillary to engineering. Advanced geography was needed to acquaint students with the history of the earth as part of the solar system. Anthropology was essential to lay a scientific foundation for other subjects. The study of hygiene and the practical application of physiological and hygienic principles to athletic development belonged in the College of Science. Second, courses beyond the introductory level were imperfectly developed; advanced work attracted few. And third, the recognition of original investigation as a duty of instructors and a normal ambition of the superior student was lacking. Nothing was more essential to advancement of the college than research in the various sciences. Forbes deplored the lack of an official policy on the matter. Nowhere on record was there an expression of the views of the trustees in reference to scientific research by the departments. A declaration of University policy on research would be particularly helpful to the younger faculty.[11]

Graduation requirements enabled a student to pursue the subjects in the four groups in the college either as general education or as specialties. A student could take a year each in any four of the principal subjects of the college, plus electives, or concentrate on any one of the subjects in which major courses were offered, or steer a middle way. Each of the four groups of science studies was divided into required and elective subjects. Departments offered separate courses for "majors" and "minors." In 1901 the college began to award only the B.A. degree rather than the B.S.

Forbes had some latitude in identifying new faculty. In the decade between 1894–95 and 1903–4, many science instructors were recent graduates of the University, with only a bachelor's degree at the time of appointment. Much of the teaching burden was carried by a small number of faculty members, who "worked like dray horses and were paid like oxen."[12]

## PHILOSOPHICAL GROUP

The Philosophical Group embraced psychology, pedagogy, philosophy, and economics (including sociology), all of which had departmental homes in the College of Literature and Arts. These studies afforded students in science an opportunity to widen their horizons by electing liberal arts subjects, and they trained prospective high school teachers of science.

Forbes emphasized the latter. The schools had a great demand for such teachers, but the University had no candidates to offer. It did not draw students for this purpose. In 1897–98 only seven students in the college were registered in the Philosophical Group. Forbes feared that if intelligent science teaching was lacking, high school students would graduate "as ignorant as so many horses of the facts and laws of the natural world." In 1904, on a visit to the universities of Chicago, Wisconsin, Michigan, and Minnesota, Forbes discovered that there was no point at which Illinois seemed so comparatively weak as in the preparation of teachers for secondary school work. All four of these competitors had a system by which they testified to the fitness of students as high school teachers, a field into which the normal schools were pushing. Forbes wanted Illinois to adopt such a plan, but the Philosophical Group remained a negligible entity in the College of Science.[13]

## MATHEMATICS GROUP

The Mathematics Group included all of the University's offerings in mathematics, physics, and astronomy. In mathematics and astronomy, three senior professors and a number of junior faculty members carried the instructional load in the years from 1894 to 1904. Samuel W. Shattuck (b. 1841), a Massachusetts native who had taken B.S., A.M., and C.E. degrees at Norwich University in Vermont, headed the department from 1868 to 1905. In 1893 Edgar J. Townsend (b. 1865), a native of Michigan with a bachelor's degree from Albion College and a master's degree from the University of Michigan, joined the faculty. In 1900 Townsend, whose taste ran to pure mathematics, earned a doctorate at the University of Göttingen. George W. Myers (b. 1864), a Champaign County lad, did not think himself good enough in mathematics to take engineering courses when he entered the University, so in 1888 he graduated with a B.L. Appointed an instructor in mathematics in the Preparatory School that fall, in 1890 he became an assistant professor of mathematics.

Most of the instructional load in mathematics was carried by junior staff members. A baker's dozen, including one woman, served for varying periods from 1894 to 1904. At the time of appointment, eight of this group had bachelor's degrees, three had master's degrees, and two had doctorates.

In March 1894 Shattuck, Townsend, and Myers drew up a plan for creating a course of study in astronomy and for broadening the mathematics work, which had been with the College of Engineering since the earliest days. The Mathematics Group was designed to meet the requirements of those who needed mathematics as a tool for engineering work, of those who wished to teach the subject, and of those who studied mathematics for the love of it. In parallel with the pure mathematics focus of the junior and senior years, two lines of associated work in applied mathematics, physical and astronomical, were offered. One led from the physics of the sophomore year through the mathematical theory of electricity, magnetism, heat, light, and sound; the other led through surveying and mechanics to celestial mechanics and to general and mathematical astronomy. The two courses of study (mathematics and physics, mathematics and astronomy) were identical for the freshman and sophomore years. The prescribed course in mathematics encompassed twenty-one subjects, of which fifteen were in mathematics. In addition, a student following the applied mathematics route had to take at least one line of associated work in either astronomy or physics, and could take both. In addition to the prescribed courses, the number needed to graduate could be made up by election from three lists, one for astronomy, one for physics, and one containing seventeen subjects in both Science and Literature and Arts.

In 1894–95 the catalog showed the mathematics department offering nineteen courses. Judging from the course names alone, four or five of these would now be regarded as high school courses. There was a heavy emphasis on geometry, which was the subject of six courses.

Over the next ten years the curriculum was substantially revised and enlarged. Two of the geometry courses, including the course on conic sections, were dropped. In 1903–4 twenty-six courses were listed. Some of these, such as Partial Differential Equations and Functions of a Complex Variable, were in areas that are still very active research fields. Several others would not be out of place in a modern curriculum. No separate courses for graduate students were available at the turn of the century, but starting in 1903–4, twelve of the undergraduate offerings could be counted toward graduate work.

From this evidence it appears that the Mathematics Group transformed itself in this period into a modern mathematics department. The change is surprising, considering that in 1894 Shattuck had been department head for twenty-six years.[14]

At the turn of the century discovery in physics was so rapid and fruitful that physics enjoyed predominance among the sciences. Nevertheless, physics at the University of Illinois was the least developed of all the sciences, having long been subordinated to the practical needs of engineering students.

Sometime in 1901–2, President Draper, acting on impulse and supposing that all would agree, transferred the departments of physics and mathematics from the College of Engineering to the College of Science. Engineering interests strongly objected and questioned his authority to do such a thing. Draper admitted that they were right as to his lack of authority, and he agreed to undo his impulsive action. This curious affair is impossible to understand or explain, and the earlier arrangements were quickly restored.[15]

Astronomy, the most ancient of sciences, is dependent on observation associated with mathematical modeling and reasoning. Its great practical use is in furnishing the means of determining positions on land and sea, in mapping the earth, and in navigating the oceans. Astronomers, however, are often motivated by the desire to know the universe and the place that humanity occupies in it, and in the late nineteenth century astronomical science progressed rapidly.[16]

Forbes wanted more work in astronomy than the four courses offered in 1894–95, and Myers was eager to provide it. Since 1890 the authorities had assured Myers that he could take over the astronomy work if an opportunity arose, and in 1894 he secured a leave of absence and went to Munich to study with Hugo Seeliger, the best man for mathematical astronomy in Europe. Myers spent two years with Seeliger, earning a doctorate in 1896 with mathematics and physics as subordinate fields.[17]

When Myers returned the catalog listed him as teaching all eight astronomy courses. These included the four courses previously taught plus Cosmogony, Theory of Orbits, and Special Perturbations, all of which showed the influence of Seeliger, and Astronomical Seminary and Thesis. The department was devoted to work known as the astronomy of precision, but Myers proposed to add studies known as the "new astronomy," whose central idea was the application of spectroscopy and photometry to the study of the heavenly bodies.[18]

In 1897–98 three new courses were added in astronomy and cross-listed with mathematics: Calculus of Variations, Spherical Harmonics, and Potential Functions. In that same year William C. Brenke (b. 1874), a native of Berlin who had graduated from the University with an A.B. in 1896, became an assistant in astronomy. For the next two years Myers and Brenke taught this curriculum, slightly enlarged.

Progress in astronomical science led to an observatory boom in which Illinois was an eager participant. In 1895, while in Munich, Myers was advanced to associate professor, and he sent home plans for a students' observatory and a list of telescopes and equipment needed for such a facility. Later that year the legislature appropriated $15,000 for the purpose. A site was chosen on a little knoll near both the Morrow Plots and what later became Smith Memorial Music Hall (erected about 1913), and in 1896 construction began. A year later Myers was named professor of astronomy and applied mathematics and director of the observatory, which had a twelve-inch refractor telescope. With additional funds provided in 1897, the observatory was well-equipped for instruction and the practice of spherical and positional astronomy.[19]

An excellent teacher, Myers attracted many students. He did not report enrollments, but a published study of the number of undergraduate and graduate students who took astronomy in thirty-five leading American colleges and universities in 1896–97 shows that at Illinois, with 1,062 students, 38 undergraduates were taking required work and 38 were taking elective courses in astronomy. Only Columbia, Dartmouth, Mount Holyoke, and Yale had more undergraduates in required astronomy courses. As Myers boasted, the University had the largest attendance in lectures on celestial mechanics of some four or five leading universities in the country. But in elective or advanced work, Illinois lagged behind California, Michigan, Boston University, Bowdoin, Cornell, Harvard, and Princeton. Illinois had three graduate students in astronomy, a number exceeded by seven schools.[20]

Myers discovered the cause of light changes in Beta Lyrae and in U Pegasi, publishing his findings in *Popular Astronomy*,[21] and he invented a method of computing the orbit of close double variables from the light curve of the variable. His own star was ascendant, and in 1900 he resigned from the University, where he was being paid $2,000 and was offered $2,500 to remain, for a position at the Chicago Institute at a salary of $3,500. A year later he became professor of the teaching of mathematics and astronomy in the College of Education at the University of Chicago, a position from which he retired in 1928.

In 1903 astronomy gained a more solid foundation with the appointment of Joel Stebbins, a native of Nebraska with a fresh Ph.D. from the University of California, as instructor of astronomy and director of the observatory.

## CHEMICAL GROUP

The Chemical Group included programs devoted to "pure" chemistry, applied chemistry, and pharmacy. By the 1890s structural organic chemistry, which dealt with the composition of substances and the arrangement of atoms within the molecule, was the great achievement. Instruction took a taxonomic approach, emphasizing the composition of compounds and its expression in formulas, the valency of elements, quantitative analytical methods of determining composition, and the synthesis of new compounds. Germany, a growing commercial and industrial nation whose dye industry relied heavily on chemistry, was the preeminent center of the science.

Organic chemistry was considered basic to understanding the field, but Wilhelm Ostwald of Leipzig, Jacobus Henricus van't Hoff of Rotterdam, and Svante Arrhenius of Sweden wanted to study physical chemistry—the conditions under which compounds formed and decomposed, chemical affinity and equilibrium, mass action, and reaction velocity. By the turn of the century physical chemistry was rapidly enlarging our knowledge of the conditions under which chemical changes occur, and it could not be excluded from any instruction in the subject. We must evaluate chemistry at Illinois in the context of this transition.[22]

Chemistry had always occupied a prominent place at Illinois, and in 1894 the times were ripe for the work to flourish. The nation was rapidly industrializing, and the chemical industry, agriculture, mining, metallurgy, and pharmacy all required trained chemists. The University could help meet the need.

The senior faculty members in chemistry were among the best and brightest of the University's own. Arthur W. Palmer, who was born in London in 1861 and grew up in Elgin, Illinois, graduated in 1883 with a B.S. in chemistry. From 1884 to 1886 he studied at Harvard, taking a doctorate in science and then joining the faculty. During 1888–89 he studied in Berlin and Göttingen. In 1889 he became an assistant professor, and in 1890 a professor.

Samuel W. Parr, who was born in Granville, Illinois, in 1857, graduated in 1884 (at age twenty-seven) with a B.S. in chemistry. He was an outstanding student in many activities. After earning an M.S. at Cornell in 1885 he went to Illinois College as an instructor. In 1891 he joined the Illinois faculty as professor of analytical chemistry. During 1900–1 Parr took a leave to study at the University of Berlin and the Polytechnic in Zurich.

Harry S. Grindley, who was born near Mahomet, Illinois, in 1864, graduated in 1888 with a B.S. in agriculture. He served as an assistant in the Agricultural Experiment Station and later in chemistry until 1892, when he became a fellow at Harvard. T. W. Richards, a Harvard chemistry professor, remembered Grindley as "a forceful but uncultivated youth of unusual promise," somewhat uncouth and ungrammatical, but possessing "mental power and energy."[23] In 1894 Grindley earned an Sc.D. at Harvard and joined the Illinois faculty as an assistant in chemistry.

In August 1894 the trustees divided the responsibility for the work in chemistry between Palmer and Parr. Their departments were to be separately organized as agreed upon by themselves. Palmer took over the Department of Chemistry and the Chemical Laboratory, a two-story building with a basement and mansard, and Parr took over the Department of Applied Chemistry. The departments were of equal rank and completely independent as far as their courses were concerned. This organizational arrangement lacked tidiness, but both men seemed satisfied with it.[24]

Forbes regarded chemistry as one of the strongest, best-equipped, and best teaching departments in the University. Palmer wanted to provide for those who studied chemistry as part of a liberal education, but he recognized the commercial and industrial demand for well-trained chemists. He designed a curriculum to train chemical analysts, teachers of chemistry, and managers or superintendents of works. In practice, chemistry was one of the most highly specialized programs at the University.[25]

Parr's work in applied chemistry was a new specialty. In 1888 the first program of this type was established at M.I.T. The Illinois course in engineering chemistry dated from 1894 and was apparently second in the nation. Parr was a missionary for this "most progressive and pioneering science." Upon applied chemistry, he argued, depended urban public health, safety in railway travel, the development of mineral wealth, and the saving of waste products. People trained in applied chemistry were needed for all sorts of mining and manufacturing operations as well as in the preparation and conservation of food.[26]

To graduate in chemistry a student needed to complete forty-one full term credits (one more than in any other curriculum) and present an acceptable thesis. Much of this work was required, with the emphasis on the scientific side. In 1894–95 the catalog listed twenty courses in chemistry, making no distinction between chemistry and applied chemistry. In addition, there were courses in investigations and thesis, a seminary, special advanced courses, and an elementary course in quantitative analysis for students of other departments. The textbooks and manuals used were by both Americans and Germans.

Chemistry 1, although required of all regular chemical students, was arranged primarily to provide students of other departments with an understanding of the fundamental principles of general chemistry. It enrolled large numbers but was a bugbear for students and an affliction for the department. Often those who took the course were entirely unfamiliar with the methods of experimental science and needed constant supervision. Lectures, lab practice, and quizzes required thirteen hours a week of students, many of whom failed or were conditioned. "There is no reason," complained one, "why a student who works hard and honestly and does moderately good work should be flunked in Chemistry 1 any more than in anything else." Palmer scrambled to obtain enough instructors to teach the course. Many people, including a few men with doctoral degrees and three women with lesser degrees, taught chemistry during the years studied.[27]

The courses offered in 1894–95 remained the core of the curriculum for a decade, but the enterprise suffered a severe blow on 16 August 1896, when a fire largely destroyed the Chemical Laboratory. The two departments restored their labs as best they could, operating under the handicap of disagreeable quarters and enrollments that outpaced the instructional force. In March 1901 the College of Science faculty declared that they regarded "the present Chemical Laboratory as so far inadequate and unfit for its present use to be a reproach to the institution and a disgrace to the State." A new laboratory was completed in 1903, but it was only slowly equipped.[28]

Despite hardships, the chemistry curriculum changed over time to meet the needs of students, to accommodate faculty research interests, and to keep up with advances in the field. "The line of work which it is particularly desirable that we should develop here is work in physical chemistry," Palmer wrote in 1899. "All about us other institutions are making much of this branch of the subject which is gradually coming to the fore and taking the place which a decade ago was occupied by organic chemistry." Advances in chemistry were now coming largely through physical chemistry. "Students ask for this work

TABLE 7

ENROLLMENTS IN CHEMISTRY AND APPLIED CHEMISTRY,
1894–1904

| Year | Chemistry | Applied Chemistry | Total |
|------|-----------|-------------------|-------|
| 1894–95 | 261 | 47 | 308 |
| 1895–96 | 372 | 57 | 439 |
| 1896–97 | 147* | NA | NA |
| 1897–98 | 175* | NA | 456 |
| 1898–99 | 181* | NA | NA |
| 1899–00 | 237* | NA | NA |
| 1900–01 | 301* | NA | NA |
| 1901–02 | 362* | 36* | NA |
| 1902–03 | 739 | 88 | 827 |
| 1903–04 | 830 | 105 | 935 |

*Fall semester only.
NA: Not available.
Source: These data are from scattered sources, primarily the annual reports of Forbes, Palmer, and Grindley, 2/4/2, B:2, 4.

and we are obliged to advise them to go elsewhere because of the lack of facilities and the lack of men to do the work of instruction."[29] Accordingly, in 1896–97 Palmer transformed the course in advanced general chemistry into physical chemistry, and in 1903–4 the offerings in physical chemistry were expanded.

Data on enrollments in chemistry are scant, but the figures in Table 7, with all their limitations, are revealing.[30] In 1894–95 104 students were enrolled in Chemistry 1. A year later the same course drew 148, and in 1903–4 261 students enrolled. Pure chemistry drew most of the other students. Applied chemistry attracted 47 in 1894–95 and 57 a year later. The study of both pure chemistry and applied chemistry was dominated by men.

Although the University was geared to the teaching of undergraduates, the senior chemistry professors were engaged in research intended to yield results of value to the people of Illinois. While studying in Berlin, Palmer began work on arsine, a compound of arsenic and hydrogen, which culminated in 1892 with his establishing the existence of the series of arsines. Later, Palmer's laboratory work was devoted primarily to a survey of the waters of the state. The water survey is a classic example of science pursued for the common good.

At the time most Illinois residents still lived in small towns or rural areas. Half of them drank surface waters, the other half drank well water, and sewerage discharge contaminated much of the water supply. Water-borne infectious diseases, especially typhoid fever and diphtheria, were prevalent, and as the population increased, impure water and epidemics of disease became more problematic. In 1894 Palmer proposed a water survey, the legislature provided the funds, and the board endorsed the task.

On 1 September 1895 the Illinois State Water Survey began in the Department of Chemistry. Its aims were to determine the sanitary status of water samples drawn from wells, streams, and lakes, to formulate standards of purity for drinking water, to prevent disease from the use of impure water, and to publish the results of these investigations to conserve the public welfare. Most of its early work was concerned with developing testing methods to define safe water. In its first fifteen months the Water Survey analyzed 1,787 water samples sent in from throughout the state. Some records perished in the fire that ravaged the Chemical Laboratory, but Palmer salvaged what he could and published his results along with standards of purity in *Chemical Survey of the Water Supplies of Illinois: Preliminary Report* (January 1897). Over the next seven years Palmer was responsible for a total of 3,715 chemical analyses of potable water samples submitted by 478 towns, representing all but two counties of the state.

In addition, Palmer expanded his survey to include sanitary chemical examinations of the waters of the Illinois River before and after the opening of the Chicago Main Drainage Canal (the Sanitary Canal). Palmer's assistants took water samples at ten points related to their study, starting at Lake Michigan in Chicago and including the Mississippi River at Quincy. Although focused on the Illinois River, the study included tributaries that fed into it. Palmer published his conclusions, along with many plates and tables of analyses, in *Chemical Survey of the Waters of Illinois: Report for the Years 1897–1902* (1903). His report remained a valuable reference book for a generation.

The success of Palmer's research stimulated a flow of requests for the chemistry department to analyze all sorts of substances, leading him to suggest that the time was ripe for establishment at the University of state laboratories, analogous to the State Laboratory of Natural History and the State Water Survey, to carry on such work. Nothing came of the proposal.[31]

Parr initiated various lines of investigation. In the years under review he published seven papers in the *Journal of the American Chemical Society*. The first of these, "Sodium Peroxide as a Third Group Reagent" (1897), evidently grew out of his experience teaching qualitative analysis. The method of using sodium peroxide that he described was extensively used for decades. Parr's most important research had reference to the wider utilization and increased economic value of Illinois coals. He requested funds to continue a work beneficial to the people of the state, but the board often denied them. His second important paper, "A New Coal Calorimeter" (1900), described a device he had developed for determining the heat of combustion of coals. The "Parr Peroxide Calorimeter" was extensively used as a rapid and quite accurate method for the valuation of coals. From the peroxide calorimeter came methods for determining the sulfur content in coals and in organic compounds and mixtures. Parr also developed a method for determining the carbon content in coal, in soils, and in carbon compounds and mixtures by burning them with sodium peroxide, liberating the carbon dioxide formed, and measuring the volume of the gas. When he found that tables of constants needed for his calorimeter were not accurate enough, he worked out new tables. By 1904 Parr was well launched on a career as a researcher on the properties and uses of coals.[32]

Grindley coauthored four published papers on chemistry early in his career, but he soon turned to the chemistry of foodstuffs. His study of human and animal nutrition was apparently shaped by local conditions more than by an interest in physiology. Illinois produced both meats and cereals. Grindley began his nutrition work in 1896 in association with Wilbur O. Atwater, a chemistry professor at Connecticut Wesleyan, and A. C. True, director of agricultural experiment stations for the U.S. Department of Agriculture. Atwater was concerned with metabolism as a problem in physiology and with establishing a dietary standard for the working class; he prompted Congress to support nutritional research. He and True exerted a decisive influence on the administrative policies of agricultural experiment stations, and they wanted to make Illinois a center of food investigations.

Grindley studied the chemical composition, digestibility, and nutritive value of meats. He was interested in the chemical and physical changes that occurred in boiling, roasting, frying, and broiling meats. In April 1897 he began a dietary study on his own family, and in July he began a similar study on a boarding-house family of fourteen workers, analyzing 150 samples of food. In December 1898 the trustees provided $500 to continue this research. Grindley published the results of his early studies in reports and bulletins. In 1902 he requested $3,000 to continue his work. One of his early publications, coauthored with Timothy Mojonnier, was *The Artificial Method for Determining the Ease and the Rapidity of the Digestion of Meats* (1903).[33]

Palmer's sudden death on 3 February 1904 at the age of forty-three was a grievous loss. Since Draper had resigned in March and left for Albany on 1 April, the choice of Palmer's successor was virtually left to Forbes.[34] Charles L. Jackson of Harvard strongly recommended Grindley, his former student, but Forbes thought Jackson was prejudiced in favor of Harvard men. Forbes wanted a man clearly superior to either Grindley or Parr.[35]

Since the very best organic chemists in the nation were unavailable, the leading candidates soon became Moses Gomberg, of the University of Michigan, J. F. Norris, of M.I.T., and Joseph H. Kastle, of the University of

Kentucky. Forbes was much impressed with Kastle, but Draper, who continued to advise, thought that southern men did not usually prove to be very strong.[36]

As the search progressed Charles S. Palmer, chief chemist of Anaconda Mining Company, became a candidate. Holder of a Ph.D. from Johns Hopkins, Palmer had been in charge of the chemistry department at the University of Colorado and president of the School of Mines at Golden, Colorado. He had taken a year off to learn about the new physical chemistry from Ostwald at Leipzig, which led to his translation of Walther Nernst's *Theoretical Chemistry from the Standpoint of Avogadro's Rule and Thermodynamics* (1895). In mid-May Forbes was prepared to appoint Palmer. But a question arose as to Palmer's professional standing, and he was dropped.[37]

On 1 June Forbes was prepared to make Gomberg a proposition after he had looked over the University, but Gomberg wanted a proposition *before* he looked over the University. So the vacancy was not filled at this time. After further consultation, Forbes recommended and the trustees approved the appointment of Richard S. Curtiss as an assistant professor of organic chemistry. A Yale graduate (1888) who had taken a Ph.D. from the University of Würzburg and spent a year at the Sorbonne, Curtiss had taught at the University of Chicago and Hobart College before going to Union College, from which he was appointed. The Department of Applied Chemistry was now discontinued and a unified Department of Chemistry was formed. Parr continued as professor of applied chemistry, and Grindley was promoted to full professor and made professor of general chemistry. The headship of the department was divided: Parr was in charge of matters relating to instruction and instructors, while Grindley, as director of the laboratory, was in charge of all business affairs.[38] Forbes may have picked up the idea of a division from Charles L. Jackson, who said that it had worked at Harvard. But the compromise was almost certain to cause friction, and it soon did.[39]

The Chemical Group included a two-year course in pharmacy whose purpose was to train pharmacists and persons wishing to work in the pharmaceutical industry. In 1894–95 the catalog listed six courses in this area. William E. Sandford (b. 1871) was in charge of most of these courses. Sandford had entered the University with the class of 1892 but had left after three years because of his dissatisfaction with student rowdyism directed against Regent Peabody. He went to the University of Michigan, which he found much farther advanced than Illinois, graduating in 1892 with a Ph.C. (pharmaceutical chemistry). Sandford returned to Illinois that year as an assistant in chemistry. In 1894–95 twenty-six students were enrolled in the five courses taught by Sandford; a year later thirty students were enrolled in three of these courses. After Sandford left, in 1896, the pharmacy program was discontinued at Urbana and established in Chicago as a branch of the University.

## NATURAL SCIENCE GROUP

By the late nineteenth century natural history was beginning to divide into a number of fields, the practitioners of which were being challenged by exciting new ideas, including the germ theory of disease and, above all, Darwin's evolutionary hypothesis.

The Natural Science Group was designed to prepare students for careers in botany, entomology, geology, physiology, or zoology; to lay a liberal foundation for a course in medicine; and to prepare teachers for high schools and colleges. To graduate in natural science a student had to complete a number of required courses, take nine terms of work in one major elective or twelve terms of work in more than one such major, take at least minor courses in all the other electives, and submit a thesis. A total of forty full-term credits were required for graduation. Special courses were arranged as preparation for a course in medicine.

The Natural History Museum had at one time been an important part of the University's scientific equipment, but by 1897 it had declined to a position of relative insignificance. It was overcrowded, distant from classrooms, and without supervision. Forbes wanted a curator and plans made for its development. In 1900 he achieved part of his goal with the appointment of Frank Smith as acting curator.[40]

Geology and zoology at Illinois were united until 1884, when Charles W. Rolfe took over the former. Rolfe had earned two degrees from the University, a B.S. (1872) and an M.S. (1878). After some time as a teacher, principal, and superintendent of schools, Rolfe taught natural science in the Preparatory School from 1881 to 1884, when Peabody named him assistant professor of geology. During the years under review Rolfe had the assistance of five young colleagues. Four were graduates of the University; none had more than a master's degree at the time.

Rolfe had ambitions for his field, and his plans are best seen in historical context. Geologists had been instrumental in establishing the American Association for the Advancement of Science in 1848, and state-sponsored geological surveys were one of the earliest examples of public patronage of science in the United States. In the years between 1823 and 1853 twenty-four states established geological surveys to conduct inventories of their natural resources. Illinois, in 1851, was next to last of this group. Joseph G. Norwood, a medical doctor, became the first state geologist. His failure to submit the required annual report—he submitted only three in seven years—weighed against him, and in 1858 a new Republican governor dismissed Norwood, a Democrat, and appointed Amos H. Worthen, a Republican, to the post. Worthen's interests were primarily paleontological—he built a collection of fossils for the state and a private collection that ranked among the best in the country—whereas the public's interest was primarily economic. The General Assembly failed to appreciate the need for basic studies, and in 1875 it discontinued all appropriations for the survey. Worthen's pioneer work led to publication of eight volumes of the highest scientific character, and in 1877 he was named director of the new state Natural History Museum. But the state lacked an office of geological survey.[41]

In August 1894 Rolfe laid plans for his department before Draper. He proposed to stress economic geology, both because of its importance and because the University's location made fieldwork in stratigraphic or dynamic geology impossible. He also wanted a laboratory where geological materials could be tested, noting that the geological survey of the state was admirable from the paleontological side but had left the economic side almost untouched. Illinois had no state geologist, while demand for an economic survey of the state was growing. The University could occupy this field. Rolfe proposed surveying one area each year and publishing the results. He wanted Draper to ask the General Assembly to support the proposed laboratory with an annual appropriation and to call on those interested to aid in passage of a bill for the purpose.[42]

Rolfe also sought Draper's assistance in obtaining for the University the large and valuable collection of fossils left by Worthen. The State Museum Board in Springfield had purchased both this collection and Worthen's library and had passed a resolution donating these treasures to the University, which had received only a portion of this material. Draper pressed the matter, and Governor Altgeld's private secretary promised that the entire collection would go to the University.[43]

In 1894 Rolfe's vision as to who should assume prime responsibility for a state geological survey was a bit imprecise. Years later he said that in 1894 the University had asked for an appropriation for equipping a laboratory for research work in coal mining and ceramics and for establishing a geological survey, but that Draper thought that the sciences were absorbing too large a share of the support given to the University, so Draper asked that the bill be withdrawn and reintroduced later. The coal and clay interests of the state were prepared to support the bill, said Rolfe, who thought it would have passed.[44]

Perhaps such a bill was drafted, but the General Assembly did not meet in 1894, and no such bill was introduced in the 1893 or 1895 sessions. In late 1896, however, Rolfe proposed offering a course in field geology, to be known as the University Geological Survey of Illinois; he suggested that the trustees provide $500 for this purpose. In addition, Rolfe reiterated his request that Draper ask the legislature to appropriate funds for a laboratory of economic geology. This was the project that had failed as a separate bill two years earlier.[45]

Rolfe later returned to the subject of a state geological survey, but meanwhile he had instructional duties in geology and cognate subjects. For several years the department's curriculum remained fairly constant. In 1894–95 it consisted of courses in geology for majors and minors, geology for engineering students, plus investigation and thesis. A year in duration, the major course treated dynamic, petrographic, historical, and economic geology as well as paleontology. In 1898–99 the course in engineering geology was dropped; a year later a course in economic geology was added. For three years Rolfe also taught a course in meteorology, although he considered meteorology more closely allied to astronomy than geology. In addition, from the academic year 1894–95 through 1900–1, his department offered elementary and advanced courses in mineralogy. The latter included both crystallographic and optical mineralogy. In 1900–1 the department introduced a course in physiography that treated the general principles of meteorology, oceanography, and climatology along with the physical geography of North America and Europe.

In 1901–2 the department's offerings, which had been listed under various headings in the catalog, were brought together under the rubric of geology. The catalog showed thirteen courses, including the four geology courses of former years (the major course was renamed Dynamic and Historic Geology), a mineralogy course divided into five sections, one continuing course (Physiography), two reintroduced courses (Meteorology and Engineering Geology), and a new entry, Agricultural Geology. Four additional courses were planned at the request of other departments on the understanding that Rolfe would receive an additional assistant. Forbes endorsed such an appointment.[46]

In June 1902 Draper recommended that the board grant the department $300 for a half-time assistant and $300 for equipment and supplies. When the trustees did not act on the matter, Rolfe complained that Draper had always expressed sympathy for and offered to aid Rolfe's work, but that he had not permitted the department to take a single step forward. Draper had stopped the growth underway in the direction of advanced mineralogy and economic geology and had failed to see the advantages that would arise from pushing work in geology. Perhaps Draper did not wish to invest in what he regarded as a weak department. (It is worth noting that after Draper persuaded the trustees to fund his quixotic venture in the domestication of squirrels on the campus, he assigned Rolfe the job of squirrel master.)[47]

Enrollment figures, while incomplete, suggest that numbers impressed Draper. In 1894–95 the courses offered under Rolfe's direction drew sixty-six students. In 1904–5 enrollment was seventy-eight (including fifteen women), a slight increase in ten years. Not one was in the major course.

In 1895–96 Rolfe introduced three courses for graduates: Paleontology, Economic Geology, and Illinois Geology (especially as related to surface water). They were offered through 1900–1. None was listed as available the following year. Starting in 1902–3, however, five undergraduate courses could be taken for graduate credit and three others were offered for graduates: Economic Geology, Dynamic Geology, and Physical Geography.

Dean Forbes thought it undesirable to abandon permanently the advanced courses in geology that had been temporarily dropped when Rolfe did not get an assistant, and he was concerned that Rolfe had not published. Wanting someone who would publish, Forbes said it was not creditable that so important a department should take no part in the rapid development of its field.[48]

In 1904 Rolfe sent Draper a manuscript, "The Nucleus of a Clayworking School," that he wanted to publish. Draper criticized the manuscript as not well prepared and for stating that the University had committed itself to a clayworking school when no University authority had passed on the matter. Distinguishing between pure and applied science, Draper informed Rolfe that his department was to do the former. Rolfe was not to continue in the piecemeal development of a work to which the University was not committed and that, if the University were to undertake, it might prefer to put in other hands. "I trust that in the course of time you will get this point," Draper snorted, and stop "until the whole subject may be carefully considered and authoritatively acted upon." Chastened, Rolfe agreed to confine his work to pure geology—historical, dynamic, and economic. Forbes asked Draper whether Illinois should continue the development of economic geology, and if so, whether Rolfe should be encouraged to develop his plan or a new man should be found for this work.[49]

Rolfe's troubles reveal the tensions inherent in the transition to a university, and they persisted as he urged the establishment of a state geological survey. Its creation in 1905 is said to have resulted from the collaboration of Professor Thomas C. Chamberlin of the University of Chicago and Governor Charles S. Deneen. But Rolfe had suggested the survey in 1894, and he played a part in its creation.[50]

By November 1900 the idea of a state geological survey had matured to the point that professors of geology at leading universities of the state met in Chicago to confer on the appointment of a University of Illinois faculty member as state geologist and to agree on a plan of procedure to promote the interests of geological science. Draper sent Forbes rather than Rolfe because the meeting was likely to concern organization and plans for legislative action rather than geology. Forbes met with Chamberlin, formerly president of the University of Wisconsin and a distinguished scientist who at the time was a professor of geology at the University of Chicago, Professor U. S. Grant, of Northwestern, and Professor J. A. Udden, of Augustana College in Rock Island. Udden was an announced candidate for the curatorship of the Geological Museum.

The conferees drew up a plan for a geological survey whose main features included creation of a state board charged with the duty of making a geological survey, appointing a director of the survey, and placing the collections of the survey in the museum at Springfield, at the state university, and at other state educational institutions in such a manner as to promote the best interests of science and education. The plan suggested an appropriation of $10,000 a year for the work. As one of several alternatives, Chamberlin suggested that the geological collection and control of the survey should go to the University. Grant objected, saying that this would give the University an unfair advantage over other schools. Forbes replied that the University belonged to the state as much as did the proposed geological survey.[51]

Meanwhile, the University's trustees, unaware of the Chicago conference, had appointed a committee consisting of Draper, Burrill, and Rolfe to secure the appointment of a member of the University faculty as state geologist. Writing Draper about the tangle that had arisen over establishment of a geological survey, Chamberlin put Rolfe in a bad light for bungling the attempt to create the agency. The University's committee asked the board for authority to act for the University in drafting a bill and securing its passage. Rolfe asked Chamberlin to comment on this draft, and in January 1901 Rolfe asked Draper to enlist the Illinois Society of Engineers and Surveyors, which was to hold its annual meeting in Bloomington in a few days, in support of the proposed geological survey.[52]

By 1904, when Deneen was seeking the governorship, the time was ripe for a state geological survey. Chamberlin urged Deneen, his neighbor in Chicago's Hyde Park, to establish the agency if elected. On 9 January 1905 Deneen asked the General Assembly to appropriate funds for a geological survey, noting that the immense mineral resources of Illinois awaited development. On 17 January the University's trustees authorized the president and its legislative committee to introduce a bill entrusting the conduct of the survey to the University of Illinois. Two days later a Chicago legislator introduced a bill to establish at the University of Illinois a state geological survey. The bill passed by a unanimous vote, was signed into law, and became effective 1 July 1905.[53]

Rolfe had helped prod the state of Illinois into establishing the State Geological Survey, whose first director was H. Foster Bain, a former student of Chamberlin's. Under Bain the survey made progress in mapping the vast natural resources of Illinois, preparing topographical studies, and publishing bulletins. It was soon learned that oil, coal, and clay were the most valuable mineral products of Illinois, and with studies of these resources by the Geological Survey and its consulting staff members the value of Illinois mineral production increased rapidly. The Illinois coalfields were the largest known in any American state. Samuel W. Parr of the chemistry department began an association with the Geological Survey in which he made valuable studies of the caloric content of Illinois coals. After oil and natural gas were discovered in southeastern Illinois in 1905, the Geological Survey made petroleum studies that helped open up these vast riches. Clay, which was used in brick and tile and for other products, was available in vast quantities in Illinois. Bain called on Rolfe to study its use in construction.

The work in botany was led by Thomas J. Burrill, an accomplished scientist. Born in 1839 in Massachusetts, Burrill had moved at the age of nine with his family to Stephenson County in northern Illinois. He grew up on a farm, acquiring an education in log schools and the district school and attending high school in Freeport and later Rockford. In 1862 he entered the State Normal University at Normal, where he was inspired by the work being done in natural history. After graduating in 1865 he began teaching in Urbana; two years later he went as botanist on John Wesley Powell's first expedition to the Colorado Rockies. He joined the faculty in 1868 when the University opened, and was appointed assistant professor of natural history and botany when Major Powell did not take up his chair at Urbana. Two years later he was promoted to a full professorship in botany and horticulture.

Burrill viewed science as an agency of human welfare, and in his teaching and research he demonstrated alertness to scientific advances. He pioneered the new field of plant pathology. In his botany courses he taught the use of the microscope, he dealt with fungi and vegetable diseases, and he opened the virtually uncultivated field of cryptogamic botany. He was probably the first to teach plant pathology and the first to use microscopes in botanical instruction. At the time, the study of bacteria in botany was still in the primitive stage. It had long been known that diseases attacked plants, and fire blight, a contagious disease of pear, apple, quince, and other trees, was a major problem for Illinois fruit-growers. But no one had satisfactorily explained the cause of pear blight. In fact, bacterial diseases of plants were far rarer than fungal diseases, and when Burrill began his study of fire blight, he leaned to the belief that fungi were the source of trouble. As late as 1877 he believed that the presumed fungal origin of the fire blight of the pear and the twig blight of the apple was well-founded. But a year later he identified the "minute oscillating particles" that exuded from affected limbs as bacteria. His finding "that *bacteria* cause disease in plants," which had been abundantly proved in the case of animals, was entirely new. Burrill did not publish his results until 1881, a delay probably caused by the press of other University duties, but an authority on the subject later credited Burrill with discovering that pear blight could be attributed to bacterial origin and nothing else. The Society of American Bacteriologists congratulated Burrill on founding the science of plant pathology through his work on the cause of pear blight. Burrill's achievement brought him world renown as a scientist. In addition, Burrill was an able administrator. From

1891 to 1894, while the trustees searched for a new president, he served as acting regent.[54]

From 1894 to 1904 Burrill was the senior professor in botany. Forbes occasionally taught in the department, and the junior staff included George P. Clinton and Charles F. Hottes. Both took bachelor's and master's degrees from Illinois (Clinton in 1890 and 1894, Hottes in 1894 and 1895) and went elsewhere for doctorates. From 1890 to 1902 Clinton was an assistant at the Agricultural Experiment Station and in botany. He earned an M.S. at Harvard in 1901 and a Ph.D. in 1902, when he received an offer at $2,000 from the Connecticut Agricultural Experiment Station. Since the University could not pay that much, it allowed him to accept the post. Hottes began as an assistant in botany in 1895. In 1898 he was given leave to go to Germany for two years, where he studied vegetable physiology with "the best masters the world affords," and in 1901 he earned a Ph.D. at the University of Bonn.[55]

From 1894 to 1904 the curriculum in botany remained fairly stable. In 1894–95 seven courses were available. General Botany offered an introduction. Majors could take Histology, Morphology, and Physiology; Bacteriology; Systematic Botany; Plant Reproduction and Development; Pharmaceutical Botany; and Investigation and Thesis. The changes over time were minor. Years later the total number of offerings was thirteen, including a course taught by Burrill that dealt with bacteria and one taught by Hottes titled German Readings. Enrollments in botany went from 80 students in 1894–95 to 220 in 1904–5, with 79 (including 49 women) taking the introductory course and 107 taking Burrill's course on bacteriology.

Forbes, a man of broad experience in biology and a broad outlook on nature, earned distinction in several scientific fields. A pioneer ecologist, he early became impressed by the significance of the interrelationship between organisms and their environment, an interest that dominated both his teaching and his research. From 1875 to 1882 he studied the microscopic life of fresh inland waters; his writings on biology and zoology established him as the leading worker in America in the study of aquatic biology. He also pioneered study of the fauna of the region, especially the food of fishes, birds, and insects.[56]

On 1 April 1894 Forbes opened the Aquatic Biological Station, later named the Illinois State Biological Experiment Station, on the Illinois River near Havana under the joint sponsorship of the University and the State Laboratory of Natural History. This venture, patterned after the marine biological stations at Naples, Italy, and Woods Hole, Massachusetts, was one of the first freshwater biological stations in the world. Forbes made the main object of the station, which was housed in a floating laboratory, investigation rather than instruction. Its field was the study of the aquatic plant and animal life of the Illinois River and its dependent waters, including their interactions as living associates. From 1894 to 1900 Forbes and others surveyed the plankton of that stream prior to the opening of the Chicago Drainage Canal, later reporting on the destructive effect of sewage on the life of this river.[57]

Insect pests were a problem for Illinois agriculture. Forbes had begun to publish on entomology in the early 1880s, and in 1882 he became state entomologist. Thereafter he wrote primarily on insects and gained eminence as an economic entomologist. In 1893, at the request of the Illinois Board of World's Fair Commissioners, he prepared for the State Laboratory of Natural History an exhibit of the zoology of Illinois for the World's Columbian Exposition.[58]

Zoology was taught in a number of courses that provided an introduction to the subject and opened up three lines to specialists, one leading toward entomology, a second toward physiological and medical study, and a third toward advanced zoology—anatomical, systematic, or ecological. In the years from 1894 to 1905 Forbes, head of the department, shared instructional duties with ten colleagues. Two (Hottes and Summers) were from other departments, and two (Frank Smith and Charles A. Kofoid) were from the State Laboratory of Natural History. Of the eight instructors in the zoology department, one was a graduate assistant, four had master's degrees, and three (including Kofoid) had doctorates.

In 1894–95 the zoology department offered nine courses. Five were in zoology proper. Three were variations on a course in general zoology, another was Embryology (of the chick), and still another was Advanced Zoology, which was divided into systematic zoology, including paleontology; ecological zoology; and comparative anatomy and embryology, or other morphological work. Three courses were in entomology: General Entomology, Advanced Entomology, and Practical Entomology (for agricultural students). The ninth course was Thesis and Investigation.

Starting in 1895–96 the zoology department offered courses for graduate students. Three of these were in zoology, one in entomology, and one in pedagogical zoology. In 1900–1 courses in plankton zoology, freshwater ichthyology, and freshwater and terrestrial annelids were added, and starting in 1903–04 graduate students in entomology and zoology could take various undergraduate courses for graduate credit.

In 1897–98, the first year for which data are available, enrollment in zoology and cognate subjects was 168. The basic course in general zoology drew 73, the introductory course 27, Advanced Zoology enrolled 18, and Elementary Entomology enrolled 18. The figures for 1903–4 are fragmentary but suggest a drastic decline in enrollment in both zoology and entomology.

The study of physiology was often tied to anatomy, biology, or chemistry. Physiological chemistry, a branch of physiology in the late nineteenth century, was a stage in the evolution of biochemistry.[59] Prior to 1894–95, the University had offered instruction in anatomy, physiology, and hygiene for premedical and biology students and as a basis for future studies in hygiene. In 1894–95 physiology was a program within the zoology department and was not taught as a subject valuable in its own right. It was often the route from academic study into medicine. Having spent a year as a medical student, Forbes wanted to devise a strong program for premedical students, and physiology fit that plan.

Even so, the curriculum in physiology was thin and lacked focus. In 1894–95 the available offerings were Major Course, Advanced Physiology, Investigation and Thesis, and Minor Course. In 1896–97 two new courses were introduced, on the nervous system and hygiene. The following year Advanced Physiology replaced Nervous System; in 1900–1 this course was renamed Special Physiology. These offerings remained in force through 1903–4.

From 1893 to 1897 Henry E. Summers was in charge of physiology. He had earned a B.S. at Cornell in 1886 and had studied abroad in 1891–92; in 1892 he worked under Forbes as an entomologist in preparing an exhibit for the World's Columbian Exposition. Draper found Summers and Krohn, a psychologist, lacking in desirable personal characteristics; moreover, he wanted a physiologist and a psychologist who would supplement each other's work. Draper and Forbes tried to get Summers to improve his ways, but in June 1897 Draper terminated both Summers and Krohn.[60]

In 1897 George T. Kemp replaced Summers. Born in Baltimore in 1861, Kemp had earned a B.A. (1883) and a Ph.D. (1886) from Johns Hopkins University. While serving as associate director of Hoagland Laboratory in Brooklyn he had taken a medical degree from Long Island Medical College and then practiced medicine in Brooklyn. Abandoning his practice, he returned to Johns Hopkins to engage in research. He had made two trips abroad for study—one to Leipzig, for physiology, and the second to Paris, for neurology. Kemp did not wish to assume responsibility for both psychology and physiology but wanted to give a thoroughly up-to-date course in physiology. He also wanted an opportunity to do "first-class research," and therefore considered the University's attitude toward science important. He was appointed professor of physiology at $2,000 a year. His investigations came to focus on the human blood.[61]

Forbes regarded Kemp as a man of eminent qualifications and experience. He viewed the work in physiology as the backbone of the premedical course and an important link to the College of Medicine in Chicago. He supported Kemp's efforts to build up physiology by securing equipment and increasing the department's enrollments. Although classes were small, the instruction was of a high order. Forbes described Kemp as an able physiologist, a stimulating but unmethodical instructor, irregular in his work habits, and "inclined to depend too much upon his personal qualities and relations for the maintenance of his university standing."[62]

## SUMMARY: FORBES AND UNIVERSITY SCIENCE

An eminent scientist with a broad perspective on nature, Forbes contended that general science courses offered a liberal education and that the College of Science, the only one of its kind in the state, had an obligation to strengthen high school science studies. Forbes was a pioneer in introducing the study of the natural sciences into the educational system of Illinois.[63]

In 1901 and again in 1904, overburdened by his multifarious duties, Forbes asked for relief from part of his load in order to perform the remainder with success. Draper did not grant his request.[64] Forbes's taxing assignments prevented him from concentrating on the college, but he protected its interests while stating its needs with moderation.

The problems of the college were fairly intractable. Much of the work remained at the elementary level and in the hands of young instructors. Departmental contours were not yet well defined. Early in 1904 Forbes reported that registration in general science courses had fallen off relatively or even absolutely in recent years. He attributed the decline to the lucrative jobs open to graduates of technical and agricultural courses and to students' heading for business and political careers. Science courses were taken mainly by prospective teachers and premedical students.[65]

Forbes was a spokesman for research within the University and a major contributor to the school's scientific eminence. He was interested both in expanding the boundaries of knowledge and in the practical applications of science, and he urged faculty and students to pursue original investigations, especially in directions likely to yield results of practical value. Several faculty members in the college were highly reputable scholars. In addition to Forbes, Burrill, Palmer, Parr, Grindley, and Rolfe all conducted research designed to promote the economic welfare of Illinois. In 1905, in recognition of his accomplishments, the University conferred on Forbes an honorary LL.D.

## NOTES

1. 15/1/6, 44, 85; *18th Report*, 70; Forbes to Draper, 7 March 1895, 2/4/2, B:1, F:Forbes.
2. This sketch of Forbes is based on Solberg, 247–49; Henry B. Ward, "Stephen Alfred Forbes—A Tribute," *Science*, n.s. 30 (11 April 1930), 378–81; L. O. Howard, "Stephen Alfred Forbes, 1844–1930," *National Academy of Sciences, Biographical Memoirs*, 15 (1934), 3–25; Ernest B. Forbes, "Stephen Alfred Forbes: His Ancestry, Education, and Character," *In Memoriam: Stephen Alfred Forbes, 1844–1930*, 43/1/25, Forbes Papers; and Robert A. Lovely, "Mastering Nature's Harmony: Stephen Forbes and the Roots of American Ecology" (Ph.D. diss., University of Wisconsin, 1995), 20–27. The quotation is from Forbes, "War as an Education," *The Illinois*, 3 (October 1911), 9.

3. The first number was issued as the *Bulletin of the Illinois Museum of Natural History*, and succeeding numbers as the *Bulletin of the Illinois State Laboratory of Natural History*.

4. Milton D. Thompson, *The Illinois State Museum: Historical Sketch and Memoirs* (Springfield: Illinois State Museum Society, 1988), 1–9.

5. Published in the *Bulletin of the Illinois State Laboratory of Natural History*, 1 (1882), 3–32.

6. Stephen A. Forbes, "The Illinois State Laboratory of Natural History and the Illinois State Entomologist's Office," *Transactions of the Illinois State Academy of Science*, 2 (1909), 54–67; *16th Report* (1892), 242–43; Lovely, "Mastering Nature's Harmony," 31–62, 80, 115–30.

7. Forbes's annual reports for the academic years ending in 1896, 1898, 1899, 1902, and 1903 have been located. The first three are in 2/4/2, B:2, 4, 5, F:Forbes; the others are in 2/4/4, B:2, F:Departmental Reports 1902, 1903 (1903 is also in 15/1/13). Forbes to Draper, 7 March 1895 and 5 June 1897, are in effect annual reports. Both are in 2/4/2, B:1, 3, F:Forbes.

8. *Catalogue* (1894–95), 58; Forbes to Draper, 7 March 1895, 2 November 1903, 2/4/2, B:1, 10, F:Forbes.

9. Forbes to Draper, 31 May 1902, 2 November 1903, 2/4/2, B:8, 10, F:Forbes.

10. Forbes to Draper, 7 March 1895, 30 May 1896, 2 June 1898, 17 May 1899, 2/4/2, B:1, 2, 4, 5, F:Forbes; W. L. Pillsbury (Registrar) to Professor W. G. Raymond, 7 December 1904, 15/1/3, B:2, F:1905–07–P; Forbes to Pillsbury, 21 May 1904, 15/1/2.

11. Forbes to Draper, 7 March 1895, 2/4/2, B:1, F:Forbes. On research policy, see Forbes to Draper, 2 June, 19 November 1898, 20 May 1899, ibid., B:4, 5, F:Forbes.

12. As quoted in Solberg, 251.

13. Forbes to Draper, 3 June 1895, 2 June 1898, 20 May 1899, 18 January 1902 (the quotation), 4 January 1904, 2/4/2, B:1, 4, 5, 8, 10, F:Forbes.

14. I am indebted to Professor Richard Jerrard of the University of Illinois for help on the previous three paragraphs.

15. Forbes to Draper, 3 June 1902, 2/4/4, B:2, F:Departmental Reports, 1902; Draper to Forbes, 16 October 1902, 2/4/3.

16. Simon Newcomb, "The Aspects of American Astronomy," *Popular Astronomy*, 5 (October 1897), 351–67.

17. Myers to Draper, 5 December 1894, 28 August 1895, 2/4/2, B:1, F:Myers, B:2, F:L–Z.

18. Myers to Draper, 5 December 1896, 2/4/2, B:3, F:H–P.

19. Myers to Draper, 19 June 1895, 5 December 1896, 2/4/2, B:1, F:Myers, B:3, F:H–P; G. W. Myers, "The Astronomical Observatory of the University of Illinois," *Popular Astronomy*, 6 (August 1898), 319–21; Michael T. Svec, "The Astronomical Observatory of the University of Illinois" (a paper written in 1986 and revised in 1987), 15/3/2, LAS, Astronomy, Observatory History, B:1.

20. G. D. Swezey, "Astronomy in Our Universities and Colleges," *Popular Astronomy*, 5 (September 1897), 255–57; Myers to Draper, 6 March 1897, 2/4/2, B:3, F:H–P.

21. G. W. Myers, "Light Fluctuations of Variables as Related to Changes in Positions of Periastron and in Orbital Eccentricity," *Popular Astronomy*, 6 (March 1898), 7–15; idem, "The Light Changes of Beta-Lyrae," *Popular Astronomy*, 6 (July 1898), 268–88.

22. John W. Servos, *Physical Chemistry from Ostwald to Pauling: The Making of a Science in America* (Princeton: Princeton University Press, 1990), 3–20; David Knight, *Ideas in Chemistry: A History of the Science* (New Brunswick: Rutgers University Press, 1992), 1–53, 157–70; Alexander Smith, "The Teaching of Physical Chemistry," *Electrochemical Industry*, 1 (June 1903), 385–86.

23. Richards to Edwin A. Alderman, 26 April 1906, as quoted in Robert E. Kohler, *From Medical Chemistry to Biochemistry: The Making of a Biomedical Discipline* (Cambridge: Cambridge University Press, 1982), 375 n. 25.

24. *17th Report* (1894), 268; *Catalogue*(1894–95), 64; W. A. Noyes, "Samuel Wilson Parr," *Journal of the American Chemical Society*, 54, pt. 1, *Proceedings* (1932), 1; Forbes to Draper, 7 March 1895, 2/4/2, B:1, F:Forbes.

25. Forbes to Draper, 30 May, Forbes's endorsement of Palmer to Draper, 26 November 1896; Palmer to Draper, 3 March 1895, 26 November 1896, 2/4/2, B:1, 2, F:Palmer.

26. Samuel C. Prescott, *When M.I.T. was "Boston Tech": 1861–1916* (Cambridge: Technology Press, 1954), 119; J. W. Westwater, "The Beginnings of Chemical Engineering Education in the USA," in *History of Chemical Engineering*, ed. William F. Furter, vol. 190 in *Advances in Chemistry* (Washington, D.C.: American Chemical Society, 1980), 141–52 (which offers a view slightly different from the one stated here); Parr to Draper, 2 March 1895, 2/4/2, B:1, F:Parr.

27. *Illini*, 13 March 1896, 356.

28. 15/1/6, 211.

29. Palmer to Forbes, 24 May 1899, 2/4/2, B:5, F:Forbes.

30. See the table in 2/4/2, B:4, F:Forbes.

31. Palmer to Forbes, 21 May 1898, 2/4/2, B:4, F:Palmer.

32. Edward Bartow, "Samuel Wilson Parr," *Industrial and Engineering Chemistry*, 17 (September 1925), 985; Noyes, "Samuel Wilson Parr," 1–2, 5.

33. "The Nutrition Investigation at the University of Illinois," 2/5/3, B:84, F:Filbey; 2/5/15, H. S. Grindley Folder; Palmer to Forbes, 18 June 1898, 2/4/2, B:4, F:Forbes; Grindley to Palmer, 1 October 1902, ibid., B:9, F: Palmer.

34. Forbes to Draper, 23 February 1904, Forbes to W. T. Sedgwick, 6 April 1904, 15/1/2.

35. Jackson to Forbes, 3, 13 March 1904, 2/5/6, B:2, F:E–L; Forbes to Draper, 15 April 1904, 15/1/2.

36. Draper to Forbes, 18 April 1904, 15/1/3, B:1, F:1904–D.

37. Forbes to Charles S. Palmer, 16 May 1904, Forbes to Draper, 17 May 1904, Forbes to Ira Remsen, 23 May 1904, Forbes to Charles S. Palmer, 23, 26, 30 May 1904, 15/1/2.

38. Forbes to Acting President T. J. Burrill, 27 June, 13 August 1904, 15/1/2; *22nd Report* (1904), 329.

39. Parr to Forbes, 20 December 1904, 15/1/3, B:2, F:1905–07–P; Forbes to Parr, 22 December 1904, 15/1/2.

40. Forbes to Draper, 5 June 1897, 17 May 1899, 19 December 1900, 2/4/2, B:3, 5, 6, F:Forbes.

41. Robert G. Hays, *State Science in Illinois: The Scientific Surveys, 1850–1978* (Carbondale: Southern Illinois University Press for the Board of Natural Resources and Conservation of the Illinois Institute of Natural Resources, 1980), 8–12; Charles W. Rolfe, "Investigations Previous to the Founding of the Present State

Geological Survey," Illinois State Geological Survey, *Bulletin*, 60 (1931), 23–28; Lovely, "Mastering Nature's Harmony," 88–113; M. M. Leighton and Don Carroll, "The Historical Development of the Illinois Coal Industry and the State Geological Survey," *Proceedings of the Illinois Mining Institute* (1942), 43–52.

42. Rolfe to Draper, 21 August 1894, 2/4/2, B:1, F:Rolfe. Nothing came of Rolfe's first request, so he reiterated it. Rolfe to Draper, 7 December 1896, ibid., B:3, F:Rolfe.

43. Rolfe to Draper, 24 August 1894; Altgeld's private secretary to Draper, 27 August 1894, 2/4/2, B:1, F:Rolfe. In 1893 a bill to transfer a collection from the State Geological Museum to the University had been tabled. See *Journal of the House of Representatives of the Thirty-Eighth General Assembly* (1893), cxxviii, and *17th Report* (1894), 98. On the delay, see Forbes to Draper, 25 January 1897, 2/4/2, B:3, F:Forbes, and Sam. M. Inglis to Draper, 22, 26 January 1897, 2/4/1, B:1, F:Inglis.

44. C. W. Rolfe, "Investigations Previous to the Founding of the Present State Geological Survey," Illinois State Geological Survey, *Bulletin*, 60 (1931), 28.

45. Rolfe to Draper, 7 December 1896 (two letters of this date), 2/4/2, B:3, F:Rolfe.

46. Forbes to Draper, 14 February 1902, 2/4/2, B:8, F:Forbes.

47. Rolfe to Draper, 14, 21 June 1902, 2/4/2, B:8, F:Rolfe. On the squirrels, see *21st Report* (1902), 107, and Rolfe to Draper, 6 May 1901, 2/4/2, B:7, F:Rolfe.

48. Forbes to Draper, 25 June 1903, 2/4/2, B:9, F:Forbes. Rolfe published "Use of the Aneroid Barometer in Geological Surveying," *Journal of Geology*, 3, no. 2 (1895?), 128–37, and a little book titled *Guide to the Life-Histories of Rocks* (n.p., [1904]), primarily for students. He has three entries on clays in *Paving Brick and Paving Brick Clays of Illinois*. Illinois State Geological Survey, *Bulletin*, 9 (1908).

49. Draper to Rolfe, 21, 26 January 1904, 2/4/3; Rolfe to Draper, 21, 28 January 1904; Forbes to Draper, 12 February 1904, 2/4/2, B:10, F:Rolfe, Forbes.

50. Both Morris M. Leighton, "Recollections and Reflections of the Illinois Geological Survey, 1905–1954" (1964), and the *Announcement of Activities Commemorating the Fiftieth Anniversary of the State Geological Survey, 1905–1955* (1955), 44/1/810, Geological Survey, Histories and Anniversary Celebration Programs, trace the origins of the survey to the efforts of Chamberlin and Deneen. Leighton was chief of the Illinois State Geological Survey from 1923 to 1954. Hays, *State Science in Illinois*, 70–72, suggests much the same but is more modulated.

51. Draper to Chamberlin, 10 November 1900, Draper to Rolfe, 23 November 1900, 2/4/3; Rolfe to Draper, 24 November 1900, 2/4/2, B:7, F:Rolfe; Forbes to Draper, 26 November 1900, ibid., F:Forbes.

52. *21st Report* (1902), 14, 25, 32; Chamberlin to Draper, 6 November 1900, 2/4/1, B:1, F: Chamberlin; Draper to Chamberlin, 10 November 1900, 2/4/3; Rolfe to Chamberlin, 7 December 1900; Rolfe to Draper, 22 January 1901, 2/4/2, B:7, F:Rolfe.

53. *Journal of the House of Representatives of the 44th General Assembly of . . . Illinois* (1905), 71–72, 100, 972, 993, 1076, 1279; *23rd Report* (1906), 25, 38.

54. On Burrill, see Solberg, 152–55, 331–36.

55. Burrill to Forbes, 24 May 1898, 2/4/2, B:4, F:Forbes (the quotation).

56. Lovely, "Mastering Nature's Harmony," offers a comprehensive view of the scientific career of Forbes.

57. *17th Report* (1894), 311–18; *18th Report* (1896), 114–15, 302–336; Forbes, "Biennial Report of the Director, 1893–1894," *Reports to the General Assembly of Illinois* (1894), 9:46–52; Howard, "Biographical Memoir," 11–12; Lovely, "Mastering Nature's Harmony," 16.

58. Lovely, *Mastering Nature's Harmony*, 243–44.

59. Kohler, *From Medical Chemistry to Biochemistry*, treats this development.

60. Forbes to Draper, 31 August 1896, 2/4/2, B:3, F:Forbes; Draper to Summers, 12 May 1897, 2/4/3; *19th Report* (1898), 113.

61. Draper to Kemp, 21 May 1897, 2/4/3; Kemp to Draper, 26 May 1897, 2/4/2, B:3, F:H–D.

62. Forbes to Draper, 20 September, 15 December 1897, and extracts on Kemp from Forbes's annual reports to Draper, in 2/5/1, B:10, F:Kemp.

63. Forbes to Draper, 18 January 1902, 2/4/2, B:8, F:Forbes.

64. Forbes to Draper, 10 May 1901, 12 February 1904, 2/4/2, B:6, 10, F:Forbes.

65. Forbes to Draper, 9 January 1904, 2/4/2, B:10, F:Forbes.

# CHAPTER 5

# REVITALIZING A CORPSE

## AGRICULTURE

Despite the importance of agriculture in the founding of the University, the study of agriculture developed slowly for a quarter of a century after the University opened. In 1894 the College of Agriculture was by far the smallest of the four colleges in the University. Enrollments in agriculture had plummeted starting in 1878, and in 1893–94 only three students were enlisted in the regular course. The college was about to be swallowed by the waters of oblivion.

The reasons for this sad state of affairs were largely beyond the control of any individual or institution. The slow growth of agricultural science meant that the college had little of value to teach in the early years; careful training was not necessary for success in farming. In addition, farmers who worked western lands believed in the eternal fertility of their soil and did not look to the University for aid.

These circumstances had rendered George E. Morrow's position as professor of agriculture and dean of the college precarious. Morrow was ahead of his time, a voice crying in the wilderness, and in addition his personal limitations made him vulnerable. A poor practical farmer, destitute of mechanical skill, he had allowed the University farms to fall into deplorable physical condition. In the 1892 elections the Democratic party gained a majority on the Board of Trustees for the first time since the University opened. An agricultural committee appointed to evaluate conditions was critical, and in the face of persistent criticism from one trustee, on 13 March 1894 Morrow resigned.[1]

Because of the powerful influence of agricultural interests in Illinois, Draper and the governing body should have realized that the success of the University depended on the treatment of agriculture. But the president, an easterner, had no knowledge of western agriculture, and at the time of his appointment he reportedly had informed the trustees that he would not be responsible for growth in that area. Education in agriculture was at a turning point, but the board had no clear notion of how to proceed. Most members of the board thought that the agricultural staff should not try to train students but only do research, and that relations between the College of Agriculture and the Agricultural Experiment Station needed better definition.[2]

Decisions on these matters would depend largely on the new leadership. The University wanted a man to serve as both professor of agriculture and director of the experiment station. Draper and the trustees considered a number of candidates. Three of them visited Urbana, were offered the position, and declined it. They were Thomas F. Hunt of Ohio State, an 1884 graduate of the University who was very exacting in his conditions; H. J. Waters of Pennsylvania State, who did not seem very forceful; and Clinton B. Smith of Michigan State.[3]

When Smith refused, Eugene Davenport submitted his own name. Draper replied that Davenport had not written much and that he seemed to lack an aptitude for scientific experiments. Davenport responded by describing his research and his ideas on agricultural organization and instruction. He impressed Draper and received glowing recommendations, and on 5 December the board appointed Davenport dean of and professor in the College of Agriculture, agriculturist of the Agricultural Experiment Station, and a member of the station's board of direction. He was to receive $2,000 a year and the use of a house, the salary to increase by $100 a year until it reached $2,500. Use of the house was considered to be worth $200 a year.[4]

## DEAN EUGENE DAVENPORT

What manner of man had the trustees chosen? Davenport was born in a log house in the hardwood area near Woodland, Michigan, in 1856. His parents were Universalists, although they attended Calvinist and revivalist churches. An only child, Davenport went to the district school and a private school, taught school briefly, and in 1898 graduated from nearby Michigan Agricultural College (later Michigan State University) with a B.S. For the next ten years he helped his father operate the family farm; when he turned twenty-one his father deeded him a half-interest in the property. Returning to Michigan State in 1888, he served as assistant to Professor William J. Beal, a pioneer of the "new botany" who had studied under both Louis Agassiz and Asa Gray at

Harvard. Davenport also worked closely with Manly Miles, who advised him to read Lawes and Gilbert on their agricultural experiments at Rothamsted, England, and he earned a master's degree in agriculture. From 1889 to 1891 Davenport was professor of practical agriculture and superintendent of the college farm.

In 1891 Louis Queroz, a wealthy Brazilian, invited him to establish an agricultural college, a "little Lansing," at Piracicaba in the state of São Paulo. When Davenport's superiors denied him a year's leave of absence, he resigned and left for Brazil. Conditions in that country made this venture premature. Queroz could not deliver on his promises, and political unrest ruled out state support. In April 1892 Davenport left Brazil, returning to the United States by way of England in order to study the methods of scientific agriculture practiced at Rothamsted. Back home he resumed the life of a farmer until he accepted the Urbana appointment. He later gave three reasons for going to Illinois: first, he and his wife were still childless, and he hoped to do something that would live after him by working with the children of others; second, the art of farming was giving way to the science of agriculture; and third, he wanted to affiliate with an institution organized as a university.[5]

On 1 January 1895, at the age of thirty-eight, Davenport took up his duties. When he arrived in Urbana, the experiment station overshadowed the college and the college was on the verge of extinction. It had one classroom in the attic and another in the basement of Natural History Hall; its only property was a few picture frames and an old model of underground drainage, valued at five dollars. Davenport heaved the lot out the window so he could start afresh. His budget for the remainder of the year was sixty dollars. The farm building and the livestock showed the results of indescribable neglect.

The faculty was a negligible quantity. Donald McIntosh, who taught veterinary science, opposed the theory that animal diseases were caused by microorganisms. George W. McCluer, a horticulturist who had graduated from the University in 1884 and taken an M.S. there in 1892, divided his time between the college and the station. So too did Cyril G. Hopkins (b. 1866), a chemist hired the previous November. Hopkins had studied at Cornell for four terms and had spent six years at the South Dakota Agricultural College. Thomas J. Burrill, a botanist and horticulturist, and Stephen A. Forbes, an entomologist and zoologist, were greatly interested in the welfare of agriculture. The college had become an asylum for incompetents. Out of a student body of about eight hundred, only nine were enrolled in agriculture in 1894–95—four freshmen, three sophomores, and two "specials." Agricultural instruction was not offered until the junior year, by which time students were lost to other subjects. As a result, the few regular students were put into the short course on agriculture, which was held during the winter months.[6]

A king without a kingdom but not without territory, the dean acted quickly to revitalize the languishing operation. His first proposal went to the trustees in March, and a fuller scheme was presented in September. Observing that the subject of agriculture was too large to be handled by one person, Davenport called for division into agriculture proper (soils and crops, later called agronomy), animal husbandry, dairy husbandry, and horticulture, with a head in charge of each division. He proposed reducing the instruction in veterinary science to that concerning the common diseases of domestic animals. And he emphasized the need for equipment and space. The experiment station owned all of the property and equipment that was devoted to agriculture, but it was not called on to teach. The college needed its own lands, implements, crops, and livestock, and it needed a hall with classrooms, offices, and laboratories. This building, the greatest need, would cost not less than $100,000 with a dairy annex. The same property and persons should serve the interests of both the station and the college, with a fair proportion of the expense assigned to each. The equipment must precede the students. Build the facilities, Davenport pleaded, and students will come.[7]

Draper gave no evidence of support for agriculture, so in May 1896 Davenport again pressed his case in a letter to Draper. One of his concerns was lack of staff. He was now the only instructor in agriculture, which was unfair to students, who expressed regret that they had not gone elsewhere. Moreover, the college had to draft station people to handle instruction, which was illegal. In the number of its agriculture instructors, Illinois ranked behind sixteen other states. Davenport wanted a professor of agricultural physics (soil and crops), an assistant in dairying, and an associate professor or assistant in horticulture. He also reiterated the need for a building. Frustrated by inaction, he closed by bluntly asserting, "we are suffering from a kind of dry rot, and no half way measures will ever effect a reorganization." Davenport was "at a loss to understand the situation, and not a little disconcerted by the evident unwillingness to attack the problem boldly and provide an organization for this College."[8]

A month later the authorities finally addressed Davenport's proposals. First, Draper and the board put the relations between the College of Agriculture and the Agricultural Experiment Station on a sounder footing. Since its founding in March 1888, the station had been under a board of direction; the dean of the college had no more to do with it than any other professor. Now the trustees created the position of director of the station, made the dean of the college the director ex officio, and transformed the board of direction into an advisory board. As director, Davenport was charged with entire responsibility for carrying out the policies of the University's Board of Trustees or the Agricultural Experiment Station's Advisory Board and reporting to the president. The station was to have a staff of ten, with their salaries and duties to be divided equally between the college and the station.

In addition, the board enlarged the faculty of the college. In March 1895 the trustees had changed Davenport's title to professor of animal husbandry; now they appointed Perry G. Holden an assistant professor of agricultural physics and Wilber J. Fraser an assistant in dairying. Holden (b. 1865) held bachelor's and master's degrees in agriculture and pedagogy from Michigan State, where he had been Davenport's assistant. Fraser (b. 1869) had taken a B.S. in agriculture at the University in 1893. Each man was to serve half time in both the college and the station.[9]

## DAVENPORT AND THE ILLINOIS FARMERS' INSTITUTE

Davenport, a midwestern farmer who had given considerable thought to agricultural education, was eager to put agriculture on the same basis as other University studies. He understood, however, that the president and the trustees were in no haste to rejuvenate the college. Draper liked horses, but he had no knowledge of midwestern agriculture, and no one knew what he thought about agricultural education until he addressed the topic in 1898. Aware that he lacked backing from the administration, Davenport was convinced that vastly over half of the constituency of the University were rural people who would support his college. So he took matters straight to the farmers without the slightest reference to the president or the trustees. Burrill sustained Davenport in this effort, but Davenport was careful not to compromise Burrill by confiding in him before acting.[10]

The appeal to the husbandmen of the state revived an earlier practice. Some years earlier the University had pioneered in organizing Illinois agriculturists. Farmers' institutes were held in Urbana and elsewhere under University auspices from 1869 to 1873. They lapsed because farmers and professors failed to understand each other, but the idea was kept alive by various agricultural organizations. In the 1880s the State Board of Agriculture sponsored institutes for the farm community.

Efforts to form a new farmers' organization were underway when Davenport became dean. During the state fair in September 1894, Charles F. Mills of Springfield, secretary of the State Board of Agriculture and editor of *Farm Home* magazine, served as secretary of a committee to draft a plan to organize the farmers. On 24 June 1895, after Davenport assumed office, the governor signed a bill creating the Illinois Farmers' Institute (IFI). Its purpose was to encourage useful education among the farmers and to develop the state's agricultural resources. On 21 August the IFI was organized as a public corporation in Springfield. (In 1897 the General Assembly began appropriating funds to support the IFI.) Its board of direction consisted of five members. The IFI did its work largely through county institutes and an annual meeting, to which each county elected three delegates. Mills assured Davenport that the college would succeed if the farmers could be enlisted to support it. The dean became a member of the IFI's Board of Directors as well as chair of its Committee on Agricultural Education, and he often spoke at county farmers' institutes and IFI annual meetings.[11]

These gatherings provided Davenport a forum in which to express his views on agricultural education, which reflected the dominant intellectual currents of the time. Strongly influenced by the theory of evolution, Davenport insisted that the comparative study of agriculture over time revealed a close correspondence between the condition of a people and the kind of agriculture it maintained. The great laws of evolution and survival of the fittest operated in the interest of progress. When people struggled under equal conditions, the ultimate victory would be with the group that had the better food supply. Agriculture was an economic industry that would prove the racial superiority of the best husbandmen. Superior people maintained their high standard only by skillful manipulation of the soil. Since soil fertility was already failing, even on western lands, it was the racial, national, and individual duty of Anglo-Saxons to foster an intelligent, progressive, but conservative agriculture. Agriculture was an industry "upon which depends more than upon any other single factor the final supremacy of races."

Davenport viewed agricultural education as part of universal education. He wanted high schools and universities to teach agriculture and vocational subjects as a matter of course. If they failed to do so, trade schools would take their place and instruction rather than education would prevail. He labored tirelessly to make industrial education part of secondary education, to introduce courses in agriculture and domestic science into the public high schools. He saw agriculture as a science and the production of food as important as the production of literature.

Davenport weighed three different conceptions of the purpose of a college of agriculture. One was the German philosophy that agricultural colleges were to impart technical information only. Such a philosophy had tinctured many American institutions, but it would create an American peasantry. Another was the American idea of training men to become scientific investigators. This notion was objectionable because it was too narrow. What the nation needed was a new, universal education in the name of efficiency and culture. The mission of a college of agriculture was to give students a liberal education of a scientific character. Davenport lacked sympathy with those who would eliminate disciplines that could not show immediate application to utilitarian ends. Philosophical and literary studies must be taught along with industrial and technical education. Students should devote equal time to agricultural studies, scientific studies, and elective liberal studies. An agricultural student was a future citizen of a free government, and an agricultural college should stand for the building of a class that Davenport called "the American Country Gentle-man." When Davenport addressed IFI meetings, he pleaded for help in getting a building for agriculture, wanting to make the College of Agriculture at the University second to none. No other kind of college could adequately repre-sent the interests of "the greatest agricultural state of the Union."[12]

The new organization of agriculture began in the fall of 1896. Teaching took on new life with more instructors. Holden and Fraser, hired in June, were joined by Joseph C. Blair (b. 1871), who was appointed in August as assistant horticulturist in the station and an instructor in the college. Born in Nova Scotia, Blair had graduated from and later taught at the Provincial School of Agriculture at Truro, Nova Scotia. He attended Cornell for four years, where he studied with Liberty Hyde Bailey and fulfilled all requirements for a B.S. except for one language. He had no academic degree when he joined the staff. With Davenport and McIntosh there were five instructors, each of whom had eight to ten hours of classwork a week in two or three subjects. But the course of instruction remained much the same as in 1894–96, with more of the agri-cultural work moved into the first two years. The Winter School continued to be offered through 1898–99. In 1896–97 seventeen students registered in agriculture and sixteen attended the Winter School.[13]

Davenport continued to emphasize the need for a building. The Farmers' Institute had asked for it, he told Draper, and the agricultural press of Illinois had pledged to support it. In December 1896 the trustees requested $80,000 for an agricultural building with a dairy annex, ranking the item behind a new central heating plant and a chemistry laboratory in a plea for an emergency appropriation bill. This effort failed, but Davenport and the IFI continued their campaign to enlist public support for agricultural education.[14]

Meanwhile, the work of the Agricultural Experiment Station had begun to fire public enthusiasm. The experiments covered a wide range of topics, in-cluding the digestibility by cattle of various types of ensilage, smut in broom corn, damage by insects, variation in crop yields, repeated planting and "soil sickness," bacteria on roots of leguminous plants, the effects of subsoiling, contamination in milk production, the city milk supply, and fruits and grapes. The station disseminated the results of its studies by means of lectures and publications. County institutes called on the University to provide speakers, and the experts carried their knowledge around the state. While valuable in winning support, these lectures became so burdensome that the University could not respond to all of the requests. In addition, the station published its findings in bulletins or technical reports printed in small quantities, and in circulars, which were short abstracts printed for mass distribution.

Two areas of investigation were especially significant. In the late 1890s en-thusiasm for sugar beets swept over the country. This plant seemed promising for certain sections of Illinois, which consumed over $12 million worth of sugar annually. The United States had less than a dozen factories that converted beets into sugar, compared to over 700 in Germany. Perry Holden distributed 500 pounds of seed received from the U.S. Department of Agriculture for planting in over 500 places in various parts of the state. The chemistry laboratory of the station examined over 300 samples of the crop to see whether factory production of sugar would be commercially viable in Illinois. Holden lectured on the subject to county institutes and meetings of the IFI, he went to Nebraska to study sugar production, and, together with Hopkins, he published *The Sugar Beet in Illinois* (1898), which the station issued in 3,000 copies as Bulletin No. 49. Davenport described the report as the most exhaustive public document ever issued on this subject. A four-page abstract was issued in 17,000 copies.

In February 1898, when the University was host to a sugar beet convention and the annual meeting of the IFI, Holden read a paper titled "The Sugar Beet Industry for Illinois." A year later the IFI urged the state to grant a bounty for the production of sugar beets, and about this time a factory for converting beets into sugar was established in Peoria. The frenzy over beet sugar posed dangers—Holden restrained some communities from irrational and hasty action—but the station's work brought rewards. "Nothing the University has ever done," Davenport wrote, "has made us so many friends over the state."[15]

Sugar beets enjoyed a transient vogue, but Illinois is corn country, and the experiment station devoted much of its effort to the study of *Zea mays*.[16] Illinois, as Davenport said, was "doing more with Indian corn than all the world besides."[17] Hopkins, who took leave for the first six months of 1898 to complete his Ph.D. at Cornell, wrote his dissertation on the chemistry of the corn kernel. The station published this work as its *Bulletin* 53. It attracted favorable attention.

In February 1898 the IFI held its annual meeting at the University. The program included a tour of the college, and for the first time many farmers saw how little the state provided to promote agricultural interests. It was on this occasion that Draper first addressed the subject of agricultural education. Called on to fill time when bad weather delayed a speaker, he may have spoken impromptu. In any case, he rambled. He began by declaring that he had very decided ideas about agricultural education (but he had decided opinions on every subject he addressed!), and that since his arrival in Urbana they had been gaining ground. He then announced that it would be better for the University to make "a special agricultural school of high grade, or high school, rather than a university or college grade, with a view to taking boys directly from the farm and giving them two or three years of practical work and not a university degree, but a certificate or diploma at the end of the course to show just what they have done."[18]

As these remarks reveal, Davenport and Draper held diametrically opposed views on agricultural education. Davenport looked forward to well-educated farmers, whereas Draper looked backward to a farm school. Davenport had known for some time that the two were proceeding on a collision course, which is why he had gone over the president's head to the IFI.

In the same address Draper declared that it was almost hopeless to build a great university when there was discord on the board or the faculty or between the faculty and the trustees, or when insubordination or lack of confidence was exhibited by everybody who ought to help. Some of these shafts seemed aimed at Davenport.

A month later Davenport obsequiously and disingenuously made amends for what Draper probably viewed as "insubordinate" conduct by one of his deans. Knowing that Draper had an offer to become superintendent of schools in New York City, Davenport urged him to remain at Illinois. "I could not have asked for a more steady, helpful support," he added, "and I could not hope for the same interest and assistance from a successor."[19]

## THE NEW AGRICULTURAL BUILDING

Throughout the summer and fall Davenport pushed hard for support for the college. He enlisted the aid of the agricultural press, trustees, influential farmers, leaders of state farm organizations, and the IFI. He asked others to bring pressure to bear on President Draper, insisting that supply had to precede demand. In September the IFI passed a resolution requesting an appropriation sufficient to provide buildings and equipment for a worthy college of agriculture and agreeing to campaign throughout the state for the funds.[20]

Meanwhile, Davenport pressed his case. Fourteen other states had supplemented the federal funds designed for agricultural instruction and research with state funds for the purpose, he demonstrated, whereas in Illinois the state had given nothing for agriculture. The University's agriculturalists were located in attics and basements, he pointed out, and "no amount of hard work can offset a situation so palpably inferior to other interests here, or to similar interests in other states." He wanted working facilities second to none. "I see no legitimate reason why we should occupy even a secondary position." The public pulse was healthier than ever before; therefore Davenport asked for liberal provision for agricultural instruction. Draper found this pressure objectionable, and on 26 October Davenport assured him that the IFI committee was only trying to be helpful and that "above all things they do not desire to be irritable to the management of our university."[21]

Draper's difference with Davenport on an agricultural building was one of degree. Writing to Trustee Mary Turner Carriel, Draper expressed interest in an agricultural building and confessed that the state had not done what it should in that direction. But the trustees were not at fault. Federal money was slated for both agriculture and mechanic arts, and the former had received more of its share than critics admitted. Moreover, the demand for engineering education was fifty times greater than the demand for agricultural education. Indiscriminate talk against the course of the trustees was without foundation, and Draper admitted that he was a little sensitive to unwarranted attack.[22]

To all outward appearances, Carriel, the daughter of Jonathan Baldwin Turner, was Davenport's closest ally on the board. But as Lucy L. Flower informed Draper, Alice Asbury Abbott was a strong partisan of both Davenport and the College of Agriculture, and she had gained strong influence over Carriel. As we saw in Chapter 1, Abbott was behind the board's resolution that undermined the authority of the president. Moreover, said Flower, Abbott had tried to get the board to buy a vehicle that Davenport greatly desired from agricultural funds. And Davenport told Flower that Abbott had asked him to advance Abbott the money for a trip Abbott wished to take. As Flower added, "was not that a queer request from a trustee to a professor?"[23]

On 13 December 1898 a committee from the IFI appeared before the trustees in Urbana to plead their cause, only to learn that the board had already decided to ask for $150,000 for the building and furnishings. Draper was annoyed that Davenport had left him in the dark as to cost estimates for the new building and had sent him important data only the previous day, when the board was already halfway through its business. Davenport may have known exactly what he was doing, but he replied that he had no intention of acting without Draper's advice and approval.[24]

On 13 January 1899 a special meeting of the Board of Trustees was held in Chicago. Four elected members and Draper were absent, but Governor John R. Tanner was present. According to the official record, he spoke of the "great desirability of strengthening in every way the agricultural department of the University." The interests of the state demanded that agriculture be made one of the most prominent departments of the University, and Tanner "pledged himself to favor most heartily liberal appropriations for its enlargement and maintenance."[25]

According to the next day's Chicago *Inter Ocean*, however, Tanner had given those present some plain talk. The federal government had endowed the University as an agricultural college, he charged, but the school had been converted into a literary institution. Illinois was the greatest agricultural state of the Union, and it should have the greatest industrial University. As it was, more students from Illinois attended the agricultural college of Wisconsin than the one at Illinois. Tanner knew nothing about the occupant of the chair of agriculture except that he was a clever fellow. The University needed a dean who could make his influence felt at the level of the state legislature. Tanner was getting tired of the present management of the University. If the proper kind of instruction were given at Urbana, the farmers and dairymen would send their sons to the University instead of to neighboring states. Tanner intimated that unless a radical change in management was made, he would oppose future appropriations.[26]

These seemingly discrepant accounts are easily reconciled. Although Tanner displayed a good deal of ignorance about University affairs, he probably both criticized the course of development and offered his support. This thesis is borne out by the fact that another newspaper quoted Tanner as saying that he would give his hearty cooperation to securing money for a new building to be devoted exclusively to teaching agricultural science. "If you ask the legislature for the necessary funds," he said, "I will see that they are forthcoming." After the governor left, the board agreed to ask for a special appropriation of $150,000 for a new building and equipment.[27]

In January leaders of the Farmers' Institute, although dismayed at Tanner's criticisms, made strong representations to the Illinois Senate and House on the appropriation. When Davenport appeared before the appropriations committee, he named nineteen states that were ahead of Illinois in agricultural education. In February, at the annual meeting of the IFI, Mrs. Carriel pleaded the case for a building, and delegates adopted a resolution supporting the bill for the appropriation. On this occasion Carriel also praised Draper fulsomely, probably in an attempt to reduce tensions between Draper, on the one hand, and Davenport and the IFI on the other hand.[28]

The IFI officially endorsed the bill, and every agricultural organization in the state supported it. Draper apparently opposed the larger appropriation for an agricultural building as unnecessary and wasteful. As a result, according to Davenport, who provided the only account of the episode, the IFI, having lost confidence in Draper, made an effort to relocate the college. Amos F. Moore, president of the IFI, went to Davenport's home at 4 o'clock one morning (the date is not specified, but in all likelihood the event occurred at this juncture in affairs).[29] The appropriation would go through, Moore reported, but the farmers were jealous because the legislature had allocated $160,000 for an engineering building. Thus the IFI wanted to take the college away from the University and bring it under their control with Davenport as head. But Davenport threatened to resign if the college was removed from the University.[30]

Davenport's appeal to farm leaders was about to bear fruit, but Draper was annoyed with the machinations of his dean. On 27 January 1899 he complained to Trustee Lucy L. Flower, "Professor Davenport has run amuck among farmer politicians and political leaders in the State and against my constant advice." Davenport had not informed him of the plans for the proposed agriculture building, and he had gone behind Draper's back to the governor. His conduct was reckless and dangerous.[31]

The legislature approved an appropriations bill that included funds for an agricultural building. But additional funds were needed for instruction. At the time, under the terms of the Morrill Act (1862) and the Second Morrill Act (1890), the University received about $56,000 a year, of which about $7,000 went to the College of Agriculture. With the backing of the Farmers' Institute, Davenport drafted a bill calling for more, and in March Duncan M. Funk of Bloomington introduced in the lower house a bill that set aside one-half of the funds derived from the two acts for agricultural education. In mid-April this bill passed in both chambers with but one dissenting vote.[32]

This measure was awaiting the governor's signature when, on 19 April, Draper, unwilling to surrender, laid before the board a plan to which he had given "much thought and investigation for several months." He proposed establishing an agricultural high school that would admit students fourteen years of age and over and would award a diploma at the end of a course in elementary agriculture. The "ag" high school would replace the University's Preparatory School. The College of Agriculture would continue to carry on all work in technical agriculture, while related work of college grade within the scope of other scientific departments would be kept with those departments. Draper wanted to use the funds appropriated for an agricultural building to erect a beautiful home for a new, model Preparatory School.[33]

The board referred Draper's proposal to a special committee that included Abbott and W. H. Fulkerson, president of the State Board of Agriculture. The committee disapproved of the idea and recommended that the entire appropriation be devoted to the agricultural college. The board then decided that a committee should visit other agricultural colleges to study their methods, buildings, and equipment, and it appointed J. C. Llewellyn architect for the building. In May, Davenport, Holden, Llewellyn, and trustees Fulkerson, McKay, Hatch, and Abbott visited Wisconsin; Michigan State; the Agricultural Experiment Station at Geneva, New York; Cornell; and Ohio State. The trustees then made four recommendations: increase the size of the agricultural faculty, strictly separate the funds of the college and the experiment station, publicize the College of Agriculture by distributing ten thousand circulars, and construct a large agricultural building. The full board endorsed the report, opted for a classical style of building, fixed its location on the campus, and expressed the wish that the building be finished and ready for use by September 1900.[34]

Construction proceeded with occasional delays, generating tension in official circles. "I do not care to say much about agricultural building matters," Draper wrote Flower on 4 December 1899. "Unless the Board is very careful it will be unpleasantly involved." He added, petulantly, "the agricultural people never come to me about the building, nor indeed about anything else, and matters in that college are far from satisfactory." Draper warned his confidante that difficulties touching the agricultural building might arise at the December board meeting.[35]

When the governing body met it ordered that two inscriptions be placed on the cornice of the building. One was to read " 'Industrial education prepares the way for a millenium [sic] of labor.'—Turner." The other was to read " 'The wealth of Illinois is in her soil and her strength lies in its intelligent development.'—Draper." The trustees also directed that a tablet be erected at the main entrance to the memory of Jonathan Baldwin Turner. These orders were carried out to the letter. The building, which was practically ready for occupancy by December 1900, consisted of four separate structures built around an open court and connected by corridors. The main edifice was 248 feet long, from 50 to 100 feet deep, and three stories high. The Agricultural Building, which was formally dedicated on 21 May 1901 with addresses by various dignitaries, including Davenport but not Draper, was described as the largest single edifice in the world devoted to agriculture.[36]

## THE REJUVENATED COLLEGE

The Agricultural Building was the visible symbol of the new dignity and importance of agriculture at the University. The new era actually began with the Funk Bill of 1899, which directed that half of the funds from the two Morrill Acts be devoted to teaching agriculture. As a result, the money available for this purpose increased from about $6,000 to nearly $27,000 a year.[37] Accordingly, in June Davenport proposed salary increases for some staff members and the creation of four new positions. During the summer Holden became a professor of agronomy, and five new faculty appointments were made.[38] In July, at the board's request, the dean submitted a detailed plan of instruction for the college, which the trustees later adopted with changes made by the board's Committee on Instruction. In August the trustees agreed that the college be organized into agronomy, animal husbandry, dairy husbandry, horticulture, and veterinary science departments.[39]

By the fall of 1899 a vastly expanded curriculum was in place. The new era in agriculture attracted more students than ever before. Enrollment figures for the College of Agriculture are spotty at best, but from 1894 to 1899 the number appears to have averaged less than 20 a year. In 1899–1900, 68 students were registered in the first semester and 88 in the second semester. In 1900–1 enrollments exceeded 100 for the first time, with 135 students registered in the fall semester and 140 in the spring semester. And students kept coming. In 1903–4 enrollments ranged from 340 to 406.[40]

The increased attendance was largely due to a scholarship program offered through the IFI beginning in 1899. Davenport undoubtedly devised the program, which Alice Abbott and Fred Hatch presented to the board. Under the plan the University, upon recommendation of the executive committee of the IFI, agreed to receive into the college for the period of two years each one student from each county outside of Cook County and one from each of the seven congressional districts of the state. All term fees of such students were to be remitted, provided that the students recommended had not previously been in the University and that they complied with all conditions of admission to the college. By 1899 seventy-one scholarships had been granted.[41]

Davenport also increased attendance by creating "special students" in agriculture. Since the University's admission standards could be met only by high school graduates, Davenport secured approval of a plan to admit boys over sixteen without examination on condition that they take English and other courses that they had the ability to pursue profitably. The scholarships authorized for the college applied to special students, who entered the Preparatory School until they met matriculation requirements. Trustee Lucy Flower, Draper's ally and Davenport's critic, reported that someone told her that many of the specials could not pass the simplest examination in English. But when special students did well, Davenport boasted that Illinois had pioneered in taking such a radical step.[42]

Davenport realized that the University's policy on salaries and continuous service throughout the year risked the loss of his best faculty members. Perry Holden was a case in point. In 1900 his salary was $1,600. Davenport wanted to raise it, and perhaps for this reason Draper argued that Holden had been treated fairly in rank and pay. Holden would have remained for $2,500, but he resigned to accept a job as superintendent of the agricultural department of the Peoria Sugar Refining Company at $4,000. He departed not for the salary but for the chance to secure money and time for study and travel abroad in order to improve himself. Davenport viewed Holden's departure as an irreparable loss, and to forestall future losses he urged Draper to support competitive salaries and a policy of regular leaves at half pay.[43]

## DOMESTIC OR HOUSEHOLD SCIENCE

In the 1870s the study of household economics entered American higher education. The University of Illinois pioneered in this field, opening a School of Domestic Science and Arts in 1874 which its founder called "the first college course of high grade in domestic science in the United States, if not in the world." This attempt to combine liberal and practical education for women won at least moderate success until 1880, after which it foundered. Meanwhile, a number of cooking schools arose in eastern cities and contributed to better standards in food preparation.[44]

In June 1895 Draper declared that the best interests of the University called for a course in domestic science, and the board's Committee on Instruction urged that such a department be established as soon as practicable. The women affiliated with the IFI agreed. Mrs. Henry M. Dunlap, whose husband was a prominent fruit-grower in Savoy and a state senator, spoke on household economy at the annual meeting of the IFI on 9 January 1896. Captivated by the ideas of Sarah T. Rorer of Philadelphia, a cookbook author and food demonstrator at the World's Columbian Exposition, Dunlap reiterated the notion that "what a man eats that he is." In 1895 the women associated with the IFI formed the Illinois Association of Domestic Science.[45]

Draper found the matter of a domestic science department difficult. The University needed a lunchroom, he informed the trustees in April 1898, and they might accomplish two desirable purposes at once by establishing a department of domestic economy and having it operate a lunchroom. Domestic science had little scientific content, he warned, and there was little demand for it. Draper was more interested in "the practical than in the theoretical side of this domestic science movement."[46]

Draper's ideas on the subject soon changed. In February 1899 Mrs. Dunlap, addressing the annual meeting of the IFI, declared that the women wanted a woman's building and a household science department at the University.[47] About this time Ellen H. Richards, a chemist and a leader in applied and domestic science on the faculty at the Massachusetts Institute of Technology, visited the University, and she gave Draper the names of two women in her field—Henrietta I. Goodrich of Boston and Isabel Bevier of Lake Erie College in Painesville, Ohio. Draper wrote them identical letters, informing them that the University was thinking of employing, "as an instructor in our department of chemistry," a young woman "whose tastes would run in the direction of food analysis and who would be especially interested in household matters, and who, perhaps, eventually would become the head of a department of household economics and domestic economy." Draper did not want a teacher of cooking; rather, he wanted to develop a department of college or university grade. He inquired whether they would be available in September.[48]

By March Draper had a clearer vision of his course. Mere expertness in household duties was not up to the grade of college work, but analysis of foods and the study of nutrition and household sanitation were college work. So he recommended appointment of a properly qualified woman in this field as an instructor in the Department of Chemistry. In 1899 the General Assembly appropriated $5,000 for the organization of a department of domestic science, but the governor vetoed the item.[49]

On 13 March 1900 the board approved the establishment of a department of domestic science and authorized Draper to search for a "suitable person of scientific attainments and organizing qualities" to head it. This department was to fix the standards and have oversight over the lunchroom. The new "Department of Domestic Arts," as Draper explained, was put in the College of Agriculture because the University could accommodate it there and because there was money for the purpose, derived from the 1899 law that directed that half of the proceeds of the two Morrill Bills go to agricultural education. He expected to make domestic science a scientific department, and no one short of a well-educated scientist would be put in charge of it. At this same time the Illinois Association of Domestic Science passed a resolution favoring the establishment of a department of domestic science, which the IFI endorsed.[50]

Learning from Mrs. Richards that Goodrich planned to remain in Boston and that two other women who had been available were on the point of accepting positions elsewhere, Draper immediately wired Bevier to come for an interview. She visited the University on 7–9 April 1900. Draper found her to be a "woman of excellent qualities" and substantial character, good general scholarship, with special strength in chemistry, physiology, and physics, modest about her own attainments, and bright and attractive in her ways. Where she fell short was in "lack of organizing power, and in independent self-confidence and general aggressiveness." She would assume a very creditable place among the University faculty, and she would not make mistakes, for she was "rarely sensible and well balanced." Draper recognized that this department would have to do some things in the way of cooking in order to meet the demands of poorly prepared students and the public, but such work must be subordinate to scientific standards. Draper wanted "the most thoroughly educated, scientific woman whom we can find." Although Bevier was the best they had seen, Draper, Davenport, Burrill, and Forbes were not satisfied when Bevier left on 9 April; they wanted to see a Miss Albro. Nine days later, however, the board appointed Bevier professor of household science at a salary of $1,500 a year.[51]

Isabel Bevier was born in 1860 on a farm in north-central Ohio, the youngest of nine children. In 1885, after two years of high school in nearby Plymouth and study at the Wooster (Ohio) Preparatory School, she graduated with a Ph.B. from the University (later College) of Wooster. She was then a principal and a teacher in Ohio high schools, and in 1888 she received a master's degree in Latin and German from Wooster.

Her fiancé drowned that same year, and to be near friends she accepted a professorship of natural sciences at Pennsylvania College for Women in Pittsburgh, preparing for the vacancy during the summer by studying chemistry at Case School of Applied Science in Cleveland. A colleague convinced her that the future for women in chemistry lay in work with food, so she continued her education during the summers at Harvard and then at Wesleyan University, where she worked with Wilbur O. Atwater, a pioneer in agricultural chemistry and calorimetry. Under his direction she conducted nutrition studies in

Pittsburgh and among Negroes near Hampton, Virginia. The results were published, along with the results of similar research undertaken later at Lake Erie College, in *Bulletins* 52 (1898), 71 (1899), and 91 (1900) of the Office of Experiment Stations, U.S. Department of Agriculture.

Dissatisfied with life in a women's college, in 1897 Bevier resigned her Pittsburgh post for a year of study at Western Reserve University and at Massachusetts Institute of Technology, where she specialized in the chemistry of food and in sanitary chemistry with Ellen H. Richards. In 1898 she became professor of chemistry at Lake Erie College. She still longed for a coeducational setting in which to work out her ideas for the liberal education of women.[52]

Her inaugural visit to the University promised to fulfill her hopes. "I shall never forget my first impressions of Champaign that April day when I arrived to be looked over," she later wrote of her initial visit to the University. President Draper took her for a drive after luncheon. "I thought I had never seen so flat and so muddy a place," she recalled, "no trees, no hills, no boundaries of any kind. This lack of boundaries, physical and mental, the open-mindedness of the authorities and willingness to try new experiments, indeed their desire to do so, opened up a whole new world to me."[53]

Bevier took up her duties at the University at a critical time in the development of household science as a field of study. Social and economic changes were altering the role of the home, and home economics was in its infancy as a university subject. Although other land-grant institutions with courses in the field had organized them on a cooking-school basis, Bevier and the University authorities both insisted on providing scientific rather than merely utilitarian work.

The Department of Household Science, organized in 1900–1, occupied temporary quarters in Natural History Hall and then moved to the second floor of the north wing of the new Agricultural Building. Bevier designed a curriculum that treated home economics both as part of a liberal education and as education in a profession. Students who specialized in other subjects could acquire a general knowledge of household science by taking basic courses offered by the department, while those specializing in household science were to complete a number of prescribed courses and take additional elective offerings. The prescribed list was heavy on pure science and included several household science courses. Since household science was a new field that had to win its way, Bevier declared that the subject was treated "as one of a strictly scientific character, and the training in it, while not losing sight of the practical aspects, [was] therefore severely scientific."[54] Yet she recognized the importance of artistic and literary training for home life, and the required subjects included a considerable amount of art and design, English, history, and foreign language.

Since the department was designed to serve the interests of women, particularly in relation to home and family life, Bevier built the curriculum around the topics of food, shelter, and clothing, with institutional management added later. The initial curriculum included five courses: Principles of the Selection and Preparation of Food, Home Sanitation, Elementary Household Decoration, Chemistry of Food and Nutrition, and Hygiene and Dietetics. The department opened with an enrollment of twenty students, and to avoid acquiring a reputation as a "cooking school," only Home Sanitation was taught the first term. Bevier and James M. White of the architecture department offered the course. During the second semester the food course was taught by Cornelia E. Simon (b. 1865), a graduate of Lewis Institute in Chicago who had previously taught domestic science at the Illinois Soldiers' Orphan's Home, while Bevier taught Household Decoration.[55]

These five courses remained in the curriculum, joined by four others that were added in 1901–2: Economic Uses of Food, Textiles, Personal and Public Hygiene (as related to food and sanitation), and Seminary. In 1903–4 two graduate courses were added to meet the demand for teachers. Bevier's colleagues included Esther Beatty (b. 1876), a graduate of Iowa State College and Teachers College, Columbia University, and Gertrude C. Sober (b. 1866), a widow with a B.S. degree from the University of Michigan and a former high school science teacher.[56]

In 1900–1 twenty students were enrolled in household science, with less than half from the College of Agriculture and the rest from the other colleges. In 1901, to encourage enrollments and demonstrate that the University considered household science important, the trustees agreed to grant a free scholarship in the department to one woman from each county of the state, on the same terms as the scholarships granted to men in the College of Agriculture. Deans of the other colleges opposed this special treatment, so in 1903 the Council of Administration recommended that household science scholarships be open to all women in the University. The board agreed to open the scholarships to women outside the College of Agriculture on condition that the recipient take not less than eight hours of work each year in household science or in courses in science strictly precedent to them. The compromise created a new problem: in 1904 two women who had held household science scholarships in Agriculture asked to graduate from the College of Science, whose requirements they could meet, instead of from Agriculture, without having to pay the fees that had been remitted through the scholarships. As a result, early in 1905 a new president recommended extending the scholarships to the College of Science. David Kinley, dean of the College of Literature and Arts, protested on the grounds that such a policy offered a premium for registration in Science and therefore discriminated against Literature and Arts. So the board extended the scholarships to Literature and Arts also.[57]

Registrations in household science grew steadily. Bevier reported twenty in the first year, forty in the second, sixty in the third, and eighty in the fourth year (1903–4). The first class of three graduated in 1903, and a class of four graduated in 1904.[58]

## THE DEPARTMENTS

These advances—the new building, additional financial support, the increase in student numbers, creation of the Department of Household Science— all testified to a new era for the College of Agriculture. In late 1900 Davenport reported that Illinois had moved from its old place of about seventeenth to a new place as one of the foremost agricultural colleges. And the progress continued, with considerable turnover in the faculty. Davenport regarded young people as preferable for appointments both because salaries at Illinois were comparatively low and because older people could not be readily trained for new lines of work.[59]

In 1902 Davenport reported that the University offered no less than eighty-two courses in agriculture—eighteen in agronomy, eighteen in animal husbandry, thirteen in dairy husbandry, nineteen in horticulture, nine in household science, three in veterinary science, and two in thremmatology (the study of the improvement of domestic animals and plants and the principles on which such study rests). "No such list of studies," he boasted, "is offered in any other college of agriculture." A year later twenty-one of the twenty-four instructors in technical agricultural subjects devoted their entire time to agriculture. A survey of the college in 1903–4, Draper's last year as president, reveals impressive strength.[60]

The Department of Agronomy, described by Davenport as the chief advantage of the College of Agriculture at Illinois, had a staff of six, including Davenport and Hopkins.[61] Together they taught sixteen courses related to the field and its affairs.

The Department of Animal Husbandry, with a staff of five, offered nineteen courses covering the separate study of sheep, swine, beef cattle, and horses, the management of farm herds, and feeding and breeding. Three courses for graduates were available. Much of the teaching work in this subject, Davenport's specialty, was briefly carried by William J. Kennedy (b. 1876), who had studied at the Ontario Agricultural College in Guelph, Canada, and completed his bachelor's degree at Iowa State. When Kennedy accepted a position at Iowa State, Davenport secured Herbert W. Mumford (b. 1871) as a replacement. Mumford had graduated with a B.S. in agriculture from Michigan State. He was well situated as a faculty member in Lansing. But he wanted to specialize in animal husbandry, which he could not do at Michigan State.

Mumford had had more literary training than most agricultural people, said Davenport, "but he is in no sense of the term a brilliant man. He is honest, industrious and solid." He came as professor of animal husbandry and chief of the same in the station at a salary of $2,200.[62]

In the Department of Dairy Husbandry, four instructors gave thirteen courses related to milk, the dairy cow, the management of dairy farms, factory management, dairy bacteriology, and city milk supply. From 1899 to 1903 Fraser, the senior faculty member, was assisted by Oscar Erf (b. 1874), who held a B.Sc. from Ohio State, and in 1902–3 additional assistance was provided by Arthur J. Glover (b. 1873), who held a B.Agr. from the University of Minnesota. Erf's criticisms of Fraser were so bitter that Glover left after one year.[63] By 1903–4 conditions in the department had settled down.

The Department of Horticulture, with five faculty members, conducted a total of nineteen courses in orchard management, small-fruit culture and vegetable gardening, nut culture, floriculture, landscape gardening, forestry, fruit propagation, greenhouse management, the evolution of cultivated plants, and commercial horticulture and nursery management. Apart from Burrill, Blair was the senior professor.

When Mumford was appointed in animal husbandry, Davenport recommended that his own teaching continue with the position and title of Professor of Principles of Variation and Selection in Domesticated Animals and Plants (Thremmatology). The catalog of 1902–3 was the first to list thremmatology as a department. Davenport taught one course and directed theses.[64]

The Department of Veterinary Science was staffed by McIntosh, the senior member of the faculty in length of service if not in professional standing. (Draper strenuously opposed any advance in his salary.)[65]

The relative strength of the departments in 1902–3 is indicated by the following figures: animal husbandry led, with 15 courses and 785 students, followed by agronomy, with 12 courses and 440 students. Horticulture had 9 courses and 111 students, dairy husbandry had 9 courses and 61 students, veterinary science had 3 courses and 169 students, and household science offered 8 courses and enrolled 105 students.[66]

## THE AGRICULTURAL EXPERIMENT STATION

With the Funk Bill and developments since 1899, the college enjoyed a new prestige. To Davenport, however, the task was not simply to instruct students but to aid in the agricultural development of the state so far as academic methods could contribute. That meant investigation into the farming problems of the commonwealth and finding methods for their solution, which required close relations with men engaged in farming who could help identify problems and test solutions. Davenport felt his way to a scheme for rebirth of the experiment station.

He lost no opportunity to develop closer relations with the agricultural community of the state. He strengthened ties with the IFI, whose members frequently sought the expertise of the college and station staff. Their calls for lectures, which interrupted work and laid claim to funds, became a heavy burden. Several solutions addressed the problem. In December 1900 the board asked the legislature for $6,000 a year to provide more agricultural teachers to meet the demands for instruction at farmers' institutes; the General Assembly appropriated this sum for 1903 and 1904. In addition, at Davenport's request the board created the position of Institute Visitor to correspond with the farmers' institutes, schedule the attendance of faculty members at institutes, represent the interests of the University at the institutes, and correspond with people of the state concerning scholarship in connection with farm work in Illinois. In September 1901 Fred H. Rankin, who came from a wealthy and cultured farm family in Athens, Illinois, and was secretary of the Illinois Live Stock Breeders' Association, was appointed to this post.[67]

These measures whetted the appetite of the IFI, which in June 1903 asked the University's governing board to establish a correspondence school as a department of the college. To gain freedom to act in the matter, the trustees renewed Rankin's appointment from month to month, subject to termination at one month's notice. The board's Committee on Instruction then studied the matter. Its report, submitted in December, balanced water on both shoulders. After describing the work of the college and the station in research, teaching, and outreach and the experience with correspondence schools elsewhere, the committee concluded that a correspondence school, if established, should be adapted to three groups: young farmers unable to attend college; young people who took extension work, outgrew it, and passed the age for which it was adapted; and teachers in rural schools who needed a better agricultural education. But a correspondence school was such a departure from established lines that no funds under existing appropriations could be used for it. While the committee was favorable to the enterprise, it recommended that those interested in agricultural advance devote another year to discussion of the matter.[68]

Closer relations with the organized farmers of the state were also formed through advisory committees. By about 1900 nearly every agricultural society of the state had taken formal action favoring the extension of the work of the college and the experiment station through state appropriations. These groups were instrumental in revitalizing the experiment station.

On 7 February 1901 a conference of delegates representing the IFI and the various agricultural organizations met in Springfield and agreed to pursue the idea of state development by systematic investigation of the natural resources and the controlling conditions, climatic and economic, under which agricultural interests worked. With that idea uppermost, the group drafted what became known as Bill 315. The proposal, introduced in the lower house on 13 February 1901, sailed through both chambers with minor amendments and became law.

Bill 315 made it the duty of the Agricultural Experiment Station to conduct investigations along six independent lines, to be agreed upon by the director of the station and a committee of five that was to be appointed by the agricultural society most nearly representing the interests of some existing agricultural organization; and it appropriated funds annually for the years 1901 and 1902 for this purpose. The law brought a total of $54,000 annually for two years, of which $8,000 was to be used for livestock and $46,000 for extending the work of the station. None of the money could be used for salaries in the college.

The college and station now had unprecedented financial resources. The total funds available for agricultural work had more than doubled in 1899, and, with the appropriations of Bill 315, they more than doubled again in 1901, yielding a sum of over $104,000 annually. Nothing approaching it, Davenport exulted, had ever before come to Illinois or to any agricultural college or experiment station. Davenport now pressed hard for increases in rank and salary for the existing staff and for additional help to develop the agricultural conditions of the state by investigation.[69]

Davenport planned the lines of work under Bill 315 in conference with station workers and advisory committees from the various agricultural societies. The Agricultural Experiment Station had long had an advisory board, but its meetings rarely attracted a quorum. Now the agricultural associations with a member on the station's advisory board were also represented on the committees of five from the various societies. The chief interest of these advisors was in immediate results, whereas the station staff was mainly concerned with theoretical questions and fundamental principles. Of the many valuable studies carried out with available funds, two deserve special mention. Both were directed by Cyril G. Hopkins.

## Two Key Experiments—Corn and Soil Fertility

Indian corn was a leading agricultural staple in Illinois. As we have seen, Hopkins wrote his doctoral dissertation on the chemistry of the corn kernel. He obtained leave to study agricultural chemistry in Germany for a year, starting on 1 September 1899, and the following June he was promoted to full professor of agronomy in the college and special assistant in agronomy at the station. Hopkins apparently began his corn-breeding project soon after returning from Europe. Studies of animal nutrition were being actively pursued at the time;

they centered on the proper balance of carbohydrates, fats, and proteins. Corn, the great American feed crop, was deficient in both proteins and fats for an animal diet, but it showed great variation in chemical composition. These wide variations suggested that the chemical composition of corn might be considerably improved by breeding. Hopkins conducted selection experiments on maize with the object of increasing its protein and fat content. He employed two assistants to conduct chemical analysis of the kernels grown under his program. Louie H. Smith, who graduated from the University with a B.S. in chemistry in 1897 and earned an M.S. in chemistry two years later, joined the station staff as assistant chemist in 1899. Edward M. East, who graduated from the University with a B.S. in chemistry in 1901, became an assistant chemist at the station that year. In 1903 Hopkins, Smith, and East published *The Structure of the Corn Kernel and the Composition of Its Different Parts*, which the station issued as its Bulletin No. 87. The Illinois experiments in selective breeding to alter the chemical composition of corn attracted wide attention.[70]

Although trained as a chemist—he earned an M.S. in chemistry at the University in 1904—East became dissatisfied with the routine job of analysis. He was eager to understand the genetic mechanisms involved in corn breeding. His curiosity was aroused at a propitious time, for the rediscovery of Mendel's laws, which had lain unnoticed since they were first published in an obscure journal in 1865, had been announced almost simultaneously in 1900 by the Dutchman Hugo DeVries, the German Carl Correns, and the Austrian Eric Tschermak. According to the agricultural journalist A. Richard Crabb, East learned about Mendel's laws in a course he took from Charles F. Hottes. Crabb may be right, but evidence to support his position is lacking. Hottes had taken both bachelor's (1891) and master's degrees (1895) in natural science at the University and then joined the faculty in botany. Since no graduate courses in plant physiology were available in the United States at the time, in 1898 he went to Germany for further study. He was at the University of Bonn, where he took his Ph.D. in 1901, when Europeans learned about the rediscovery of Mendel's laws. East's decision to shift to plant sciences, Crabb writes, had crystallized by late summer 1903.[71]

East believed that Hopkins and Smith were overlooking potentially rewarding avenues of experimentation. The pedigree records showed that all of the high-protein lines descended from one of 163 ears selected at the start, but increases in protein and oil content resulting from selection were accompanied by decreases in yield. This finding doomed to failure Hopkins's effort to introduce to Illinois farmers a new kind of corn unless some means could be found to increase protein and fat without at the same time decreasing yield. East suspected that the problem might be the result of inbreeding. Would the reduction that followed inbreeding be accompanied by increased growth from crossbreeding?

East devised an experiment to test the effects of inbreeding so as to preserve the advantage of the unusual ear and avoid low yield. He secured permission from Hopkins to make his study part of the corn-breeding project. In 1905 East laid out the first corn-inbreeding plot of its kind and obtained good results. When Hopkins, who was busy with other research and losing interest in the corn-breeding experiment, finally inspected the test plot during the summer, he ordered the work discontinued.

East left in September for a position at the Connecticut Agricultural Experiment Station in New Haven, where much of the pioneer American work in nutrition had been conducted in close collaboration with Yale University. Here he continued the experiment he had initiated at Illinois with seed that a former co-worker sent him from ears that East had developed in Urbana. East's work, together with the independent investigations of George H. Shull of the Carnegie Institution for Experimental Evolution at Cold Spring Harbor on Long Island, finally led to the development of hybrid corn, which revolutionized corn growing in America and throughout the world.[72]

"There is a certain justice," writes A. Richard Crabb, in this inbred material moving from Illinois to Connecticut and being molded into "the first successful strain of the new hybrid corn." Crabb finds it especially fitting that Hopkins should make some tangible contribution to the result. As he writes:

> For all his limitations as a plant breeder, which became so evident as his corn-improvement project progressed at the University of Illinois, Hopkins' work and that of his institution will ever stand as the connecting link between the ageless practice of corn improvement by selection methods and the modern plant-breeding achievement we know today as hybrid corn.

Hopkins set out to develop a grain with qualities never before associated with maize:

> He was the first to breed corn on a field scale, first to make wide use of the pedigree in corn improvement. His program aroused an intense desire in the possibilities of breeding better corn in Edward Murray East, the man whose role was to be a determining one in making hybrid corn possible in our time.[73]

East remained in New Haven for four years. While there he received his Ph.D. from the University of Illinois in 1907, and in 1909 he left Connecticut for the Bussey Institution of Harvard University, a graduate school of applied biology. In 1914 he became a full professor at Harvard. East's most important contribution was in the development of hybrid corn, a project he had initiated while at Illinois.[74]

In addition to his corn-breeding project, Hopkins also directed an important study of soils. Corn and other field crops robbed the land of its productive capacity, a problem to which Hopkins had given considerable thought.[75] Convinced that American agriculture was absolutely dependent on soil fertility, he envisioned a permanent agriculture based on maintaining the original productive capacity of soil. The Farmers' Institute supported a systematic study of the soils of the state. Bill 315 provided funds for such a study to develop the economic possibilities of the state and to protect its people against the calamity of reduced production through exhausted lands. The bill laid the duty on the University. On 18 June 1901 the advisory committee on soil investigations met in Urbana with Davenport, Hopkins, and other station staff members and laid out a plan. On 20 September Hopkins reported back on his research strategy. Davenport hailed these efforts as "the first attempt of a state to systematically study its natural resources with a view to their development."[76]

Hopkins believed that soil fertility could be maintained by preserving the good physical conditions of the soil and returning to the land the fertility that was removed both by cropping and by soil erosion. His studies showed the amount of essential mineral elements—nitrogen, phosphorus, and potassium—taken from the soil by corn. Farmers could restore fertility by using commercial fertilizers or by guarding the stock of mineral elements in the soil. Commercial fertilizers promised larger yields quickly, but they were costly and risked future exhaustion of the soil. Hopkins wanted a system of permanent agriculture that would enable Illinois to support its population indefinitely.

He invoked science to halt the ravishing of the earth by man. In one investigation, he located experimental fields of old and worn-out soils in fifteen different places throughout the state, including Urbana, and divided them into two parts. On one part he applied to the crop all of the more important elements of fertility (nitrogen, phosphorus, and potassium), both separately and in different combinations, and tested the results at the end of the year. On the other part he conducted a series of rotation experiments with corn and leguminous plants over three or four years to test the effect on the soil of these important elements of fertility. In a second investigation he collected soil samples from five places around the state and conducted similar experiments at the University in four-gallon containers.

These studies enabled Hopkins to formulate some simple rules for improving soils and feeding plants. If the soil was acid or sour, he urged farmers to apply lime to make it sweet. Lime was readily available at low cost. If the soil lacked nitrogen only, he suggested growing clover or some other legume that could secure nitrogen from the atmosphere. This advice was based on studies Hopkins conducted on leguminous crops. If the soil was poor in phosphorus or potassium, Hopkins urged farmers to supply the need not by applying highly manufactured commercial fertilizers, whose use he opposed, but by recycling farm products, such as dried blood for its nitrogen and bone meal for its phosphorus, both of which could be obtained inexpensively from the Chicago slaughterhouses, along with ground rock or ground slag phosphate and potash. He also counseled farmers to use barnyard manure and to make liberal use of green manures to maintain the supply of organic matter in the soil.[77]

These soil studies were complemented by a soil survey of Illinois that the experiment station conducted in cooperation with the Bureau of Soils of the U.S. Department of Agriculture beginning in 1902. This enormous task involved the mapping and analyzing of every type of soil, down to ten-acre fields, in a state with boundaries that paralleled Massachusetts on the north and Virginia on the south.[78]

## Summary and Conclusion

In 1894, when Andrew S. Draper became president and the University began to remodel itself, the College of Agriculture was comatose. In 1895 Eugene Davenport assumed leadership of the college. When his attempt to enlist Draper and the trustees in revitalizing the agricultural enterprise met resistance, he went over their heads to enlist the support of the IFI. The first great job of this farm organization was rejuvenation of the College of Agriculture. By 1899 these joint efforts had succeeded, as witnessed by the fact that the legislature appropriated funds to construct an agricultural building and to vastly expand the course work in the college. In 1901 the task of revitalization was accelerated when House Bill 315 more than doubled the money available for agricultural activities, directing that the funds be used to support investigations conducted by the Agricultural Experiment Station. These studies promised to yield enormous economic and material benefits for the people of Illinois.

By late 1903 Davenport was able to say that he had accomplished the larger part of what he came to Illinois to do.[79] He fought a continuing battle with Draper to revitalize the college and the station. "Dr. Draper and I bumped together head on in more than one way," he later wrote. He viewed Draper as an autocrat of autocrats, a man with a military attitude toward faculty members. According to Davenport, Draper bitterly resented the determination of the farmers of the state to build up a real college of agriculture, and he tried to stop the movement for an agricultural building and increased funding for agricultural instruction. To Draper's humiliation, the trustees went ahead. All this occurred in the first half of Draper's administration, while Draper "was still filled with the idea that HE was dictating the policy of the institution."[80]

After this incident, however, Draper informed Davenport that henceforth he would approve every recommendation Davenport might make if it did not injure the rest of the University. Things went well, and in Davenport's view the rapid development of the College of Agriculture spurred unprecedented growth of the University as a whole, as the legislature and the people of the state for the first time caught the vision of what a state university might become.

In October 1905 Draper returned to the campus for the inauguration of his successor. On this occasion, Davenport recounted, he assembled the agriculture faculty to meet Draper, who confessed that "the most significant thing that happened here during my administration was the development of the College of Agriculture, and I did all I could to prevent it."[81]

Like the prophet Ezekiel, Davenport had been set down in the middle of a valley of dry bones. These bones were the College of Agriculture and the Agricultural Experiment Station. Davenport was instrumental in causing flesh to come upon the bones and in breathing life into them that they might live.

## NOTES

1. Thomas J. Burrill to Maj. Henry E. Alvord, 16 April 1894, 2/4/3; Eugene Davenport, "Rejuvenation of the College of Agriculture of the University of Illinois,", 8/1/21, B:6, 19–21; *17th Report* (1894), 240. See also Richard G. Moores, *Fields of Rich Toil: The Development of the University of Illinois College of Agriculture* (Urbana: University of Illinois Press for the College of Agriculture, 1970), 101–43.
2. Thomas J. Burrill, "Eugene Davenport," *Illinois Agriculturist*, 19 (June 1915), 736; James E. Armstrong to Draper, 27 April 1894, 2/4/5, B:1; Burrill to Armstrong, 8 May, 1 June, 1894; Burrill to Nelson W. Graham, 17 May 1894, 2/4/3.
3. Draper to Hunt, 26 September; Draper to Waters, 9 October; Draper to trustees Nelson W. Graham, 8 October, Napoleon B. Morrison, 9 October, Francis McKay and James E. Armstrong, 18 October; Draper to Smith, 26 October; Draper to Armstrong, 31 October, 27 November 1904, 2/4/3.
4. Davenport to Draper, 3, 26 November 1894, 2/4/2, B:1, F:Davenport; Draper to Davenport, 22 November, 6 December 1894, 2/4/3; *18th Report* (1896), 42.
5. Davenport, "What One Life Has Seen: Personal Recollections of an Epochal Era, 1856–1935," 8/1/21, B:4, Binders 1, 2, and 3:1–2; Davenport, "Experience in Brazil," *Speculum* [of Michigan Agricultural College], 11 (11 July 1892), 121–25 (copy in 8/1/21, B:19).
6. Davenport, "What One Life Has Seen," Binder 3:3–10. Davenport gives 810 as the size of the student body. In 1894–95 the official count was 751; in 1895–96 it was 815. For enrollments in the colleges in the 1890s, see 15/1/11, 1898–99.
7. *18th Report* (1896), 72, 159–60; Davenport to Draper, 4 March, 24 August 1895, 2/4/2, B:1, 2; a copy of the 24 August letter, titled "First Formal Report," is in 8/1/21, B:16, bound with Davenport's "Rejuvenation of the College of Agriculture."
8. Davenport to Draper, 15 May 1896, 2/4/2, B:3, F:Davenport.
9. *18th Report* (1896), 249–50, 264.
10. Davenport, "What One Life Has Seen," Binder 3:11.

11. Solberg, 139–40; Davenport, "Rejuvenation of the College of Agriculture," 31–34; *Annual Report, Illinois Farmers' Institute . . . for the Year 1896*, 146–76; (hereafter cited as IFI, *Annual Report*, followed by the year in parentheses); A. B. Hostetter, "History of Farmers' Institute Growth in Illinois," in IFI, *Annual Report* (1904), 243–47; Davenport, "A Record Illinois Should be Proud Of: Historical Sketch of Farmers' Institute Activities," *Orange Judd Farmer*, 66 (4 January 1919), 5.

12. IFI, *Annual Report* (1896), 100–2; (1897), 34–38, 217–21; and articles by Davenport in 8/1/21. Quotations are from Davenport, "Subdivision of Agriculture for Purposes of Instruction and Research," *Proceedings of the Society for the Promotion of Agricultural Science*, 22 (1901), 160; Davenport to David Kinley, 22 May 1896, 2/4/2, B:2, F:Davenport; and IFI, *Annual Report* (1896), 102.

13. Davenport to Draper, 31 May 1897, 2/4/2, B:3, F:Davenport.

14. Davenport to Draper, 15 May 1896, 2/4/2, B:3, F:Davenport; *19th Report* (1897), 53. In 1894 the board included $40,000 for a dairy building in its appropriations request, but the funds were not forthcoming (*18th Report* [1896], 51).

15. The three preceding paragraphs draw on Davenport's reports on the experiment station; for the quotation see Davenport to Draper, 1 November 1898, 2/4/2, B:5, F:Davenport. Holden's paper is in IFI, *Annual Report* (1898), 62–66.

16. John C. Hudson, *Making the Corn Belt: A Geographical History of Middle-Western Agriculture* (Bloomington: Indiana University Press, 1994).

17. Davenport to Draper, 3 November 1897, 2/4/2, B:4, F:Davenport.

18. IFI, *Annual Report* (1898), 27–31 (quotation at 29).

19. Davenport to Draper, 15 March 1898, 2/4/2, B:4, F:Davenport.

20. For Davenport's correspondence during this period, see 8/1/1.

21. Davenport to Draper, 26 May, 1 June (Supplement to Director's Report), 19 September (first and second quotations), 26 October (third quotation), 8 December 1898, 2/4/2, B:4, 5, F:Davenport. Davenport was willing to be obsequious. If the matters he was discussing, he later wrote, should be in the slightest degree sources of irritation to "the management of the University," it would cause him the deepest regret, for he was animated only by a desire to serve faithfully. "In all matters of administration the slightest wish of the President shall be my law" (Davenport to Draper, 9 March 1899, 8/1/1).

22. Draper to Mary Turner Carriel, 30 November 1898, 2/4/3.

23. Flower to Draper, n.d. [November 1899], n.d. [Fall 1899], 2/4/1, B:4, F:1896–1900; Davenport to Abbott, 20 September 1899, 8/1/1.

24. *20th Report* (1901), 32–33; Draper to Davenport, 14 December 1898, 2/4/3; Davenport to Draper, 16, 17 December 1898, 2/4/2, B:5, F:Davenport; Davenport to Carriel, 18 January 1899, 8/1/1.

25. *20th Report* (1901), 50.

26. *Inter Ocean*, 14 January 1899 (copy in 2/4/10, B:1, vol. 2).

27. Clipping from unidentified newspaper in 2/4/10, B:1, vol. 2.

28. Charles F. Mills to Davenport, 14, 20 January 1899; Mills to Amos F. Moore, 17 January 1899; Mills to S. Noble King, 17 January 1899, 8/1/50, IFI Letterbook, B:1; IFI, *Annual Report* (1899), 225–26, 61; Davenport, "Rejuvenation of the College of Agriculture," 35–36.

29. Moore was president of the Illinois Farmers' Institute from 1 March 1898 to 1 March 1899.

30. Davenport, "Rejuvenation of the College of Agriculture," 37–38.

31. Draper to Flower, 27 January 1899, 2/4/3.

32. *Journal of the House of Representatives of the Forty-first General Assembly of the State of Illinois* (1899), 524, 785.

33. *20th Report* (1901), 70–71.

34. Ibid., 78, 103–07, 111; Flower to Draper, n. d. [c. August 1899], 2/4/1, B:4, F:Flower, 1896–1900; Davenport, "Rejuvenation of the College of Agriculture," 39–41.

35. Draper to Flower, 4 December 1899, 2/4/3, B:5.

36. *20th Report* (1901), 239; *Addresses. Dedication. Agricultural Building. University of Illinois*, May 21, 1901. The word *millennium* was also misspelled on the cornice of the building. The architect was willing to let the error stand, arguing that the terra cotta firm that had made the inscription had dissolved. Davenport protested, "I cannot feel that it is right to leave the word misspelled . . . to be for all time an eyesore to all good people and an offense against good scholarship." The wrong was righted (Davenport to Draper, 16 October 1901, 2/4/2, B:8, F:Davenport).

37. Governor John R. Tanner to the 42nd General Assembly, 9 January 1901, *Journal of the Senate* (1901), 17.

38. *20th Report* (1901), 119, 133, 136–37.

39. Ibid., 117, 128–33, 134, 138–39, 140.

40. Enrollment figures are scattered throughout Davenport's reports to Draper on the college and the experiment station and in letters to Draper.

41. *20th Report* (1901), 109, 140; Davenport to Draper, 9 October 1899, 2/4/2, B:6, F:Davenport.

42. *20th Report* (1901), 137, 140; Lucy L. Flower to Draper, 14 March [1900], 2/4/1, B:4, F:Flower, 1896–1900; Davenport, "What One Life Has Seen," Binder 3:7–9. The minimum age of special students was later raised to eighteen.

43. *20th Report* (1901), 85; Davenport to Mary Carriel, 3, 7 March 1900, 8/1/21, B:1, F:Personal Letters; Davenport to Draper, 17 February, 6 March 1900, 2/4/2, B:6, F:Davenport.

44. Solberg, 161–63 (quotation at 162).

45. *18th Report* (1896), 96, 106; Mrs. H. M. Dunlap, "Household Economy," in IFI, *Annual Report* (1896), 129–34 (quotation at 134); Davenport, "Notable People I Have Known," p. 42, 8/1/21, B:4; Mrs. E. J. Davenport to the secretaries of various county institutes, 30 July 1898, 8/1/50, IFI Letterbook B:1.

46. *19th Report* (1898), 247–48, Draper to Lucy L. Flower, 15 September 1898 (the quotation), 2/4/3.

47. Mrs. H. M. Dunlap, "The Women Students at Our State University," in IFI, *Annual Report* (1899), 52–54.

48. Draper to Goodrich, Draper to Bevier, 18 February 1899, 2/4/3.

49. *20th Report* (1901), 56–57; Draper to Helen Kinne, 12 May 1899, 2/4/3.

50. *20th Report* (1901), 259–60, 262, 269; IFI, *Annual Report* (1899), 164; Draper to Ellen H. Richards, 20 March 1900, 2/4/3.

51. Draper to Lucy L. Flower, 20 March, 6, 9 April 1900; Draper to W. O. Atwater, 9 April 1900, 2/4/3; *20th Report* (1901), 275.

52. This account draws on Winton U. Solberg, "Isabel Bevier," in *Notable American Women*, ed. Edward T. James, Janet W. James, and Paul S. Boyer, 3 vols. (Cambridge, Mass.: Belknap Press of Harvard University Press, 1971), 1:141.

53. Isabel Bevier, "History of the Home Economics Department," 11–12, 8/11/20, Bevier Papers, B:5.
54. *Catalog* (1901–2), 134.
55. Isabel Bevier, "The History of the Dept. of Home Economics at University of Illinois[,] 1900–1921," 20, 8/11/20, Bevier Papers, B:3.
56. Isabel Bevier, "Household Science at the University of Illinois," *Illinois Agriculturalist*, 12 (February 1908), 127–29.
57. *21st Report* (1902), 69; *22nd Report* (1904), 48–49, 284–85; Kinley to the Board of Trustees, 20 February 1905, 15/1/4; *23rd Report* (1906), 38, 41–42.
58. Bevier, "Household Science at the University of Illinois," 129, Bevier, "The History of the Dept. of Home Economics at University of Illinois, 1900–1921," 29–30.
59. Davenport to Draper, 1 December 1900, undated [probably June 1901, 14 pp.], 2/4/2, B:7, F:Davenport.
60. Davenport, "The Work of the College of Agriculture," in IFI, *Annual Report* (1902), 353; *Register [Catalog]* (1903–4), 126.
61. Davenport to Draper, 6 March 1900, 2/4/2, B:6, F:Davenport.
62. Davenport to Draper, 15 August (the quotation), 16, 17, 20, 22 August 1901, 2/4/2, B:8, F:Davenport; *21st Report* (1902), 181.
63. Davenport to Draper, 15 June 1903, 2/4/2, B:9, F:Davenport.
64. *21st Report* (1902), 181–82.
65. Davenport to Edmund J. James, 7 September 1915, 2/5/3, B:82, F:Davenport, Sept.–Oct '15.
66. Davenport to Draper, 4 May 1903, 2/4/4, B:2, F:Departmental Reports 1903 (1).
67. Davenport to Draper, 6 March, 5, 27 September 1901, 2/4/2, B:7, 8, F:Davenport; *21st Report* (1902), 30; *22nd Report* (1904), 87. Also see 43rd General Assembly, Senate Bill 131.
68. *22nd Report* (1904), 87, 103, 244–46.
69. Davenport to Draper, 20 June 1901, 2/4/2, B:7, F:Davenport.
70. Donald F. Jones, "Edward Murray East, 1879–1938," in National Academy of Sciences, *Biographical Memoirs*, vol. 23 (Washington, D.C.: National Academy of Sciences, 1945), 219–20.
71. Ibid.; A. Richard Crabb, *The Hybrid-Corn Makers: Prophets of Plenty* (New Brunswick: Rutgers University Press, 1947), 23–24. Crabb asserts, without documentation, that East studied botany with Hottes. According to East's student record, as a graduate student he took Botany 5, Bacteriology, during the second semester of 1900–1, when Hottes was in Bonn.
72. William B. Provine, "East, Edward Murray," in *Dictionary of Scientific Biography*, ed. Charles C. Gillispie, 16 vols. (New York: Charles Scribner's Sons, 1970–80), 4:270–72. See also Grant G. Cannon, *Great Men of Modern Agriculture* (New York: Macmillan Co., 1963), 217–28, and Deborah Fitzgerald, *The Business of Breeding: Hybrid Corn in Illinois, 1890–1940* (Ithaca: Cornell University Press, 1990), 17–22, 29–41.
73. Crabb, *The Hybrid-Corn Makers*, 37–38.
74. Provine, "East, Edward Murray," *Dictionary of Scientific Biography*, 4:272.
75. Cyril G. Hopkins, "The Elements of Fertility Taken from the Soil by a Crop of Corn, and How to Restore Them," in IFI, *Annual Report* (1901), 83–89.

76. "Report of Committee on Soil Investigations and Experiments," in IFI, *Annual Report* (1902), 128–73; Cyril G. Hopkins, "Methods of Maintaining the Productive Capacity of Illinois Soils," in IFI, *Annual Report* (1903), 119–20; Eugene Davenport, "Fertility," in IFI, *Annual Report* (1904), 108 (the quotation).

77. Hopkins, "Methods of Maintaining the Productive Capacity of Illinois Soils," 119–42.

78. "Report of Committee on Soil Investigations and Experiments," 170.

79. Davenport to Draper, 17 October 1903, 2/4/2, B:10, F:Davenport.

80. Davenport's evaluation, on which the present account draws, seems just and accurate. See Davenport, "Notable People I Have Known," 2–5, 8/1/21, B:4.

81. Ibid. (the quotations).

Students spent much of their time in classrooms and laboratories. Here some mathematics students are engaged with Professor Edgar J. Townsend in University Hall in 1895. Courtesy of the University of Illinois Archives.

In 1897 the University established a medical department in Chicago, effecting a temporary merger with the College of Physicians and Surgeons in the state's metropolis while envisioning a permanent union, with a view to the University's ultimately acquiring title to the property. In the academic year 1902–3 the medical school enrolled 689 students, including 73 women. This photo was published in the *Illio '03*.

In the fall of 1900 a Department of Domestic Science opened under Professor Isabel Bevier. Circumstances placed it in the College of Agriculture rather than, as originally intended, as an adjunct of the chemistry department in the College of Science. Home economics was still in its infancy as a university subject, but Bevier took a scientific rather than a utilitarian approach to the subject. Courtesy of the University of Illinois Archives.

Physical education, viewed as a science, entered the halls of learning along with the rise of the city in the late nineteenth century. The University responded slowly to this new field, but the Draper administration strove to provide physical training for both men and women. In 1898 Jennette E. Carpenter became director of the women's gymnasium. She gave systematic class drill in gymnastics, including exercises on various pieces of apparatus. The emphasis was on building a strong body as the basis for a strong brain, and on preparing students for life. Courtesy of the University of Illinois Archives.

Jennette E. Carpenter, director of the women's gymnasium, included Maypole dancing in the gymnastics classes she taught. On 16 May 1899 the Watcheka League, a women's organization, held a May party for the entire University at which a Maypole dance was given under the direction of Professor Carpenter. A year later the campus was the scene of what was being called the annual Maypole dance. Ladies, dressed in white, wound the maypole with streamers of University colors to the music of the military band, after which the YWCA served ice cream, cakes, and fudge. Courtesy of the University of Illinois Archives.

Military education was an integral part of the life of the University. All male students were required to enroll in military science during their first two years. Those who completed four years of study were eligible to receive commissions as brevet captains in the state militia. The regiment consisted of two battalions and eight companies, plus a battery of artillery. A military band provided music for drills and marches. Courtesy of the University of Illinois Archives.

CHAPTER 6

# COLOSSUS
# OF THE CAMPUS

In the United States the formal education of engineers is a fairly recent phenomenon. In America, apprenticeship training or shop culture gave way to school culture during the nineteenth century.[1] The United States Military Academy at West Point, founded in 1802 and reorganized after the War of 1812, was the first American institution of higher education to produce engineers. Rensselaer Polytechnic Institute, established in 1824 at Troy, New York, was the pioneer American school devoted to training civil (or civilian) as opposed to military engineers. During the next four decades perhaps a dozen schools of collegiate rank began to provide some kind of instruction in engineering.[2]

Meanwhile, a social and educational reform movement arose that culminated in the Morrill Act of 1862, which mandated that the colleges established with the aid of funds provided by the act should teach "such branches of learning as are related to agriculture and the mechanic arts."

The University of Illinois was founded on the assumption that the agricultural and mechanical arts were the peers of any other studies, and that mastery of these arts required an education different in kind but as systematic as that required for the learned professions.[3]

Soon after the University opened, engineering education eclipsed all other studies. Under able leaders the work in civil and mechanical engineering flourished, and Illinois shared with the Massachusetts Institute of Technology the honor of pioneering in architectural education. The study of physics developed slowly and unevenly, partly because that basic science was viewed as ancillary to engineering. Electrical engineering was introduced, along with a start in mechanics.

By 1894 the College of Engineering was well underway. Rapid urban and industrial growth made the nation hungry for engineers to increase production in manufacturing enterprises, trade, transportation, mining, and related areas. The state of Illinois ranked third among the manufacturing states of the Union, and manufactured products were growing much faster than agriculture.

## BUILDING ON THE FOUNDATIONS

In 1894 the college enrolled 320 out of 604 undergraduates (53 percent), including two women. The University was largely an engineering school, and in size the college ranked fourth in the nation.[4]

Nathan C. Ricker was dean of the college. At fifty-one he was five years older than President Draper. Eager to advance the college, and thoroughly sensible of its reputation, Ricker devoted about two-thirds of his time to administrative duties. Knowing that Draper favored a centralized administration, Ricker sought prior approval before making decisions even on routine matters.[5]

In 1894–95 the college consisted of five departments: civil engineering, mechanical engineering, physics and electrical engineering, municipal and sanitary engineering (to which theoretical and applied mechanics was attached), and architecture and architectural engineering. Each was headed by what Ricker usually called a chief, and all except physics and electrical engineering were in the hands of experienced professionals with one or more assistants. The instructional corps numbered twenty.

Faculty in engineering received higher salaries than faculty in other colleges in the University. In 1894–95 all heads of departments were paid $2,000 except the head of mechanical engineering, who received $2,250. Noting that he had been dean for seventeen years and that the job required the greater part of his working time, Ricker complained that he had never received a cent or even "the empty compliment of thanks" for this extra service, and inquired whether such injustice was to be perpetuated. Ira O. Baker of civil engineering, who had completed twenty-one years of service, noted that he had recently declined an offer for $2,500 on the understanding that his salary would be increased; he asked for consideration of his case on its merits.[6] Salaries in engineering were low compared to those at peer institutions.[7]

The physical facilities of the college were the best on the campus, but even so, the buildings, machinery, and apparatus were inadequate to the college's

### TABLE 8
### COLLEGE OF ENGINEERING ENROLLMENTS

| Year | Under-graduates | Graduates | Total | Instructors | Ratio of Students to Teachers |
|------|------|------|------|------|------|
| 1894–95 | 309 | 10 | 319 | 20 | 16.0 |
| 1895–96 | 312 | 8 | 320 | 25 | 12.8 |
| 1896–97 | 277 | 19 | 296 | 24 | 12.3 |
| 1897–98 | 273 | 27 | 300 | 25 | 12.0 |
| 1898–99 | 289 | 19 | 308 | 25 | 12.3 |
| 1899–00 | 291 | 30 | 321 | 26 | 12.3 |
| 1900–01 | 385 | 33 | 418 | 27 | 15.5 |
| 1901–02 | 474 | 23 | 497 | 32 | 15.5 |
| 1902–03 | 610 | 24 | 634 | 31 | 20.5 |
| 1903–04 | 789 | 37 | 826 | 35 | 23.6 |

needs and far inferior to what could be found at the best engineering schools in the East.[8]

The mission of the college was to educate engineers and architects for professional careers. Students who followed prescribed engineering programs had almost no time for anything other than technical studies. Despite efforts to ensure that entering students were properly qualified, the failure rate in engineering was probably the highest of all of the colleges.[9]

The emphasis in Engineering was on teaching undergraduates. Classes were ideally limited to twenty students. Seniors were required to write a thesis, and the best of these were published in the *Technograph*, a journal sponsored by several student clubs.[10] The college enjoyed the advantage of growing public respect for engineers and an abundance of jobs in the field. Employers wanted students who had completed a full course of studies; often the supply of graduates fell short of the demand.

Despite the favorable environment, in 1896–97 the college began to suffer declining enrollments, as Table 8 shows.[11] Ricker attributed the decline to unfavorable economic conditions, noting that the decline was more marked at a public university like Illinois than at private engineering schools. In addition, many students did not complete a full four-year program. In 1901–2, for example, apart from 52 special students, the college enrolled 172 freshmen, 122 sophomores, 63 juniors, and 65 seniors. Moreover, because the field of engineering was changing and students were alert to job opportunities, some subjects were more popular than others. The data in Table 9 reflect these dynamics.[12]

While emphasizing undergraduate education, Ricker urged the development of graduate work as well as faculty research and publication. The

TABLE 9

DEPARTMENTAL ENROLLMENTS IN ENGINEERING, 1894–1904

| Depart-ment | 94–95 | 95–96 | 96–97 | 97–98 | 98–99 | 99–00 | 00–01 | 01–02 | 02–03 | 03–04 |
|---|---|---|---|---|---|---|---|---|---|---|
| CE | 73 | 59 | 66 | 70 | 74 | 99 | 120 | 167 | 197 | 232 |
| ME | 66 | 60 | 55 | 47 | 66 | 79 | 105 | 124 | 182 | 219 |
| EE | 91 | 97 | 86 | 89 | 82 | 84 | 88 | 109 | 137 | 172 |
| MSE | 2 | 3 | 3 | 2 | 6 | 5 | 5 | 3 | 8 | 8 |
| Arch. | 73 | 69 | 56 | 47 | 42 | 41 | 43 | 40 | 56 | 47 |
| Arch. E. | | 17 | 13 | 14 | 15 | 14 | 12 | 19 | 27 | 43 |
| Total | 305 | 305 | 279 | 269 | 285 | 322 | 373 | 464 | 613 | 752 |

CE, chemical engineering; ME, mechanical engineering; EE, electrical engineering; MSE, municipal and sanitary engineering; Arch., architecture; Arch. E., architectural engineering.

University of Chicago, he said, required each professor to devote half the workday to private advanced research and study. Ricker wanted the Illinois faculty to be required to publish technical papers, and he implored the trustees to provide better facilities for postgraduate work and research. Despite his pleas, the faculty had little time for research, and most practicing engineers felt little need for postgraduate study. In 1900 the heads of the engineering departments agreed that under present circumstances, the degree of doctor of engineering should not be offered at Illinois.[13]

The main work of the college was in its departments. They all pleaded for more faculty and for more and better equipment, they lamented the loss of faculty members to better-paying jobs, and they found it difficult to fill vacancies because of the low salaries offered by the University.

## Civil Engineering

In 1894–95 civil engineering was a well-developed field. Ira O. Baker (b. 1853), who had graduated from the University in 1874 and earned a C.E. in 1878, had become head of the department in 1879 and a full professor a year later. From 1894 to 1904 the course of study in civil engineering remained fairly stable. Most of the courses dealt with surveying, railroad engineering, masonry construction, bridges, tunneling, structural design and details, and variations on these subjects. In 1896–97 a course in practical astronomy was transferred to the College of Science.

With graduates readily finding jobs, civil engineering was the largest department in the college. In America, only three similar departments were larger. As Table 9 shows, in 1894–95 the department enrolled 73 students;

attendance then declined for three years, after which it steadily increased. Many students entered the department with advanced standing.

Baker had ten assistants during the decade under review. All but one had a B.S. from Illinois (the exception had a B.S. from Purdue). Most of them remained only briefly. This group included Milo S. Ketchum, who served as an assistant professor from 1899 to 1903, earning a C.E. in 1900. In 1922, after a long absence, Ketchum returned as dean of the College of Engineering. Few engineers planned to teach, so the demand for graduate work in civil engineering was weak.

Baker's writings grew out of his teaching. His handwritten lectures on geodesy, railroad engineering, engineering instruments, stadia surveying, underground surveying, and friction were blueprinted and used as textbooks. Some of these works were published. His *Leveling: Barometric, Trigonometric and Spirit* (1897) was translated into French and published in Paris.

During much of Baker's career the state of Illinois lacked improved highways, and his main professional interest was the principles of road building. His Cement and Masonry Laboratory, established in 1889 and one of the first if not the first of its kind in an educational institution, contained all the materials and appliances necessary for testing the ingredients of concrete and concrete materials.[14] Concrete was being used in all sorts of structures at the time, and the cement industry of the country was growing rapidly. Baker's classic work, *A Treatise on Masonry Construction* (1889), went through ten editions and was widely influential. Baker continued his experiments on roadbed materials such as stone, gravel, and brick. His *Treatise on Roads and Pavements* (1903), which took the place of lectures he formerly gave, went through three editions and was adopted in many schools. Both volumes sold thousands of copies.

Baker took a keen interest in the education of engineers. Wanting to train literate engineers, he encouraged participation in literary societies, and he was instrumental in founding the Illinois Society of Engineers (1886), now the Illinois Society of Professional Engineers. In 1893, at the World's Engineering Congress in Chicago, he chaired the committee that established the Society for the Promotion of Engineering Education (now the American Society for Engineering Education), later serving as its president. In addition, Baker made many inspection trips and consulted. His report on pavement contracts in Chicago exposed incompetence and graft amounting to nearly $400,000.[15]

## Mechanical Engineering

Mechanical engineering is concerned with the generation and transmission of power, with machinery, and with the application of machinery to the regulation of modern industry. In the late nineteenth century the number of graduates in this field began to exceed the number in civil engineering throughout the nation, but at Illinois it ran a close second.[16]

Lester P. Breckenridge (b. 1858) headed the department. After receiving a Ph.B. at Yale's Sheffield Scientific School in 1881 and engaging in engineering practice, he taught at Lehigh University and Michigan Agricultural College before joining the Illinois faculty in 1893. Breckenridge was most interested in the experimental side of engineering. He enjoyed warm personal relations with Draper, and his salary was $250 larger than that of other engineering department heads.[17] Ricker commented on the salary discrepancy to Draper. Other heads worked as hard, he pointed out, and they thought it unjust that much more money had been spent on mechanical engineering than on all the other departments of the college. This injustice discouraged other heads and showed that going to members of the board, or exercising "pull," might be essential for the development of a department.[18]

In 1894–95 Breckenridge introduced an improved curriculum in his department. It required work in shop practice, machine design, steam engines, boilers, thermodynamics, estimates, valve gears, and related studies, plus considerable laboratory work.[19] The emphasis was on shop and laboratory instruction, machine design, and the steam engineering laboratory. During the following decade the curriculum changed little, but in time students took up the design and manufacture of farm implements.

In 1894–95 the department enrolled 66 students. Thereafter enrollments declined for several years, then steadily rose, and by 1903–4 they approached the number in civil engineering. In that year the shop courses were providing instruction to 522 students.[20]

Breckenridge gave attention to railway engineering. In 1898 the department received a dynamometer car (a railway test car) designed for use in locomotive road tests under actual service conditions. This car was jointly owned by the University and the Peoria and Eastern Division of the Big Four (Cleveland, Columbus, Cincinnati, and Indianapolis) Railroad. In 1899 Breckenridge recommended establishment of a separate course in railway mechanical engineering. A year later the department received another dynamometer car. This one, owned jointly with the Illinois Central Railroad, was equipped with all the appliances necessary for carrying on train resistance experiments as well as with auxiliary apparatus used during locomotive tests. From 1900 to 1903 eleven students were enrolled in railway electrical engineering.[21]

Breckenridge had twenty-four assistants during the years under review. Apart from shop foremen and others who lacked any degree, fourteen had bachelor's degrees (nine from the University of Illinois) when appointed, and five had M.E. degrees. Most assistants served only briefly, but there were exceptions.

In 1895 Breckenridge brought George A. Goodenough, whom he had known at Michigan Agricultural College, to Urbana. Goodenough later rose to full professor and became an authority on thermodynamics. Edward C. Schmidt served from 1898 to 1903, doing important work with the railway test car, especially in and near New York City, "attracting very favorable notice from prominent eastern engineers, and extending the fame of the University."[22] Oscar A. Leutwiler, who received B.S. (1899) and M.E. (1900) degrees from the University and joined the faculty as an assistant professor in 1903, wrote textbooks on machine design and headed the department from 1935 to 1945.

## Physics and Electrical Engineering

Electrical engineering had emerged as a separate division of the engineering profession by 1884, when the American Institute of Electrical Engineers was founded in Philadelphia. With the development of electricity as a source of light and power came the electrical expert whose knowledge rested on theoretical science and advanced mathematics. As in other branches of engineering, the education of electrical engineers gradually moved from home laboratories and small shops to colleges and technical schools, and it generally began in physics departments. In 1883 Cornell set up one of the nation's first electrical engineering programs within its physics program. During the 1880s other electrical engineering programs arose in association with physics departments at M.I.T., Harvard, Yale, Stevens Institute of Technology in Hoboken, New Jersey, the Case School of Applied Science in Cleveland, and the University of Texas.[23]

Physics remained somewhat marginal in the College of Engineering at Illinois until about 1890, when Samuel W. Stratton's work in the subject captured attention. He aroused the enthusiasm of students through his able presentations, well-designed experiments, and ability to make the apparatus he needed. In June 1891 Stratton was promoted to full professor, and during the following academic year he introduced in the Department of Mechanical Engineering what was intended as a full course in electrical engineering, the first two years of which were identical with the first two years in mechanical engineering. Stratton also established a laboratory in electrical engineering.

At the end of the academic year, however, owing mainly to his low salary, Stratton resigned to accept an appointment in the physics department at the University of Chicago. His loss was a severe blow. Stratton, who later became the first director of the National Bureau of Standards and president of M.I.T., would probably have given both physics and electrical engineering better leadership than they were to experience for the next several years.

Daniel W. Shea (b. 1859), Stratton's successor, had taken bachelor's and master's degrees at Harvard (1886, 1888) and a doctorate at Bonn (1892). That

September he accepted a position at Illinois as assistant professor, and in March 1894 he won promotion to full professor.

Shea was in charge of physics and electrical engineering, which were not yet separate departments although they were often referred to as such. He had three assistants. Bernard V. Swenson, who had earned a B.S. in both mechanical and electrical engineering from the University in 1893, joined the staff that year. Also in 1893 William Esty, an Amherst College B.A. who had earned a B.S. from M.I.T., became an instructor. A year later Fred A. Sager, holder of a B.S. from the University of Michigan, became an assistant.

In 1894–95 the catalog listed eight courses in physics and ten in electrical engineering; the latter "department," with 91 students, was then the largest in the college. During the fall term Shea and his assistants each spent an average of 29 hours a week instructing a total of 116 students. During the winter term the four men each averaged 45.5 hours of teaching a week, with a total of 182 students in four physics and four electrical engineering courses, plus seminars and theses. During the spring term each faculty member averaged 43.25 hours' teaching 173 students who were taking two physics courses and seven electrical engineering courses. Shea taught mainly physics and Sager taught only physics, while Esty and Swenson taught primarily electrical engineering.[24]

On 10 January 1895 Draper presented the trustees with a letter from Shea tendering his resignation effective 1 September 1895. The board, unanimously declining to accept the resignation, assured Shea that it would assist him in every way in promoting the growth of physics and electrical engineering, and it authorized Draper to employ a "practical electrician" as an assistant in the electrical department.[25]

On 2 March 1896, reporting on his department to the dean, Shea declared its equipment inadequate for the number of students and the undergraduate work not satisfactory in proportion to the efforts of the teachers. The students were weak in mathematics and languages, the department should aim higher than elementary instruction, and each teacher and student should carry on original investigation. With more resources, an independent department of electrical engineering could be created, and each department should have its own head. Shea praised Swenson and Sager, but he was not entirely satisfied with Esty.[26]

On 12 March Shea again submitted his resignation, and a day later the board again expressed its unanimous wish that he withdraw it. Shea was bargaining for increased support; his 29 May letter to the board requested promotions for Swenson and Sager, more assistants, another instructor in physics, and $10,000 for equipment and operating expenses for 1895–96—a tenfold increase over the $1,000 authorized a year earlier for these purposes![27]

On 16 September Shea "again and finally" tendered his resignation. He could not let pass opportunities that constantly presented themselves, he explained, and it was evident that his teaching duties at Illinois would prevent him from carrying on "work of the high scholarly character" for which he had prepared himself. Draper accepted Shea's resignation to take effect when he could arrange for Shea's classes. On 27 September, however, Shea wrote Trustee Richard P. Morgan urging that the board deal with his request for funds. Morgan informed Draper that he had lost confidence in Shea, and on 10 October Draper wrote all board members that "it is necessary to relieve Professor Shea at a very early day." Since it was impractical on short notice to get a strong man to head the department, he proposed to split it into two departments and continue the work for the year in the hands of the younger men. He wanted approval to proceed.[28]

On 10 December the board approved Draper's recommendations to divide the department into two units, promote Sager to assistant professor and put him in charge of physics, appoint an additional physics instructor, make Swenson chief of electrical engineering, and promote Esty to assistant professor. These actions, effective as of 1 November, were to be good for at least the rest of the year. The board also approved a request for an appropriation of $1,135 for the combined department for the next year. Shea left for a professorship of physics at the Catholic University of America in Washington, D.C., where he later became dean of the Faculty of Science.[29]

In September 1896 Albert P. Carman became head of the physics department. Born in 1861 in New Jersey, the son of a Methodist minister, Carman held three degrees from Princeton—A.B. (1883), A.M. (1884), and D.Sc. (1886)—and had studied from 1887 to 1889 at the University of Berlin. From 1889 to 1892 he had been professor of physics and electrical engineering at Purdue, and since 1892 professor of theoretical physics at Stanford. A model of propriety, Carman apparently pleased Draper. He visited the University, and on 22 April the board approved his appointment as professor of physics at $2,250 a year. Carman would head the physics department until he retired in 1929. His research dealt with the resistance of thin tubes to collapse and the thermal conductivity and diffusivity of concrete. He published two short papers in the *Physical Review*, "Resistance of Tubes to Collapse" (1905), and "The Effect of Pressure on the Aluminum Rectifier" (1910).[30]

In addition to Carman, whom Ricker described as an excellent instructor, and Sager, the faculty included Burton E. Moore, who had taken a Ph.D. at Göttingen, and Oscar Quick, who held bachelor's and master's degrees from Harvard. In 1901 William F. Schulz, a Johns Hopkins electrical engineering graduate, was added; in 1902, Floyd R. Watson, a Cornell Ph.D.; and in 1903 Charles T. Knipp, also a Cornell Ph.D.

The combined department carried on with no discernible disruption until April 1898, when twenty members of the senior class in electrical engineering submitted a petition against retention of Carman as head of electrical engineering on the ground that he lacked competence in the field. Having spoken with those involved, Ricker concluded, among other things, that Carman was more interested in physics than electrical engineering and had not kept up with the latter, that Carman had been overworked, that the discontent sprang partly from electrical engineering being a new field, and that Swenson had fomented dissatisfaction by discussing the matter with students. He advised relieving Carman from electrical engineering, employing a head for that work, and terminating both Swenson and a mechanician who allegedly had helped foment discord.[31]

Before the Board of Trustees met in June, Francis M. McKay and perhaps other board members meddled in this matter. They questioned Esty and Swenson in regard to Carman's competency. "It is evident to me," Ricker added, "that Swenson is actively engaged in endeavoring to injure Carman now."[32]

When the board met, Draper followed Ricker's advice. He praised Esty, whom Ricker had recommended to head a separately constituted electrical engineering department, and criticized Swenson as a man who would not be thought of "as a safe head for any University department." His undue familiarity with students, his antagonism to his associates and superior officers, and his loose talk had caused friction and demoralization. Swenson had amazed Draper by volunteering statements to Draper concerning Carman "which were not only without justification but were absurd." They showed such bad judgment as to preclude his continuance in the faculty.[33]

Draper proposed that electrical engineering be organized as a separate department, that Carman be made head of physics, that Esty be promoted to associate professor, that Swenson leave by 1 September, and that the board empower the president to engage a professor of electrical engineering. The board approved with one exception—that Draper make a serious effort to bring Swenson "into more satisfactory relations with his associates in his department," and if that did not prove practicable, to end his connection with the University.[34]

President McKay called a special meeting of the board on 7 July to consider these matters. Draper, as usual during the summer, was in New York. Piecing together the available cryptic evidence, it appears that McKay presented Swenson's resignation at this time. Some members, probably including McKay, felt that refusing Swenson the chance to resign was too severe. So further consideration of the matter was postponed until September. At that meeting the board took no further action on the case. So Draper's decision stood.[35]

In 1898–99, with Carman as head of the department, six physics courses enrolled 239 students; a year later eight courses drew 346 students.[36]

Meanwhile, Draper had begun the search for a head of electrical engineering. A teachers placement agency apparently suggested William S. Aldrich, professor of mechanical engineering and director of mechanic arts at the University of West Virginia. Born in Philadelphia in 1863, Aldrich had graduated from the U.S. Naval Academy in 1883, taken a degree at Stevens Institute of Technology in 1884, taught in high schools from 1885 to 1889, and pursued graduate studies in electrical engineering at Johns Hopkins University from 1889 to 1892. He then went to West Virginia, where he taught the electrical engineering courses from an engineering perspective. Because his laboratory had recently been destroyed by fire, he was open to a bid.

Aldrich was offered $2,250 but insisted on $2,500, which Worcester Polytechnic was willing to pay him. After visiting the campus and agreeing on a salary, Aldrich accepted, and on 13 June 1899 the board approved his appointment. He believed that engineering education benefited from a university environment as much as law and medicine did,[37] and he vigorously promoted the work in electrical engineering. He improved the department's methods of instruction and prepared a laboratory manual for students that proved very valuable. The Mechanical and Electrical Engineering Society arranged a series of lectures by eminent engineers on the uses of electricity for light and power. During his time at Illinois, Aldrich published two papers. One, extracts from a paper he read before the American Society of Mechanical Engineers, appeared as "Electrical Power for Factories" (1900), the other as "Mechanical and Electrical Features of the Pan-American Exposition" (1901).[38] The former difficulties between instructors and students disappeared.[39] Enrollments in electrical engineering remained static, however, and on 20 May 1901 Aldrich resigned to accept the presidency of the recently founded Clarkson School of Technology (later Clarkson University) in Potsdam, New York.

So Draper beat the bushes for a qualified replacement, and on 11 June the board approved the appointment of Morgan Brooks to the vacancy. Born in Boston in 1861, Brooks graduated from Brown University and overcame the strong opposition of his father to study engineering rather than law. In 1883 he graduated from Stevens Institute of Technology in mechanical engineering, and until 1886 he worked in Boston, mainly in research for the American Bell Telephone Company. He spent the next eleven years as an engineer in St. Paul, and in 1898 he went to the University of Nebraska as professor of electrical engineering.

Brooks was eminently qualified, and during his first year in charge he admirably managed a department with a new and exciting subject. Enrollments began a dramatic growth, and as a bonus Brooks was useful in practical ways. In 1903 he supervised installation of a telephone system at the University.

By June 1902, then, both physics under Carman and electrical engineering under Brooks had finally found firm footing. During 1901–2, however, Draper, "acting on impulse and supposing that all would agree," as he said later, suddenly transferred the departments of physics and mathematics, which had been in the College of Engineering since the earliest days, to the College of Science. He met strong opposition from the engineering faculty. They rightly questioned his authority, Draper admitted, and he agreed to undo his act. In the end, mathematics remained in the College of Science. It would have been better for the University if physics had also.[40]

Despite apparent success in promoting electrical studies, Brooks encountered difficulties in advancing his department. He had to plead constantly for equipment, laboratory assistants, instructors, and reimbursement for authorized expenses incurred in taking the seniors on a tour of electrical installations in Chicago.[41]

By 1904 relations between Brooks and Draper were strained. When Brooks learned that a requisition for electrical instruments needed for thesis work by students had long been held up in the president's office, he requested an interview. By letter Draper refused to grant it. "Evidences are plentiful enough," Draper added, "that you have not assimilated very well with our work here, and have not developed any special enthusiasm in it." The circumstances seemed to indicate "that you will prefer to make some other disposition of your services after this year, and that it may be as well for the University that you should do so." If so, the purchase of additional equipment ought to wait.

"Since my relations with the Executive of the University have become so unfortunately strained," Brooks shot back, "it is true, as you say, that I would prefer to make other arrangements for the future. Indeed that probability has been in my mind for some time." Returning to the matter later, Brooks said that he did not wish his earlier reply to be interpreted as a resignation or as expressing an intention of voluntarily leaving at the close of the year. In addition, Brooks was surprised at Draper's belief that Brooks was not enthusiastic about his work or that he had not assimilated with colleagues or students. "I believe you are mistaken about this, and as I do not admit the facts I am unwilling to acquiesce in action based on them." Four days after Brooks stood his ground, Draper announced his own resignation. He later admitted that before leaving he had made up his mind that Brooks was "not of any permanent value to the institution" and should go. Brooks remained, however, giving valuable service for another quarter of a century.[42]

## Municipal and Sanitary Engineering and Mechanics

Arthur N. Talbot is best identified with two specialties—municipal and sanitary engineering, and theoretical and applied mechanics—that brought distinction to the College of Engineering. Born in Cortland, Illinois, in 1857, Talbot entered the University in 1877, studied under Ira O. Baker, compiled an outstanding academic record, and graduated in 1881 with a B.S. In 1885, after four years of railroad work in the West, he returned to the campus, received a C.E. for his practical experience and the preparation of a thesis, and became an assistant professor of engineering and mathematics.

The rise of the city in the late nineteenth century created a host of new urban problems. Sewage-polluted waters affected many population centers, and typhoid epidemics were common. Chicago in particular had to face a gigantic task in sanitation. Although Koch had discovered the typhoid bacillus in 1882, the chemistry and bacteriology of sewage as well as water analysis had yet to be developed.[43] The new problems called for municipal and sanitary engineers, so in June 1890 the University extended the course in civil engineering to include roads, streets, and pavements; water supply and hydraulics; and sewers and sewerage. Talbot was promoted to full professor with the title of professor of municipal engineering.

In 1891–92 he introduced a program in municipal engineering that may have been the first of its type in a land-grant college. The four-year curriculum, a modification of the one in civil engineering, included as much chemistry and bacteriology as was necessary to understand questions involved in water supply and sewage disposal. In addition to the work in civil engineering, the catalog listed five advanced offerings in the new field: Road Engineering, Water Supply Engineering, Sewerage, Botany, and Bacteriology. Ricker believed that municipal and sanitary engineering, which Talbot headed, would soon become of more importance to the state than any other branch of engineering.[44]

Talbot was also in charge of theoretical and applied mechanics (TAM).[45] Mechanics is the science that deals with the principles of equilibrium and motion that must be considered in the design and construction of bridges, buildings, machines, and other structures. At least the theoretical part of TAM might properly have been included in the physics department, but physics had a curious organizational history at Illinois. TAM was even more of an anomaly. It was not a department but a group of courses. In 1891–92 the initial course offerings included Analytical Mechanics, Resistance of Materials, and Hydraulics—all taught by Talbot, who signed himself, "Professor of Municipal and Sanitary Engineering (In Charge of Theoretical and Applied Mechanics)."

A devoted and excellent teacher, Talbot molded and inspired generations of young engineers. His curriculum in municipal and sanitary engineering remained basically unchanged from the early 1890s through 1903–4. In 1896–97 work in bridges was rearranged to accord with the course in civil engineering, the course in botany was dropped, and new subjects were introduced in water purification, sewage disposal, and general sanitation. The list of subjects offered for graduate study was transferred from civil engineering to municipal and sanitary engineering. These twenty graduate offerings included seven in water supply engineering, five in sewerage, two in road engineering, and six others.

The fire of 9 June 1900 that destroyed the Mechanical Building and Drill Hall ruined the records, machinery, and apparatus of the department, and work did not fully resume until a new testing laboratory was completed in 1902. The hydraulics laboratory was excellent for all forms of experiments, and the department continued its original work in the testing of paving bricks, which produced results of importance to Illinois cities. In 1900 the National Brick Manufacturer's Association adopted the University's method of testing paving brick.[46]

Ricker emphasized the importance of the municipal and sanitary engineer, but the specialty failed to attract a decent following. In 1894–95 only two students enrolled, and by 1903 only ten students had graduated from the department. The numbers may have been limited by the popular notion that municipal engineers were usually selected by political favor rather than by merit.[47]

Over time TAM increasingly absorbed Talbot's attention, and without a change in title his teaching emphasized mechanics and engineering materials. In 1894–95 TAM included the original three courses plus Applied Mechanics and Strength of Materials. A year later Talbot added four courses in mechanics and materials at the graduate level. Thereafter the curriculum remained essentially unchanged through 1903–4. In 1902–3 TAM attracted 125 students and a year later 145; since students were by then well prepared in higher mathematics, failures were rare.

In the late 1890s Talbot began making important contributions to the engineering profession. Two of the earliest were formulas, one for areas of waterways for bridges and culverts, the other for rates of maximum rainfall; both were published in the *Technograph* and widely used. His treatise, *The Railway Transition Spiral*, published in 1899, described a flexible transition or easement curve that could be used to connect circular curves with tangents for the purpose of avoiding the disagreeable lurch of trains due to an instant change in the relative position of cars or to a sudden change from level to inclined track. By 1927 this little book had gone through twelve editions and sold thousands of copies.

Most of Talbot's research resulted in publications after 1904.[48] His tests of paving brick for strength and abrasion, his pioneer work in water purification, sewage treatment, and hydraulic problems, his laboratory tests of such engineering materials as plain and reinforced concrete (a new structural combination material in which iron rods were embedded), brick, and steel—all these made possible notable advances in engineering and brought distinction to both Talbot and the University.

## Architecture and Architectural Engineering

Ricker was largely responsible for the development of formal architectural education in the Midwest, and for two decades he directed the only architectural school west of the Atlantic seaboard. He and William R. Ware of M.I.T. and later Columbia University, the fathers of architectural education in the United States, drew inspiration from different sources. Ware was under the influence of the École des Beaux-Arts, whose styles the World's Columbian Exposition of 1893 had established as the model for American architecture. Most American schools of architecture followed the French lead.[49]

Steering an independent course, Ricker drew on eclectic sources, especially the German theories of the Bauakademie, which emphasized study of the past, functionalism, organic design, and the exploitation of new materials and new building types. Opposing the replication of classical models and the obsession with style in the French tradition, Ricker stressed the science of construction and the history of culture, convinced that America would in time develop its own architectural style.[50]

At the turn of the century the Midwest, and particularly Chicago, had a great demand for architects. Ricker sought to prepare students for the practice of the profession; his pedagogy involved a few basic principles. First, he prohibited imitation in the design of buildings, although he viewed history as a guide to design. Architects needed a knowledge of construction and structure because function determined the proportion of building elements. Second, architects must adapt the forms of the past for modern use. Third, good architecture was defined by good taste. Aesthetics was a tool for good design, which was the "nucleus or soul of all architectural training." The course of study comprised the theory and practice of construction, drawing applied to all purposes, the principles of design and their application to the planning and designing of buildings, the history and aesthetics of architecture, draftsmanship, and office practice so far as it could be taught in a professional school.[51]

By way of contrast with William Ware of M.I.T., who looked to a general liberal arts education, not a technical education, to furnish the profession with well-educated men with the qualities of "good sense and good taste,"[52] Ricker's prescribed four-year curriculum leading to a B.S. degree in architecture was narrow and technical. Starting in 1893–94 the course offerings were increased from fourteen to twenty-one. Apart from twenty architecture courses—only Advanced Graphics was not required—and a thesis, Illinois students studied only French or German, rhetoric, mechanics, and physics. In architecture, first-year students took Shop Practice (carpentry and joinery, turning and cabinet-making, and construction) and second-year students took Wood Construction, Stone, Brick, and Metal Construction, Sanitary Construction, and Roofs. In the third year they took two courses in the history of architecture, three in architectural drawing, Architectural Seminary, and one of two Architects' Art Courses. The fourth-year courses were Superintendence, Estimates, and Specifications; Heating and Ventilation; Architectural Perspective; Requirements and Planning of Buildings; Architectural Design (two courses); Esthetics of Architecture; and Thesis.

Always abreast of the most progressive developments of the day, Ricker led in another significant phase of professional education. The development of skeleton construction for tall buildings in Chicago created a demand for personnel trained in the new techniques. At the suggestion and with the support of Dankmar Adler, a prominent Chicago architect, Ricker initiated a program in architectural engineering, the first in the nation.[53] According to the 1893–94 catalog, the course was intended for students who preferred the mathematical and structural side of architecture to its artistic side, and those who wished to acquire a thorough knowledge of iron and steel construction as it was then being executed in architectural structures. The course was identical with that in architecture except that hydraulics was required; masonry construction, bridge analysis, and bridge design replaced freehand drawing; the orders and history of architecture were omitted; differential and integral calculus were added; and advanced graphics replaced architectural perspective.

In 1895 Ricker observed that the engineering side of the instruction in architecture at Illinois was fully developed, probably more so than at other schools of architecture, and it was time to devote more attention to the artistic side, especially drawing and designing. He proposed to emphasize freehand drawing, chiaroscuro, architectural rendering, study of color, and water color plus sketching.[54]

Actually, the curriculum set out in the catalog of 1895–96 differed only slightly from that of the previous year, but four new courses appeared, all of which were to be taught by special arrangement only. Three were in design (Renaissance, Gothic, and Romanesque) and the fourth was Composition of Ornament. In addition, several courses for graduates were introduced. This core program remained largely unchanged for many years, except for the occasional addition of a course. For example, in 1896–97 Architectural Composition and Vacation Sketches was added, in 1898–99 Domestic Architecture, and in 1899–1900 Mural Decoration.

During the decade ending in 1903–4, Ricker had the assistance of eight colleagues. Seth J. Temple, who had earned a Ph.B. in architecture from Columbia in 1892, served from 1896 to 1904. Both Frank F. Frederick and Newton A. Wells of the art department taught courses in architecture. In 1903 Wells became professor of architectural decoration.

Along with Ricker, the mainstay of the department was James M. White (b. 1867), a native of Chicago who had graduated from the University in 1890 with a B.S. in architecture and who joined the faculty as an assistant. In 1893 he was promoted to assistant professor; in 1894–95 he was granted a leave of absence to study in Europe. While in Paris he met Hugh Tallant and urged Ricker to appoint him to teach architectural design. Ricker wished to do so, believing that Tallant could introduce the best features of the French system of instruction and practice. But Tallant remained in Paris to complete his studies. White went from Paris to the Technische Hochschule in Munich, concluding, like Ricker, that the German schools were more thorough than the French and enjoyed much superior facilities and equipment. In 1896 White was promoted to associate professor. Ricker believed that White associated too freely with "certain society women in Champaign," which involved "risk for an innocent man." He wanted White to devote more time to his work and less to society, to marry and settle down.[55] Despite such doubts, in 1901 White became a professor of architectural engineering.

Ricker usually taught the history of architecture, the aesthetics of architecture, and the architectural seminary. Often he taught architectural composition, and with White he co-taught courses in Romanesque design and composition and ornament. Ordinarily White assumed responsibility for engineering, drawing, and designing related to architecture, and for heating and ventilation, estimates, and planning of buildings.

Ricker's teaching methods evolved in response to the interests and capacities of his classes. Lectures, he found, were of limited value because students became drowsy and took poor notes, so he prepared syllabi, duplicating them by the blueprint method. Some of these efforts became books, the first of which was *Elementary Graphic Statics and the Construction of Trussed Roofs* (1885), while others remained in blueprint, such as his "Elements of Architectural Construction" (2 vols., 1887).

Finding no suitable English texts on the history of art and architecture or on special topics, Ricker translated, typed, and duplicated foreign works for his students. In 1884 he began, with Rudolf Redtenbacher, *The Architectonics of Modern Architecture* (1883), offering an abridged translation in 1888. More than forty manuscript volumes followed, including translations of Viollet-le-Duc's *Rational Dictionary of French Architecture from XIth to XVIth Centuries*, in eleven volumes, and such standard German works as Josef Durm's volumes on architecture from the ancient Greeks through the Italian Renaissance and Wilhelm Lübke's four-volume history of the Renaissance in France and in Germany.[56]

Ricker's alertness to European developments was evidenced in his translation of Otto Wagner's *Moderne Architektur* (1896 and later editions), a book that made a definitive break with the past. A father of European modernism, Wagner emphasized the need for a new architecture in response to new functional requirements, materials, and structural methods. In 1901 Ricker's translation of the second edition of Wagner's book (1898) appeared in the *Brickbuilder*, and a year later as a book.[57]

Since his students lacked the opportunity to see grand buildings in Champaign-Urbana and access to such magnificent libraries as existed at other American schools of architecture, Ricker devoted himself to building an architecture library. He insisted on reference books for the seminary room and a card index to the books and periodicals in the general collection, and he bought books whenever funds permitted, laying the foundations for what became an outstanding art and architecture library.

As Table 9 demonstrates, architecture and architectural engineering attracted a sizable following. In 1896, 25.3 percent of all regular students in American architectural schools were enrolled at Illinois.[58] Ricker trained students to be sensitive to the past and yet free to search for an American tradition. When Walter Burley Griffin of Elmhurst, Illinois, one of nine students who graduated in architecture in 1899 (along with two in architectural engineering), won first prize in 1912 for his design for Canberra, the new capital city of Australia, his international reputation called attention to architecture at Illinois. Ricker also educated a number of worthies of lesser light who contributed to midwestern architectural development.[59]

Architectural evidence of Ricker's eclecticism and respect for history can be found in the University buildings he designed—the Chemistry Laboratory (1878), later Harker Hall, in the Second Empire Style with a mansard roof; Military Hall or the Old Armory (1890), now Kenney Gymnasium Annex, with exposed wood and steel trusswork; the first unit of Natural History Hall (1893); and the Library (1897).

In 1897, along with Dankmar Adler, Ricker helped secure passage of an act that required architects to be licensed and that regulated the practice of architecture as a profession, the first such legislation in the United States. The Illinois State Board of Examiners of Architects was organized that September. Ricker was a board member for twenty years and president from 1904 to 1922.

Although the new law stipulated that after 1 January 1898 licenses could be granted only to those who passed an examination, Ricker won the diploma privilege for the University. After 1 July 1898 all candidates for license to practice architecture in Illinois who presented to the board a diploma of graduation from the architecture or architectural engineering departments at the University were not required to pass the examinations prescribed by the law. They had only to present the diploma and proof of adequate practical experience in the design and superintendence of construction of buildings. No similar privilege was granted to graduates of any other institution. This privilege gave the University an advantage over competing institutions and afforded students an inducement to complete the full course of study.

In 1898, when eleven candidates took the licensing examinations, Ricker proudly reported that three graduates and one special student from the

University ranked higher than the graduate of the École des Beaux-Arts, which was generally considered the "highest" institution of architectural instruction in the world. Five candidates failed, including one University graduate, who was eighth in rank and had never been a strong student.[60]

By 1903 the American Institute of Architects was ready to admit graduates from the University's Department of Architecture to membership without being required to pass any entrance examination. This privilege placed Illinois on an equal footing with M.I.T., Cornell, Pennsylvania, Columbia, and Harvard.[61]

A leader in the development of modern architectural education, Ricker gave long service to his department and made an important contribution to the advancement of American culture. In 1900 the University recognized Ricker's achievements by conferring on him an honorary degree of doctor of architecture.

## A New Departure

Enrollments in the College of Engineering began to climb dramatically in 1900–1 (see Table 8) and, along with growing strength in the departments, spurred efforts to elevate the quality of the programs. The first of several steps in this direction occurred on 16 December 1901, when the University Senate agreed to raise the number of high school credits required for admission to the University from thirty-six to forty starting in 1902–3, and to forty-two starting in 1905–6.[62]

This move precipitated an exchange between Draper and Ricker. While praising the work done in Ricker's college, Draper did not think it desirable that the college should be different from other colleges in entrance requirements. The college could be made stronger by insisting that it was not merely a technical school but a University college entitled to entrance requirements no lower than those of any other college.[63]

Ricker found Draper's high appreciation of the college "exceedingly gratifying," all the more since he thought that "the University authorities" had habitually applied "more inflexible tests and sterner criticism" to its management than to other colleges of the University. But Ricker did not think that the quality of the preparation in math and English was likely to be improved by tightening the admission requirements. He challenged the assumption that a literary training produced a broader mental development than an engineering training. The engineer already exerted wider influence in society than the literary theorist. The ability to compare and interpret the poems of Homer, Virgil, and Dante did not necessarily place one in a higher rank than the conduct of great business enterprises.

According to Ricker, if his college was a professional one, it was too much under the control of professors in other colleges, who were ignorant of engineering and how it had to compete with similar institutions. But if his college was a university college, it had outgrown its present organization. Ricker proposed dividing it into twelve or fifteen departments of study that would be arranged in groups, as in the other colleges, each group comprising the technical studies required for graduation in a professional course.[64]

The Draper–Ricker exchange aired basic issues. Draper viewed the college as willing to settle for less than the best. Ricker's narrower approach revealed an acute sensitivity to the status of engineering but little awareness of the value of the liberal arts.

On 30 June 1902 the second stage in the effort to upgrade the college began when the trustees adopted a motion by Trustee McKay that the board appoint a committee to investigate and report on the College of Engineering.[65] During August this committee visited eastern schools, and in September the committee asked Ricker for a statement of the needs of his college. McKay wanted a plan that would place the college on a footing equal to Cornell's. One trustee invited Ricker to indicate what would be needed to place the college "distinctly and confessedly at the head of all similar institutions in this country."[66]

Ricker responded by stating the needs. Illinois engineering graduates were as well equipped for their professional work as those of any other engineering college, he said, and maintenance of this rank was all that the state could properly be expected to provide. To solve the problem of overcrowding, Ricker wanted a separate building for the physics department, which no longer belonged to the College of Engineering. And since the state appropriation for equipment had been used partly to pay for the increased cost of buildings, he wanted an increased appropriation for equipment as well as for current expenses.

Low faculty salaries, said Ricker, were the most serious obstacle to the progress of the college. The salaries of assistants were fixed by those paid men of equal rank in other colleges of the University, where the supply exceeded the demand and the faculty could do nothing with market value beyond the University. The case was different for engineering, where under good business conditions the demand for its graduates exceeded the supply threefold. Faculty salaries in engineering should therefore be based on the salaries of engineering graduates in professional work. Conditions in other colleges should not control the relations of the College of Engineering to the engineering professions.

Ricker described the problem of low faculty salaries in engineering accurately, but low salaries prevailed throughout the entire University. Ricker's logic was impeccable if one granted his premise, but to grant his premise—

the market should be able to dictate University policy and thereby to advance the interests of one faculty group—risked undermining faculty morale.

Noting that the mathematics department had recently been transferred from Engineering to Science, Ricker said that since mathematics was "probably the most important foundation of all later engineering studies," it was important that math should be taught with reference to its future practical application and in such a manner that the student of average ability might reasonably understand it, both to make it more useful to the student and to prevent a failure rate that had sometimes amounted to 30 percent. Since mathematicians insisted that math be studied for itself, without regard to applications, Ricker wanted instruction in engineering mathematics placed under control of the engineering college, either by transferring it back to the college or by creating a department of engineering mathematics in the college.[67] And since the full year of physics was rarely pursued by nonengineers, Ricker wanted the Department of Physics transferred back to the College of Engineering.

Lastly, Ricker proposed reorganization. General Engineering Drawing, a required course that had grown large, should be made a distinct department instead of being continued under the charge of the dean. Because the engineering shops had become such a great enterprise, they should be made a department and separated from the Department of Mechanical Engineering, freeing Breckenridge for original research. Moreover, the Department of Municipal and Sanitary Engineering should be subdivided so that research in the testing and hydraulic laboratories could proceed independently instead of being restricted to class demonstration.[68]

In addition to making his own recommendations, Ricker asked department heads what they needed to place their units on a footing equal to that of Sibley College at Cornell (which was devoted to mechanical engineering and had gained fame under the direction of Robert H. Thurston; Cornell also had a college devoted to civil engineering).[69]

On 9 December the special committee reported to the full board on the needs of the college. The committee recommended appropriating a total of $530,250 for new buildings, laboratories, and equipment. At its 9 December meeting the board modified these proposals. The board's Committee on Legislative Appropriations recommended that the trustees request the next session of the legislature to provide, among other items, $150,000 for a physics laboratory and $75,000 for engineering equipment. The full board struck out the item for a physics building, adopted the report, and then agreed to ask for $300,000 in a separate bill for enlargement of the College of Engineering.[70]

The college quickly organized a campaign to lobby for the appropriation. Department heads were assigned tasks, with expenses met by an appeal to students, graduates, railways, manufacturers, and members of engineering societies. With so little time and money, and with the College of Agriculture competing for funds in Springfield, Ricker thought the college had little chance of winning. But the state legislature granted $150,000 for the next biennium for enlarging the engineering equipment.[71]

Draper was unwilling to see this money divided among the different departments on the basis of either courtesy or the supposed relative importance of the departments. It was to be divided, he declared, "through the most thorough examination of our relations to the mechanical and constructive industries and . . . with a purpose to lead all engineering colleges in the United Sates in some lines if we can not in all."[72]

The third step in the effort to upgrade the college came later in 1903. Ricker and Draper conferred with each other and with department heads on the disposition of the money provided. To be fair, Ricker submitted the minutes of his conferences with department heads to Draper along with his own recommendations. Ricker wanted to use the appropriation to improve undergraduate instruction, to place the college on a par with other well-equipped engineering colleges, and to enable it to engage in research in an engineering experiment station. Accordingly, he and the department heads unanimously recommended that the $150,000 appropriation be distributed among the various departments and the college as they indicated.[73]

Concluding that the faculty could not wisely spend $75,000 annually, Draper informed Ricker that some new use must be suggested for half the sum available. Although Breckenridge had previously advocated the establishment of a national engineering experiment station, nothing had come of it. Ricker, drawing on the agricultural model, now proposed an engineering experiment station.

The idea was new as applied to engineering, Ricker said, yet the manufacturing and railway interests in Illinois were as large and as important as the agricultural interests, and the need of such investigations in engineering was just as pressing. The proposed station was to engage in experimental work in engineering just as the Agricultural Experiment Station did in agriculture, to bring the college into intimate relations with manufacturing and railway interests and with professional engineers, to aid advanced work by students and faculty, to make commercial tests when advisable, and to publish a bulletin with its results. The new station was to be placed under the charge of a board of direction, consisting of the dean of the college and the chiefs of the departments, that was to operate along the same general lines as a similar board of the Agricultural Experiment Station. Ricker did not recommend a new building for the station; to avoid duplication and promote full utilization of equipment, he proposed that the machinery and apparatus in the different departments be used for research as well as instruction. The engineering experiment station was the readiest method that could be employed to enhance the reputation of the college and the fame of the University.[74]

Accordingly, at a meeting of the Board of Trustees on 8 December Draper recommended $30,000 for equipment to improve undergraduate instruction, with nearly half going to mechanical engineering and electrical engineering and the rest distributed among the other departments, $13,000 to purchase land to enlarge the engineering operations, $20,000 to erect and equip a steam engineering laboratory, and $10,000 to enlarge the machine shops or erect a new foundry. He also recommended establishment of an engineering experiment station, assigning the remainder of the appropriation ($77,000) to purchasing apparatus for advanced work in engineering research. This sum was to be divided among units in the college as he indicated. The board approved these recommendations and established the Standing Committee on the College of Engineering. The only other standing committees of the board related to the work of academic units were on agriculture and medicine.[75]

By 1903, then, the college had erected an impressive superstructure on its earlier groundwork. One evidence of this came in June 1903, when the University conferred honorary doctorates of engineering on three graduates of the college—John A. Ockerson (1873), Ira O. Baker (1874), and Samuel W. Stratton (1884)—and Richard P. Morgan, a civil engineer and member of the Board of Trustees (1891–97).

Another evidence, the capstone of the new structure, was the Engineering Experiment Station, the first of its kind in connection with an engineering college. The station was to be a public service research laboratory dealing with fundamental problems; it was designed to benefit manufacturing and industrial enterprises, add to the wealth of the state, and improve the health and comfort of the people of Illinois. On 2 June 1905 the Engineering Experiment Station was organized as a separate department of the University under the direction of Breckenridge, who was instrumental in developing many lines of experimental work of great importance to the industries of the state as well as to the railroads.[76]

In 1894, Engineering was the dominant college within the University. Ricker and his faculty built well, and in 1904 the college remained the colossus on the campus. For the University as a whole the results were mixed. On the one hand, the excellence of the work in engineering was well known. If engineers at Illinois were educated narrowly, they were well-trained within their own specialties. On the other hand, the commanding position of technical studies gave the institution a reputation as a school for engineers and delayed the full development of the arts and sciences that is essential to a complete university.

# NOTES

1. Peter Lundgren, "Engineering Education in Europe and the U.S.A., 1750–1930: The Rise to Dominance of School Culture and the Engineering Professions," *Annals of Science*, 47 (1990), 33–75, and Monte Calvert, *The Mechanical Engineer in America, 1830–1910: Professional Cultures in Conflict* (Baltimore: Johns Hopkins University Press, 1967).

2. George S. Emmerson, *Engineering Education: A Social History* (New York: Crane, Russak & Co., 1973), 132–65; Daniel H. Calhoun, *The American Civil Engineer: Origins and Conflict* (Cambridge, Mass.: Technology Press, 1960), 43–46. See also the series on engineering schools in *Engineering News*, 27 (19 March 1892) to 28 (22 December 1892), and James G. McGivern, *First Hundred Years of Engineering Education in the United States (1807–1907)* (Spokane: Gonzaga University Press, 1960).

3. *1st Report* (1868), 47–64.

4. *18th Report* (1896), 63. M.I.T. enrolled 890, Cornell, 700, Purdue, 345, Illinois, 320, Michigan, 300, Ohio State, 245, and Wisconsin, 215. See "Growth of Attendance at Engineering Schools," 11/1/1, B:1, F:Reports . . . 1900–7.

5. Ricker to Draper, 22 June 1897, 25 September 1901, 2/4/2, B:3, 8, F:Ricker.

6. Ricker to Draper, 23 May 1895; Baker to Draper, 24 May 1895, 2/4/2, B:1, F:Ricker, Baker.

7. In 1866, instructors at Rensselaer Polytechnic Institute averaged $2,400 and hoped to obtain $3,000 by 1868 (Raymond H. Merritt, *Engineering in American Society, 1850–1875* [Lexington: University Press of Kentucky, 1969], 114).

8. Ricker to Draper, 6 March 1895, 2/4/2, B:1, F:Ricker.

9. Ricker to Draper, 1 March 1904, 12 April 1895, 2/4/2, B:10, 1, F:Ricker.

10. M. E. Jansson, "A History of the *Technograph*," *Technograph*, 35 (March 1923), 142–43; Kenneth W. Cook, "History and Evaluation of the Illinois *Technograph*, 1885–1965" (master's thesis, University of Illinois, 1965).

11. Table 8 is from a document in 11/1/1, B:1, F:Reports . . . 1900–7, to which the Total column is added. The figures in this document do not always agree with those in other official records. But the differences are minor, and I cite the sources without altering them.

12. Table 9 is from the *Technograph*, 50 (September 1935), 7 (omitting the figures for three transient programs having a total of sixteen students). Totals in the article cited often do not add up correctly, and the comment about discrepancies in the previous note (applicable to Table 8) also applies here.

13. Ricker to Draper, 6 March 1895, n.d. [March 1895], 1 June, 18 November 1897, 19 April 1900, 2/4/2, B:1, 3, 4, 6, F:Ricker.

14. Ira O. Baker and Everett E. King, "A History of the College of Engineering of the University of Illinois, 1868–1945," 2 vols. (Urbana, n.d.), 1:247.

15. Ira O. Baker, *Report upon Pavements Recently Built by the Board of Local Improvements of the City of Chicago* (Urbana, 1916).

16. "The Engineering Schools of the United States," *Engineering News*, 28 (28 July 1892), 87; 28 (11 August 1892), 139 graph.

17. Trustee James E. Armstrong credited himself with this increment, which he considered a breakthrough in boosting small salaries for department heads (Armstrong to Stewart S. Howe, 13 January 1929, 26/4/1, J. E. Armstrong Folder).

18. Ricker to Draper, 23 May 1895 (two letters), 2/4/2, B:1, F:Ricker.
19. Breckenridge to Draper, 14 August 1894, 2/4/2, B:1, F:Breckenridge.
20. For slightly variant figures, see Breckenridge to Ricker, 2 October 1902, 2/4/2, B:9, F:Ricker; Ricker to Draper, 1 May 1903, 11/1/1, B:1, F:Reports . . . 1900–7; Breckenridge to Ricker, 16 May 1904, ibid., F:Mechanical Engineering Department, 1902–7.
21. Breckenridge to Draper, 7 March 1899, 2/4/2, B:5, F:Breckenridge. The enrollment data are from the source cited in n. 12.
22. Ricker to Draper, 22 May 1902, 11/1/1, Engineering Dean's Office, B:1, F:Reports . . . 1900–7.
23. A. Michal McMahon, *The Making of a Profession: A Century of Electrical Engineering Education in America* (New York: IEEE Press, 1984), 1–59, esp. 36, 40, 43–47.
24. The data are from a table prepared by Shea in 2/4/2, B:1, F:Shea.
25. *18th Report* (1896), 57–58.
26. Shea to Ricker, 2 March 1895, 2/4/2, B:1, F:Shea.
27. *18th Report* (1896), 73, 79–80; Shea to the Board of Trustees, 29 May, undated note (probably 29 May), 22 June 1895, 2/4/2, B:1, F:Shea; *18th Report* (1896), 43.
28. Shea to Draper, 16 September 1896, 2/4/2, B:2, F:L–Z; *18th Report* (1896), 184; Shea to Morgan, 27 September 1895; Morgan to Draper, 2, 14 October 1895, 2/4/1, B:10, F:Morgan; Draper to Morgan, 10 October 1895, 2/4/3. At the time of Shea's "final" resignation, 198 students were enrolled in physics courses and 53 in electrical engineering courses. Shea to Ricker, 28 September 1895, 2/4/1, B:2, F:Ricker.
29. *18th Report* (1896), 187, 188.
30. Carman to Draper, several letters, esp. 25 October 1895, 6 January and 29 April 1896, 2/5/15, Albert P. Carman Folder.
31. The petition is dated 5 April 1898; Ricker to Draper, 9 April, 23 May 1898, 2/4/2, B:4, F:Ricker.
32. Ricker to Draper, 30 May 1898, 2/4/2, B:4, F:Ricker.
33. *19th Report* (1898), 257–58.
34. Ibid., 266.
35. Ibid., 280; W. L. Pillsbury to Draper, 8 July 1898, 2/4/2, B:4, F:P–Z; *20th Report* (1901), 1.
36. Carman to Ricker, 8 June 1899, 2/4/2, B:5, F:Ricker.
37. William S. Aldrich, "Engineering Education and the State University," *Proceedings of the . . . Annual Meeting of the Society for the Promotion of Engineering Education*, 2 (1894), 268–92.
38. The former appeared in *Cassier's Magazine*, 18 (July 1900), 194–97; the latter in *Engineering Magazine*, 21 (September 1901), 839–62.
39. Ricker to Draper, 1 June 1901, 2/4/2, B:7, F:Ricker.
40. Draper to Forbes, 16 October 1902, 2/4/3; Forbes to Draper, 17 October 1902, 2/4/2, B:9, F:Forbes.
41. Ricker to Draper, 22 May 1902, 11/1/1, B:1, F:Reports . . . 1900–7; also Brooks to Draper in 1902–3, 2/4/2, B:9, F:Brooks.
42. Brooks to Ricker, 17 February 1904, 2/4/2, B:10, F:Brooks; Draper to Brooks, 17 February 1904, 2/4/3; Brooks to Draper, 17 February, 5 March 1904, 2/4/2, B:10, F:Brooks; Draper to Edmund J. James, 19 April 1905, 2/5/1, B:6, F:D. Enrollments

reflected the turmoil in the department. Electrical engineering attracted 91 students in 1894–95 and 97 a year later. With Shea's departure, concerns about Carman, and Swenson fomenting discord, enrollments declined for the next five years. With the arrival of Brooks the flow of students reversed course, reaching 172 in 1903–4.

43. James K. Finch, *The Story of Engineering* (Garden City, N.Y.: Doubleday & Co., 1960), 297–98, 510–11.

44. Ricker to Draper, 6 March 1895, 2/4/2, B:2, F:Ricker.

45. James W. Phillips, comp. and ed., *Celebrating TAM's First Hundred Years: A History of the Department of Theoretical and Applied Mechanics, University of Illinois at Urbana-Champaign, 1890–1990* (Urbana, 1990); idem, *Arthur Newell Talbot* (Urbana, 1944).

46. Talbot to Draper, 28 September 1900, 2/4/2, B:7, F:Talbot.

47. For slightly variant figures on enrollments, see the document on Municipal and Sanitary Engineering, 11/1/1, B:1, F:Reports to Engineering Faculty, 1895–1903.

48. See, for example, Talbot's essay in *Paving Brick and Paving Brick Clays of Illinois*, ed. C. W. Rolfe, R. C. Purdy, A. N. Talbot, and I. O. Baker. Illinois State Geological Survey, *Bulletin*, 9 (Urbana, 1908), 47–131.

49. J. A. Chewning, "William Robert Ware at MIT and Columbia," *Journal of Architectural Education*, 33 (November 1979), 25 (quotation), 26–27; Anthony Alofsin, "'Tempering the École': Nathan Ricker at the University of Illinois, Langford Warren at Harvard, and Their Followers" (typescript in author's possession), 1; and Turpin C. Bannister, ed., *The Architect at Mid-Century: Evolution and Achievement*. Report of the Commission for the Survey of Education and Registration of the American Institute of Architects, vol. 1 (New York: Reinhold Publishing Corp., 1954), 81–104.

50. Alofsin, "Tempering the École," 1–2; Roula Geraniotis, "The University of Illinois and German Architectural Education," *Journal of Architectural Education*, 38 (Summer 1985), 17.

51. Alofsin, "Tempering the École," 2–3; Ricker, "The School of Architecture at the University of Illinois," *Building Budget*, 3 (October 1887), 124, quoted in Geraniotis, "The University of Illinois and German Architectural Education," 17; *15th Report* (1890), 207–11; *Catalogue* (1894–95), 41.

52. Chewning, "William Robert Ware at MIT and Columbia," 25.

53. Turpin C. Bannister, "Pioneering in Architectural Education," *Journal of the American Institute of Architects*, 22 (August 1953), 78–79.

54. Ricker to Draper, 31 May 1895, 2/4/2, B:1, F:Ricker.

55. Ricker to Draper, 6 March, 18 May 1895; 28 January 1898, 2/4/2, B:1, 3, F:Ricker.

56. Thomas E. O'Donnell, "The Ricker Manuscript Translations," *Pencil Points*, 7 (October 1926), 621–22. The bound volumes of Ricker's translations are in the Ricker Library of Art and Architecture at the University.

57. *Brickbuilder*, 10 (1901), 124–28, 143–47, 165–71.

58. Bannister, "Pioneering in Architectural Education," 77.

59. Alofsin, "Tempering the École," 4–5. Lynn M. Allen's "Nathan Clifford Ricker and His Students: A Legacy in Architectural Education" (master's thesis, Western Illinois University, 1971) traces the careers of Ricker's students who settled in western Illinois after graduating. A copy is in the Ricker Library of Art and

Architecture.

60. Ricker to Draper, 2 May, 30 June 1898, 2/4/2, B:4, F:Ricker.
61. Ricker to Draper, 4 May 1903, 2/4/2, B:9, F:Ricker.
62. 4/2/1, 23 November to 16 December 1901. In 1895 a faculty committee had rec-
    ommended equalizing the requirements for admission to all four of the Universi-
    ty's colleges, but in 1897 a report on entrance requirements for engineering
    colleges included Illinois among the engineering schools with the highest
    requirements (Ira O. Baker to Draper, 28 March 1895, Baker to Draper, 8 June
    1897, 2/4/2, B:2, 3, F:Baker).
63. Draper to Ricker, 17 December 1901, 2/4/3, B:7.
64. Ricker to Draper, 31 December 1901, 2/4/2, B:8, F:Ricker.
65. *21st Report* (1902), 288.
66. Breckenridge to Draper, 18 August 1902, 2/4/2, B:8, F:A–F; Ricker to Draper,
    16 October 1902, Ricker to Special Committee, 8 September 1902, 2/4/2, B:9,
    F:Ricker.
67. In 1911 a subcommittee of the International Commission on the Teaching of
    Mathematics reported that mathematics teachers generally agreed that mathe-
    matics should be taught as a science by professional mathematicians and not as a
    tool by engineers. See Mann, *Study of Engineering Education*, 39.
68. Ricker to the Special Committee, 8 September 1902, Ricker to Draper, 9, 18 Sep-
    tember 1902, 2/4/2, B:9, F:Ricker. On the need to break up each professional
    course into specialties or departments, also see Ricker to Draper, 27 October 1903,
    2/4/2, B:10, F:Ricker.
69. See the letters in 2/4/2, B:9, F:Ricker.
70. *22nd Report* (1904), 31–33.
71. Ricker to Draper, 21, 24 February 1903, 2/4/2, B:9, F:Ricker.
72. *22nd Report* (1904), 72.
73. Ricker to Draper, 19, 27 November 1903, 2/4/2, B:10, F:Ricker.
74. Ricker to Draper, 7, 8 October 1903, accompanied by Ricker, "Results of Con-
    ferences," and Ricker, "Extension of Equipment and the Work of the College of
    Engineering," 2/4/2, B:10, F:Ricker; Ricker, "The Story of a Life," 29–30, in
    12/2/1, Fine and Applied Arts, Architecture, B:15, F:Ricker.
75. *22nd Report* (1904), 238–41, 104, 243.
76. Lester P. Breckenridge, "The Engineering Experiment Station and Its Relation
    to Illinois Industries," *Journal of the Western Society of Engineers*, 14 (August 1909),
    487–528, Russell H. Chittenden, *History of the Sheffield Scientific School of Yale Uni-
    versity*, 2 vols. (New Haven: Yale University Press, 1928), 2:346. For a description
    and illustrations of the station at a later period, see *The College of Engineering and
    Engineering Experiment Station of the University of Illinois: A Pictorial History*. Uni-
    versity of Illinois, *Bulletin*, 16 (6 January 1919), no. 19.

# CHAPTER 7

# NEW VENTURES

In 1894 the University was on the threshold of a new era. Although the academic work was still largely conducted within four colleges, some of it began to spill over the boundaries. Art and design and music carved out separate identities, while the Library School made its appearance as a vital component of the institution. These units helped create the structure of a complete university.

## ART AND DESIGN

In 1894 art and design was a department in the College of Literature and Arts, but the subject was not part of the four academic groups in the college. The work was well established under Frank F. Frederick (b. 1866), a native of Massachusetts who had graduated from the Massachusetts Normal Art School in 1890 and joined the faculty that fall as a professor of industrial art.

The purposes of the department were to afford students the opportunity to learn the freehand drawing techniques they might need for other courses and to offer "such as have a talent or taste for art the best facilities for pursuing studies in industrial designing or other branches of fine arts."[1] A four-year course was adapted as necessary for students from every part of the University. The Art and Design Gallery, a large room containing thirteen full-sized casts of celebrated sculptures, forty statues of reduced size, and a large number of busts, bas-reliefs, and other works, was of special value to art students.

In 1895 a new purpose was added, that of offering potential teachers of drawing opportunity for study, and the department listed thirteen courses as available. Edward J. Lake (b. 1871), a native of Scotland who grew up in Wisconsin and graduated from the University in 1895 with a B.S. in architecture, joined the faculty. The program remained substantially the same for four years. In 1898–99 Stanley M. Lewis assisted Frederick while Lake took a leave to study at the Pratt Institute in Brooklyn, and a total of twelve courses were offered.

In 1899–1900 the department announced that its aim was to offer courses that would assist students in their University studies, cultivate their aesthetic taste, and equip them for future art work. The new departure emancipated the study of art from its close ties with industrial design. To facilitate this goal, twenty courses were made available.

In 1897 Newton A. Wells (b. 1852) arrived in Urbana. He had taken a bachelor of painting degree at Syracuse University, taught drawing at Union College and Syracuse University from 1877 to 1889, and in 1889–90 served as dean of the School of Art at Western Reserve University. In 1886 he studied at the Académie Julien in Paris for four months, and from 1895 to 1897 for another twenty months. While in Paris he won the competition to decorate the rotunda of the University's new library building. By 1898, having executed some of the work, he returned to Paris to prepare a series of designs for the mural compositions. In the fall of 1899, as these neared completion, Wells was appointed professor of the history and practice of painting to serve one semester of each year at $1,000.

The courses as well as the faculty of the department remained substantially the same for a few years. In 1902, when Frederick was on leave, Isabel E. Jones, an 1891 alumna who had studied art at the Pratt Institute, was called in as an instructor. She taught still-life painting.

From 1894 to 1904 the work in art and design made unusual progress. Enrollments rose from 117 at the beginning to 454 at the end of the period, an average of 298 students a year. A high proportion were women. Kinley rated the instruction highly; in 1897 he proposed for the near future a school of fine arts with a separate faculty, a degree, and a separate building.

But the department lacked apparatus, its rooms were terribly dilapidated, and faculty salaries were low. In 1898 Frederick requested a salary increase equal to that of the heads of other departments in the College of Literature and Arts. A year later Kinley recommended an increase for Lake; when Draper would not agree to it, Kinley offered to take the matter to the trustees. In 1900 Wells was offered a professorship at the Chicago Institute at $3,000, with increases to follow. At the time Wells was employed half-time at the rate of $2,000 a year. He preferred to stay in Urbana, and was appointed full-time at $2,000 a year.

Both Frederick and Wells had what Kinley saw as the artist's disregard for administrative detail, and they showed little interest in general University matters. Also, their theories of art differed. By 1903–4 harmony between the two was lacking. Wells wanted to transfer to architecture. In 1904 he went to that department as a professor of architectural decoration. By then the art and design department had grown to the point that it had to refuse applications for admission.

## THE SCHOOL OF MUSIC

For some time after the University opened, music was not included in courses leading to a degree in any part of the University. In 1892, however, Acting Regent Burrill recommended that music be included in the regular system of instruction, and by June 1894 a proposal had been made to introduce such work. We know little about the plan except that it borrowed from the University of Michigan's program. No space was available for a "musical department," but Burrill did think it was important to offer instruction in music theory and history and to make private music lessons available. And music would help make the University attractive to women students.[2]

In 1894–95 the study of music entered the curriculum. A so-called Department of Music offered two courses, History of Music and Theory of Music, as well as instrumental and vocal lessons. The courses were intended to provide a thorough foundation for a music education and to prepare students for admission to any school devoted exclusively to the study of music.[3] President Draper supported the effort to develop a department of music, which he hoped would in time be self-sustaining.

Shortly after taking office Draper appointed Charles W. Foster (b. 1854), director of the Foster Concert Trio and the Foster School of Music in Champaign, to supervise the musical work. A native of England, Foster was educated by private tutors before entering the University with the class of 1874. He took an academic course, but as a student he organized and conducted the first University orchestra and led the male chorus. At his family's insistence he later studied law, but his first love was the violin, and reportedly he was once a member of the London Philharmonic Orchestra.

Foster's duties were to organize a University orchestra, to aid in reorganizing the Mandolin and Guitar Club and the Glee Club, to train these organizations and with them to furnish music at meetings held under the University's authority, and to give occasional musical entertainments. He was to be paid $300 a year.[4] Foster's wife taught piano, and Mary H. Steele taught voice.

Foster wished to inculcate in students the great classical tradition of music. But he became restive; in the spring of 1895 he informed Draper that he would be pleased to stay if music were made a regular part of University study with examinations. Without such, music was only a "diversion and amusement for the young ladies," and his position was "superfluous." He advised abolishing it, saying that Michigan and other universities made music part of the regular course of study, and his wife asserted that the culture acquired through the study of music was at least equal to the culture derived from the study of a modern language. "Music study," she added, "is the study of a language and a literature." At the end of the year the Fosters resigned.[5]

Meanwhile, both Dean Kinley and President Draper had urged the introduction of the study of music. The board advised Draper to prepare a plan, and he reported that it would be possible to establish a department of music at a cost not to exceed $1,500 to $1,600 a year.[6]

## Launching the School

On 12 June 1895 the board established a School of Music (for some time official publications used *department* and *school* interchangeably) and approved the appointment of Walter Howe Jones as assistant professor at a salary of $700 a year and half of the music fees in excess of $700. Jones (b. 1862), who was born in Hastings, Minnesota, and attended high school in Clinton, Iowa, had studied music in both Chicago and Berlin. Since 1892 he had been professor of piano at DePauw University in Indiana. The board also authorized the appointment of an assistant in vocal music at $500 for ten months.[7]

Both Kinley and Draper praised the progress Jones made in his first year, and in 1896 he was promoted to professor of music.[8] As head or director, Jones devised a curriculum that included History of Music, Theory of Music, Courses for the Piano, Courses for the Organ, and Courses for the Voice. Students in music could receive a certificate of graduation by completing the entire course specified for their instrument or voice, passing an examination in the history of music, and writing a thesis on some musical subject.

Students in music paid no matriculation or term fee, but they paid fees for music lessons and also for classes in harmony, counterpoint, and fugue, each class of which admitted only four students. Other students could take vocal and instrumental lessons for a fee, but music students paid higher fees than the other students (presumably because they received more lessons).

Draper proposed appointing a violin teacher, but he also wanted this person to lead the band and to assist in the music work generally. In 1896 a course in violin was added; a year later courses called University Orchestra and University Oratorio Society (later, University Choral Society) were introduced.

The faculty was almost evenly divided between men and women. Jones recruited many of his former DePauw colleagues. He shared the piano instruction with Jessie Y. Fox (b. 1873), an 1895 graduate of DePauw who arrived in 1897;

he himself taught all the organ courses. Jones also directed the University Band, the University Orchestra, and the Glee Club, and he organized the Oratorio Society. A composer, Jones wrote the words and music for several University songs and the music (but not the words) for "Illinois," a song that begins "By thy rivers gently flowing, Illinois" and celebrates the state rather than the University. Adeline W. Rowely (b. 1873), another 1895 graduate of DePauw, taught voice from 1895 to 1897; her successor was Alison M. Fernie (b. 1866). A native of England, Fernie had studied at the Royal Academy of Music in London, the Philadelphia Academy of Music, and in Germany, France, and Italy before heading the vocal department at DePauw. Fernie made a deep impact on the musical life of the campus. From 1899 to 1901 Emma Q. Fuller (b. 1872), who had studied at the American Conservatory of Music in Chicago, was a voice instructor. Draper had special difficulties in obtaining a satisfactory violin teacher. His first four appointments in this area were misfits, none of whom cooperated with the teachers in the other music departments.

Since enrollments in the department were few and almost entirely female, music remained peripheral at the University. Trustee Thomas J. Smith of Champaign, a former attorney for the Wabash Railroad Company, was eager to remedy the situation. In April 1897, at the second board meeting he attended, he called for reorganization of the music department, proposing that it be made a college, that no greater tuition be charged to students in music than to students in other departments, and that diplomas and degrees be granted to graduates of the college. At a June board meeting, Smith invited four Champaign women to reinforce his recommendations.[9]

He was premature and perhaps also brash; the trustees rebuffed his proposal. While affirming that "first-class courses in musical instruction" should be available to those with proper preparation and that diplomas and degrees should be conferred for satisfactory completion of such courses, the board concluded that "to offer such courses without extra compensation would be unwise and detrimental to the best interests of the University." Class instruction in vocal music to students of the University should be continued free, but "the School of Music should be conducted on the same basis as the Schools of Law, Medicine, etc., and be as nearly self-supporting as circumstances may permit."[10]

In the fall of 1897, however, on Jones's recommendation, the faculty approved a slate of courses leading to a degree in music. Under the new policy, the preparatory course in music was open to anyone desirous of taking it, while the collegiate course was open to two groups—those who desired to become candidates for the degree of bachelor of music and those who desired to do special work in music but were not working toward a degree in music. The requirements for admission to the B.Mus. degree program were made identical with those for admission to the College of Literature and Arts, except that in place of four years of Latin a student could substitute one year of Latin and three years of French or German. The faculty announced a list of credits required for the B.Mus. Special students could obtain admission by satisfying the music faculty of their fitness for pursuing such work, with respect to both general education and musical preparation. In addition to music, special students were required to pursue other lines of study sufficient to fill their spare time. Students who completed at least three years of work satisfactorily were to receive a certificate showing the amount of work done. Credit was to be given for work in the University Orchestra and the University Oratorio Society.[11]

In 1898 these requirements went into effect. Graduation with the B.Mus. degree required 130 semester hours, 80 of which were to be in music. Students enrolled in the department paid music fees but not semester fees. In 1899 the University awarded its first B.Mus., to Alice Putnam.[12]

In June Thomas Smith resumed his campaign by introducing a resolution that the board adopted in September. One part stated that all matriculated students were entitled to instruction in all departments of the School of Music at no higher rates than were charged students in other departments of the University. Another part held that all persons desiring to enter the School of Music were subject to the rules in force in other departments of the University touching qualifications and course of study. An examination was to be held as in other departments to ensure that each pupil "shall maintain the required standing." These new policies were to become effective 1 September 1901.[13]

Salaries in music were low, and dependence on fees made instructors peculiarly vulnerable to shifts in student numbers and sentiments. In March 1900, for example, Jennie Y. Fox requested a raise, noting that she was being paid $400 and 50 percent of all above that amount received from fees, which amounted to $360, making her total compensation $760, for which she had to teach thirty-four hours a week. During the year she had taught seventy-seven students, all women except two or three. Fox asked for $800, a sum needed to meet her living expenses, and no percentage from fees. Jones endorsed her request.[14]

Jones also was discontented with his salary, which was lower than that of some of his assistants and considerably lower than that of other full professors, and in October 1900 he repeated an earlier request that Draper reconsider the matter and take it to the board. In December the board filed his letter without action, whereupon Jones informed Draper that nominally he was head of music but actually he had been ignored without being given any reason for this treatment. If his work was not satisfactory, he added, he should have been told so long ago. If he did not receive the position and salary he deserved, he would resign effective 1 September 1901.[15]

Before Jones could resign Draper fired him. To Draper, Jones discredited himself by his conduct in June 1900. He had accepted an invitation to appear on the program of the Illinois Music Teachers' Association in Springfield on condition that a Steinway piano be provided. When Allen Spencer, the program chairman, declined to pay to have the piano brought from Chicago, Jones asked that his name be removed from the program. Spencer, who believed that Jones was using the Steinway as an excuse for withdrawing, threatened to humiliate Jones before the convention by reading his letter of withdrawal. Parties to the conflict complained to Draper, who thought that an artist had a right to set conditions but did not approve of Jones's conduct. There are pianos other than the Steinway, he wrote, "and if you cannot use one [of the others] you are not fit to represent the University in a State meeting."[16]

This episode was probably the last straw. In 1896, Draper had described the work of Jones's first year as highly satisfactory from an artistic point of view. The implication was entirely clear: Jones lacked administrative ability. In any case, Draper found Jones wanting. In March 1900, rehearsing the great difficulty he had had in getting a department of music started, he said that the problem was in finding musical artists who were also managers. Draper wanted a director who was strong on the business side and who could teach some instrument without excelling in musical work.[17]

## A New Director

In December 1900 the trustees agreed to ask the legislature for $5,000 for maintenance of the School of Music, and they appointed a committee to consider reorganization of the school. In January 1901 Draper hired Frederick L. Lawrence as director of the school and professor in charge of the piano department at a salary of $1,800. In March the board accepted the resignations of Jones and Fox as of the end of the academic year.[18]

Lawrence (b. 1869) was a fine pianist who had studied at the Royal Conservatory of Music in Leipzig in 1896–97 and taught for seven years in the music school at Northwestern University before becoming director of the School of Music at Carleton College in Minnesota. He had a reputation for business ability.

Lawrence made little change in the program of study. The number of offerings greatly increased as courses with several component parts became separate courses. In 1903 Lawrence introduced ear-training and sightsinging courses as well as Public School Methods.

Under the new regime the faculty was largely reconstituted. With various assistants Lawrence led the work in piano. Almeda F. Mann (b. 1874) came with him from Carleton as instructor of piano and director of the Musical Preparatory School. Eunice D. Daniels (b. 1865, wife of the head of the philosophy department), who had been a private teacher of piano and harmony in Boston and Lowell, Massachusetts, became an instructor of piano. In 1901–2 Maurice Eisner of Champaign (b. 1880), who went to Europe at age fourteen to study piano and attended the Royal Academy of Music in Budapest for six years, taught piano. Eugenie Glodery (b. 1875), formerly of Carleton College, replaced Eisner, and a year later Bertha I. Howe succeeded Glodery.

In 1901 the voice faculty was strengthened by the addition of Benjamin W. Breneman (b. 1873) and his wife May Emory Breneman (b. 1872). Both had studied with private teachers in New York and in Dresden and Paris and had engaged in singing and teaching in New York City for years before joining the faculty. May Breneman had also studied in Berlin and taught at Millersville Normal School in Pennsylvania. In 1903 Mary Wendell Greene (b. 1866) and Constance Barlow-Smith joined the voice faculty.

In 1902 George F. Schwartz (b. 1872) became instructor of violin and theory. A graduate of the College of Wooster, Schwartz had studied at the Cincinnati College of Music and had taught in conservatories for several years. He was the first person at Illinois to make a success of the violin and theory work, and he served on the faculty until he retired in 1938.[19]

The cost of instruction in music was a continuing problem. When the board's decision to make tuition in music free to matriculated Illinois students became effective in 1901, the music faculty objected on the grounds that the policy seemed to extend the privilege to students without musical preparation. Responding to the protest, Draper declared it "more than doubtful if the Board intended that free instruction should be furnished in preparatory and elementary work any more than in academic lines of study." Draper wanted the division between preparatory and collegiate departments in the School of Music fixed by the faculty at a point that assumed two years of previous competent instruction and serious musical study. All students in the preparatory department were to be charged the prescribed fees; in the collegiate department tuition was to be free to matriculated residents of Illinois who carried regular University work.[20]

Thus the School of Music emerged. It made a modest contribution to the intellectual life of the campus. Many of the relatively young instructors in the school had received part of their education on the Continent. The faculty carried a heavy load and were poorly paid. Apparently few students registered for degrees in music. Most students of music were "specials," and the vast majority were women. By 1904, however, the study of music had moved from the periphery to the mainstream, and the School of Music was well positioned for the years ahead.[21]

## THE LIBRARY SCHOOL

In 1897 Katharine L. Sharp transferred her library school at the Armour Institute from Chicago to the University. Melvil Dewey was her mentor; Sharp was his favorite pupil and one of a coterie of women librarians devoted to Dewey. Sharp made her mark as director of the Library School at the University. Her work there is best seen as an extension of Dewey's remarkable influence on the library profession.

Dewey's great contribution to American intellectual and cultural development was the promotion of public libraries and the training of librarians. In the late nineteenth century public libraries grew rapidly in response to changing conditions in America. In 1876 a government report listed 3,682 libraries of 300 volumes or more containing 12,276,964 volumes, whereas in 1896 the statistics revealed 7,191 such libraries with 34,596,258 volumes. At the end of 1900, according to one estimate, the nation had 8,000 libraries of 300 volumes or more with a total of 40,000,000 volumes.[22]

This dramatic expansion created a demand for trained library personnel. Librarians had long been initiated into their careers by the apprentice system, learning the necessary skills by in-service training and by reading the relevant literature. This system was endorsed by leading librarians, who regarded a well-managed library as the best school for educating librarians.[23]

Melvil Dewey pioneered in advocating a new approach to the training of librarians. A prime mover in establishing the American Library Association (ALA) in 1876, Dewey was the first secretary of the ALA and managing editor of its *Library Journal.* The time had at last come, he wrote in the inaugural issue, when a librarian could speak of his occupation as a profession.[24] Although the ALA was reluctant to endorse his proposal, Dewey urged a formal library school to train people for librarianship.

A driven man devoted to causes, the greatest of which was the public library, Dewey was born in 1851 in West Adams, New York. He was a child of the Burned-Over District, an area in which repeated religious revivals had spawned a wide variety of reforms. At an early age the boy became preoccupied with efficiency and standardization as a way of redeeming the time. His evangelical heritage helped instill in him an obsessive desire for reform as a means of uplifting humanity—and a fierce determination to win a fortune.[25]

While a student at Amherst College, starting in 1870, Dewey made the spread of public libraries stocked with good books his mission field. As a library assistant he hit upon the idea of using decimals to number a classification of all human knowledge in print, and in March 1876, after developing the plan, he sought a copyright on the Dewey Decimal System.

In April 1876 Dewey moved to Boston, where he established commercial enterprises designed to make his fortune and promoted free public libraries. The youngest among the founders of the ALA, Dewey was at odds with the elders who had long dominated the organization. By 1883 not only was he alienated from the leading Boston librarians, he was without remunerative work, and in debt.

President F. A. P. Barnard rescued Dewey by inviting him to become librarian-in-chief of Columbia College. Dewey accepted. Although the college was almost hermetically sealed against women,[26] Dewey hired as assistants seven women who had just graduated from Wellesley College. He regarded librarianship as an excellent profession for college-bred women. They had the right character for a library, were grateful for jobs, and were willing to work for less pay than men. By recruiting a work force with high character for low cost, Dewey contributed significantly to the feminization of librarianship.[27]

Dewey transformed a dormant library into a model college library, but his arrogant manner, lack of tact, and drain on the Columbia treasury irritated both faculty and trustees, and on 20 December 1888 he submitted his resignation from Columbia. On 1 January 1889 he took over as secretary of the Board of Regents of the University of the State of New York and director of the New York State Library in Albany.

Dewey transferred the School of Library Economy from Columbia to the State Library at no cost to the state, and the regents authorized the New York State Library School to award degrees in library science. At first, admission required only a high school education, and most of the students were women. The emphasis of the two-year program was on practice rather than theory.

Although he gave little time to his school, Dewey "reigned over his admiring staff and students like a benevolent but imperious lord."[28] He rushed in at the last minute for his lectures, paced back and forth, talked rapidly, and made the case for libraries as agents of conservative reforms while also inculcating "library spirit," meaning a commitment to service. Most students were in awe of Dewey. They were aware of his influence and shared a sense of being pioneers in library history. Dewey created disciples who later built up his image by repeating bromides remembered from their student days, such as the exhortation to "work at 'concentrating cordiality.'"[29]

Although Dewey had conceived the ALA motto, "the best reading for the largest number at the least expense," he emphasized technique and procedures rather than a thorough knowledge of books and their potential audiences. He advised librarians, "look to your position as a high-grade business one." For Dewey, the spirit of the library should be that of a merchant anxious to please customers.[30]

In September 1890 Katharine Sharp entered the New York State Library School. She was quickly recognized as easily the best student in the second class, which produced many library leaders. Sharp earned a B.L.S in 1892 and became Dewey's devoted disciple. He was the prime mover behind the establishment of the Department of Library Science at the Armour Institute (later the Armour Institute of Technology) in Chicago, of which his friend Frank W. Gunsaulus, a Congregational minister, was president. When Gunsaulus asked Dewey to recommend "the best man in America to start the library and the library school and carry out your ideas," Dewey replied, "the best man in America is a woman," meaning Sharp. In September 1893 the department opened under Sharp's direction. It was the first library school in the Midwest and the fourth in the nation.[31]

Sharp's school was designed to train library assistants. A high school education or its equivalent plus an examination in general literature, general history, and current events was required for admission to the course, which in 1895 was extended to two years. The Armour Institute department imitated the school at Albany, laying even greater emphasis on technique, the practical things of library life, but paying no attention to the purposes that technique was designed to further. The school taught what was called library economy—ordering, reference, selection of books, shelf listing, cataloging, loan systems, classification, binding, and bibliography. Students also did apprentice work. The program was elementary, but the dearth of books on the subject and the lack of uniformity in library practice allowed little more. Sharp wanted an expanded program and higher standards; she even suggested a four-year course culminating in a degree, a radical proposal for the time.[32]

Sharp was restive at Armour Institute because the school could not meet the demands made on it without larger quarters and more generous equipment. The available evidence does not clearly reveal who initiated the move, but it seems that Sharp decided to relocate in consultation with Dewey and with the goodwill of President Gunsaulus, and that President Draper endorsed the result. As late as 15 March 1897 Sharp had taken no overt action to reposition the department, and to this time Draper had said nothing about establishing a library school.[33]

On 10 April 1897 Dewey wrote Draper, whom he had known in Albany, about the University's adopting Sharp and her department. Dewey's description of Sharp as "the best woman librarian in America" impressed Draper, who replied he was glad that Sharp was willing to come. He would like to have the library school at Illinois, he added, but wanted to postpone its opening for a year. What Dewey and Sharp desired, Draper informed Sharp, was precisely what he desired.[34]

Interviewing Sharp in Chicago, Draper learned that the University of Wisconsin had invited her to resettle in Madison, where Sharp had directed a summer school for the Wisconsin Library Association in 1895 and 1896. At Wisconsin Sharp would have been director of the library school but not librarian, a division she did not like. She wanted control over both the school and the library, and she wanted library school teachers to engage in library practice. Draper countered by offering Sharp an appointment at Illinois on the same basis as any other University professor and with whatever assistance might be required to manage both the library and the school, subject to the board's approval.[35]

Sharp visited Urbana and agreed to accept the Illinois offer to become head librarian, professor of library economy, and director of the library school at $2,000 a year. She was to have three assistants in the administration of the library and the work of the school.

In September 1897 the Library School was transferred to the University and the boundaries of its usefulness were broadened. Sharp saw the move as beneficial: the school now had ready access to a larger collection of books, was housed in a fine new building, and had the advantage of a university atmosphere. The State Library School, as Sharp invariably called it, offered a four-year course of study leading to the B.L.S. divided between two years of regular college work and two years of technical library work. Students were encouraged to complete four years of college before applying for admission. This high standard was justified on the grounds that conditions in library work were rapidly changing.

The school offered to provide instruction in each department of library administration, to teach "elaborate methods" to enable students to work in large libraries where bibliographic exactness was required, and to emphasize the "higher side" of library work. Its purpose was to graduate librarians not only trained in technical details but also filled with an appreciation of their high calling to furnish "the best reading to the greatest number at the least cost."[36]

Sharp was thirty-two when she arrived in Urbana. She exhibited great personal charm but could be severe when occasion demanded. Amply endowed with qualities that Draper admired, she secured his prior approval before acting on even minor matters. An efficient administrator, she was adept at flattering Draper. The two had cordial personal relations.

Library School policy called for each faculty member to be engaged in active library work so that the instruction would be practical, and the faculty and staff, cut from the same cloth as Sharp, personified Dewey's idea of the type of persons best suited for librarianship: college-educated, high-minded, and altruistic women. Such women had limited opportunity for paid employment; forced to choose a career or marriage, few married.

In assembling a faculty and staff, Sharp looked for persons with "characteristics which would make a desirable librarian," and usually found them in her former students.[37] She brought two colleagues with her to Urbana. Margaret Mann, a native of Cedar Rapids, Iowa, who had attended Englewood High School in Chicago, had been a student in the library school at Armour Institute. Mary L. Jones, holder of a B.L.S. and Sharp's former Albany classmate, came from the University of Nebraska library, but resigned after one semester. A year later Maude W. Straight joined the faculty. A native of Illinois, she had attended Oak Park High School, graduated from Wellesley in 1892, and completed the library course at Armour Institute four years later. She served as a librarian in Dubuque and Oshkosh until 1898. In 1900 she married Albert P.

Carman, professor of physics at the University. Grace O. Edwards, whose father was a wealthy businessman in La Crosse, Wisconsin, graduated from Wellesley in 1894 with high aims and ideals. She attended the Armour library school in 1896–97, earned a B.L.S. at the University in 1898, and joined the faculty and staff that year, serving until 1901. Isadore G. Mudge was born in Brooklyn and earned a Ph.B. at Cornell. In 1900 she earned a B.L.S. at the New York State Library School, and that fall she joined the faculty. In 1903 she left to become head librarian at Bryn Mawr College, later becoming the reference librarian at Columbia University. Frances Simpson, a native of Burtonsville, New York, took a bachelor's degree at Northwestern in 1884, after which she received a master's degree and studied one year in Berlin. She taught high school for several years, spent the year 1898–99 in the Library School, and then worked as a cataloger at the Chicago Institute. In 1903, after earning a B.L.S. at the University, she joined the faculty. Simpson spent her entire career at the University. In 1912 she became assistant director of the school, serving in that capacity until her retirement in 1931.[38]

A number of Sharp's younger colleagues were revisers, people who checked for accuracy the cataloging done by students. Sharp's appointment of women who graduated from the Library School led President Draper to suggest that it would be well to hire teachers trained in different schools. In principle Sharp agreed, but in practice she found "our own graduates better able to meet our conditions here and to live contentedly in this part of the country," and that "the available women are superior to most of the men who enter the library field."[39] She hired three men as clerks during their student days, and she tried but failed to hire two men to the staff and faculty.[40] In 1903 Francis K. W. Drury, an assistant librarian at Rutgers for several years who had studied one summer at the New York State Library School and wished to complete his training at Illinois, was made an order assistant in the library. In 1905 he earned a B.L.S. and became the first man to teach in the Library School.[41]

Sharp wanted to elevate the standards of library school education, but the curriculum of the Library School started by emphasizing the practical side of library work and remained basically the same for five years. The catalog listed the library courses under the heading of Library Science, a term that was coming into use but that some regarded as bearing little relation to reality. In the absence of suitable textbooks, instruction was given largely by lecture and laboratory (i.e., the University library).

Juniors, first-year library students, took elementary courses in library economy, reference, bibliography, and apprentice work, along with Selection of Books. Elementary Library Economy covered the logical library routine: order, accession, classification, shelving, cataloging, loan, binding, and library handwriting. Seniors took advanced and comparative technical courses in the four elementary subjects, plus Selection of Books, History of Libraries, and

Book-Making. They were required to write a thesis or prepare a bibliography, and to visit other libraries to make a comparative study of methods. In addition, the school offered a course in general reference open to all students to teach the use of the library and familiarity with reference books.

The apprentice work, which was later dignified by being called laboratory work, involved an average of two hours a day in the University library for two years. At eight hours a day the work was the equivalent of four months of practical instruction. The juniors once spent two months stamping and cutting leaves in books and periodicals and doing other mechanical work to prepare material for the shelves. Cheap student labor saved expense—Sharp estimated its value in 1897–98 at $1,000—but it provided little educational value and risked alienating students.[42]

In 1900–1 Margaret Mann introduced a course in Public Documents. Illinois was the only library school which gave an extended course on publications issued by the U.S. government both for their value as reference books and for the correct methods of cataloging.

Under Sharp the Library School became a jewel in the University's crown. Librarianship offered career opportunities, and people rushed into the program. In 1897–98 the school enrolled 24 students, including 6 who transferred from Armour Institute. A year later attendance rose to 41, in 1902–3 to 79, and in 1903–4 to 84. In the years from 1897–98 to 1903–4 women outnumbered men by 208 to 9. Although Illinois supplied more students than any other state, over half of those enrolled came from nineteen other states and the District of Columbia. Canada sent two; Hawaii, Japan, Norway, and Sweden sent one each. Upon admission 11 students presented three years of college work, 64 entered with a bachelor's degree, and 7 with a master's degree.

Women entered the Library School because they viewed it as the road to economic independence and intellectual fulfillment and as less physically taxing than teaching. Tuition was free, but fees amounted to $63 over two years, and students had to provide their own room and board. Of the 349 women in the Library School from 1893 to 1907 (a period that includes figures for the school at Armour Institute), 119 (34 percent) did not complete the program and receive a degree. They dropped out for various reasons, including academic difficulties, lack of money, and personal or family illness. In the years from 1897 to 1907 a total of 172 individuals, including 12 men (7 percent), earned the B.L.S., and another 29, including one man, earned a B.A. in Library Science. Of the 349 women in the school from 1893 to 1907, 149 (43 percent) completed their studies and earned the B.L.S. For women with a degree the average age on leaving was twenty-six.[43]

The school's graduates were in great demand, and Sharp took pride in the positions taken by her students. The most talented ones rose to important library offices, but most had to accept the fact that in the early twentieth century, women librarians were typically employed as clerks, assistants, and heads of small public libraries. Of the fifty-seven students who attended the library school before 1900, only 18 percent married.[44] Male alumni fared better on the job market. Torstein Jahr and Willard O. Waters joined the staff of the Library of Congress, and Adam J. Strohm, after a brief stint in the Trenton, New Jersey, library, became head of the Detroit Public Library.[45]

Sharp was able to teach any course in the Library School, and she transmitted her own inspiration to her charges. She took an interest in each student, developed a spirit of unity among them, and maintained an interest in the success of her "old library girls." In 1898 she organized the Illinois Library School Alumni Association (ILSAA) to serve as a means of communication between the school and its graduates. The ILSAA was one of the first alumni groups representing a school or college rather than the whole student body of the institution. The reason for forming the group was that in the early years many library students were graduates of other universities who felt loyalty to their own school. Sharp and the ILSAA stressed loyalty to the library profession as well as loyalty to Illinois.[46]

Despite the progress, Sharp felt that on official occasions the Library School had no place in the University, and in May 1901 she suggested that the school become a college. Because the Library School required four years beyond high school for graduation whereas the College of Law required only three, she argued, it drew to the University more advanced students than any other department, the library students (women) contributed materially to the improvement of social conditions in the University, and the school's standards had been steadily improving. The ALA seemed to recognize the Albany and the Illinois schools as the leaders, she noted, and many said that the teaching was superior and the students more practical at Illinois. The request met silence.[47]

That autumn Sharp concluded that the time had come to raise standards. Growth in enrollment was already taxing both the faculty and the physical facilities of the school, and parallel growth in the University library helped create a heavier workload than the staff could endure. A teacher could lecture to any number, but the amount of careful catalog revising one person could do was limited. Sharp recommended that, in the interest of better scholarship, starting in 1902–3 a college degree be required for admission to the Library School. The New York State Library School was the only school with requirements equal to those of Illinois, but it restricted admission, which the University could not do, and as a result many students with liberal arts preparation were weak and inexact, having missed the necessary mental drill. Sharp's proposal would undoubtedly have reduced enrollment, but nothing came of it.[48]

In early December 1902 Sharp proposed a number of changes to raise the standards in the Library School starting in 1903–4. The Council of Administration approved most of them, and on 9 December the trustees adopted two resolutions to implement her plan. One enabled candidates for a bachelor's degree to take a B.A. in library science by completing the first year of library science work. Such a course would be valuable to general students as part of a liberal education, Sharp argued, and to library students who could spend only one year in preparing for minor positions. In addition, all seniors in the University could elect any library subject for which they were prepared. According to Sharp, the Illinois Library School was the only one that offered work to college students.

The other resolution made the B.L.S. available to those holding a B.A. in library science for one year's additional study, so distributed that candidates had two full years of library work proper. Sharp had also proposed that an M.L.S. be offered for an additional year of study beyond the B.L.S. or a total of three full years of library work. The council approved of this recommendation but advised against publicizing it.[49]

Under the new plan library students began their specialized work with a better general education. The basic requirements of the earlier program remained in force, but the introduction of electives allowed for personal preferences and some specialization. The fifth-year course in bibliography became an important part of the curriculum. Earlier, Sharp had asked various University professors to lecture on bibliography in their own fields, but this venture did not work well. Students did not get practice in the subject, and specialists did not understand the problems facing the library in selecting books. Sharp gave the course a practical orientation, teaching students to use *Publisher's Weekly* and reviews in critical periodicals to become familiar with books. A library seminary for fourth- and fifth-year students also became important. In this course Sharp considered library publications in their relation to library history, biography, and administration, and once a week she met the fourth-year students alone to discuss various library topics.

Some of the theses and bibliographies presented for the B.L.S. made valuable contributions to knowledge. Two studies from 1900 on problems of interest to librarians won wide recognition. These were Torstein Jahr and Adam J. Strohm's "International Bibliography, Cooperative Cataloging, and Printed Cards: A Bibliography, 1850–1899," and Ida E. Sawyer's "A Study of Printed Catalog Cards for Sale by Subscription." Both were exhibited in June at the Montreal conference of the ALA, with the result that an ALA committee recommended that they be printed. Jahr and Strohm's thesis was a chronological study of the growth of the literature about plans and enterprises in cooperative cataloging and international bibliography. Revised and updated, it was published as *Bibliography of Cooperative Cataloging and the Printing of Catalogue Cards . . . (1850–1902)* (1903), a reprint of the Report of the Librarian of Congress for 1902. Sawyer's study, which included samples of the catalog cards that were becoming widespread, was apparently never published.

Sharp recommended several other theses for publication by the appropriate public agencies in Illinois and other states. Edith Clark's 1902 thesis was published as "Niagara Falls: A Partial Bibliography" in *Bulletin of Bibliography* (July 1903). Adelaide Hasse, chief of the Public Documents Department at the New York Public Library, saw Edna M. Hawley's 1903 thesis, "Laws Affecting the Printing, Sale, and Distribution of Public Documents," in Niagara at a library meeting. She was impressed and wanted it published.[50]

Sharp enhanced the usefulness of the Library School by involving it beyond the University. She regularly attended annual meetings of the ALA and in July 1898 was elected one of its three vice-presidents. Sharp brought prominent librarians to the campus to speak to library students and general audiences. She arranged with the Champaign and Urbana public libraries for students to help them by making reference lists for schools and women's clubs programs, talking to children on Saturday afternoons, and staffing branch libraries. Students also assembled three traveling libraries of fifty to sixty volumes each to circulate in rural Champaign County. Sharp was active in the Illinois State Library Association (ISLA), and Dewey aided her in the effort to have the Library School and the ISLA promote the library interests of the state. "Your reputation up to this time is easily first among all American universities for what you are doing," Dewey wrote Draper, "and you can hold the leadership in this rapidly growing department easier than you can build up a new one."[51] Dewey urged the University to take the lead in promoting libraries around the state because the legislature had failed to establish a state library commission. The Library School served as a bureau of information for the ISLA, and students in the bureau compiled the statistics that Sharp used in *Illinois Libraries*, a descriptive survey of over 600 pages published in Urbana from 1906 to 1908.

Sharp had to make her way in a male-dominated world—despite the feminization of librarianship, men still held the best library jobs—and she may have felt that, to be taken seriously, she had to excel. Her duties as director and librarian constituted a heavy burden. She pushed herself hard, setting an example for others. Working beyond the limits of their natural strength, Sharp and some of her colleagues paid a high price in nervous exhaustion.

Neurasthenia was a common malady in the late nineteenth century. S. Weir Mitchell, a Philadelphia physician and neurologist, discussed this nervous disorder in *Wear and Tear* (1871), and in *Fat and Blood* (1877) he advocated as a remedy for the ailment complete rest and rich food. George M. Beard, a lecturer on nervous diseases at New York University and an American pioneer in neurology, increased public awareness of the affliction and made a notable contribution to its study in *American Nervousness* (1881). By 1900 neurasthenia was claiming many victims, especially women.[52]

The faculty of the Library School was no stranger to the illness. As Sharp reported, Margaret Mann was "so constituted that she cannot shirk anything," and she had "overworked and over-worried for years." By early October 1898, she was so exhausted that her doctor commanded a rest for the remainder of the month, and in November the doctor ordered Mann to go home at once and rest for the remainder of the year.[53]

In December 1900 Cecilia McConnel, who had joined the faculty and staff in 1899, became sick and took to her bed two weeks before the holiday recess. She could not return to duty until the following February.[54] Laura R. Gibbs, who became the loan (circulation) librarian in 1898, was so worn out by May 1899 that Sharp advised a two-month vacation. In the fall of 1900 Gibbs was reported to be not as well as usual, but her determination kept her at work until the middle of January. By October 1901 her illness was so serious that her physician and her parents thought she must give up all thought of work for a year at least after her recovery.[55]

Sharp herself frequently suffered from the ailment. Some time before December 1900 she had needed a rest cure, and by the summer of 1902 she needed complete rest. On this occasion Dewey interceded on her behalf. Describing Sharp as "easily the finest product of our own school," "my favorite pupil," and "the best woman in the world for the [Illinois] library school," Dewey wrote Draper that he and others who had recently seen Sharp at a library conference agreed that she "showed the effects of overwork and the need of rest in a stronger degree than any one else there." Dewey convinced her that she could do the University no greater injustice than to cripple her own efficiency by overwork, and at his prompting she went with Mrs. Dewey to a lodge in the heart of the forest near Lake Placid, New York, to grow strong. Believing that Sharp ought to have "substantial rest, and at once," Dewey urged Draper to grant her leave until November. "She is a woman of rare character and ability and has a great future ... if we can keep her well and strong.... In the whole company there is not one in whom I have more faith than in Katharine Sharp." Sharp admitted to Draper that she did not sleep much, did not eat more than once a day save under compulsion, and that she needed more rest before returning to cope with home conditions. Draper gave her a paid leave through early November so that she could gain "reserve energy" before resuming duty.[56]

Female students in the Library School also fell prey to the affliction. Perhaps many reasons accounted for their proneness to become ill. Sharp shared with students all the learning she had acquired, she called for the best in them, and she fired them with a determination to succeed. Many women library students were anxious about entering a largely male University and having to find their own room and board. They had to give the program their full time, the courses required great concentration, the work was very confining, and on account of the number of details that required attention the work was very wearing on the nerves. Moreover, Sharp held her students to high standards.[57]

Of the 349 women in the school from 1893 to 1907, eleven withdrew or took a long break because of stress or nerves, a few dropped out, never to return, for the same reason, and fourteen withdrew or took a long break because of unspecified physical illness.[58]

In December 1900 Sharp suggested that May L. Martin take a rest cure. Sharp knew from her own experience "that nothing but absolute rest gives any relief." What Martin needed was "to go to bed and stay there and be waited upon, eating and sleeping as much as she will. . . . Nervous exhaustion will not yield to medicine. It must have rest and fresh air."[59]

When Ruth R. Cummings absented herself from school in 1903, her doctor refused to let her return to college for ten days or two weeks. "She is overworked, and must have complete rest," he said, "for if this nervousness is not checked immediately," she would break down.[60]

According to Sharp, Helen S. Dickson had entered as a student when she should have been resting. Sharp recommended that Dickson spend the following winter in a sanitarium in New York. "What she needs is absolute rest in a place where it is considered the proper thing to rest."[61]

One woman who entered the school in 1903 succumbed to nervous exhaustion after some unidentified illness. As she recovered, her sister explained, she had "nerve exhaustion to such an extent that she has had to lie still for days in a darkened room and none of us could talk to her."[62]

In 1903 Laura B. Warder, a sophomore, described the tension under which library students worked in letters home. She had never seen "so many tired, wornout, nervous people." Impending examinations were the whole topic of conversation. Laura's roommate, Genevieve, a Library School student, was "working so hard that we are all afraid she will break down. One Library girl is at home with nervous prostration, one or two others have had nervous collapses, and all of them are just worked to death. We can't prevail on 'Gene' to stop, but this week she has been compelled to stay home at night." In a later letter Laura reported "the death of a girl in the Library School from overwork & under-diet, probably." (In January 1903 Ethel A. Reed, a library student, died.) Laura's father, a lawyer in Marion, Illinois, informed Draper of these details, adding that the work required was too heavy and the risk to health and the nervous system was too great.[63]

This evidence of neurasthenia in the Library School raises some intriguing questions. The sufferers were all women. We know that these women worked hard, but presumably women faculty and students in Household Science also worked hard, and so too did male faculty members and students throughout the University, including the males in the Library School. Yet the records of these other individuals and groups contain no suggestion of nervous exhaustion. Was the malady in the Library School an occupational disease? Did physical symptoms find expression in a "fashionable" illness? Or was something else at work?

Sharp added to the University's growing fame by developing a school that won a reputation as one of the best places in the nation for training as a librarian. Her major contribution was to carry on the tradition of formal education for librarianship shaped by Dewey. She assembled a first-rate faculty, introduced a curriculum appropriate for its time, and trained a large number of librarians who gave useful service in public and collegiate libraries across the land.[64] Sharp convinced her students that no line of work was more absorbing than librarianship. Indeed, it was "second only to the church in its possibilities for good."[65] But in promoting careers for women as librarians she glorified women's service role in society.

Sharp flourished under Draper, and she demonstrated loyalty to both Draper and the University by refusing an offer from Simmons College in Boston, explaining that the environment, the climate, and the increased salary were all attractive, but the encouragement Draper gave her induced her to stay.[66]

Her best years at Illinois ended with Draper's departure, although she remained until 1907. The strain of long years of hard work began to tell, a strain exacerbated by the discovery that the Library School was not high among the priorities of the new president, who emphasized collection development and the building of a first-class library on the prairie.

## NOTES

1. *Catalogue* (1893–94), 70–71.
2. *16th Report* (1892), 205; *17th Report* (1894), 251. The early years of the School of Music are treated in Paul F. Lester, "The Development of Music at the University of Illinois and a History of the School of Music" (master's thesis, University of Illinois, 1943), and Ann L. Silverberg, *A Sympathy with Sounds: A Brief History of the University of Illinois School of Music to Celebrate Its Centennial* (Urbana: University of Illinois, School of Music, 1995).
3. *Catalogue* (1894–95), 9, 33, 148.
4. Draper to Foster, 1 September 1894, 2/4/3.
5. Charles W. Foster to Draper, 5 March 1895; Mrs. Charles W. Foster to Draper, 7 March 1895; Mr. and Mrs. Charles W. Foster to Draper, 18 March 1895, 2/4/2, B:1, F:Foster.
6. Kinley to Draper, 6 March 1895, 2/4/2, B:1, F:Kinley; *18th Report* (1896), 73, 77, 95–96, 99.
7. *18th Report* (1896), 102.
8. Ibid., 250; *19th Report* (1898), 19; Kinley to Draper, 3 June 1896, 2/4/2, B:2.
9. *19th Report* (1898), 107, 113.
10. Ibid., 124–25.
11. 4/1/1, 3:346, 348–50.
12. *Catalogue* (1898–99), 143–45, 265–66.
13. *20th Report* (1901), 111, 212–13, 255.

14. Fox to Draper, 12 March 1900, Jones to Draper, 12 March 1900, 2/4/2, B:6, F:Walter H. Jones.

15. Jones to Draper, 9 March 1899, 2/4/2, B:5, F:Jones; *20th Report* (1901), 85, 287; Jones to Draper, 2 October 1900, 1/1/6, Board of Trustees, Secretary's File, B:4; Jones to Draper, n.d. [early 1901], 2/4/2, B:7; F:F–K; *21st Report* (1902), 26, 27.

16. W. D. Armstrong (President of the Illinois Music Teacher's Association) to Draper, 23 June 1900; Draper to Armstrong, 25 June 1900; Jones to Draper, 26 June 1900; Draper to Armstrong, 27 June 1900, Draper to Jones, 27 June 1900 (quotation); Jones to Draper, 28 June 1900; Allen Spencer (Program Chairman) to Draper, 30 June 1900 (letters to Draper in 2/4/2, B:6, F:Jones; letters from Draper in 2/4/3.

17. *18th Report* (1896), 250; Draper to President Swain, 1 March 1900, 2/4/3.

18. Lawrence to Draper, 30 January 1901, 2/5/15, Frederick L. Lawrence Folder; *21st Report* (1902), 52.

19. Lawrence to Burrill, 20 April 1904, 2/4/2, B:10, F:Lawrence.

20. *21st Report* (1902), 184.

21. Lawrence to Burrill, 20 April 1904, 2/4/2, B:10, F:Lawrence.

22. U.S. Bureau of Education, *Public Libraries in the United States of America: Their History, Condition, and Management.* Special Report, pt. 1 (Washington, D.C., 1876), 1010–11; R. R. Bowker, "Libraries and the Century in America: Retrospect and Prospect," *Library Journal*, 26 (January 1901), 5.

23. Sarah K. Vann, *Training for Librarianship before 1925* (Chicago: American Library Association, 1961), 4–21. See also Carl M. White, *The Origins of the American Library School* (New York: Scarecrow Press, 1961).

24. *American Library Journal*, 1 (30 September 1876), 5–6. The name of the publication was later changed to *Library Journal.*

25. Wayne A. Wiegand, *Irrepressible Reformer: A Biography of Melvil Dewey* (Chicago: American Library Association, 1996), supersedes all previous biographies. Dee Garrison, *Apostles of Culture: The Public Librarian and American Society, 1876–1920* (New York: Free Press, 1979), pt. 3, places Dewey in the context of American library development. Garrison interprets Dewey as having an "obsessive-compulsive" personality (107).

26. As quoted in Wiegand, *Irrepressible Reformer*, 85.

27. Ibid., 85–86; Garrison, *Apostles of Culture*, 173–85. Dewey's clearest statement on this matter is *Librarianship as a Profession for College-Bred Women* (Boston, 1886). An address delivered before the Association of Collegiate Alumnae on 13 March 1886 and reprinted in Sarah K. Vann, ed., *Melvil Dewey: His Enduring Presence in Librarianship* (Littleton, Col.: Libraries Unlimited, 1978), 98–112.

28. Garrison, *Apostles of Culture*, 140.

29. Wiegand, *Irrepressible Reformer*, 94, 204–11 (quotation at 205).

30. Ibid., 60 (motto), 206–9 (quotation at 207).

31. Dewey to Frances Simpson, 21 March 1922, 18/1/22, Katharine Sharp Memorial Correspondence, B:1, F:Photogravure of Sharp memorial tablet.

32. Margaret Mann, "A History of the Armour Institute Library School, 1893–1897," in *Fifty Years of Education for Librarianship* (Urbana: University of Illinois Press, 1943), 12, says that fifty-nine students matriculated in the library school at Armour Institute from 1893 to 1897, twenty-five completed the one-year course, and eleven

completed the two-year course. All were women (22–23). The "Register of Students, 1893–1897," 2/4/2, B:2, F:Sharp, lists fifty women students trained by Sharp at Armour Institute. See also Laurel Grotzinger, "The University of Illinois Library School, 1893–1942," *Journal of Library History*, 2 (April 1967), 129–35, much of which is also in idem, "Remarkable Beginnings: The First Half Century of the Graduate School of Library and Information Science," in *Ideals and Standards: The History of the University of Illinois Graduate School of Library and Information Science*, ed. Walter C. Allen and Robert F. Delzell (Urbana-Champaign: Graduate School of Library and Information Science at the University of Illinois, 1992), 1–9.

33. Laurel Ann Grotzinger, *The Power and the Dignity: Librarianship and Katharine Sharp* (New York: Scarecrow Press, 1966), 78; years later, on 30 July 1902, Dewey wrote to Draper, "You asked me to give you the best woman in the world for the library school and I did it" (2/4/1, B:2, F:Dewey).

34. Draper to Dewey, 12 April 1897; Draper to Catherine *[sic]* Sharp, 12 April 1897; Draper to J. E. Armstrong, 12 April 1897 (the quotation), 2/4/3. Draper sent Dewey's letter of 10 April to Armstrong. Apparently it was not returned; it cannot be located.

35. Draper to Dewey, 22 April 1897, 2/4/3.

36. *Catalogue* (1897–98), 131–34. Sharp slightly misquoted quoted the ALA motto, which was "the best reading for the largest number at the least expense."

37. Sharp to Draper, 2 September 1899, 2/4/2, B:6, F:Sharp.

38. For biographical information see the entries in the *Alumni Record*, 2/5/15 Folders, 26/4/1 Folders, and, on Edwards, Albert Hardy to Sharp, 15 June 1896, 18/1/20, Katharine L. Sharp Papers, B:2, F:Applications from Students, Armour Institute, 1895–96.

39. Sharp to Draper, 17 May 1904, 2/4/2, B:10, F:Sharp.

40. Sharp to Draper, 10 June 1900, 7 September 1903, 2/4/2, B:6, 10, F:Sharp.

41. During his first year at the University Drury gave as his address the address of President Draper's house.

42. Sharp to Draper, 20 November 1902, 2/4/2, B:9, F:Sharp; Sharp, "Our State Library School," 18 October 1901, 18/1/20, Katharine L. Sharp Papers, B:2, F:Our State Library School; Sharp, "Report of the Director of the Library School," 3 June 1898, 2/4/2, B:4, F:Sharp.

43. Elizabeth R. Cardman, "Interior Landscapes: Personal Perspectives on Professional Lives: The First Generation of Librarians at the Illinois Library School, 1893–1907" (Ph.D. diss., University of Illinois, 1996), 127–31; *19th through 24th Reports* (1898–1908). The figures for the period from 1893 to 1897 are those for the department at the Armour Institute.

44. Garrison, *Apostles of Culture*, 176.

45. Sharp, "Report of the Director of the Library School," 3 June 1898, 2/4/2, B:4, F:Sharp; idem, "Report of the Director of the Library School," 1 June 1899, 2/4/2, B:5, F:Sharp; Sharp, "Our State Library School," 18 October 1901, 18/1/20, Katharine L. Sharp Papers, B:2, F:Our State Library School; Sharp to Draper, 19 September 1902; "Roster of Students," both in 2/4/2, B:9, F:Sharp; Sharp, "Annual Report of the Director of Library School," May 1903, 14–15, 2/4/4, B:2, F:Department Reports, 1903. Much of this information is summarized in *University of Illinois State Library School: Report and Student Record, 1893–1903* (Champaign

and Urbana, 1903), 37–71. The degree recipients are listed in the annual reports of the Board of Trustees. Joanne E. Passet, *Cultural Crusaders: Women Librarians in the American West, 1900–1917* (Albuquerque: University of New Mexico Press, 1994), discusses the careers of some of Sharp's graduates.

46. Josie B. Houchens, "Looking Backward," in *Reminiscences: Seventy-Five Years of a Library School*, ed. Barbara O. Slanker ([Urbana]: University of Illinois Graduate School of Library Science, 1969), 14–15.

47. Sharp to Draper, 27 May 1901, 2/4/2, B:7, F:Sharp.

48. Sharp to Draper, 21, 27 September 1901, 2/4/2, B:8, F:Sharp.

49. Sharp to Draper, 1 December 1902, 2/4/2, B:9, F:Sharp; 3/1/1, 4, 5 December 1902; *22nd Report* (1904), 30; Sharp, "Annual Report of the Director of Library School," May 1903, 2–4, 2/4/4, B:2, F:Department Reports, 1903.

50. Sharp to Draper, 1 December 1900, 20 October 1903, 2/4/2, B:7, 10, F:Sharp.

51. Dewey to Draper, 18 November 1902, 2/4/2, B:1, F:Dewey.

52. See F. G. Gosling, *Before Freud: Neurasthenia and the American Medical Community, 1870–1910* (Urbana: University of Illinois Press, 1987), and Tom Lutz, *American Nervousness, 1903: An Anecdotal History* (Ithaca: Cornell University Press, 1991).

53. Sharp to Draper, 8 October, 21 November 1898, 2/4/2, B:5, F:Sharp.

54. H. E. Tredway to Sharp, 31 December 1900; Sharp to Draper, 21 January 1901, 2/4/2, B:6, F: Sharp.

55. Sharp to Draper, 24 May 1899, 21 January, 1 October 1901, 2/4/2, B:5, 7, 8; F:Sharp.

56. Sharp to A. B. Martin, 11 December 1900, as quoted in Cardman, "Interior Landscapes," 145; Dewey to Draper, 30 July, 5, 6 August 1902, 2/4/1, B:2, F:Dewey; Sharp to Draper, 4 August, 19 September 1902, 2/4/2, B:8, 9, F:Sharp.

57. Sharp to Draper, 7 June 1901, 2/4/2, B:7, F:Sharp.

58. Cardman, "Interior Landscapes," 136, 142–43.

59. Sharp to A. B. Martin, 11 December 1900, as quoted in Cardman, "Interior Landscapes," 145.

60. Victoria Cummings to Sharp, 6 January, 4 February 1903, as quoted in Cardman, "Interior Landscapes," 143–44.

61. Sharp to J. F. Walker, [c. 15 May 1903], as quoted in Cardman, "Interior Landscapes," 144.

62. Electra Doren to Sharp, 17 January 1904, as quoted in Cardman, "Interior Landscapes," 143.

63. William H. Warder to Draper, 29 January 1903, 2/4/1, B:16, F:Warder, William.

64. Garrison, *Apostles of Culture*, 192.

65. As quoted in Passet, *Cultural Crusaders*, 81.

66. Sharp to Draper, 10 February 1903, 2/4/2, B:9, F:Sharp.

# CHAPTER 8

# MILITARY SCIENCE

## AND

# PHYSICAL TRAINING

From the start, military training figured prominently at the University. The Morrill Act, framed when the Union felt an acute need for trained officers during the Civil War, directed land-grant colleges to offer instruction in military tactics. The Board of Trustees implemented this requirement with a plan that envisioned close federal–state cooperation in recruiting military officers and promoting student discipline.

With military drill and manual labor already required of students, a program in physical training was slow to develop. But as people moved from farms to cities, collegiate institutions began to introduce work in physical culture.

## MILITARY TRAINING

Although the Morrill Act did not explicitly make military tactics compulsory in land-grant colleges, the authorities interpreted the law as if it did. The board's plan for military training had the goal of making the University a military academy along the lines of West Point. The School of Military Science was formed as an administrative unit of the University, and all male students were required to enroll in it. For a decade the state alone sponsored the military work. Enthusiasm for military study led to completion, in 1872, of the first Military Hall (also called Drill Hall or Armory). In 1878 the federal government assumed responsibility for training in military science, providing arms and accoutrements and a West Point graduate to direct activities.

Although officials viewed military education as on balance advantageous to the University, the school was the source of continuing trouble. Disruption in the military department occurred late in the administrations of both of the first regents of the University. But the captain in charge of military affairs for the next few years restored stability. By 1894 military science was well established in the University.[1]

## The Military Curriculum

The military program remained under the charge of a graduate of West Point. The course was designed to train officers of the line. Every male student not excused for sufficient cause was required to drill twice a week for two years and to study drill regulations for infantry once a week for two terms during the freshman and sophomore years.

Appointments in the battalion were made on nomination by the professor of military science and tactics and confirmation by the faculty. Students were eligible for appointment as corporals, sergeants, lieutenants, and officers of higher rank. An artillery detachment, drawn mainly from the sophomore class, received practical instruction twice a week.

In the spring a faculty committee examined candidates for commissioned rank as brevet captains in the state militia. Candidates had to be members of the senior class in full standing at the time of the examination, had to have completed the course of military studies, and had to have served three terms as captains or lieutenants. In addition, the faculty had to attest to the candidates' good reputation as scholars, officers, and gentlemen. Names of the candidates were submitted to the governor of Illinois, who had final commissioning authority.

As prescribed by the trustees in June 1894, cadets wore a uniform of gray, the coat trimmed with black mohair braid, the trousers with black cloth stripe, cut after the West Point pattern. Cadet officers wore a uniform of dark blue cloth, army pattern, with the University badge embroidered on it in gold bullion, and white gloves. The University Military (or Cornet) Band, an auxiliary to the battalion, was composed of students. Every full term of service in the band counted as one term of drill.

The military science curriculum consisted of three courses. Military Science 1 covered the basics: school of the soldier and bayonet exercise, and school of the company and both close and extended order drill. Military Science 2 dealt with more basics: company and battalion in close and extended order drill, school of the cannoneer and of the battery dismounted, and target practice. Military Science 3 was obligatory for officers and noncommissioned officers and open to others. It treated some of the basic topics along with advanced subjects, including school of the battalion; ceremonies; review and inspection; military signaling; guard, outpost, and picket duty; military administration; reports and returns; theory of firearms and target practice; organization of armies; field fortifications; and the art of war.

## The Military Science Faculty

In 1894 Captain Daniel H. Brush was appointed professor of military science and tactics. A native of Carbondale, Illinois, Brush graduated from West Point in 1871, with the rank of a second lieutenant. On 2 May 1892 he was promoted to captain. An exemplary officer, Brush served at Illinois for four years, winning the esteem of students, faculty, and President Draper. Brush was "an unusual man for getting on well with college boys," Draper wrote. "He has done more to popularize the military department at the University and to uplift the tone of honor among students since he has been here than any one else connected with the University."[2]

Brush gave his time to teaching, supervising drill, and administration. He appointed and assigned the officers and noncommissioned officers with approval of the faculty. In addition to parades and inspections, the battalion of four companies was used for ceremonial purposes. To celebrate special occasions, such as the birthday of Ulysses S. Grant, the battalion attended convocation in a body.

Brush devoted considerable effort to discipline. Resenting the military requirement, many students sought to be excused from drill or simply absented themselves from it. Brush reported derelictions of duty to Draper, who retained sole authority to excuse from drill. He called offenders to his office and told those who were physically fit to report for drill or withdraw from the University.[3]

The military program was subject to an annual inspection by an army officer who reported to the Inspector General of the U.S. Army. In May 1895 the visiting officer reported that the arms were in good condition, all movements were executed with snap and precision at the battalion drill, and the cadet officers seemed thoroughly conversant with their duties. Of the 239 cadets, thirteen were absent, three with and ten without leave. The inspector declared Brush well-fitted for his position.[4]

Two years later Brush earned another favorable evaluation with a battalion that numbered 255. Brush had accomplished as much as could be expected with the time at his disposal, yet the inspector noted some weaknesses. Space for drill was insufficient because the Drill Hall was also used both as a gymnasium and as a storehouse for artillery pieces. Moreover, members of athletic teams were excused from a large portion of the military course, which placed the program on a level below athletics and deprived the department of many of its best men.[5]

Draper heartily favored the military department, and the authorities supported the work with a liberal appropriation for military instruction and scholarships for the commissioned officers. Brush was a decided asset to the University. Draper wanted his detail to the University continued for life. But on 20 May 1898, after the battle of Manila Bay signaled the outbreak of the Spanish-American War, Brush was called to join his regiment. A large crowd gathered at Military Hall and later at the depot to say farewell. On 14 June he set out with the American expeditionary force from Tampa for Cuba, and on 1–2 July he commanded a battalion in the Santiago campaign. On 22 August Draper began a long campaign to secure reappointment of an officer he described as "sagacious, wise, unyielding, exact."[6]

As a land-grant institution the University was legally entitled to have an officer detailed to duty, and with a thousand young men Draper held that it could not accept an inexperienced officer. Draper wanted to secure the return of Brush for as long a time as was practicable.[7]

Hoping for a successful outcome, the University did not organize the military department in the fall of 1898. Draper felt lost without it. Visiting the University in September, Brush spoke at convocation, describing the campaign he had just finished and depicting the life of a soldier. In late December Draper and Brush devised a scheme to secure his services. Brush would apply for retirement on condition that the trustees appoint him and pay the difference between a captain on the active list and a major on the retired list, about $61 a month. Or, if he went with his regiment and was promoted, which seemed almost certain, he would retire and take charge of military science without added compensation. A decision had to be made within days, since Brush's regiment was to ship out by 15 January.[8]

The plan was risky, however. Brush might go with his regiment, take his chances on promotion to major, then retire, and join the faculty in 1899. But the trustees differed as to the wisdom of assuming for an indefinite time an obligation to pay the difference in his salary when the War Department was required to detail an officer without expense to the University. The board finally decided that it could not appoint Brush for life because it could not bind its successors; Draper had to conclude that the plan could not be implemented. In January Brush sailed for Manila in command of a battalion.[9]

The Spanish-American War revealed a limitation in the cooperative federal–state military relations envisioned at the time the Morrill Act was passed. During the summer of 1898 the University sent forty to fifty men into military service; the greater number had to go as privates when they were in fact thoroughly trained officers. An amendment to the congressional bill reorganizing the army provided that meritorious graduates of military departments in universities under an army officer might be commissioned in the army after West Point graduates had been provided for. Draper strongly supported the amendment, and he urged every Illinois member of Congress to do likewise.[10]

During 1898–99 the University's military department remained unstaffed while Draper negotiated with Dillard H. Clark of Roswell, New Mexico, about an appointment teaching military science. A native of Kentucky who graduated from West Point in 1873, Clark had been professor of military science and tactics at the University of Kentucky from 1887 to 1890. On 15 June 1891, owing to lung trouble, he had retired from the army with the rank of captain. Draper agreed to appoint Clark on the understanding that the University would pay him the difference between his pay as a retired captain and the pay of a captain on active service, $52.50 a month, plus a sum to cover remission of tuition and fees for his children in the Preparatory School, $12.50 a month. The board did not wish to remit fees, however, so it appointed Clark at $65 a month to cover both salary and fees.

Draper then requested that the army pay Clark as if he were in active service, and the army agreed.[11] So the University paid Clark only $12.50 a month, and he paid his children's fees. Clark proceeded on these terms. In May 1900 Draper asked Clark to remain another year. Clark wished to do so but insisted that if he were to remain, the University should pay him $52.50 a month, as initially agreed. The board declined to do so. Clark refused to remain on the terms of the year just concluded. He later sued the University for what he thought was his due, but the jury found for the University.[12]

On 31 July 1900 Major Edmond G. Fechét was detailed as professor of military science and tactics. Born in 1844 in Port Huron, Michigan, Fechét entered the U.S. Volunteers on 19 May 1861 and had been in the U.S. Army ever since. He had been honored for gallant and meritorious services in the battle at Antietam. From 1866 to 1895 Fechét had been almost continuously engaged in active opposition against hostile Indians. His most important engagements were against chiefs Victoria, Geronimo, and Sitting Bull. Fechét had planned and commanded the movement that resulted in the death of Sitting Bull and the defeat of his forces.[13] From 1895 to 1898 he had been engaged in instructing the Nebraska National Guard. In his own view, Fechét was by experience and disposition well-equipped for the military training of college men. A widower whose sole recreation was hunting and fishing, he was willing to accept the detail for the salary provided by the government. In addition, the University paid him $48 a month in lieu of quarters.

Major Fechét brought the weight of his experience and authority—and his considerable girth—to the position. In November he lectured publicly on his Sitting Bull campaign, and the following February he gave a talk on his pursuit of the famous Indian chieftain of the Southwest, Geronimo.[14] On 14 January 1901 Fechét and the regiment attended the inauguration of Governor Yates in Springfield. Yet students continued to object to compulsory drill, especially beyond the first year. In 1901 nearly two hundred petitioned that drill be suspended during the varsity's baseball games with the Chicago National League team in Urbana.[15]

In October 1902 Draper wrote Secretary of War Elihu Root regarding military instruction at educational institutions. He objected to an army order that no officer above lieutenant was to be detailed to universities. The University had over six hundred students in military studies, a regimental organization with two battalions and eight companies, a battery of artillery, and a military band of thirty-five, all fully uniformed. So formidable an organization required an officer of higher rank. Draper also wanted an officer to stay with the men for four years, and asked if Fechét could serve out the period of his detail.[16]

The inspector who evaluated the regiment in 1903 reported favorably. The military department was beneficial to the good tone of the institution and the students, he wrote, and the authorities appropriated every needful expenditure the military professor recommended. Although the University was not a military school, discipline was excellent.[17] Fechét served until 1909, providing stability and strength and making military science an integral part of the life of the University.

## PHYSICAL TRAINING

With the rise of the city, the gospel of physical well-being spread across the land, and physical education, now viewed as a science, entered the halls of learning. In 1860 Amherst College pioneered in appointing Edward Hitchcock, a physician, to a chair of hygiene and physical education, and in 1878 Harvard erected Hemenway Gymnasium.

The University responded slowly to these new developments. In the early years at Illinois, military drill and manual labor provided students with physical exercise. Wanting more, in 1870 students formed a gymnastics club. The professor of military science and tactics was later put in charge of gymnastics. In 1889, with 110 students in gymnastic classes, he recommended that a skilled instructor be employed as soon as resources permitted. But, as authorities admitted, the University lagged behind similar institutions in providing physical culture for students.[18]

Acknowledging the great desire for gymnastic exercises, in December 1890 the regent of the University appointed Mauritz Schmidt, a graduate of the Normal Turner Gymnasium in Milwaukee who was employed in the Chicago public schools, as instructor in gymnastics. He held classes during the day to accommodate the men, and at stated hours during the week for women. The board provided funds to make a room in Military Hall serviceable.[19]

For a time physical training and organized athletics developed in tandem. In 1892 Edward K. Hall was appointed director of the gymnasium and instructor in athletics; he was also the first full-time professional coach at Illinois. Hall systematized the work in physical training for men. In November the board appropriated $100 for gymnasium apparatus. In 1894 Fred H. Dodge, an 1884 Yale graduate, replaced Hall, and Anita M. Kellogg, who also taught elocution, took charge of physical culture for women.

Shortly after assuming office President Draper declared these arrangements highly unsatisfactory. He wanted the same plan to apply so far as was practicable to men and women alike. He decided to dispense with the services of Dodge and Kellogg and to combine physical training for both sexes in one department. The money saved could be used to employ "expert coaches," and perhaps the director of physical training could also coach.[20]

On 11 June 1895 Henry H. Everett was appointed director of physical culture at a salary of $1,200 for the first year, rising to $1,600 by the third year. Everett (b. 1866), a former Chicago high school athlete, had been a member of the football team and had won medals in track at the University of Chicago. He had been in charge of gymnasiums in various places and had studied medicine for a year, going in 1894 to the University of Wisconsin as instructor in gymnastics and trainer of the athletic teams. In effect, Everett became director of athletics. George A. Huff was made assistant director of the gymnasium and coach for athletic teams.

Also on 11 June, Ella H. Morrison was named director of physical culture for women, at a salary of $700. She had taught music for several years in Ohio and knew a bit about elocution. Applying for a job, she had offered to teach either music or physical culture. To prepare herself, she studied for three months at the normal school of physical education run by Dudley A. Sargent, a medical doctor who directed Hemenway Gymnasium at Harvard and enormously influenced physical training in American colleges. A year later Morrison's title was changed to director of physical training for women.[21]

At the time, the facilities for physical training were inadequate. The men's gymnasium was in Military Hall, where a floor space of 100 by 150 feet served for both physical exercise and military drill. The women's gymnasium was located on the third floor of Natural History Hall. In 1895 the trustees appropriated $600 for gymnasium apparatus for both men and women, and Morrison was assigned an outdoor "pastimes" area with a running track, tennis courts, basketball fields, and a large grassy plot for jumping, rolling, and tumbling.[22]

Taking an anthropometric approach, Morrison provided each woman with a Wellesley chart showing the woman's exact measurements and permitting graphic comparison with the average woman of her age. Morrison introduced basketball, which the women played outdoors until December and then in the small gym. Visiting, Draper and the trustees admired what they saw. Women delighted in the rings, climbing poles, ropes, trapeze, and friction rowing machine—all designed to develop sound bodies for sound minds.[23]

During the summer of 1897 Draper's greatest concern was how to provide better physical training for the men. Under existing conditions, there was practically no opportunity for work of this sort among the entire student body. Military activities monopolized Military Hall, which had never been well adapted to gymnasium purposes. In September, Draper informed the board as to how the Mechanical Building and Drill Hall could be reconfigured to make the entire second floor into a gymnasium. He urged early and decisive action, insisting that it was more important that the entire student body should have accommodations for physical exercise than that a few should be trained for teamwork and intercollegiate games. The trustees provided $4,000 for the changes, and on 12 March 1898 the men's gym was moved to the top floor of the Mechanical Building and Drill Hall.[24]

At the time, the emphasis in physical training at the best schools was on building a strong body as the basis for a strong brain and preparing students for life. A physician gave students a physical examination, often using a universal dynamometer to get an accurate picture of the living human being. He noted physical defects and recommended exercises to develop the body, maintain its health, and keep it in good condition.[25]

Illinois followed this model. The stated object of the physical training department was to teach and put into practice the best methods of preserving health, correcting imperfect development, and avoiding injury and disease. Special attention was given to those who did not reach the norm in strength or harmonious bodily development.

Women who took physical instruction were expected to undergo a physical examination each year so that their physical condition could be known and suitable advice and exercises provided. Special attention was given to graceful carriage and to correcting inequities of the hips, shoulders, and vertebrae, which were said to prevent the harmonious development of the body.

Credits toward graduation were given for completion of the course work. For men, Everett offered two courses. Physical Training 1, Gymnasium and Field Practice, was required in the winter term as part of military science. Physical Training 2, Lectures and Practical Demonstrations, was optional. During the fall term the course dealt with applied anatomy, first aid, physical deformities, and physical exercises. During the winter term it covered the effects of exercise on the organs of the body; the prevention and cure of diseases caused by overwork; and personal hygiene, sleep, diet, exercise, bathing, colds, and tobacco and alcohol use. For women Morrison offered Physical

Training 3, Gymnasium and Field Practice, three times a week, with instruction in applied anatomy, physiology, and hygiene once a week when required. Physical Training 4, Hygiene, could be taken by both men and women; it was taught by Henry E. Summers, a specialist in human physiology and vertebrate anatomy. The course treated the theory of bodily exercise, ventilation and heating, the composition and nutrient value of foods, and contagious diseases. To graduate, men had to obtain two credits in military and physical training, whereas women might obtain two credits in physical training.

In 1898 Everett resigned and was replaced by Jacob K. Shell. A Philadelphian, Shell had taken a medical degree in 1881 at the University of Pennsylvania, where he set records in nearly all branches of athletics. After a decade at Swarthmore College as a physical instructor and trainer, he was appointed professor of physical education and director of the men's gymnasium at a salary of $1,600 a year.

Ella Morrison also left the University, under conditions that are difficult to ascertain. On 7 June 1898 she had been reappointed at a salary of $100 a month. On 15 August, however, she wrote from Ohio requesting permission to return to the campus on 11 September, in time for registration. Draper approved her request. The events of the next few days are clouded. Morrison may have resigned as an alternative to returning; in any event, on 8 September Draper offered her job to Jennette E. Carpenter, a native Ohioan who had studied at the Boston School of Oratory and Physical Training and had taught both subjects in various places. Carpenter was appointed director of the woman's gymnasium for ten months at $90 a month.[26]

Male freshmen were required to take Physical Training 1, Gymnasium Practice, and a related course, Physical Training 3, Lectures. Those who had completed this work could take two advanced courses on the same subjects. Shell also offered two courses to those who wished to prepare as instructors of physical training or coaches of athletic teams.

Carpenter offered Physical Training 7, Practice, which was required of women, and Physical Training 8, Practice, an advanced course. Physical Training 9, Hygiene, the same as Physiology 6, was also required of women and was taught by George T. Kemp, a physiologist.

In 1899–1900 Carpenter began giving systematic class drill in Swedish, Delsarte, and American gymnastics, including free and light exercises, the use of dumb-bells, clubs, and wands, marching, fancy steps, maypole, games, basketball, and exercises on the various pieces of apparatus. A year later she added military drill. Women wore a gymnasium uniform of navy blue serge blouse and divided skirt, with black slippers.

In June 1901 Carpenter's salary was raised to $95 a month, and George A. Huff was appointed director of the Department of Physical Training at $1,800 a year. Since a fire on 9 June 1900 had destroyed the Mechanical Building and

Drill Hall, in September the men's gymnasium was moved back to Military Hall. Here it remained until 1901, when a new, three-story men's gymnasium opened at the northeast corner of Springfield Avenue and Wright Street. The first floor had a swimming pool, locker room, offices, and a large room with a dirt floor for vaulting, jumping, and putting the shot. The entire second floor was one large room fitted out with modern gymnastics equipment. On the third floor was an elevated running track. In the fall of 1902 the women's gymnasium was moved to the Laboratory of Applied Mechanics, immediately north of Engineering Hall.

Huff and Carpenter constituted the core faculty. During 1902–3 Huff reported an average of 435 students in physical training courses during the year, while Carpenter had an average of 206 students in her classes.[27]

Huff gave stability to the work in physical training for men as director of the department until 1936. Carpenter is best remembered in connection with the Maypole Festival. This annual spring rite owed its origins to the Watcheka League. In 1899 the league decided to hold a May party for the entire University. On Tuesday evening, 16 May, at an open-air concert by the University Band, Watcheka presented a Maypole dance under the direction of Carpenter. A year later the South Campus was the scene of what was already being called the annual Maypole dance, offered under the auspices of the Watcheka League. Seventy-two ladies dressed in white wound the maypole with streamers of University colors to the music of the military band. Carpenter supervised the dance, after which the Y.W.C.A. served ice cream, cakes, and fudge.

Thus the Maypole dance won favor and became "one of the pretty events of the spring festivities."[28] Carpenter was apparently not the original inspiration for the ceremony, but by supervising the exercise and publishing books on the maypole, she became prominently identified with a hoary pagan custom that presented such a seemingly innocent countenance.

## NOTES

1. On the background, see Solberg, passim. George Chapin's "The Military History of the University of Illinois, 1868–1923," 4/5/50, Senate Committee on the History of the Participation of the University in World War I File, B:14–15, is a compendious manuscript with special reference to the Spanish-American War and the First World War.
2. Draper to Frank A. Vanderlip, 22 August 1898, 2/4/3.
3. See the correspondence between Draper and Brush in 2/4/3 and 2/4/2, B:1, 2, F:Brush.
4. *18th Report* (1896), 93–94. The report for 1895–96 (see Draper to Brush, 12 June 1896, 2/4/3), cannot be located.
5. This report, dated 22 June 1897, is in 2/4/4, B:1, F:Misc. Papers, 1894–99.

6. *Illini*, 27 May 1898; Draper to Frank A. Vanderlip, 22 August 1898, 2/4/3; Draper, "Report of the University of Illinois," *Twenty-first Biennial Report of the Superintendent of Public Instruction of the State of Illinois* (1894–96), 145.

7. Draper's campaign, which continued into early 1899, can be followed in 2/4/3.

8. *Illini*, 23 September 1898; Draper to Brush, 26 December 1898; Draper to (Trustee) Samuel A. Bullard, 26 December 1898, 2/4/3.

9. Draper's letters on 26 December 1898 to other trustees; Draper to Brush, 31 December 1898, 7 January 1899, 2/4/3. In 1901 Brush became a major and in 1908 a brigadier general.

10. Draper's letters, dated 9 January 1899, in 2/4/3.

11. Draper to the Adjutant General, U.S. Army, 19 September 1899; endorsed "approved," 27 September 1899, 2/4/4, B:1, F:Misc. Papers, 1902–3.

12. *20th Report* (1901), 288; Draper to Clark, 17 May, 25 September 1900, 2/4/3; Clark to Draper, 18 May 1900, 2/4/2, B:6, F:D. H. Clark; Clark to Draper, 25, 26 September 1900; Clark to the Business Manager, 11 February 1903, 2/4/4, B:1, F:D. H. Clark Case.

13. Edmond G. Fechét, "The True Story of the Death of Sitting Bull," *Cosmopolitan*, 20 (March 1896), 493–501.

14. *Illini*, 25 February 1901.

15. Captain John J. Bradley Report to the Inspector General, 11 August 1902, 2/4/4, B:1, F:Misc. Papers, 1902–3.

16. Draper to Elihu Root, 31 October 1902, 2/4/4, B:1, F:Misc. Papers, 1902–3.

17. Captain Charles Smith Report to the Inspector General, 25 May 1903, ibid.

18. *15th Report* (1890), 115.

19. *16th Report* (1892), 21–22, 38–39.

20. *18th Report* (1896), 72–73.

21. 2/5/15, Ella H. Morrison Folder.

22. *18th Report* (1896), 72–73, 92, 95, 102; *19th Report* (1898), 184–85; *Illio '97*, 214, 216–17.

23. *Illini*, 18 December 1895.

24. *19th Report* (1898), 184–85.

25. William G. Anderson, "Physical Training at the Universities," *Cosmopolitan*, 21 (May 1896), 61–69.

26. *19th Report* (1898), 254; Morrison to Draper, [15 August 1898], 2/4/2, B:4, F:F–M; Draper's secretary to Morrison, 20 August 1898; Draper to Carpenter, 8 September 1898, Draper to Sargent, 19 September 1898, 2/4/3; *20th Report* (1901), 2.

27. Huff to Draper, 1 May 1903; Carpenter to Huff, 24 April 1903, 2/4/4, B:2, F:Departmental Reports, 1903 (Folder 2).

28. *Illini*, 19 May 1899, 23 May 1900, 8 May 1901 (the quotation). See Jennette E. C. Lincoln, *May-Pole Possibilities, with Dances and Drills for Modern Pastime* (Boston: American Gymnasia Co., 1907); idem, "How To Give a Maypole Dance," *Ladies Homes Journal*, 28 (15 March 1911), 33, 42; and idem, *The Festival Book: May-Day Pastime and the May-Pole* (New York: A. S. Barnes Co., 1912).

# CHAPTER 9

# THE GRADUATE SCHOOL

## AND THE

# COLLEGE OF LAW

The University stood at the summit of the public school system in the state, and in 1894 its most important function was one of undergraduate instruction. Yet a variety of social, economic, and intellectual forces were making American universities places for advanced study and research and for professional education. The University had to respond to these trends or be relegated to the academic backwater.

## THE GRADUATE SCHOOL

In 1860 Yale became the first American university to announce its readiness to award the doctorate, and in 1876 the opening of Johns Hopkins University signaled the rise of the university as the paradigmatic form of American higher education. President Daniel Coit Gilman sought to make Johns Hopkins exclusively a graduate institution by emphasizing research, the seminar, the training of researchers, acquisition of the Ph.D., publications, and the learned journal as an outlet for the fruits of scholarship—all the hallmarks of a revolution in education.

Harvard, Clark, Chicago, and other schools followed the path blazed by Gilman, and the contours of the modern university soon became discernible.

A symbol of the new order was the meeting in 1900 of representatives of four-teen major graduate institutions to form the Association of American Univer-sities. Designed to strengthen and promote American graduate education and to make it the equal of the best of the German universities, the AAU was a declaration of educational independence: America was no longer dependent on Germany for advanced study.[1]

The University of Illinois was not a charter member of the AAU, and it was slow to develop a graduate program. But the semblance of one soon evolved. In 1869 the University admitted its first resident graduate—that is, a college graduate who pursued additional studies.[2] In 1874 five resident grad-uates were enrolled in as many different fields.[3] In March 1878 the authorities decided to award the master's degree or its equivalent for a year of study after the completion of a collegiate course. The following June the University awarded its first master's degrees to six faculty members. These degrees per-petuated the custom of conferring the M.A. on graduates who, after earning a B.A., gave evidence of further intellectual achievement. In 1879 the Universi-ty bestowed its first master's degrees for a year of postgraduate study on Emma Page (M.L.) and Henry L. Reynolds (M.S.).[4]

In the years from 1880 to 1891 forty-four graduate students in the Uni-versity can be identified: eleven resident students and thirty-three nonresi-dents. The latter were graduates of the University of Illinois (and no other universities) who, after receiving their first degree, completed in absentia, after not less than three years of professional activity, a course of study equivalent in grade and amount to that required of students in residence. In all cases an acceptable thesis was required. Most nonresidents were in engineering or architecture. These master's degrees were to be earned degrees.

Thomas J. Burrill, who became acting regent in 1891, favored advanced study. Graduate students would promote the University's reputation and add tone and quality to the undergraduate work, he argued; they could also assist in instruction. He recommended fellowships for postgraduate education. Re-search was inseparably linked to good teaching, said Burrill, who also valued research in itself. "Our institution may as well sell out at once," he warned, "as to dry up within its dusty class rooms and make no marked addition to the world's knowledge."[5]

During 1891–92 the Graduate School was established in name. The cata-log announced that advanced study and research were offered to graduates of the University and of other colleges and universities without fees or payments of any kind except for laboratory expenses. The diploma of any college or uni-versity in good standing was accepted for admission. No formal courses of study were prescribed; special arrangements were to be made to meet the wish-es of each applicant. Four fellowships each worth $400 a year were provided. Recipients were to provide instruction for five to ten hours a week.

In 1892–93 a faculty committee was entrusted with control over the graduate program. Under the rules, master's degree candidates were to spend one year in residence or three years in absentia, pass examinations in one major and two minor subjects, and present an acceptable thesis. The number of resident graduate students rose from three in 1890–91 to eight in 1891–92, nine in 1892–93, and twenty-two in 1893–94. Initially, those enrolled pursued almost exclusively undergraduate studies in areas other than those in which they had earned their first degrees. But in 1893–94 ten of the twenty-two were pursuing advanced work in the area of their B.A.[6]

These efforts provided the impetus for a doctoral program. On 13 March 1894 the executive committee of the faculty asked for authority to announce the conditions under which the doctor of philosophy and doctor of science degrees would be granted. As later announced, the rules required three years of graduate work, all or most of which was to be done at the University: students had to be in residence at Illinois during either the first and second years or the third year of graduate study. For work not done in residence at Illinois, students had to present "accepted graduate work in residence at other educational institutions." Otherwise no work in absentia was accepted for a doctoral degree. No one could become a candidate for this degree who was not prepared to immediately begin research in his or her major subject, and the student had to have knowledge of French and German sufficient to conduct research in his or her chosen subject.[7]

Thus, by 1894, a beginning had been made. The Graduate School had an identity, some faculty members were eager to promote advanced study, and the best American universities were setting an example in graduate work. Yet the University lacked the capacity to advance quickly in this vital area. Most faculty members lacked a doctorate, many lacked even a master's degree, and few were prepared either to conduct their own investigations or to train other researchers.

But an impediment at a high level blocked progress. Draper and the board viewed the University's mission as undergraduate instruction. They failed to enunciate a policy encouraging original research.

Shortly after taking office, Draper named Burrill dean of the Graduate School and transferred control of the school to the Council of Administration, over which Draper presided. It was left to a small group of faculty members to plead the cause of research. On 6 April 1896 the faculty endorsed a report saying that it was important to the growth and standing of the University to extend its graduate work, that a state university should train students for service as investigators as well as for citizenship, and that graduate work had a positive value to both students and instructors and a stimulating influence on the life of the University. Since departments differed in their ability to undertake graduate work to advantage, the report added, the University would have to look to the spontaneous action of individual faculty members for the development of advanced study. And because most graduate work would have to be done with little institutional provision for it, graduate students were advised to affiliate themselves with instructors engaged in research.[8]

The deans and a few faculty members pleaded for reduced teaching loads, increased library holdings, better laboratory facilities, and funds to support original studies. But, as Kinley confided to Richard T. Ely, Draper did not seem "to appreciate the need of anything but teaching. . . . He is a public school man and has public school ideas. He is opposed to our 'using up' our time in 'writing for pay.' All our time and strength 'belongs' to the University, and 'belongs' in the narrow sense. His ideal of a successful and able man is not the scholar but the 'man of affairs.'"[9]

Even so, the Graduate School inched forward. In 1896 the number of fellowships was increased to eight, each worth $300. In 1896 the University awarded four master's degrees; in 1897 and again in 1898, twelve; in 1899, fifteen; in 1900, eighteen; in 1901, eighteen; and in 1902, twelve.

Graduate enrollment remained small, however. In 1898–99, for example, the University had 31 graduate students, whereas Kansas had 42, Indiana 73, Michigan 77, and Minnesota 132. To build up a strong graduate school, Kinley contended, the faculty should have time to write and publish, fellowships should be used to promote investigation and not to secure cheap teaching, the number of fellowships should be increased, and these awards should be assigned in advance and permanently to particular departments. To Kinley, scattering half a dozen fellowships among thirty departments was practically useless.[10]

Kinley led the drive to establish a medium for publication by faculty and advanced students, and in May 1900 the journal *University Studies* made its appearance. Ten contributions—over five hundred pages—made up the first volume. Because the University could not support a regular periodical, research results were published occasionally.

During 1902–3 the Graduate School enrolled eighty-eight students. The College of Science led, with thirty-seven, the College of Literature and Arts followed, with twenty-eight, and the College of Engineering had twenty-three. Forty-three graduate students were in residence; the others were pursuing specially arranged courses in absentia under the direction of the heads of various departments. Seventy-five were working for a master's degree. The remaining thirteen were candidates for the doctorate: three in chemistry, three in zoology, two in botany, and one each in economics, English, Latin, mathematics, and physics. Seventy-nine of the graduate students had taken their first degrees at the University of Illinois, with the other nine coming from four other universities (Harvard, Indiana, Chicago, and Wisconsin) and five colleges (Austin, Hope, Michigan Agricultural, Radcliffe, and Wabash).[11]

In June 1903 the University conferred seventeen master's degrees and its first two doctorates, which went to Henry L. Coar in mathematics and William M. Dehn in chemistry. In 1903–4 a committee "for research work in the University" was appointed. In that academic year the Graduate School had an enrollment of 118 that included 92 men and 26 women.[12]

In sum, the University recognized the challenge posed by disciplinary specialization and by the emphasis in the premier universities on advancing knowledge. Draper and the trustees contributed little along this line; they viewed undergraduate instruction as the primary mission of the University. A few faculty members took the lead in urging that the University commit itself to the pursuit of original research, arguing that it afforded new knowledge about nature and society and held the promise of benefits to humankind. They also knew that the University had to promote graduate education and research or lose ground that would be difficult or impossible to regain.

The situation bristled with irony. Draper and the trustees were justifiably concerned with undergraduate education, and the research-oriented scholars were justifiably concerned with advanced study. Neither party, apparently, gave thought to the question of how to reconcile research with the educational needs of the majority of students, the undergraduates.

## THE COLLEGE OF LAW

The law school of the University was the product of both local conditions and contemporary intellectual and social forces. In 1897, when the school opened, America was still experiencing a vast reconstruction of legal education and of theories about the nature of law, a reconstruction that had been gathering momentum since 1870. The founding of the law school is best understood in the context of this shift from the old to the new order of education for the legal profession.

The old order embraced two separate but related approaches to law. One approach regarded law as a system of basic principles reflecting the mind of the Creator. According to this notion, these eternal and immutable truths transcended human attempts to discover and elucidate them. Judges were believed not to make law but merely to discover it, using the principles gathered from cases to decide controversies.[13]

Law schools, few in number (by 1860 twenty-one existed),[14] expounded the concept of law as a science of principles. But only a small proportion of all lawyers attended such schools, most of which were proprietary institutions run for profit. Perceived as trade schools, law schools were deemed marginal to colleges and universities and were rarely an integral part of these institutions.

Even the best of the existing law schools failed to produce competent members of the bar. "For a long time," critics charged in 1870, "the condition of the Harvard Law School has been almost a disgrace to the Commonwealth of Massachusetts."[15] A similar situation prevailed at Columbia, a proprietary school in New York, then the largest and most important of the law schools. In 1876, a justice of the New York Supreme Court complained that Columbia was "a cheap, easy and *secure* road to the bar."[16]

For many, law was a practical science of procedure. Lawyers needed to know the forms of action in order to plead, and for most lawyers common law pleading organized their understanding of the law. This outlook made law largely a mechanical trade. But law offered upward mobility, and access to the profession was remarkably easy after requirements for admission to the bar were lowered during the Jacksonian period. As a result, the vast majority of lawyers got their legal education by the apprentice system, reading law while clerking in a law office.

The old order in legal education was undermined by a new order that was launched at Harvard. Charles W. Eliot, named president of Harvard in 1869, was determined to reform legal education, and a year later he appointed Christopher Columbus Langdell dean of the Harvard Law School. Eliot worked closely with Langdell in transforming the law school.

During Langdell's deanship the school raised its academic standards, replaced the practitioner who taught part-time with the full-time teacher who pursued law as a science of principles, and reformed the teaching methodology. Langdell emphasized (if he did not devise) the case system. He maintained that the reports of appellate cases in printed books were the original sources of the law. Accordingly, he had students study casebooks rather than textbooks and search for legal principles in dialogue with their teachers rather than listen to lectures. The case system was designed to teach students to think like lawyers.

New ideas about the nature of law accompanied Harvard's pedagogical innovations. Darwinism helped undermine the belief that universal and immutable truths were built into the structure of the universe and constituted the basis of law. In this changed mental climate Langdell and others reformulated their ideas about legal science along positivistic lines. Law is public force exerted through the courts.

The spread of the Harvard system incited a battle over the nature of legal education. At issue was whether law was a liberal or a professional study. Langdell regarded law as strictly a technical study, whereas the Yale Law School provided an opportunity to study not only traditional legal subjects but also Roman law, international law, and comparative jurisprudence. Nevertheless, leading law schools followed the Harvard model. By 1902 twelve of the ninety-two law schools listed in the United States employed the case method.[17]

The legal profession appealed to ambitious young men, and in the late nineteenth century many state universities created law departments or schools to meet the needs of this constituency. Among the institutions with which Illinois liked to compare itself, Michigan led the way, opening a law school in 1859; Iowa and Wisconsin followed, both in 1868; and after that Missouri, in 1872, California and Kansas, in 1878, Minnesota, in 1888, Indiana, in 1889, and Ohio, in 1891, all opened law schools.

In Illinois, several institutions offered legal education. The downstate schools included McKendree College in Jacksonville (dating from 1860), the Bloomington Law School at Illinois Wesleyan University (1874), Chaddock College at Quincy (1880), Northern Illinois at Dixon (1889), and Aurora College (1896). In Chicago, the law schools at Northwestern University and the old University of Chicago, which dated from 1859, united to form Union College of Law, which was affiliated with both universities from 1873 to 1886. In 1891 Northwestern assumed sole management and Union became the law school of Northwestern. Kent Law School dated from 1892, Chicago Law School from 1896, and the Illinois College of Law, which later affiliated with DePaul University, from 1896.[18]

The University of Illinois was laggard in legal education. In 1890, members of the Board of Trustees informally discussed a proposal to authorize establishment of a law school. Three trustees, including Oliver A. Harker, a lawyer and a judge, favored the proposal, which Regent Selim H. Peabody and Richard Edwards, the state superintendent of public instruction, strenuously opposed, maintaining that legal education was not within the province of a state university.[19]

In June 1891 Peabody resigned, and the following December the acting regent, Burrill, informed the trustees that students requested a law school. On 8 March 1892 he submitted to the board a petition from fifty-two students asking for a department of law. No valid reason prevented locating a law school outside of an urban center, Burrill said. The trustees agreed, and directed their Committee on Instruction to report a plan for the purpose. Influential members of the legal profession desired such a school, noted Burrill, who believed that the legislature would be receptive to a plea for funds to implement the idea because so many of its members were lawyers. Apparently the committee never reported a plan, but on 13 December 1892 the trustees included $40,000 for a law department and $10,000 for a law library in their request for appropriations. The legislature denied the request, opposing funds to educate men for medicine or law.[20]

There matters languished for four years. In 1894 Draper urged establishment of a law school, and Governor Altgeld supported the idea. Draper did not think legislation was necessary to start a law school except for an appropriation, but he did not feel free to move without approval of the trustees, who might not wish to jeopardize the pending appropriation.[21]

On 8 December 1896 Draper informed the board that the interests of the University demanded the organization of a law school. Although the University lacked funds for the purpose, Draper thought that with two full-time faculty, the cooperation of faculty members who taught subjects related to law, and the help of judges receiving salaries from the state, he would be justified in starting the school. From the University's own revenues the board authorized $3,500 for salaries, $3,000 for books, and $500 for expenses for the purpose. Draper expected more than twenty law students at the very beginning.[22]

Thus, at its inception the law school earned the reputation of being an illegitimate child, not duly christened. The legislature had withheld its blessing, and apparently some of the other colleges did not want a law school, "because it wasn't desirable to have too many little pigs suckling at the legislative breasts even if the last one [was] only a little runt."[23]

## Beginnings

Assured of board approval, Draper searched for a dean and a faculty. While he did not readily find a dean—he served in this capacity himself—he hired two instructors. Charles C. Pickett (b. 1862), who held an A.B. degree from the University of Rochester (1883) and had studied law in Chicago, was admitted to the bar in 1886. From 1887 to 1893 he was an assistant librarian in the Law Association Library in Chicago, then an assistant attorney at the First National Bank of Chicago and later the same at the Chicago Sanitary District. George E. Gardner (b. 1864), an Amherst College graduate (A.B. 1885, A.M. 1890) who had studied law in Elgin and Chicago, Illinois, and in Worcester, Massachusetts, was admitted to the Massachusetts bar in 1887. He was a Latin teacher in the Classical High School in Worcester. Neither man had experience in a law school as teacher or student, but Gardner had prepared men for the bar. Draper offered Gardner $2,000 because he declined to come for less, leaving $1,500 for Pickett, who considered the salary inadequate.[24]

Meanwhile, Draper was lining up state judges to serve as unpaid lecturers. Oliver A. Harker, the most important of these, was born in 1846 in Newport, Indiana, the son of a Methodist minister. He studied at Wheaton College from 1860 to 1862, served with an Illinois infantry unit during the Civil War, and in 1864 resumed his studies at McKendree College in Lebanon, Illinois, graduating with an A.B. degree in 1866. In 1866–67 he attended the Indiana University law school.[25] Principal of public schools in Vienna, Illinois, from 1867 to 1869, he read law in a lawyer's office, and in 1870 he was admitted to the bar. Starting in 1878 he was a circuit court judge in southern Illinois and later an appellate court judge, from 1889 to 1891 he was a member of the Board of Trustees of the University, and in 1895–96 he was president of the Illinois State Bar Association. He agreed to give thirty-five to forty class lectures during the year and some attention to moot court work.[26]

Draper also arranged for Charles G. Neely, a county judge of Cook County, to lecture on preparation for and the conduct of trials, and for Benjamin R. Burroughs (b. 1849), an Edwardsville attorney who had served as a circuit judge from 1889 to 1897, when he was appointed a justice of the appellate court of the third district at Springfield, to lecture on the law of real estate.

In the spring, University officials sent information on the law school to all high school seniors in Illinois, to seniors in Illinois colleges, and to every lawyer in the state. Graduates of approved high schools who were at least eighteen and of "unquestioned character" along with graduates of colleges and scientific schools of approved standing were eligible for admission without examination. On 24 September 1897 the school opened in four rooms in University Hall. The entering class numbered thirty-nine, including two women. Twelve students were from Champaign, four from Chicago, and six held a college degree.

Initially, the course of study was planned for two years, as required under the rules of the Supreme Court of Illinois in force since 1 September 1895, but it was changed to accommodate new rules of the Illinois Supreme Court in force on 4 November 1897 that required for admission to the bar a high school education or its equivalent, a three-year course of study in a law school or law office, and the passing of an examination given by the State Board of Bar Examiners.[27]

When the school opened, legal study was correlated with University work. A student could apply credits earned in the law school to other University work, and law students could take courses in certain departments of the College of Literature and Arts, subject to prior approval of the instructors involved.

The prescribed course of study included ninety term hours of work, all in technical subjects.[28] The only "liberal" study was a seminar in English legal history taught jointly by law and history professors, for which a reading knowledge of Latin and French was essential. A thesis embodying the results of original research on a subject approved by the faculty was required for a degree. Gardner and Pickett recognized the value of occasional lectures and the use of texts to supplement some lines of work, but from the beginning they made the study of cases the chief means of attaining legal knowledge and proficiency.[29]

When Gardner left after one year for the University of Maine, Draper engaged two new men. Thomas W. Hughes (b. 1858), a native of Canada with a normal-school training, had taught for about ten years before graduating from the University of Michigan law school in 1891, where he then became a subordinate instructor. His dean described him as probably "the best drill-master" at Michigan, adding that Hughes would never be promoted to full professor. He came as an assistant professor, willing to accept a comparatively low salary ($1,200).[30]

William L. Drew (b. 1864), a native of Iowa, had earned bachelor's and law degrees from the University of Iowa and had then studied for a year at Harvard Law School, where he was an editor of the *Harvard Law Review*. He practiced law in Omaha for three years, was an assistant professor of law at the University of Wisconsin for two years, and came highly recommended as a full professor at a salary of $2,000.[31]

Draper also recruited more judges as adjunct professors. Francis M. Wright (b. 1844), a former Urbana attorney who had served as a circuit judge, was an appellate court judge. Orrin N. Carter (b. 1854) had been a Cook County judge since 1984.[32] Calvin C. Staley was a judge of Champaign County.

In 1899–1900, with the change to the semester plan, sixty-six semester hours were required for graduation. The course of study remained largely the same as before.

The University had been late in opening a law school, and the school had started modestly. Perhaps Draper was wise in forging ahead without waiting until greater resources were in hand. A beginning had been made, and in the second year enrollment increased to sixty-nine, including two special students, two women, and six students with a previous degree. The "little runt" had a future.

### Dean James Brown Scott and a New Era

Draper had long tried to find an "archangel" to head the law school. He wanted Harker, who was not disposed to resign as judge to become dean; the position did not pay enough. Draper was unwilling to appoint from within; Pickett did not mind as long as Drew was not chosen.[33] Casting a wide net, Draper interviewed John H. Wigmore of the Northwestern Law School, and on 22 April 1899 he wrote to both Ernest W. Huffcut, professor of law at Cornell, and James Brown Scott of the Los Angeles Law School, asking if they were interested. Huffcut was not; Scott was.[34] He and Draper exchanged letters. Scott was strongly recommended by Professors Eugene Wambaugh and Samuel Williston of the Harvard Law School and by President Nicholas Murray Butler of Columbia. On 13 May, sight unseen, Draper offered Scott the deanship. Scott accepted at $2,500—"a life preserver thrown to a drowning man," he confessed to a Harvard classmate—telling Draper that $3,000 was merited. The negotiations took only three weeks![35]

Scott was a polished young man on the threshold of a brilliant career. Born in Kincardine, Bruce County, Ontario, in 1866 of American parents, he spent his childhood in Philadelphia, graduated summa cum laude from Harvard with a B.A. (1890) and an M.A. (1891), was awarded a fellowship that enabled him to spend the next three years studying in Berlin, Heidelberg, and Paris, and earned a doctorate (J.U.D.) in civil and canon law at the University of Heidelberg (1894), specializing in Roman and international law and theories of constitutional government. In 1893 Scott had met and favorably impressed Nicholas Murray Butler, the future president of Columbia University. Early in 1895 he settled in Los Angeles and began a law practice; in 1896, when sixty law students studying in various law offices in the city agreed to form an association and secure a lawyer to act as their preceptor, they chose Scott. When the Spanish-American War broke out Scott enlisted as a private in the 7th Regiment of California Volunteers and was mustered out as a corporal. After the war the legal association he had served as preceptor was incorporated as the Los Angeles Law School with Scott as dean. He made the school, which later became the law department of the University of Southern California, a scholarly and popular success.[36]

In their letters, Williston described Scott as a man of considerable attainments, overflowing with energy and enthusiasm, almost a "hustler." Wambaugh informed Draper that Scott did not have a systematic training in English and American law beyond what he had gained in practice and as a teacher.[37]

On 27 April Scott informed Draper that he used the Harvard case system in its entirety in his school, and if he came to Illinois he would introduce the case system as taught at Harvard and Columbia, varying the course given at Harvard by introducing the subject of jurisprudence as taught at Columbia, using William A. Keener's *Selections*, and if the third-year students were equal to it, he would offer "a course such as Dean French of Cornell gives." Illinois offered no course in Roman law, Scott observed, but Roman law had influenced the development of the common law too profoundly to be neglected. Scott was pleased that Illinois had the courage to place international law in the law school rather than in an academic department, because it was a branch of the positive law whether or not one accepted Austin's criticism regarding the sanction. The lack of a course in common law pleading at Illinois was a serious omission.[38]

Scott's bold self-assurance impressed Draper, but a critical reading of his letter might have suggested a certain glibness. Scott was steeped in the Roman or civil law of the Continent, but he overstated the influence of Roman law on the development of the common law.[39] And as Wambaugh warned, Scott had no systematic training in English and American law. Scott proposed to follow Harvard in using the case method and to teach law as both a liberal and a technical subject.

Draper described Scott as "a thorough scholar, who yet walks upon the earth, and displays great energy and good judgment."[40] In discussing teaching assignments, Scott wrote that his favorite subjects were equity, real property, constitutional law, and international law, but since these courses were already assigned, he thought it unwise to make changes at present. He would be willing to teach either Domestic Relations or Criminal Law but not Wills or Administration, all unassigned. He did not want to take the courses of other faculty members.[41]

Scott became dean in the fall of 1899 at the age of thirty-three. He liked the simplicity and social informality of the community—in 1901 he married Adele C. Reed, class of 1900—to which he added a cosmopolitan dimension.[42] On 9 February 1900 the school officially became the College of Law, and during that year it became a charter member of the American Association of Law Schools. A year later the General Assembly recognized legal education at the University for the first time when it appropriated $8,000 to reconstruct the former Chemical Laboratory so as to make it available to either the College of Law or the School of Music. The trustees awarded law the prize, and Scott proposed to use the dedicatory exercises of the refurbished building (later Harker Hall) to advertise the college.

In early years the law school library contained fewer than five hundred volumes. Pickett served as law librarian.

During Scott's deanship law teachers were hard to recruit at the salaries Illinois offered. In 1900 both Pickett and Tooke received their own law degrees from the University. Pickett had passed examinations in the subjects of the third-year work or their equivalent, thereby complying with the rule of the Illinois Supreme Court that members of the bar be given the degree on completing one year's study in a law school. Tooke had compiled sufficient credits to receive a law degree.[43] In 1900–1 the state judges gave their last lectures; thereafter the faculty was a law-teaching body rather than a law-practicing one.

In 1901 Frank H. Holmes, class of 1901, joined the faculty as an instructor at $75 a month. At the same time, for reasons to be explained, Draper approved of Tooke's transfer from Literature and Arts to Law, with his work to be assigned between the two colleges according to the character of the different courses.[44] A year later Tooke went on leave, never to return.

Scott assumed the initiative in faculty recruiting, while leaving actual appointments to Draper. In 1902, while in Cambridge at the Harvard Law School library during the summer, he solicited names from the deans of the Harvard and Columbia law schools. The prime candidate was a Mr. Moss, whom Dean James Barr Ames of Harvard had also recommended for a position at Wisconsin that carried a salary of $2,000. Moss accepted the Illinois offer, but he reneged and went to Wisconsin, leaving Elliott J. Northrup, a graduate of Amherst and Cornell Law School who had practiced law in Syracuse for seven years, as the candidate. Northrup was very agreeable in manner and scholarly in tastes, Scott wrote, but a trifle overdressed and fussy, a gentleman from a gentlemanly family. Scott persuaded Draper to make him an assistant professor rather than an instructor.

In the fall, after Holmes resigned, Draper appointed William Cullen Dennis (b. 1878) as an instructor. Dennis was born in Richmond, Indiana. After preparatory studies at the Gymnasium of Bonn, Germany, the Royal High School of Edinburgh, Scotland, and the preparatory department of Earlham College, he graduated from Earlham (1896) and went to Harvard, where he earned a second A.B. (1897), an A.M. (1898), and an LL.B. (1901). In 1901–2 he was secretary of the Lake Mohonk Conference on International Arbitration, and in 1902 he was admitted to the bar.[45]

Ever the optimist, in 1901 Scott reported that a spirit of harmony and confidence prevailed in the college.[46] But there were problems. In June 1900 Scott asked Hughes to resign. But a few students rallied around Hughes, he promised to cooperate, and Scott relented. Now Hughes and Pickett quarreled, and each felt free to speak about the other, which did not enhance the school's reputation. Students were against Northrup on account of his manner of teaching, his unfamiliarity with the subject of property, and his unsympathetic bearing in class.[47]

Scott himself made an indelible impression on others. A reader as well as a talker—Samuel Williston once said, "James, I have never been able to make up my mind whether you are a brilliant conversationalist or just an incessant talker"[48]—he remembered almost everything he read. Some thought his reasoning power was not equal to his memory. In the classroom he dressed up the dry bones of his subjects with the flesh and blood of historical facts and theories in such a way as to hold attention. When he got into a tight place, it was said, he would take up the rest of the hour with comments on the judge who decided the case, and the next day, after conferring with Dennis, return to the point of law. Yet Scott placed himself on a level with students and endeared himself to them; he could rarely bring himself to flunk one.[49]

Scott was young, bright, and cosmopolitan, but other deans criticized him, perhaps because of what a friend called "jealousy of a genius beyond their capacities" and for playing cards late at night with his students.[50] On 12 June 1900, at the end of Scott's first year, Trustee Francis McKay made a motion to ask for his resignation.[51] But Draper and Scott enjoyed cordial relations. On many occasions Scott praised Draper generously, and in 1902, announcing his intention to dedicate his first book to Draper, Scott wrote, alluding to the McKay incident, "I owe this mark of recognition to you, for had you not been loyal and sympathetic my law teaching would have ended two years ago."[52]

Yet Draper held Scott to a high standard. So far as Draper could see, he wrote in 1902, the teaching in the College of Law seemed to be going very well, but Scott should give more time to administration. "You must be sure of the quality and regularity of the work. The college is gaining a bad reputation on the score of irregularity of doing things at some other time than the right time." The dean must be held responsible for this defect. "Procrastination is, I fear, your own worst enemy. You will do yourself needless harm . . . if you do not determine at once that you will never delay till tomorrow what needs to be done today." And Scott needed to bestow more thought and time on building up the college through increased enrollments. "Do not infer more than I have said plainly," Draper added. "On the whole, I think matters are going very well, better than in recent years. But I think they may go yet better and stronger. I think you may be the instrument of it. And my interest in the college and in you leads me to say so much to the end that it may be so."[53]

Scott expressed profound regret that Draper should have considered it necessary to write such a letter; he promised to take care that Draper need not feel called upon to write another one like it. Though he thought that Draper's expectations were pitched rather high for a school started only in 1897, the best way to advertise the school, he added, was by having a good record before the bar examiners, and in this the school had been very successful. Scott frequently informed Draper when Illinois law students passed the bar examinations.[54]

As requested, Scott submitted a plan for advertising the college. The College of Literature and Arts was the best nursery for prospective law students in a university-related law school, he wrote, and a program by which students could earn both a B.A. and an LL.B. in six years would prove mutually advantageous to both colleges. In addition, Scott proposed to advertise the college and recruit students by sending circulars describing the law school to colleges and high schools in the state, to men who were studying law in a lawyer's office or reading law privately, to law students from Illinois who were studying in law schools in Michigan, Wisconsin, Iowa, and St. Louis, to the judges of the state, and to members of the legislature. He also proposed placing an advertisement in the *Chicago Legal News*.

Scott also suggested that a law bulletin would make the college widely known. No law school magazine existed in the state at the time, so the field was wholly unoccupied. Scott envisioned a small monthly publication, a law review of a more eclectic nature than the existing law reviews. Dean Ames and Professors Wambaugh and Williston encouraged the enterprise.[55]

Moreover, Scott assured Draper that he was a reformed dean. He planned to devote himself to administrative work more than in the past. The administrative officer of the school needed to be on hand to direct, he admitted, and he was in his office for this purpose four hours every morning.[56]

During Scott's first year, graduation requirements were increased from sixty-six to seventy-eight semester hours. Scott and the law faculty thought that students were given more work than they could do well; they wanted the hours reduced to sixty-nine, with the work to be in subjects required for admission to the bar. Draper opposed the reduction in principle. A number of electives had been introduced, Scott explained, and they were available to students who were capable of doing extra work.[57]

Scott's professional star was ascendant, and in May 1902 he informed Draper that he had declined an offer from Northwestern that probably would have paid $4,500; in July he reported that he had been offered the deanship of the Boston University Law School and had received inquiries about his availability for a deanship in Cincinnati at $4,000. Scott considered Cincinnati attractive because the school had a good library and the County Court Library was almost as good as Harvard's. But "you need not fear of my leaving you in the lurch," he assured. "I would not leave you in a dishonorable way for all their books and all their money. Perhaps Illinois may have books one of these days and perhaps I may be wanted somewhere at the right time."[58]

When appointed, Scott had registered his desire to teach law as both a liberal and a professional subject. On 20 May 1899, after conferring with the law faculty, Draper had informed Scott that during his first year he would teach Real Property, International Law, Constitutional Law, and Equity Pleadings, and that Tooke would teach Domestic Relations and Criminal Law, as he had during 1898–99. Draper thought that Literature and Arts, which had been offering Constitutional Law and International Law, would be glad to transfer these courses. Such was by no means the case, Draper later learned, and since he did not want to force the matter, he informed Scott that Constitutional Law and International Law would be left under Tooke in Literature and Arts in 1899–1900.[59]

Despite this arrangement, when Scott arrived in September he insisted on teaching three courses taught by Tooke—International Law, Constitutional Law, and Roman Law. A conflict ensued, as described more fully in Chapter 3. Dean Kinley objected on the grounds that these courses belonged in Literature and Arts and that their loss would be a serious blow to the establishment of a political science department. Scott refused to discuss the matter with Tooke, and he declared that the law school would not give credit for the courses to a law student who had taken them in the college. As the conflict escalated, Kinley prepared a written statement objecting to the transfer of the subjects to the law school and buttressed his reasons with comments he had solicited from eminent lawyers, justices, and law school deans throughout the country, most of whom agreed that the three subjects were not solely or even primarily law subjects; they were elements of a liberal education. Draper backed Scott, however, and by early December it was decided that Scott would teach the subjects in the law school to law students. Little wonder that Scott later thanked Draper for honoring every recommendation, even every suggestion, he had made in regard to law matters since he had assumed office.[60]

The catalog of 1899–1900 listed Scott as teaching both International Law and Constitutional Law, which he continued to offer in later years. In addition, he took over Roman Law and added Elements of Jurisprudence in 1901–2; a year later (after the Spanish-American War) he introduced a course that dealt with Roman law—the civil law of the Spanish-American colonies. As the catalog of 1901–2 indicates, Elements of Jurisprudence, International Law, and Roman Law were elective for law students, while students in Literature and Arts could take Elements of Jurisprudence, Constitutional Law, International Law, and Roman Law for credit toward a bachelor's degree. Scott's behavior in the assignment of these courses was high-handed. But Draper supported Scott and undercut Kinley, and in September 1901 he transferred Tooke to the law faculty.

Apart from his effort to make law both a liberal and a technical subject, Scott did little to alter the curriculum he inherited. In 1899–1900 the course of study remained much as before. Scott's major subjects were international law and constitutional law. In 1902 he published *Cases on International Law: Selected from Decisions of English and American Courts*, an edited work based on an 1893 book by Freeman Snow, his teacher at Harvard, titled *Cases and Opinions on International Law*, which Scott had used in his classes. Catalogs also listed Scott as teaching Equity, Real Property, Mortgages, Torts, Pleadings, Sales, Admiralty, and Conflict of Laws.

Scott took pride in the success of Illinois students on the bar examinations. In 1902, when about a third of the 185 candidates who took the bar examinations failed, all 11 University students passed. During the previous four years 84 students from the College of Law had passed the examinations and been admitted to the bar. In his 1903 annual report, Scott noted that the course of instruction in the law school was the same as that offered at such leading law schools as Harvard, Columbia, Northwestern, and the University of Chicago, the chief difference being that the first year's work alone was prescribed at the others, whereas at Illinois the entire three-year course was prescribed. Illinois attempted as earnestly as the others to give a thorough legal training, but it also sought to introduce students to all the subjects prescribed by the Supreme Court of Illinois for admission to the bar. The course of instruction, Scott said, was "as thorough, fundamental, and comprehensive as any law school of the United States."[61]

Law students had their own identity within the University. In 1901 the legal fraternity Phi Delta Phi, founded in 1869 at the University of Michigan, granted a charter to the Langdell chapter at Urbana. On 11 March 1904 the Magruder chapter of Phi Alpha Delta was formed on the campus. In 1902 Theta Kappa Nu was founded at the University from the top 10 percent of the graduating class to promote scholarship among law students. This honor society established chapters at other law schools; eventually it merged with a similar group founded at Northwestern University and took the name of the Order of the Coif.

TABLE 10

LAW SCHOOL ENROLLMENT AND DEGREES GRANTED, 1897–1904

| Year | Men | Women | Total | Scott's Total | Previous Degree | LL.B. |
|------|-----|-------|-------|-------|--------|-------|
| 1897–98 | 37 | 2 | 39 | 39 | 6 | 4 |
| 1898–99 | 62 | 2 | 64 | 71 | 6 | 0 |
| 1899–00 | 75 | 3 | 78 | 92 | 12 | 26 |
| 1900–01 | 81 | 4 | 85 | 99 | 10 | 21 |
| 1901–02 | 95 | 3 | 98 | 114 | 14 | 20 |
| 1902–03 | 86 | 3 | 89 | 110 | 10 | 30 |
| 1903–04 | 115 | 0 | 115 | — | 15 | 39 |

Law students also were members of the football, baseball, and track teams. They were prominent on the debate team, and were class officers. Some participated in the hazing of students. Thomas Arkle Clark, dean of undergraduates, disliked law students, considering them rowdy and lawless.

In the years to 1902–3, a large majority of the law students whose geographic origins can be identified came from Champaign or Champaign County. The number from Chicago remained small (three to six a year), as did the number from out of state (one to four). The number of students who entered the law school with a previous degree grew. While the enrollment shot up during the second year of the school's existence and continued to rise, it remained fairly steady until 1902–3, when a decline became a cause of concern. The number of students who graduated with an LL.B. gradually rose. The data on these trends are provided in Table 10.[62]

Scott had anticipated a slight increase in 1902–3, but he put a good face on the decline. The second- and third-year classes were larger than before, he explained, while the freshman class had fallen off owing to the opening of the University of Chicago Law School and the reorganization of Northwestern. The better class of men preferred a law school where either all or most of the students were college graduates, said Scott, who expected larger enrollment when the beneficial influence of the new law building was felt. The Illinois faculty was as good as Northwestern's, he declared, and nearly if not as good as Chicago, whose library facilities made a difference.[63]

Scott admitted that it was difficult to recruit students from the northeastern part of Illinois, where many law schools were located. Moreover, the Chicago night schools, organized to make legal education readily accessible to all classes, made heavy inroads into the University's College of Law.[64]

William P. Pillsbury, registrar of the University, viewed the data less favorably. One reason for the decline in 1902–3, he explained, was that in 1901–2 three young men who had been rejected from the University on examination and sent to the Preparatory School had been induced to enter the law school. All three were dropped from that college before the end of the year. Moreover, a persistent effort had been made to induce all the young men in the College of Literature and Arts who were intending at some time to enter the law school to come at once instead of studying longer in preparation. In this way the law school got a number of students ahead of time, swelling their numbers in 1901–2 and cutting off their natural increase in 1902–3. The college should grow, not merely hold its own.[65]

In June 1903 Dean Scott suddenly resigned. At different times and to different persons, he offered two different explanations for his departure. According to what Scott told Frederick Green, at some unknown point in time (probably in early 1903) Draper said, "Scott, I have always stood up for you, but I shall not be able to stay here much longer, and you will not be able to stay after I have gone. I shall try to get you a position somewhere else, and you had better take it." As we know, in 1901 McKay had sought Scott's ouster, and some fellow deans had criticized him. Scott may have felt that he had other worlds to conquer. Green reports that Draper arranged for President Butler of Columbia to offer Scott a job, and Scott concluded that a Columbia professorship was better in the world's eyes as well as in salary than an Illinois deanship.

Although the available evidence makes this explanation plausible, a search of Draper's outgoing correspondence reveals only one letter to Butler on Scott's departure (Draper wanted to make certain that Scott's position at Columbia was secure before he began a search for a new dean). By late April, it was known that Scott would leave to go to the Columbia Law School.[66]

A second explanation comes from a statement Scott made some years after he departed. Referring to an unidentified point in time (probably in early 1903, shortly after he published his book on international law), he said that he had been invited to take up a chair of law at Columbia University. Draper was anxious to have him remain and willing to make certain financial concessions, but these did not interest Scott. Scott had told Draper that he would be glad to remain, and to remain as long as the University cared to have him, "if he [Draper] would request the trustees . . . to permit the establishment of a journal of international law. He [Draper] said that he did not see the feasibility of such a journal. Therefore, I accepted the appointment to Columbia University which had been offered to me."[67] Neither Scott's correspondence with Draper nor the trustees' minutes say anything about a journal. While these two accounts differ, each may represent one facet of a complex truth.

Scott spent three years at Columbia. Because there was no room for another professor of international law, he could not devote himself to the subject of his chief interest. While at Columbia he joined others in promoting the organization of a society for the advancement of international law and the establishment of a periodical in English. In January 1906, at the first meeting of the executive council of the American Society of International Law, Scott was elected recording secretary; at the second meeting, in June 1906, Scott's project of publishing the *American Journal of International Law* was approved. He became managing editor. Unable to teach international law at Columbia, Scott applied to Secretary of State Elihu Root for the vacant solicitorship of the Department of State. Root was so amused by the nonchalant tone of Scott's letter of application that he read it aloud at a cabinet meeting, whereupon President Theodore Roosevelt thumped the table and said, "Elihu, we must appoint that man."

Scott resigned from Columbia effective 31 January 1906 and moved to Washington, where he served as solicitor (legal advisor) to the Department of State until 1911. In 1907 he served as a technical delegate and expert in international law on the American delegation to the Second Peace Conference at the Hague. In 1910 Scott became secretary and executive head of the Carnegie Endowment for International Peace, and a year later he received a lifetime appointment as secretary and director of the Division of International Law of the Carnegie Endowment.[68]

Scott's departure was a significant loss to the University, for he was a man of "dynamic personality, vivid imagination, keen intellect, tireless energy, cultured mind, and human soul," a unique fountain of inspiration that was never replaced.[69] His insistence on teaching law as both a liberal and a professional subject had considerable merit. As Josef Redlich later observed in *The Common Law and the Case Method in American University Law Schools* (1914), law students stood to benefit by studying jurisprudence early in their careers. Nevertheless, this approach ran counter to the main current of legal education at the time, and Scott's insistence that he alone should be able to teach certain subjects was not constructive.[70] According to Green, Scott would have liked to stay in Urbana.[71] Although he was not there long enough to have left much of a mark, he might have provided brilliant leadership for the College of Law. But Scott was more a jurist and scholar than a molder of practitioners, and the law school would undoubtedly have reflected his preferences.

## Dean Oliver A. Harker

Scott's departure saddled Draper once again with the job of finding a suitable head for the law school. He solicited other presidents for names, discovered few that were suitable, and offered the deanship to Oliver A. Harker, with whom he felt less uncertainty than with a stranger.[72] Harker was reluctant to accept, though he now thought he would like the work and would have greater usefulness as dean than in practice. But he had serious misgivings, since he had no experience as a teacher of law students and no decided views as to the best methods of getting young men started. After a talk with Draper he accepted, and on 8 June 1903 he was appointed dean and professor of law.[73]

He began on a part-time basis at a salary of $2,000 with the understanding that he would give not more than three days a week to the University and have the balance of his normal salary of $3,000 to spend for the law library. Draper resigned abruptly in March 1904, and in June Harker accepted a full-time appointment at a salary of $3,000. Serving as dean until 1916, he was for all practical purposes the founding dean of the College of Law.

## NOTES

1. Richard J. Storr, *The Beginnings of Graduate Education in America* (Chicago: University of Chicago Press, 1953); Hugh Hawkins, *Pioneer: A History of the Johns Hopkins University, 1874–1889* (Ithaca: Cornell University Press, 1960); Roger L. Geiger, *To Advance Knowledge: The Growth of American Research Universities, 1900–1940* (New York: Oxford University Press, 1986).
2. *Circular and Catalogue* [1868–1869], 25. See also Frederick C. Dietz, "History of the Graduate College" [1957], 7/1/5, History of the Graduate College, and Daniel E. Worthington, "Advanced Training on the Prairie: The University of Illinois Graduate College, 1867–1980" [1990], in the author's possession.
3. *Circular and Catalogue* (1875), 13.
4. *9th Report* (1878), 94; *10th Report* (1881), 179.
5. *16th Report* (1892), 204.
6. Burrill, "Report of the University of Illinois," in *Twentieth Biennial Report of the Superintendent of Public Instruction of the State of Illinois* (Springfield, 1894), 7.
7. *17th Report* (1894), 221; Burrill to Draper, 21 April 1903, 2/4/4, B:2, F:Department Reports, 1903.
8. 4/1/1, 3:312–15.
9. Forbes to Draper, 2 June 1898, 2/4/2, B:4, F:Forbes; Kinley to R. T. Ely, 22 April 1897, State Historical Society of Wisconsin Collection, Ely Papers, Wisc. Mss., MK, B:11, F:4.
10. Kinley to The President, 28 April 1899, 2/4/2, B:5, F:Kinley; Kinley to Burrill, 22 October 1902, 15/1/4.
11. Burrill to Draper, 21 April 1903, 2/4/4, B:2, F:Department Reports, 1903. Burrill's report gives eighty-eight; the records of the trustees give ninety-three, including seventy-nine men and fourteen women (*22nd Report* [1904], xxiii).
12. *22nd Report* (1904), xxiii.
13. This background draws on Robert L. Stevens, *Law School: Legal Education in America from the 1850s to the 1980s* (Chapel Hill: University of North Carolina Press, 1983), and William P. LaPiana, *Logic and Experience: The Origin of American Legal Education* (New York: Oxford University Press, 1994).
14. Stevens, *Law School*, 21.
15. Quoted in LaPiana, *Logic and Experience*, 9.
16. Quoted in ibid., 87.
17. Stevens, *Law School*, 64.

18. [Henry L. Taylor], *Professional Education in the United States: Law.* University of the State of New York, *Bulletin,* 7 (December 1899), 179–84; M. H. Hoeflich, "The Bloomington Law School," in *Property Law and Legal Education: Essays in Honor of John E. Cribbet,* ed. Peter Hay and Michael H. Hoeflich (Urbana: University of Illinois Press for the University of Illinois College of Law, 1988), 203–16. In 1899 the John Marshall Law School opened in Chicago, and in 1902 the University of Chicago founded a law school.

19. O. A. Harker, ["History of the Law School"], May 1933, 26/1/20, B:11, F:Law School Reminiscences. The only meeting of the trustees in 1890 at which Peabody and the trustees named by Harker were all present was on 23 September; the records of this meeting do not mention the discussion (*16th Report* [1892], 15–36). In 1882 Peabody had said that "all forms of technical education, and in the wide scope of possibilities, every form of human learning which it has fallen to the fortune of mankind to devise or acquire" were legitimate subjects for schools founded on the Morrill Act of 1862 (*11th Report* [1882], 63).

20. *16th Report* (1892), 171, 205–6, 218–19, 253; *17th Report* (1894), 62, 73, 74; Anon., "Origin and Development of the College of Law of the University," 26/1/20, B:11, F:Law School Reminiscences.

21. Draper to Lucy L. Flower, 27 November 1894, Draper to Milton A. Narramore, 11 April, 16 April 1895, 2/4/3.

22. *18th Report* (1896), 73; *19th Report* (1898), 44; Harker, ["History of the Law School"]; Draper to Nathan Abbott, 19 January 1897, 2/4/3.

23. Frederick Green, "Law School Recollections," [1937], 15, 26/1/20, B:11, F:Law School Reminiscences. Green joined the faculty in 1904.

24. Charles W. Tooke of the College of Literature and Arts, a former graduate student at Cornell, had asked Ernest W. Huffcut, a professor of law at Cornell, for names of law teachers. Huffcut suggested Nathan Abbott of Stanford, Frederick C. Woodward, in practice in New York City, and Pickett, whom he described as "a man of culture and learning who desires to go into law teaching" (Huffcut to Tooke, 5 May 1896, 2/4/2, B:2, F:Tooke). See also Draper to Nathan Abbott, 22 December 1896, 19 January 1897, 2/4/3. Draper's correspondence with Pickett and Gardner is in 2/4/3 and 2/4/2, B:4, F:Gardner, Pickett. [College of Law], *Law in the Grand Manner: 1897–1967: A Popular History of the College of Law at the University of Illinois* ([Urbana, 1967]), 5–12, discusses the early years.

25. Newport is in Fountain County, Indiana; many accounts name Fountain City, Indiana, as Harker's birthplace. Frederic B. Crosskey, *Courts and Lawyers of Illinois,* 3 vols. (Chicago: American Historical Society, 1916), 895, errs in stating that Harker attended Northwestern University Law School.

26. Harker to Draper, 16, 24 May 1897, 2/4/1, B:6, F:Harker.

27. Juleann Hornyak, Clerk of the Supreme Court, to the author, 5 June 1991; *Catalogue* (1897–98), 145–46.

28. The first-year courses were Contracts, Torts, Real Property, Domestic Relations, and Criminal Law. Those of the second year were Evidence, Sales, Real Property, Pleadings, Damages, Bailments, and Guaranty and Suretyship. The third-year courses were Equity, Private Corporations, Commercial Paper, Wills, Partnership, Constitutional Law, and Equity Pleadings.

29. George E. Gardner, "The Law School and Its Function," *Illini,* 28 January 1898; *Catalogue* (1897–98), 142.

30. H. B. Hutchins (dean of the University of Michigan Law School) to Draper, 27 February 1897, 4 May 1898; Hughes to Draper, 27 April 1898, 2/4/2, B:5, F:O–H; *19th Report* (1898), 253. The board's records show that Charles A. Winston was appointed assistant professor to replace Gardner, but he seems never to have taken up this post (*19th Report* [1898], 246–47).

31. *19th Report* (1898), 253.

32. In 1902 Carter was elected a justice of the Illinois Supreme Court; he served until 1915.

33. Harker to Draper, 11, 17 March 1899, 2/4/2, B:5, F:O–H.

34. Draper to Scott, Draper to Huffcut, Draper to Eugene Wambaugh, 22 April 1899, 2/4/3; Huffcut to Draper, 25 April 1899, 2/4/2, B:5, F:O–H.

35. Wambaugh to Draper, 19 April 1899, Williston to Draper, 6 May 1899, Butler to Draper, 22 May 1899, Scott to Draper, 14 May 1899, 2/4/2, B:5, F:Scott; Green, "Law School Recollections," 2 (quotation).

36. George A. Finch, "James Brown Scott, 1866–1943," *American Journal of International Law*, 38 (January 1944), 184; Frank M. Porter, "History of the University Law School," in *Ceremonies in Dedication of the School of Law Building of the University of Southern California* (Los Angeles, 1926), 42.

37. Williston to Draper, 6 May 1899; Wambaugh to Draper, 19 April 1899, 2/4/2, B:5, F:Scott.

38. Scott to Draper, 27 April 1899, 2/4/2, B:4, F:Scott.

39. Any doubt on this matter should be removed by Frederic W. Maitland's *English Law and the Renaissance (The Rede Lecture for 1901)* (Cambridge: At the University Press, 1901), a gem.

40. Draper to Harker, 20 September 1899, 2/4/3.

41. Draper to Scott, 16 May 1899, Scott to Draper, 21 May 1899, 2/4/2, B:5, F:Scott.

42. Green, "Law School Recollections," 2.

43. 3/1/1, 30 May 1900, p. 122; Scott to Draper, 4 June 1900, 2/4/2, B:6, F:Scott; *20th Report* (1901), 286.

44. *21st Report* (1902), 204; Scott to Draper, 1 October 1901, 2/4/2, B:8, F:Scott.

45. *21st Report* (1902), 81; Scott to Draper, 2, 8, 19 July, 5, 13, 15, 20 August 1902, 2/4/2, B:8, F:Scott; *22nd Report* (1904), 23.

46. Scott to Draper, 1 October 1901, 2/4/2, B:8, F:Scott.

47. Green, "Law School Recollections," passim; Hughes to Scott, 12 June 1900; Scott to Draper, 12 June 1900, 12 September 1902, 3 February 1903 (two letters), 2/4/2, B:6, 9, F:Scott. On Hughes, see also Harker to Draper, 11, 17 March 1899, 2/4/2, B:5, F:H–O.

48. Green, "Law School Recollections," 2.

49. Ibid., 3–5.

50. Ibid., 2.

51. *20th Report* (1901), 306.

52. Scott to Draper, 19 July 1902, 2/4/2, B:8, F:Scott. See also Scott to Draper, 2 July 1902, ibid.

53. Draper to Scott, 17 January 1902, 2/4/3.

54. Scott to Draper, 17 January, 28 February, 13, 14 May 1902, 2/4/2, B:8, F:Scott.

55. Scott to Draper, 17, 28, 30 January 1902, 2/4/2, B:8, F:Scott.

56. Scott to Draper, 12 September, 7 October 1902, 2/4/2, B:9, F:Scott.

57. Scott to Draper, 2 March 1902, 2/4/2, B:8, F:Scott.

58. Scott to Draper, 27 May, 19 July, 13 August 1902, 2/4/2, B:8, F:Scott.
59. Draper to Scott, 20 May, 6 June 1899, 2/4/3.
60. Scott to Draper, 1 October 1901, 2/4/2, B:8, F:Scott.
61. Scott to Draper, 29 May 1902, 1 May 1903, 2/4/4, B:2, F:Department Reports, 1902 and 1903.
62. These data, compiled from official records, do not include "specials." The data in the "Scott's Total" column, which are in Scott to Draper, 1 May 1903, 2/4/4, B:2, F:Department Reports, 1903, include this category of student.
63. Scott to Draper, 12, 17 September 1902, 2/4/2, B:9, F:Scott.
64. Scott to Draper, 17 January 1902, 2/4/2, B:8, F:Scott.
65. William L. Pillsbury to Draper, 22 September 1902, 2/4/2, B:9, F:Pillsbury.
66. Draper to Butler, 20 April 1903, Draper to Harker, 27 April 1903, 2/4/3; Butler to Draper, 22 April 1903, 2/4/1, B:1, F:Butler; Green, "Law School Recollections," 2, 3; *22nd Report* (1904), 83.
67. Scott's remarks at a meeting of the executive council and board of editors of the *American Journal of International Law*, 23 April 1931, in *Proceedings of the American Society of International Law* (Washington, D.C., 1931), 242–43.
68. Finch, "James Brown Scott," 188–96 (quotation at 194), 200; Julius Goebel, Jr., *A History of the School of Law: Columbia University* (New York: Columbia University Press, 1955), 198–99.
69. Finch, "James Brown Scott," 183; Green, "Law School Recollections," 4.
70. James B. Scott, "The Study and Teaching of Law," *Educational Review*, 28 (September 1904), 130–51, is an entirely mainstream statement on legal education.
71. Green, "Law School Recollections," 3.
72. Draper to Harker, 28 May 1903, 2/4/3.
73. Harker to Draper, 11, 27, 29 May 1903, 2/4/2, B:9, F:G-K; *22nd Report* (1904), 77.

# CHAPTER 10

# THE MEDICAL CENTER

The land-grant colleges were not intended to educate for the learned professions. In the nineteenth century, lawyers, pharmacists, physicians, surgeons,
and dentists gained their professional skills largely through serving appren-
ticeships; only gradually did training become formalized, moving to proprietary
schools operated for profit. As the century drew to a close, universities began
to assume responsibility for educating lawyers and practitioners of the health
sciences.

The University of Illinois was part of this progression. By 1892 the Board
of Trustees had resolved to transform what was largely an engineering school
into a university, and the newly elected governor endorsed this goal. John P.
Altgeld was determined to do everything within his power to give the state
"a complete university in the highest meaning of the term."[1] Thus began a
movement to acquire schools of pharmacy, medicine, and dentistry for the
University in the state's metropolitan center, Chicago.

## THE SCHOOL OF PHARMACY

In the training of pharmacists the apprenticeship system long prevailed, but in
due time schools arose to provide a system of instruction in the subject. The
first of these was chartered in 1822. By 1878 the nation had thirteen schools of
pharmacy, and by 1899 fifty-two. The most rapid growth came between 1876
and 1900, when thirty-eight schools were founded. Near the end of the century
some proprietary schools became affiliated with universities.[2]

As early as 1892–93 the University had offered instruction in pharmacy in the College of Science. A four-year course leading to the B.S. degree furnished training to those who wished to become pharmaceutical chemists, to engage in manufacturing, or to devote themselves to scientific investigation in pharmacy. The University also offered a two-year course designed to prepare students for examinations required by the State Board of Pharmacy for registration as a pharmacist. Illinois was one of seventeen states in which a diploma in pharmacy did not admit the holder to practice. An examination was required, and to take it one had to have four years' experience in compounding prescriptions.

At the time, most of the pharmacists in Illinois were being trained in two schools of pharmacy located in Chicago. One was the Chicago College of Pharmacy. Organized in 1859, it was among the pioneer schools of pharmaceutical education in the nation and the first of its type in the Midwest. In 1884 an split within this enterprise led to the formation of a new School of Pharmacy. Efforts to unite the rival institutions were of no avail, and a new school of pharmacy was organized and soon became affiliated with Northwestern University.

By 1895 the Chicago College of Pharmacy had fallen on hard times, and in December 1895 the managers asked to be absorbed by the state university. A committee of the board investigated, and on 22 April 1896 Governor Altgeld reported that the College of Pharmacy had agreed to donate its title and property on condition that the University take over the college and run it as a branch of the University. The University agreed to assume debts of the college up to $1,500. On 2 May the deed was done.[3] Under the arrangements, the college, which had wide name recognition, was to be known as The Chicago College of Pharmacy, The School of Pharmacy, University of Illinois. The Board of Trustees was to appoint the existing faculty members to their positions, on the understanding that their salaries were to be paid out of tuition fees received by the college.[4]

On 6 October 1896 the Chicago College of Pharmacy began to operate as the School of Pharmacy of the University of Illinois. The catalog listed eight faculty members, all of whom had Ph.G. (Graduate in Pharmacy) degrees, plus a laboratory director. Frederick M. Goodman, an 1871 graduate of the college and a professor of materia medica and botany, was dean; William B. Day, an 1892 graduate and an instructor of materia medica and microscopy, was secretary and actuary.

Admission was open to any person at least sixteen years of age who presented satisfactory evidence of education equivalent to that gained in a public grammar school. The course of instruction, covering two years of twenty-five weeks each and requiring seven hours daily for three days a week, included pharmacy, chemistry, materia medica-botany, and bacteriology. The course was designed to impart a thorough knowledge of the principles of pharmacy, practice in pharmaceutical manipulations, the manufacture of many typical galenical preparations, drill in the compounding of prescriptions, and laboratory practice in qualitative and quantitative chemical analysis.

The college conferred the Ph.G. on those who were twenty-one years old, had four years of practical experience in pharmacy, including the period of attendance at the college, and had completed two full courses of instruction, the first of which might have been in some other reputable college or school of pharmacy. The diploma of the school entitled the recipient to register as a pharmacist in twenty-two states of the Union but not in Illinois, where all candidates for registration had to come before the State Board of Pharmacy for examination.

To students who completed a third year of work, embracing principally instruction in more advanced pharmaceutical chemistry and in bacteriology, and who were not less than eighteen years old, the degree of Pharmaceutical Chemist (Ph.C.) was offered. For this degree drugstore experience was not required. Now the University discontinued its short course in pharmacy at Urbana while continuing to offer courses in pharmacy, chemistry, and allied sciences leading to the B.S. in pharmacy and chemistry.

The Illinois pharmacy law was unjust to schools of pharmacy in that persons who worked in a drugstore for four years and had not attended a school of pharmacy were eligible for examination before the Board of Pharmacy, whereas persons who had engaged in pharmaceutical practice for the same period but who had devoted part of their time to attending a school of pharmacy were not eligible to take the examination.

The Chicago College of Pharmacy had taken the initiative in seeking affiliation with the University, but in absorbing the school the University took on unanticipated problems. One was low enrollment. The increase in attendance envisioned at the time of union was less than expected, and the first-year (junior) class was always larger than the second-year class. The student body was largely male, but in 1896–97 six women registered, and in the years up to 1903–4 the number of women averaged about 2.5 a year. The annual enrollment is shown in Table 11.[5]

Because the college relied on tuition income to pay its way, low enrollments created problems. In 1896–97 the balance left at the end of the year was $1,451, and in later years it was about the same. Faculty salaries were considerably less than those paid by schools of equivalent standing. The gravity of the situation prompted the college to turn to the University for aid. College officials wanted the Board of Trustees to seek a state appropriation to provide a home for the college. Officials also recommended that scholarships be given in the School of Pharmacy as a way of attracting students and raising academic standards.[6]

TABLE 11

ANNUAL ENROLLMENT IN THE COLLEGE OF PHARMACY,
1896–1904

| Year | Juniors | Seniors | Specials | Total |
|------|---------|---------|----------|-------|
| 1896–97 | 124 | 57 | — | 181 |
| 1897–98 | 89 | 50 | 1 | 140 |
| 1898–99 | 98 | 57 | 3 | 158 |
| 1899–00 | 101 | 48 | — | 149 |
| 1900–01 | 111 | 71 | — | 182 |
| 1901–02 | 100 | 54 | — | 154 |
| 1902–03 | 114 | 51 | 3 | 168 |
| 1903–04 | 117 | 68 | — | 185 |

Draper kept a close eye on enrollment. "I cannot disguise the fact that I am much troubled about the School of Pharmacy," he told Day in 1898. "We are losing $2000 this year upon the school and cannot afford to put any money into the institution beyond what it earns." Draper wanted "something heroic" done to improve matters at an early day.[7]

One such measure was to combine the two schools of pharmacy in Chicago. Consolidation was considered desirable because it would permit higher standards than possible when the two competed for existence. The Chicago College of Pharmacy seemed to favor an alliance, and in the fall of 1899 Day reported that four of the five members of the executive committee of the Northwestern University School of Pharmacy appeared to be favorably inclined to a union. According to Day, William A. Dyche, a graduate of the Chicago College of Pharmacy and a trustee of Northwestern University, thought it best for President Draper to write President Henry Wade Rogers asking him to bring before the Northwestern trustees a proposal to turn over their School of Pharmacy to the state University. Such a letter would be "indelicate," Draper replied; a movement of this type should at least appear to be started by the concurrent action of emissaries of both institutions. If Dyche would ask Draper to write Rogers on the matter, he would do so.

Shortly thereafter either Draper or Rogers remarked to the other that the two pharmacy schools should be consolidated. The other party concurred, but neither wished to yield. "I did not know but that you might be willing to give up your School," Rogers told Draper. "We should not be willing to give up ours, so matters will have to drift along in the way they are now."[8]

The level of education offered in the College of Pharmacy was a matter of concern. The course in pharmaceutical chemistry had been under consideration for some time. On 29 June 1897 the Board of Trustees resolved that the

Ph.C. degree should no longer be given for completion of the existing requirements and that the pharmacy faculty should raise the standard for graduation as rapidly as possible to that of the best schools of pharmacy in the United States.[9]

On 2 September 1897 delegates of both the University and the college met in Chicago to consider the course requirements for the advanced degree. Professor Palmer of the chemistry department at Urbana opposed the School of Pharmacy conferring the Ph.C. for less work than that required by other schools for the same degree. Those present agreed that candidates for this degree had first to complete the course for the Ph.G. and then take a third term of the same length as each of the Ph.G. terms (then seven or eight hours daily, five days a week, for twenty-eight weeks).[10]

In 1898–99 the course was lengthened by adding two weeks to each school year, making the entire course fourteen months instead of thirteen, and instruction in physiology was added to the curriculum. In 1900 Henry H. Rogers, who held both a Ph.B. and an M.D. but not a Ph.G., was appointed to teach the subject.

By 1900 the School of Pharmacy ranked fifth in size among the fifty-seven schools of pharmacy in the nation. Until 1903–4 the faculty numbered eight, then a ninth was added. The principal members, all of whom served from 1896 to 1904 and held the Ph.G., were, in addition to Goodman and Day, Carl S. N. Hallberg, professor of theoretical and practical pharmacy, and William A. Puckner, professor of chemistry. In 1899 Day became a professor of histological botany. Most of the junior staff served only briefly.

In the class of 1904, which had 108 members, 14 states were represented, with Illinois and Colorado contributing the largest number. One member characterized the class as "pillular in construction, acid in reaction; its active principles neither homocides or glucosides; its fracture tough; therapeutically destined to be a valuable agent in medicine; if properly handled, a financial success."[11]

The Alumni Association of the College of Pharmacy was active in promoting its prosperity. Alumni arranged special lectures on business subjects outside of the regular hours at the school. In 1900 the association sponsored a series of meetings to discuss the decennial revision of the United States pharmacopeia, and in 1902 an association-sponsored lecture, "Cigars as a Side-Line for Druggists," drew a large audience.[12]

Relations between the University and its School of Pharmacy were unique. Customarily, the Board of Trustees adopted the recommendations forwarded by officials of the college with respect to the appointment of faculty members, the amount of their guaranteed salaries, and the division among the faculty of any excess of receipts over expenses. School officials sought to secure more aid from the University, usually without success. In March 1902 Trustee Alice A.

Abbott proposed adoption of a generous plan of scholarships for the School of Pharmacy and the introduction of evening classes in organic chemistry at the school. The Board of Trustees rejected the former proposal and referred the latter to a committee.[13]

The College of Pharmacy was located in close proximity to many of the drugstores in Chicago from which the school drew numbers of students, but the pharmacy faculty considered the location undesirable. Officials sought to have the college moved into the University's College of Medicine building at Harrison and Honore streets, but the Board of Trustees decided to execute a lease with the University of Chicago for the premises at the corner of Michigan Avenue and Twelfth Street for the School of Pharmacy at an annual rent of $5,000, provided that it could sublease a portion of the premises for an evening medical school at $2,500 a year. By May 1904 this transaction had been completed.[14]

The School of Pharmacy trained many of the pharmacists in the state of Illinois. In the years from 1897 through 1904 the University awarded the Ph.G. to 319 graduates, including 6 or possibly 7 women. The number of graduates ranged from 35 to 49 a year, with the annual average 40. In these same years the University awarded 9 Ph.C. degrees, 7 in 1897, before the standards were raised, and 1 each in 1898 and 1902.[15]

By early 1904 the time had come to adjust the relations of the School of Pharmacy to the University. The adjustment was overshadowed by Draper's sudden departure from the University. On 9 March he formally announced his resignation effective 1 April 1904, and on 28 April the Board of Trustees recommended that the "Pharmacy Department" should be officially denominated "The School of Pharmacy of the University of Illinois" and that the salaries of the faculty should be made independent of the income from the fees of the school. Because the statutes of Illinois made no distinction between practical experience in a drugstore and technical education and college attainments in qualifying to become a registered pharmacist in Illinois, the board also requested that President Draper work with others in drafting a bill to amend the law so that graduation from a reputable college of pharmacy be accepted in lieu of at least two years of experience in a drugstore.

On 6 June the board acted on these proposals. It amended a resolution to denominate the Pharmacy Department the College of Pharmacy of the University of Illinois but approved a motion to make the name "The School of Pharmacy of the University of Illinois." The proposal to make faculty salaries independent of the income from fees was laid on the table, and a motion to ask the legislature to appropriate $3,000 to place the School of Pharmacy on a firm basis lost by a tie vote. The trustees agreed to advance the school a sum not to exceed $3,000 from time to time as needed, the sum to be repaid out of fees on or before 1 September 1905. The proposed revision of the statutes fell by the wayside. In any event, by 1904 the School of Pharmacy was a functional part of the University.[16]

## MEDICAL EDUCATION

In the late nineteenth century medical education was in a state of transition. For most of the century the French had led the way in medical science, but after the Franco-Prussian War, victorious Germany took the lead. German medical science relied on careful collection of all the facts about a patient and a diagnosis made from the complete evidence, often involving investigation in the laboratory. In Germany the development of laboratory medicine flourished in the universities.[17]

American medical education followed its own course. In early days men of means went abroad to study in Edinburgh, London, or on the Continent, while the less affluent became apprentices for a term of years to some practitioner. The states had practically no laws as to who could practice medicine. In 1765 the first American medical school was founded at the University of Pennsylvania, and by the 1890s many others had arisen across the land.[18]

During these years anybody could found a medical college. In most cases the initiative came from a group of ambitious physicians with a few medical books. Proprietary medical schools in urban areas long dominated the teaching of medicine. These joint-stock companies were operated for profit. Students were admitted to "doctor factories" with little inquiry as to their preliminary training, and for two short years they took a course without sequence or arrangement. Reform was difficult because it risked curbing enrollments and reducing profits.

In a single lifetime Chicago experienced unprecedented growth from a frontier outpost to a busy metropolis. A large population supplied an endless stream of patients to the city's clinics and teaching institutions, and the large number of physicians and surgeons in the city permitted specialization. By 1890 the city could boast a number of medical schools devoted to regular (allopathic) or sectarian (eclectic, homeopathic, and physiomedical) medicine, two postgraduate institutions, a dozen medical societies, numerous hospitals and clinics, ten medical journals, and more than twelve hundred regular practitioners of medicine.[19]

At this time three regular medical schools dominated the local scene and competed for students. Rush Medical College was the first of its type in Chicago. In 1837 David Brainard, who had trained at medical colleges in New York and Philadelphia, secured a charter for a medical school from the General Assembly, and in 1843 Rush Medical College opened with a young and able faculty that owned and controlled the institution. Rush met a strong demand for medical education, and it prospered. As scientific research increasingly found its home in universities, the faculty desired attachment to a strong university. In the 1890s the new University of Chicago, backed with Rockefeller money, offered a splendid opportunity, and in April 1898 Rush Medical College affiliated with the University of Chicago.[20]

The Northwestern University Medical School traced its origins to a conflict that split the Rush faculty in 1857. Nathan S. Davis, who joined the Rush faculty in 1849, deplored medical education as it then existed and urged a graded system of instruction. When Brainard vetoed the plan, fearing that reform would drive away students, Davis and others seceded. They organized a medical department within Lind University. When it failed they established the Chicago Medical College. In 1869 it became a department of Northwestern University, and in 1891 the Chicago Medical College became the Northwestern University Medical School.[21]

The third regular medical college in Chicago was the College of Physicians and Surgeons (CPS), which was later absorbed by the University of Illinois. In 1881 A. Reeves Jackson, Charles W. Earle, Daniel A. K. Steele, and two physicians combined to found the school. Jackson (b. 1827), who had graduated from the Pennsylvania Medical College in 1848, practiced in Stroudsburg, Pennsylvania, until 1870, when he moved to Chicago. At CPS he was president and professor of gynecology from the institution's founding until his death in 1892. Earle (b. 1845), an Illinois farm boy who had been captured and imprisoned, eventually escaping, during Civil War service, received an A.M. degree from Beloit College in 1868 and an M.D. degree two years later from the Chicago Medical College. He conducted a large private practice, especially in obstetrics and diseases of children. Steele (b. 1852), the Ohio-born son of a Presbyterian minister, grew up in Perry County, Illinois, and studied with a doctor in Rantoul while clerking in a drugstore. In 1873 he graduated from the Chicago Medical College, and for several years thereafter he was attending surgeon at Cook County Hospital.

The college was ostensibly organized to furnish a higher grade of medical education than that prevailing, but the latent if not the actual motive was to enlarge the field for a group of ambitious and capable medical men. The faculty proposed a graded curriculum designed to lead students from elementary studies to the more advanced branches. In July 1882 the capital stock was increased from $30,000 to $60,000, and each member of the faculty subscribed $2,000 worth of stock. In September the college opened in its new building on the northwest corner of Harrison and Honore streets, across from the main entrance of Cook County Hospital. By the end of the year the first session attracted 165 students.

In 1883 William E. Quine joined the faculty. Born in 1847 on the Isle of Man, in 1853 Quine emigrated with his family to America, settling in Chicago.

An apprentice in pharmacy for three years, in 1869 he received an M.D. degree from the Chicago Medical College, and the next year he became professor of materia medica and therapeutics at that institution. At CPS he was professor of the principles and practice of medicine.

During its first decade the school did not prosper. Faculty turnover was high, enrollment was low, and the college ran annual deficits. In 1892 dissension led to the expulsion of Earle from the governing board. He was replaced by Quine, who, at the urging of Jackson and Steele, reorganized the college. He established two official bodies. Jackson was elected president of the Board of Directors, which was to have the final word in matters of finance and appointments, while Quine was elected president of the Teaching Faculty, which was charged with operation of the college, subject to financial restraints imposed by the board.

In the reorganization Bayard Holmes was made secretary and director of education. A surgeon who gave considerable thought to medical education, he energetically recruited students and increased the enrollment. In addition, he effected radical changes in the composition of the faculty, the shape of the curriculum, and the methods of instruction.

These measures set the school on a new course, and in 1893, after the deaths of Earle and Jackson, Steele became president of the governing body. For the next twenty years Steele and Quine were dominant in the affairs of the college. In 1895 the faculty adopted an obligatory four-year course.[22]

## THE UNIVERSITY ACQUIRES A MEDICAL SCHOOL

In 1891, on the eve of reorganization of CPS, Bayard Holmes took the initiative in seeking a connection with the University. Feeling "very keenly the need of offsetting the sordid tendencies of our medical schools by the scholastic traditions and associations of the University," he wrote to Samuel A. Bullard, president of the Board of Trustees, urging union with the University on mutually satisfactory terms. Bullard invited Holmes to meet with the board on 8 December 1891, giving him twenty minutes. The trustees asked no questions, and Holmes left discouraged by his failure to secure their interest.[23]

The board referred the matter to its executive committee, which visited the college and asked the Illinois attorney general for his opinion on the legal questions involved. Among other things, the proposition called for one University trustee to become a member of the governing board of CPS and for the University to own some of the stock of the medical school. The attorney general advised that the board had no authority to enter into a partnership with or lend aid to a private enterprise. In March 1892 the executive committee reported this finding to the full board. It hoped that establishment of a medical department in Chicago might not be long deferred.[24]

In November Altgeld was elected governor of Illinois. He was eager to secure a medical school for the University. People understood that medical schools sought large cities in order to have an abundant supply of clinical material, so it was foreordained that the University's medical school would be in Chicago. It was to the University's advantage to connect with an existing medical college.[25]

In 1894 Holmes again raised the question of affiliation, and on 15 November the board referred the matter to a committee consisting of Governor Altgeld, President Draper, and James E. Armstrong, president of the board. On 5 December, after visiting various medical institutions in Chicago, the committee reported that the prospects of an arrangement with CPS were promising. The two other prominent medical colleges in the city were already affiliated with other universities, and CPS favored the alliance. Quine, who was present at the board meeting and authorized by his directors to negotiate, offered to sell the property and good will of CPS for a price not exceeding $160,000. The trustees agreed to absorb the college, to arrange for determining its fair market value, and to seek a legislative appropriation to pay for the same. The medical college agreed to these terms.

Draper favored acquisition of a medical department. He tried to make sure that affiliation would meet no objection from the other medical schools in Chicago. They wanted assurance that the University's fees would be comparable to theirs.[26]

On 12 February 1895 the Board of Trustees met at Governor Altgeld's invitation in Springfield. Draper read to the trustees an address in which he said that absorbing the college would accomplish "the most difficult step in the direction of developing an ideal university." Later that day the board approved a bill for the purchase of CPS at a price not to exceed $160,000. The bill provided that the University's governing board would have control over appointments and salaries, would "recognize no particular schools of medicine to the exclusion or disparagement of any other school," and would maintain tuition fees on a basis that would make the department self-supporting so far as was practicable. Two days later the bill was introduced into the General Assembly, and quickly died in both houses. The proposed union alarmed the sectarian medical schools. They secured the introduction of bills that provided for the establishment of both homeopathic and eclectic medical departments when the state purchased CPS. All of these proposals failed. Illinois legislators were willing to educate farmers and engineers but not physicians and surgeons. In 1895 Indiana, Kansas, Missouri, and Wisconsin did not yet have a medical school in their state universities, whereas California, Iowa, Kentucky, Michigan, and Minnesota did.[27]

The University and CPS remained eager to combine, and in October 1896, after renewed prompting from Chicago, a special committee of the board again visited the medical college. Favorably impressed, the committee urged acquisition of the school, and the parties arranged terms. The directors proposed to rent the property and transfer the good will of the medical school to the University if the University would assume full authority for conduct of the institution. CPS records seemed to show that tuition fees more than met expenses and could be used by the University to offset the rent, thus enabling the University to circumvent the General Assembly and acquire a medical school without expense to the state. Having agreed to this plan, the University declined an invitation to absorb the National Medical College of Chicago.[28]

According to the understanding signed on 1 April 1897, the University agreed to lease the property of the college for a period of four years beginning 21 April 1897 for the purpose of establishing a medical department in Chicago. The merger was seen as a great achievement. In 1897 Chicago was the center of medical study in the United States, having more medical students than any other city in the Western Hemisphere. These students were distributed among fourteen medical colleges. CPS was second in size and, its admirers declared, was not outranked in respect to faculty, the curriculum, and the esteem of the medical profession.[29]

The University spent generously in advertising the Chicago school, which began operations in 1897 under the aegis of the University, with Steele as actuary and Quine as dean. Relations between the two institutions were plastic in the early years of the lease. Money matters were a prime concern. Early in 1899 the medical faculty urged the University to request state funds for a medical and hygienic laboratory. The board agreed to ask the legislature for an appropriation of $50,000 for this purpose. Somewhat later, the medical faculty recommended asking $2,000 for a physiological laboratory, $2,000 a year for a professor of physiology, and certain increases in salary. When these matters came before the General Assembly, Dr. John H. Vincent, a Springfield homeopathic physician and a member of the Committee on Appropriations, violently attacked the item referring to the medical and hygienic laboratory. He went on to attack CPS and the University for having any relations with the school. So the medical faculty withdrew its recommendation.[30]

In June 1899 the trustees, convinced that the medical school benefited monetarily from its connection with the University, resolved that such a portion of the increased earnings resulting from the union as might be agreed upon be set aside each year as the property of the University, to be used as a sinking fund with which the University could purchase the stock of the college and become the owner of the property of the school.[31]

Along with money, control over academic policy and faculty appointments proved troublesome. The medical faculty asserted that the prosperity of the school, the devotion of individual faculty members, and the safety of their property interests required that the faculty be consulted in all matters pertaining to appointment and dismissal of faculty members and in all expenditures from the treasury of the School of Medicine as long as it was affiliated with the University.[32]

In late June the two parties agreed on a set of rules to govern their relations. The rules stipulated that the general statutes of the University applied to the School of Medicine, with some exceptions. The exceptions divided the faculty of the school into a teaching faculty and an executive faculty. The teaching faculty, consisting of the president of the University and the entire instructional corps, was given legislative functions pertaining exclusively to the internal work of the school. The executive faculty, which included the president of the University and members of the teaching faculty who held stock in CPS, was to have an advisory relation to University officials with respect to all matters pertaining to the School of Medicine. It was empowered to nominate from among its members a dean, an actuary, and a secretary for the school; the nominations were made to the Board of Trustees through the president. The executive faculty also had the right to nominate candidates for faculty positions and to cooperate through official channels in determining the school's educational policy. The board approved these rules.[33]

Time was running out on the lease, so in September 1899 the board appointed a special committee to confer with CPS on the terms for a permanent union, with a view to the University ultimately acquiring title to the property. President Draper, the business manager, and the chair of the board's Committee on the Medical College represented the University, while Quine, Steele, and three others represented the medical faculty. Financial records indicated that for 1899–1900 the school operated at a net profit of $9,028 and that from 21 April 1897 to 30 April 1900 the net profit was $28,380.[34] On 9 February 1900 the two parties reached an agreement that was endorsed by the Board of Trustees without dissent.

Briefly stated, the contract put the value of the property, equipment, and good will of the college at $217,000 and provided that the entire property be leased to the University for twenty-five years, or until the agreement was terminated, at $12,000 a year plus taxes and assessments. Meanwhile, the net earnings were to belong to the two institutions. Under the contract the University was to have one-third and the stockholders of the college two-thirds of the net earnings. CPS was to convey to the University in escrow all its property and good will and all properties that it might later acquire. The University's share of the net earnings was to be paid annually in cash and put in a separate fund and invested for the purchase of the property.

When this fund equaled the purchase price of the property, it was to be paid over and the conveyance delivered with the option to close the matter by paying the existing difference in cash at the end of the twenty-five years if the agreement had not already been consummated. During the period of the lease, initiative as to the policy of and appointments in CPS was to be with the faculty thereof, including the president of the University, but ultimate authority was to be with the Board of Trustees. The University was to use the revenues of the college to strengthen it and to advance medical science "without being confined to any particular branches of study or methods of instruction." Thus the agreement did not bind the state in any way financially, and it was expected to promote the general usefulness of the University. On the day the contract was executed the medical school had existing liabilities of $70,700 and the School of Medicine officially became the College of Medicine.[35]

On 1 May 1900 the new lease became effective, and by this time the need for enlarged quarters was urgent. So in June ten medical faculty members subscribed $62,000 to bonds to purchase the West Division High School. In September Quine and Steele laid the matter of purchase of the property before the Board of Trustees. A special committee of the board studied the matter. The school building adjoined the building of the college, the committee reported, but it was much larger than necessary for the immediate needs of the college. Nevertheless, the property was so valuable that the committee recommended purchase at the City of Chicago's asking price of $186,000 in order to provide larger quarters for the medical school and with a view to using the surplus room of the building to house the pharmacy school and a dental school. The full board approved the recommendation with one dissenting vote and authorized up to $5,000 to make permanent improvements in the building. The deed for the property was recorded in the Cook County recorder's office and then placed in escrow with the Secretary of State.[36]

The University had entered into the agreement with CPS believing that it could realize annually the amount needed to pay off the purchase price in twenty-five years, and it had approved buying the West Side High School property, confident that the facility would yield increased net income that would cover the increased obligations. On 25 June 1901 a fire in the original building had necessitated repairs that were partly covered by insurance, but along with the repairs, substantial improvements were made in the building, and the total cost of these items was more than $100,000. The board had also paid $17,000 to establish a dental department in the College of Medicine. As a result, the total indebtedness was $528,000, making the University's ability to receive a sufficient share of the net annual profit to pay off its debt in twenty-five years problematic.

By October 1902 the Board of Trustees was alarmed at the financial results of the past two years and the prospects for the current year. As the Committee on the Medical School reported, expenses had grown by a much greater percentage than income, profits had decreased, and the University had not received a sufficient annual return to be able to liquidate its debt in twenty-five years. The loss of a single year's net income was not of grave importance, but in prosperous times, with enrollment and income both increasing, the loss was a matter of deep concern.

The committee estimated that if the medical college reduced its estimate of expenses for 1902–3 so as to yield a surplus of $38,400, the University's share would be $12,000, the necessary amount contemplated by the contract. Thus, members recommended that the proposed budget of the college be returned to the actuary with the request that the expenses for the current year be reduced accordingly, and that in the future the actuary's estimates should adjust income and expenses so as to yield a surplus of $38,400 each year.

Taking a broader view of relations with the medical school, the committee expressed its "candid belief" that the state of Illinois could not "with honor to itself, for longer than a temporary period, employ a private corporation to educate for it the young men and women of the State." The contract between the University and the College of Medicine should not be allowed to continue indefinitely. It should be fulfilled at the earliest possible time. Such a result would be to the financial advantage of CPS and the educational enlargement of the University.[37]

The medical school's educational program operated within the institutional framework described. Requirements for admission were good moral character as certified by two reputable physicians and attainment of a certain level of knowledge, as demonstrated by a diploma from a recognized college, academy, or high school or by passing an examination in English, mathematics, physics, and Latin. The winter session ran from mid-September to late April and was obligatory. The spring session ran from late April to the end of June and offered supplementary work. The curriculum required for graduation extended over four years. The first two years were confined to the basic sciences fundamental to practical medicine. The method of instruction was about equally divided between laboratory and didactic work. During the last two years the time was about equally divided between clinical and didactic work.[38]

Enrollment rose from 235 in 1895–96 to 408 in 1897–98, the first year of the affiliation, after which, as Table 12 shows, the student body increased almost uninterruptedly. The junior and senior classes were ordinarily much larger than the freshman and sophomore classes, indicating that many students entered with advanced standing. In the April 1898 commencement at the Grand Opera House in Chicago the University conferred the M.D. degree on 106 students, including two women.[39]

The admission of women as medical students caused conflict. Quine knew that the prospect of coeducation alarmed the faculty, which feared that a good many men would drop out if women were admitted. But he had insisted that when the college united with the University it must admit women on equal

TABLE 12

ANNUAL ENROLMENT IN THE MEDICAL SCHOOL, 1897–1904

| Year | Men | Women | Total |
|------|-----|-------|-------|
| 1897–98 | 391 | 17 | 408 |
| 1898–99 | 479 | 35 | 514 |
| 1899–00 | 539 | 41 | 580 |
| 1900–01 | 625 | 48 | 673 |
| 1901–02 | 658 | 50 | 708 |
| 1902–03 | 616 | 73 | 689 |
| 1903–04 | 641 | 53 | 694 |

terms with men. That women would be admitted, Steele said publicly in June 1897, was a false alarm growing out of a misinterpretation of Quine's remarks. According to Steele, neither college officials nor the Board of Trustees favored such an innovation, and a large number of the male medical students seriously objected to coeducation. So for at least two years the policy was not likely to change.[40]

On 8 June 1897 William A. Pusey, secretary of the medical school, asked Draper if the faculty could postpone admitting women for a year by saying the instructors were not yet ready for them. Draper was willing to allow the present status to continue until the board changed the policy of CPS. In late June, however, Trustee Lucy L. Flower secured board approval of a resolution that women would be admitted starting in 1898.[41]

When women were admitted, Quine later recalled, they were treated "with undisguised hostility and contempt." But when the persecution took the form of positive vulgarity and personal abuse, the men themselves promptly repressed the offenders. Women would not inform on their persecutors. They met the situation with tact, patience, and courage.[42]

Faculty as well as students offended. In February 1899, Twing B. Wiggin, a professor of physiology, made remarks to a mixed class that raised objections, The incident got into the newspapers. Quine suspended Wiggin from the faculty, but later restored him. Draper thought the punishment sufficient. The public was very sensitive about such matters, he added, and it deserved assurance that such talk would be stopped. In April 1900 a number of male students were charged with obscene and indecent conduct, and a female student charged some students and a member of the faculty with indecent conduct in regard to her. After investigating, Quine suspended six males, warned five others, and, as the minutes state, he "privately expelled" the woman.[43]

New methods of administration under the long lease led to faculty dissension, Quine reported in 1900, but reorganization provided a cure. Several faculty members resigned, others were reassigned, and new teachers were added. The faculty, with sixty-four members, many of whom were part-time clinical instructors, gained in unity of purpose and professional standing. A physiological laboratory was established; some departments were abolished or combined with other departments. The school year was divided into three terms of sixteen weeks each. Students could enter at the beginning of any term and earn credit for not more than two terms in any year, with attendance required for eight terms. This change required attendance of eight months a year for four years. The lecture and the amphitheater gave way to personal instruction in the classroom.[44]

Quine took pride in the comparative thoroughness of the curriculum. He himself was an excellent teacher. Despite his didactic method, a relic of his own education, he was rated among the top half-dozen teachers of his subject in Chicago's medical schools.[45] He generously supported the school's library, whose foundations were laid when A. Reeves Jackson left his private collection of books to the college in 1892. In 1895 the faculty named this library after Quine and hired a trained librarian. By November 1902 the Quine Library had 7,360 volumes. Among the medical libraries of the Midwest it was second in size and first in number of patrons, who averaged 134 a day.

Archie J. Graham, who had studied for three years at Urbana before entering the medical school in 1899 as a sophomore, offered a student's perspective on CPS. Coming from small classes and quiet laboratories, he found the college in many ways deficient. It had to pay its way on fees alone. Enormous classes made it difficult to hear lectures or look carefully at specimens. To sit in a class of 200 and be quizzed struck Graham as bad pedagogy. But lecture classes were broken into quiz sections, and most subjects were supplemented by clinics. Graham thought that students received good instruction.[46]

Medical students were a rowdy lot. The average age of the class of 1900 was between twenty-five and thirty. A few bad actors led in "nefarious practices," others followed, and the result was "scholastic pandemonium." Freshmen broke the monotony by kicking the backs of seats, shouting "exam" before every lecture, and throwing a burning newspaper from the top row of an amphitheater to observe the reflexes of the unwary. "There was always an uneasiness that a professor would be late," Graham recalled, "and then the chairs would be thrown into the pit and broken into bits." Of all the nightmares, class rushes on the stairs were the worst.[47]

Disruptions sparked by class antagonisms were apparently tolerated. The faculty minutes from 1891 to 1902 record only two disciplinary cases, one involving the sophomore and junior classes on 6 November 1899, the other involving the junior class in 1902. The records do show that students cheated on examinatioms and that one student was disciplined for drunkenness.[48]

Many students had some collegiate experience before entering medical school, and they wanted to perpetuate activities with which they were familiar. Since most of the students came from Christian families—a survey in 1901 found that 51 percent were church members and 83 percent either were church members or expressed a church preference—the Christian Associations were active in the college.[49] The YMCA of the medical school was a department of the Chicago YMCA and under the management of a board consisting of three professors, three alumni, and three students. The Y's objectives were to promote Christian fellowship and to enlist members in aggressive Christian work. The Y had its own quarters—at various times a room in the college building or a house at 596 West Adams Street—where it conducted Bible classes and held prayer meetings. "An organized disseminator of helpful influences," the Y sponsored faculty lectures and helped students in many ways.[50]

In 1901 fifteen women students formed a branch of the YWCA with a view to promoting "higher and nobler ideals of Christian living." In their Bible class they studied the life of Christ using the four gospels and Sharman's *Life of Christ*.[51]

Medical students formed a Mandolin Club, a Glee Club, and a band. The Mandolin Club (also known as the Glee and Mandolin Club or the Mandolin and Guitar Club) performed in various venues, including a faculty member's home and Steinway Hall.

The *P & S Plexus* was a monthly journal of the school dating from October 1895. The *Plexus* was designed to report on college activities, to develop esprit de corps, and to keep alumni in touch with the institution. Each issue devoted some space to medical articles by faculty members. For some years two students, an editor and a business manager, owned and operated the journal, and all four classes were represented on the staff.

The *Plexus* provided valuable information on the life of the college. In February 1899 the faculty recommended financial support for it, and in 1900 or 1901 the faculty purchased the journal and leased it back to a student for three years. In April 1901 the magazine had a monthly circulation of 1,200; the following October the faculty decreed that a faculty committee was to "supervise and revise" all the matter published in *Plexus*. The designation of the journal as the official organ of the college was dropped. Thenceforth the editors published more on medicine and less on student affairs.[52]

Although college authorities provided a gymnasium and hired a director of physical training, students wanted intercollegiate sports. They formed a football team, which was managed by a student chosen by the Athletic Association. Football in the medical school was much like football in other collegiate institutions of the day. Suffice it to say that the team played several games each year against a motley assortment of opponents. For four years P&S, as the College of Physicians and Surgeons Team was known, fielded the champion medical college football team of the Midwest. The sport commanded a prominent place in the life of the college. The football banquet and ball became the highlight of the social season.

But expansive student managers ran up debts and then asked to be bailed out. The medical faculty wanted the University to provide funds to support the activity; the trustees agreed only to approve the payment of indebtedness up to $800 out of any surplus funds of the school.[53] When debts continued to mount, the medical school's Committee on Athletics recommended that the Athletic Association be placed under the control of a faculty manager and that $500 a year be appropriated for the support of athletics. Athletics was seen as "a medium of advertising and a means of engendering college spirit." But the full faculty refused to recognize any baseball or football team as a college organization and declined to appropriate any money for the support of such teams.[54]

In the years from 1896 to 1904 the College of Medicine carved out an enviable place for itself in the nation. It had the advantage of location in Chicago, which by 1902 was home to fifteen medical schools, far outstripping any other city in the nation in this respect. In student enrollment the University's medical school was the second largest in Chicago. Only Rush was larger.

Around the turn of the century, three other Chicago medical schools sought affiliation with the University. In 1896 the trustees rebuffed an overture from the National Medical College because of the commitment to CPS, and in 1903 the board turned down Harvey Medical College, a night school that had little in the way of admissions requirements. In 1903 Hahnemann Medical College asked to become part of the medical school as its homeopathic department. Trustee Bullard desired acceptance, but the College of Medicine was not agreeable. A year later the question of what to do about homeopathic medicine was still unresolved.[55]

In the years to 1904 the University awarded the M.D. degree to 1,173 physicians and surgeons, including 87 women (7.41 percent). A number of the new doctors had previous degrees, including the bachelor's degree, the Ph.G., the M.D., or some combination of the three. The number of M.D. recipients ranged from 106 in 1898 to 221 in 1902, declining slightly over the next two years to 216 in 1903 and 215 in 1904. The number of female graduates rose from 2 in 1898 to 26 in 1903, then dropped to 17 in 1904. Among the graduates in 1901 was Isabella M. Garnett, an African-American woman.[56]

Judged by the only standards available, graduates of the medical school were of high quality. An Illinois law gave the State Board of Health permission to license without examination graduates of legally chartered medical schools in Illinois, so graduates of the College of Medicine did not need to pass a qualifying examination in order to be licensed. Nevertheless, graduates of the school did very well in examinations given by state boards of health in other jurisdictions.[57] Graduates also did very well in the competition to secure good appointments in the better hospitals of Chicago.

Students in the College of Medicine organized four medical fraternities for men and one for women in these years. In 1902 a third-year student, William W. Root, founded Alpha Omega Alpha, a medical honor society, for both men and women. It was the only organization of its kind in medical schools in North America.

## THE SCHOOL OF DENTISTRY

Dentistry, in ancient times practiced as a branch of surgery, became a distinct profession in the late nineteenth century. The Baltimore College of Dental Surgery, established in 1839 and the first institution of its kind in the world, arose after an unsuccessful attempt to found dental chairs in medical schools. The dental colleges that followed—in Ohio (1845), Pennsylvania (1856), and Philadelphia (1863)—taught little medicine but paid attention almost entirely to mechanical training and to what a dentist had to know. All conferred the D.D.S. degree. In 1865 the New York College of Dentistry was founded with the purpose of educating men to practice dental surgery as a specialty of medicine. In 1867 Harvard University opened a dental department and began teaching dentistry as a branch of medicine; the universities of Michigan (1875) and Pennsylvania (1878) followed Harvard's example.

From 1878 to 1899 the number of dental schools increased dramatically, owing largely to the fact that the laws in many states required graduation from a dental school as a condition for licensure. In 1878 the nation had twelve dental schools; in 1899 it had fifty-six.

Schools of dentistry flourished in metropolitan centers with an abundant supply of clinical material, and most such schools started as proprietary enterprises. In the late 1890s Illinois had five dental schools, all in Chicago. Chicago had more of these institutions than any other city in the nation.[58]

The Chicago College of Dental Surgery (CCDS), chartered in 1884, was the pioneer. By 1894 it was the largest institution of its kind in the world.[59] The American College of Dental Surgery was organized in 1886, and the Northwestern University Dental School had its beginnings in 1887.[60] The others were the Northwestern College of Dental Surgery (1885), the German-American Dental College (1888), and Columbian Dental College (1893).

In 1897–98 the Columbian Dental College had only fifty-five matriculants. On 17 August 1898 the stockholders changed the name to the Illinois School of Dentistry, and shortly thereafter the officials applied for affiliation with the University.[61]

In January 1901 the school repeated its request. The trustees approved the proposal, and the authorities of the College of Medicine proceeded with their plans to organize a school of dentistry as a department of the college. Committees representing the medical school and the dental school agreed that it was in their mutual interest to unite. The University would establish an entirely new school, to be known as the School of Dentistry of the University of Illinois. Under the terms, CPS would acquire the Illinois School of Dentistry, taking over its equipment and good will for $17,000, payable in interest-bearing bonds of CPS. Transfer of the lease and the premises, a building at the southwest corner of Clark and Van Buren streets, was to take effect on 15 March 1901 at a rental of $3,500 annually. The lease was to expire on 1 May 1904. CPS assumed liability for the contracts of five faculty members of the school.

On 3 October the School of Dentistry opened as a department of the College of Medicine in the five-story building formerly occupied by the medical school at the corner of Harrison and Honore streets (it had been restored and improved after the fire of 25 June 1901). Adelbert H. Peck, a professor of materia medica, special pathology, and therapeutics with a D.D.S. from the Chicago College of Dental Surgery (1888) and an M.D. degree from Rush Medical College (1894), the dean of the old school, was retained as dean of the new school.[62]

Under the rules of the National Association of Dental Faculties, requirements for admission were a certificate of entrance into the second year of a high school or its equivalent. Studies in other dental schools of equivalent standing were accredited for advanced standing. The course of study required for graduation extended through three years, each of seven months.

For two years the college operated under these arrangements. In 1901–2 the faculty consisted of sixteen members and a year later nineteen, including several M.D.s who also taught in the medical college, plus demonstrators, quiz masters, anatomy teachers, and clerical assistants. In 1901–2 the three classes enrolled a total of 134 students, and a year later 132, including five women each year. In 1902 the University awarded the D.D.S. degree to 40 graduates and in 1903 to 38, including one woman each year. During these years dental students organized a football team, a band, and three professional fraternities.

But the school operated at a deficit. For 1901–2 the loss was $12,349, and for 1902–3 it was $8,621. The medical college covered the losses, but to do so ate into its profits and endangered the University's interest. So on 6 June 1903 the medical faculty accepted the resignations of Dean Peck and five other dental school faculty members. Bernard J. Cigrand, a professor of prosthetic dentistry, technics, and history who held a D.D.S. degree from Lake Forest University (1888) and an M.S. degree from Northern Indiana Normal School

(1891) was among the eight faculty retained. Formerly in charge of dental prosthetics at the American College of Dental Surgery and later at Northwestern University Dental School, Cigrand had published historical works and was known as the author of *The Rise, Fall and Revival of Dental Prosthetics* (1892, 2d ed. 1893). He was named acting dean.[63]

During the summer the authorities acted swiftly to reorient the dental department. In July 1903, hard on the heels of Peck's ouster, Truman W. Brophy requested that CCDS become the University's dental school. A graduate of the University of Pennsylvania Dental School (1870) and Rush Medical College (1880), Brophy was at the time professor of oral surgery at both CCDS and Rush Medical College, and president of the former. At a July meeting with the executive committee of the University's board, Trustee Samuel A. Bullard of the Committee on the Medical College, and officers of the College of Medicine, Brophy proposed to turn over the property of his school to the University on about the same terms as CPS had done. He wanted to retain the name of The Chicago College of Dental Surgery and add "The College of Dentistry of the University of Illinois." Brophy planned to use two buildings, the CCDS building, at the southeast corner of Harrison and Wood streets, and the University's dental building, a block to the west, and to conduct the dental college entirely separately from the medical college. The board of the medical college unanimously favored the offer on the terms outlined.[64]

In early August Bullard drew up a contract, and on 19 September the Board of Trustees held a special meeting in Chicago to consider the matter. Delegations from both the College of Medicine and CCDS were on hand. Everyone believed that a union of the two dental schools would promote "a wider and larger usefulness in professional education than at present," and the trustees approved a contract between the two parties. Although the CCDS had estimated the value of its property and good will at $260,000, the trustees valued the real and personal property at $188,000, and agreed on $200,000 for the property and the good will together. The University was to pay to acquire the CCDS out of the net earnings of the college over a period of years, as spelled out in a complex contract.[65]

The arrangements envisioned a combination of the two schools that would make, in Draper's terms, "the largest and strongest college for dental instruction in the world." Fusion of the faculties would strengthen the department, and use of both buildings would provide ample room for enlarged classes. Draper thought the new school would be a financial asset to the College of Medicine.[66]

On 7 October the new school opened for the 1903–4 session, and a day later the old school opened for the academic year with a faculty of twenty-two plus special lecturers and clinicians, demonstrators of three grades, and quiz masters. At its opening exercises, Dean Brophy praised the advantages of a connection with the University. Dean Cigrand topped him, calling the city of Chicago the medical and dental Mecca of the world and taking pride in being affiliated with "the greatest University of America."[67]

A week later Draper praised Brophy as "right up to the front in his professional work" and "a good business man who insists upon prudence and expects to have his ends meet and have some to spare." Brophy thought that there were expenses in "the Cigrand School" that might be eliminated. Cigrand, Draper confessed, was an enigma. "He may be a literary or historical genius but he certainly lacks in stability, steadiness and reliability, and I fear he lacks in fidelity." So Draper felt impelled to tie to Brophy. Success had to come via Brophy or not at all. Draper urged Steele "to put yourself on confidential and mutually helpful relations with [Brophy]" and keep him from precipitating troubles that might result in an opposition school.[68]

Draper soon became disillusioned with Brophy. A problem arose in the effort to combine the faculties of the old and new dental schools. Brophy had said that he would use all the best men of the former school, he to be the judge. Draper asked for a list of the contracts with Brophy's faculty showing their length of employment and salary, but after four requests over the course of two months he still did not have it. On 3 December Brophy finally wrote that the list would be mailed that night.[69]

It soon developed that the financial situation of CCDS was not as represented and that its officers were not carrying out the terms of the agreement. According to the contract, CCDS had an encumbrance of $75,000 in the form of bonds secured by a first mortgage and a floating indebtedness of about $25,000, and no other indebtedness. The contract authorized the college to issue bonds of the corporation to be due in ten to thirty years from 30 September 1903 to the amount of $125,000, to be secured by a second mortgage, with $25,000 of the bonds marked "preferred" and $100,000 "common." The former were to be used to pay the floating indebtedness. All tuition fees received by CCDS or the School of Dentistry of the University of Illinois were to be accounted for to the business manager of the University and credited to the dental school.

But the University belatedly discovered that the floating indebtedness of CCDS was $48,000 rather than $25,000. The officers of CCDS refused to pay the difference, insisting that the University shoulder the whole amount. The University also learned that CCDS wanted to make the bonds due in ten years rather than ten to thirty years, and that CCDS had wrongfully used tuition fees received amounting to $30,000 to pay old debts or otherwise.

When the University insisted that CCDS should pay its own debts and that the contract should be executed with exactness, the officers and stockholders of the dental college claimed that the contract was hard on them. The trustees of the University agreed to some modifications, and the two parties executed a supplemental agreement relating to the issuance of bonds. But members of the board of directors of CCDS refused to sign it.

When the University took steps to carry out the contract, W. L. Copeland, a professor of anatomy and a stockholder of CCDS who had assented to the conclusions reached, brought a legal action to have the contract nullified on the ground that it had not been authorized at a meeting of CCDS stockholders or directors, although the written contract itself was executed by Brophy, who had stated that it was executed under authority of a resolution of his board. Brophy, who personally held a large majority of the stock, refused to cooperate with the University in defending this action.[70]

Unwilling to make any further concessions or to waive the execution of any part of the agreement, and not deeming it worthwhile to contest the matter, on 8 March 1904 the Board of Trustees consented that the contract be annulled. An order of the court was entered to that effect, and the board directed its Committee on the Medical College to separate the School of Dentistry from the College of Medicine and to reorganize it as the College of Dentistry of the University of Illinois. The next day Draper submitted his resignation as president.[71]

In late April the University awarded the D.D.S. to fifty-six graduates of the School of Dentistry, including two women, and the trustees authorized the chairman of the Committee on the Medical College to confer with the president of the University and prepare for publication a refutation of "certain articles" that had appeared in the daily press and dental magazines "derogatory to the honesty and integrity of the University of Illinois." Copeland had published harsh criticisms of Draper in the *Dental Review*. On 6 June this refutation was printed in full in the records of the trustees. After briefly rehearsing the troubled relationship, Bullard, the probable author, declared that the statement that the agreement was nullified because of the purpose of the University to remove certain teachers at the dental college was untrue. Although the University had arrived at no such purpose, it had reserved to itself the right of ultimate control over the Chicago departments in order to ensure that their standards should advance to and never fall below the University grade. "Apparently the men who deserved removal were apprehensive of their dues." Brophy had insisted that not he but his associates were the wrongdoers, whereas they asserted that he was the guilty party. These conflicting statements had some bearing on the controversy, but the University did not have to settle them. It was quit of the whole matter.[72] On 6 October 1904 the College of Dentistry began its new academic year, and no more was heard of the Chicago College of Dental Surgery.[73]

In sum, when propriety schools of pharmacy, medicine, and dentistry sought affiliation with the University, the trustees agreed to absorb them as long as it could be done without cost to the state. In the years from 1896 to 1904 the venture into professional education was successful in pharmacy and medicine but problematic in dentistry. In any event, foundations had been laid for later advances in the health sciences in Chicago.

## NOTES

1. Altgeld to Draper, 6 March 1896, copy in 2/5/3, B:30, F:Altgeld and Medical School.
2. Henry L. Taylor, *Professional Education in the United States: Pharmacy*, University of the State of New York, College Department, Bulletin 10 (1900), 955–58; W. B. Day, "The School of Pharmacy," in *The Alumni Record of the University of Illinois: Chicago Departments, Colleges of Medicine and Dentistry, School of Pharmacy*, ed. Carl Stephens ([Urbana]: University of Illinois, 1921), xxv.
3. *18th Report* (1896), 195, 229, 238.
4. Ibid., 240–42.
5. These figures are from the reports of the Board of Trustees, supplemented by letters of Day to Draper in 2/4/2.
6. *21st Report* (1902), 212; Day to Draper, 26 April 1898, 18 May 1900, 2/4/2, B:5, 6, F:Day.
7. Draper to Day, 23 April 1898, 2/4/3.
8. Day to Draper, 26 April 1898, 13 November 1899 (two letters of this date), 2/4/2, B:5, 6, F:Day; Draper to Day, 16 November 1899, 2/4/3; Rogers to Draper, 15, 18 January 1900, 2/4/1, B:16, F:Rogers; Draper to Rogers, 16 January 1900, 2/4/3.
9. *19th Report* (1898), 137.
10. Draper to Day, 29 November 1897, 2/4/3; *19th Report* (1898), 188–90.
11. *Illio 1904*, 144.
12. *20th Report* (1901), 380; *Plexus*, 7 (20 March 1902), 416.
13. *21st Report* (1902), 110–11, 235–36.
14. Ibid., 242, 279, 283.
15. These figures are compiled from the reports of the Board of Trustees for the years from 1897 through 1904.
16. *22nd Report* (1904), 278–79, 306.
17. Charles Newman, *The Evolution of Medical Education in the Nineteenth Century* (London: Oxford University Press, 1957), 265–69; John H. Warner, *Against the Spirit of System: The French Impulse in Nineteenth-Century American Medicine* (Princeton: Princeton University Press, 1998).
18. Francis R. Packard, *History of Medicine in the United States*, 2 vols. (New York: Paul B. Hoeber, 1931), 1:273–337; for a list of seventy medical schools founded between 1765 and 1873, see 2:1213–14.
19. Thomas N. Bonner, *Medicine in Chicago, 1850–1950: A Chapter in the Social and Scientific Development of a City*, 2d ed. (Urbana: University of Illinois Press, 1991), 84–85.
20. Norman Bridge and John E. Rhodes, "History of Rush Medical College," in *Medical and Dental Colleges of the West: Historical and Biographical, Chicago*, ed. H. G. Cutler (Chicago: Oxford Publishing Co., 1896), 1–74. The same material is in

H. G. Cutler, ed., *Physicians and Surgeons of the West: Illinois Edition* (Chicago: American Biographical Publishing Co., 1900), 1–74.

21. Samuel J. Jones, "History of Northwestern University Medical School (Chicago Medical College)," in *Medical and Dental Colleges of the West: Historical and Biographical, Chicago*, ed. H. G. Cutler (Chicago: Oxford Publishing Co., 1896), 157–76. This account is also in Cutler, ed., *Physicians and Surgeons of the West*, 75–98.

22. Daniel A. K. Steele and William E. Quine, "History of College of Physicians and Surgeons," in *Medical and Dental Colleges of the West: Historical and Biographical, Chicago*, ed. H. G. Cutler (Chicago: Oxford Publishing Co., 1896), 341–53 (reprinted with added information in Cutler, ed., *Physicians and Surgeons of the West*, 139–52); D. A. K. Steele, "The Genesis of a Great Medical College," in *The Alumni Record of the University of Illinois: Chicago Departments* ([Urbana]: University of Illinois, 1921), vi–xiii; and Anon., "The College of Physicians and Surgeons of Chicago: An Outline of Its History," (1913), 26/1/10, B:9, F:Medicine. Anon., apparently a former faculty member of the college, offers a valuable corrective to the account of Steele and Quine. The cited Folder in 26/1/20 contains criticisms of Steele's "Genesis" article for slighting Quine's contribution. For biographical accounts of Quine and Steele, see *Medical and Dental Colleges of the West: Historical and Biographical, Chicago*, ed. H. G. Cutler (Chicago: Oxford Publishing Co., 1896), 364–67, 360–63.

23. Holmes to T. J. Burrill, 1 April 1913, 2/5/3, B:33, F:He-Hu 1912–13; *16th Report* (1892), 171–72, 196.

24. *16th Report* (1892), 220–22.

25. Ibid., 205.

26. *18th Report* (1896), 39, 41–42, 58, 64; Henry Wade Rogers (president of Northwestern University) to Draper, 24 December 1894, 2/4/1, B:16, F:Henry Wade Rogers.

27. *18th Report* (1896), 61, 64, 67 (the quotation); *Journal of the Senate of the Thirty-Ninth General Assembly of the State of Illinois* (1896), 172, 979; *Journal of the House of Representatives of the Thirty-Ninth General Assembly of the State of Illinois* (1896), 316, 367, 423; Henry L. Taylor, *Professional Education in the United States: Medicine*, University of the State of New York, College Department, Bulletin 8 (1900), 368–77.

28. *19th Report* (1898), 28, 44–45.

29. *Catalogue* (1897–98), 147.

30. 52/1/1, 116; *20th Report* (1901), 50, 125; Draper to Quine, 18 February 1899, 2/4/3.

31. *20th Report* (1901), 94.

32. 52/1/1, 141.

33. *20th Report* (1901), 125–26.

34. 52/1/2, 55.

35. *20th Report* (1901), 214, 238, 239, 241, 242, 245–54 (quotation at 246).

36. 52/1/1, 159; 51/1/2, 114; *21st Report* (1902), 1, 21–4, 29, 66–67; *22nd Report* (1904), 7–11, 20.

37. *22nd Report* (1904), 20–23 (quotations at 22, 23), 62.

38. Ibid., 148–52.

39. Enrollment figures for 1895–96 and 1896–97 are from a College of Dentistry catalog; the others are compiled from reports of the Board of Trustees.

40. Quine to Draper, 1 February 1895, 2/4/1, B:15, F:Q, 1894–1903; *Plexus*, 3 (June 1897), 35.
41. Pusey to Draper, 8 June 1897, 2/4/2, B:3, F:1897; Draper to Pusey, 10 June 1897, 2/4/3; *19th Report* (1898), 134.
42. William E. Quine, "Woman's Sphere," *Plexus* 9 (20 January 1904), 303–4.
43. 52/1/1, 116, 150–51; Draper to Lucy L. Flower, 17 February 1899; Draper to James E. Armstrong, 17, 21 February 1899; Draper to Quine, 20, 23 February 1899, 2/4/3; *20th Report* (1901), 291.
44. *20th Report* (1901), 291–94.
45. James M. Phelan, "Quine, William E.," *Dictionary of American Biography*, vol. 21, Supplement One, ed. Harris E. Starr (New York: Charles Scribner's Sons, 1944), 616–17.
46. A. J. Graham, "Lobbying Days, 1913," [written 1934–36], 15–18, 26/1/20, B:9.
47. W. T. Eckley, "Scholastic Pandemonium," *Plexus*, 5 (20 November 1899), 239–42; H. B. Hamilton, "Class History," *Plexus*, 5 (20 February 1900), 404; Graham, "Lobbying Days, 1913," 16.
48. 51/1/1, 144–45; 51/1/2, 113, 117, 257.
49. *Plexus*, 7 (20 October 1901), 220.
50. Ibid., 2 (February 1897), 200.
51. Ibid., 9 (20 July 1903), 85–87 (quotation at 86). The book was H. B. Sharman, *Studies in the Life of Christ* (1898).
52. 51/1/1, 146; 51/1/2, 136, 138, 186 (the quotation), 235; *Plexus*, 1895–1904.
53. 51/1/1, 96, 98–99, 101–2; *19th Report* (1898), 235.
54. 51/1/2, 68, 69 (the quotation).
55. *19th Report* (1896), 28, 44–45; *22nd Report* (1904), 57, 123, 302, 310, 311, 334; Bullard to Draper, 8 July, 12 August, 23 September 1903, 2/4/1, B:1, F:Bullard; Draper to Steele, 17 March 1904, 2/4/3; *23rd Report* (1906), 18.
56. These figures are compiled from the records of the Board of Trustees.
57. *19th Report* (1898), 360.
58. Henry J. Taylor, *Professional Education in the United States: Dentistry*, University of the State of New York, College Department, Bulletin 9 (1900), 749–51, 758; "History of the College of Dentistry," in *The Alumni Record of the University of Illinois: Chicago Departments, Colleges of Medicine and Dentistry, School of Pharmacy*, ed. Carl Stephens ([Urbana]: University of Illinois, 1921), xxii–xxiv (an inadequate account).
59. Truman W. Brophy, "History of Chicago College of Dental Surgery," in Cutler, ed., *Physicians and Surgeons of the West*, 153–70.
60. Edgar D. Swain, "Northwestern University Dental School," in Cutler, ed., *Physicians and Surgeons of the West*, 171–78.
61. Columbian Dental College, *Fifth Annual Announcement, 1897–98*; *Illinois School of Dentistry, Announcement, 1898–1899*, 54/1/805, Dentistry Catalogs and Announcements; Walter Sayler to Draper, 12, 31 August, 15 September, 7 December 1898, 2/4/1, B:16, F:Sa; Draper to William E. Quine, 1 September 1898; Draper to Sayler, 9 December 1898, 2/4/3; *20th Report* (1901), 3–4.
62. 51/1/2, 111, 125–26, 141, 149, 156, 171; *21st Report* (1902), 46, 49, 54–56; *Catalog* (1900–1901), 174; *Plexus*, 7 (20 July 1901), 118–39; *Catalog* (1901–1902), 25, 160.
63. 51/1/2, 348–49. Cigrand described the events of 1903, when the University operated a dental department and absorbed the CCDS, in two letters to President Edmund J. James, 20 April 1905 (2/5/6, B:2, F:A–D.)

64. Bullard to Draper, 9, 20 July 1903, 2/4/1, B:1, F:Bullard.
65. Bullard to Draper, 7 August 1903 (with a draft of the contract), 2/4/1, B:1, F:Bullard; *22nd Report* (1904), 228–37.
66. Draper to Cigrand, 24 September 1903, 2/4/3; see also *Plexus*, 9 (20 September 1903), 173; Draper to D. A. K. Steele, 29 September 1903, 2/4/3.
67. *Plexus*, 9 (20 October 1903), 216, 226; Draper to Brophy, 6 October 1903, 2/4/3. No catalog of Brophy's school can be located.
68. Draper to Steele, 15 October 1903, 2/4/3.
69. Bullard to Draper, 9 July 1903, 2/4/1, B:1, F:Bullard; Draper to Brophy, 28 October, 9 November, 2 December 1903, 2/4/3; Brophy to Draper, 3 December 1903, 2/4/1, B:1, F:Brophy.
70. [Andrew S. Draper?], "The Chicago College of Dental Surgery," [4 February 1904], 2/4/3. A summary of the dispute.
71. *22nd Report* (1904), 267, 274.
72. W. T. Copeland to the Editor of the Dental Review, *Dental Review*, 18 (15 March 1904), 285–87; *22nd Report* (1904), 279, 307–8.
73. *Catalog of Dentistry of the University of Illinois: Announcements for 1904–1905* (Chicago, [1904]), 35, 51/1/805, Dentistry Catalogs and Announcements.

# PART III

## STUDENT LIFE AND CULTURE

# CHAPTER 11

# COMMON BONDS

Universities are social institutions whose main purpose is to educate the young for useful lives. Authorities can readily determine what goes on in the classroom, but in large measure students shape "college life." They often learn as much from each other and from discussions with teachers outside of class as they do from books.

At the turn of the century the nation was changing rapidly. In 1894 the majority of Illinois undergraduates came from farms or rural communities, whereas by 1904 many came from towns or urban areas. Most students went to college uncultured, crude, and in a plastic moral state. They went to the University to put themselves in a position to make a better life. They left with their character more fully formed through college associations.

In the 1890s the University community shared a sense of inferiority about the school's standing. The institution had grown slowly. The trustees had made timid requests to the legislature, the General Assembly had provided niggardly support, and the people of Illinois were poorly informed about Urbana. Chicago newspapers disparaged the downstate enterprise.

By 1894, however, a new era was dawning. The Board of Trustees, Governor Altgeld, and President Draper were all determined to upgrade the institution. Students were convinced that they had a vital role to play in releasing the school's potential. When the institution gained fame, they reasoned, the legislature would be obliged to furnish greater financial support.

A robust University spirit and a deep sense of loyalty to Illinois were prerequisite to any advance. These qualities had to be cultivated.

## The College Class System

The college class system would prove to be a barrier to the development of University spirit. This prominent feature of American higher education had taken root at a time when college classes were small and homogeneous and a fixed curriculum was the norm. For four years a whole class marched in lock step through the same course of studies. Members formed close personal bonds and developed intense loyalty to their class.

In 1894 the class system was well entrenched at Illinois. The class more than the University provided students with their primary institutional identity. Traditionally, class rivalries were a prominent part of the class system. By the 1890s the class system was beginning to crumble, but for many years it continued, intensifying class loyalty. In 1894 the declaration that students should pledge their loyalty to the University rather than their class was viewed as radical.[1]

## President Draper and Convocation

Convocation was one of the chief means of shaping student values and creating University spirit. In 1894 convocation replaced the compulsory chapel exercises that had just been abolished. Ideally, convocation was to meet once a week. Attendance was voluntary. All regular University duties were suspended as far as possible so that everyone might attend. Programs included scripture reading and prayer, several musical selections, and at least one address. Convocation met ten times in 1894–95, nine times the following year, and thereafter with decreasing frequency. Students filled the chapel for these gatherings.

Convocation served many purposes. Draper intended to use it to deepen and quicken the religious life of the University. The meetings frequently commemorated national heroes, especially the martyred Lincoln. Draper was almost invariably the presiding officer. Convocation provided him the best forum for addressing students. Draper had a thoroughly conventional mind. He could effortlessly meet students on their own level. He liked to banter with his audience. Students punctuated his remarks with laughter and applause. Speaking with utter confidence, he carried conviction.

Draper used these occasions to dispense homely advice, to create University spirit, and to instill loyalty to Illinois. He offered practical advice on how to get along in college, praised the value of promptness, and stressed the importance of firm principles and good character. On one occasion he spoke about the proper attitude toward the law. "Men become either criminals or patriots early in life," he opined. "He who overlooks the little things in youth becomes the law-breaker in later life." A fatuous statement, it may still have impressed his auditors. Another time he said that the life of students depended as much on the life of the associations they formed as on their classroom work, but students should never lose sight of University spirit. He sometimes thought that he discerned too much class spirit and too little University spirit, but that the time would come when students would be proud not that they were members of a class but that they were graduates of the University of Illinois.[2]

Every great university, Draper asserted at one convocation, had a certain definite spirit—it stands for something. Neither buildings and equipment nor the faculty or board of trustees defined the spirit. Rather, "It is the life of the university, the product of the best that was and the best that is. It becomes a tradition and is handed down from generation to generation. It determines the character of the university, which in turn determines that of its graduates, who in their turn carry its results out into the world." Here Draper was grappling with a complex idea. He gave a short account of the founding and early history of the University, adding, "we are now determining our university spirit." It was the composite result of the thought of students, faculty, and trustees. Each class, each individual, exerted an influence on it, so each individual was responsible for the spirit that was to represent the University. "The essence of university spirit is university comradeship. If that spirit be worthy, then we as comrades must be worthy. We must have objects in agreement." Draper's remarks reveal a conservative administrator who valued order.[3]

## UNIVERSITY COLORS, SONGS, AND YELLS

Students as well as Draper were greatly concerned with generating University spirit. No one could readily define the concept, but everyone agreed that some visible symbols were needed to provide a rallying point for college activities.

For years, uncertainty existed as to the University colors. Many different color combinations had gained recognition, with the Athletic Association making the selection. For a long time old gold and black were accepted, but they were common in other colleges and therefore not a distinguishing mark of Illinois. In the early 1890s, when the athletic coach was from Dartmouth, Dartmouth green was a favorite color.

In September 1894 the editor of the *Illini* called for official action on University colors, and in October Draper urged that the matter be settled. A faculty committee met with student representatives and proposed orange and white, with green in addition on the athletic field. A committee from the Athletic Association reviewed these ideas, and the combined committees then proposed navy blue and orange. Draper submitted the scheme to a convocation, and students endorsed the recommendation. On 6 November the faculty made the colors official.[4]

At the turn of the century many colleges had their own songbook. The typical book of this type had almost no original music. Schools appropriated the same melodies.[5] At Illinois the need for suitable songs was keenly felt. No other university had so little singing of college songs as Illinois, wrote the *Illini*. "The social element introduced by the singing of songs which deal with the subjects closest to the student in his life here, and which breathe forth a spirit of love and loyalty to the alma mater, is an important one. It gives the students . . . a common bond of union."[6]

Several efforts were made to generate songs that would belong distinctively to Illinois and contribute to Illinois spirit. The YMCA offered cash prizes for the best songs of this type. Trustee Samuel A. Bullard promoted a project to produce songs that would set forth the work the University was doing and at the same time have sufficient raciness in them to commend themselves to students. A Song-Book Committee announced monetary prizes for the best Illinois songs.

These endeavors resulted in many labored tributes to alma mater that fell of their own weight, along with some lighter and often meaningless songs that enjoyed favor. In the fall of 1894, Franklin G. Carnahan, '92, and William L. Steele, '96, produced the words to "Our Dear Illinois." A year later the college newspaper published both the words and music to "Illinois," subtitled "The University Song," by these men.[7]

In 1895 Walter Howe Jones, head of the music department, wrote the words and music to "Illinois University Hymn." That same year Jones wrote the music and Steele wrote the words to "Dear Old Illinois." These tributes are readily forgotten.[8]

Jones is also identified with "Illinois," a song associated with the University that endures. On 10 December 1897 the *Illini* reported the performance of this composition at a Glee and Mandolin Club concert. It begins, "By thy rivers gently flowing, Illinois, [Illinois]," and celebrates the state, not the University, during the Civil War years. On 25 November 1898 the *Illini* published both the words and the music to this song. Jones said that he had written the music but not the words. In 1901 he copyrighted the music.[9]

Sometime in May 1901, wrote the *Illini*, Jones published the *Illinois Song Book*, with over thirty University songs, all by Jones. These productions were reportedly written for use by glee clubs and had been sung for the past six years. The book was said to contain two arrangements of "By thy rivers gently flowing," the so-called University Hymn "Dear Old Illinois," with words by Steele and music by Jones, and a University medley. This book, said Jones, was published by the *Champaign Gazette*.[10] In December 1902 Bullard sent

Draper a song with words he had written and music by Frederick L. Lawrence, director of the School of Music. The song was "Grand Illinois."[11]

In 1903 Ethel Forbes, '03, and Ethel I. Dobbins, '02, of the Song-Book Committee published *Illinois Songs*, a collection with words and music for twenty-eight songs and words alone to another three. Fifteen entries with words and music were mainly popular songs, another was a Yale college song, and thirteen items were distinctively Illinois songs. Seven of these set an Illinois text to a familiar or published tune; among them was "Fair Illinois," sung to the tune of "Fair Harvard." Another so-called University Hymn, "The Watch on the Rhine," with words by Lewis A. Rhoades, professor of German, was set to music composed by Franz von Blon for a piece titled "Die Wacht am Rhein."[12] Another six songs consisted of original words and music allegedly distinctive to the University. "Alma Mater," arranged by Ralph G. Mills, '03, was the most memorable. The first stanza goes:

> Rising midst the golden corn field,
> Grandly to the view,
> Reaches our dear Alma Mater
> Proudly to the blue.

The chorus continues:

> Swell the chorus ever louder,
> Full of cheer and joy;
> Hail to thee our Alma Mater,
> Dear old Illinois.

Two more stanzas elaborate the theme. "Alma Mater" was the only Illinois item included in *Songs of All the Colleges* (1901, 1906). But in that book the arrangement is attributed to George Rosey (George Rosenberg), a native of Dusseldorf, Germany, who came to the United States in 1883 and became a composer, arranger, and publisher.[13] In 1906 the publisher copyrighted the Rosey arrangement. "Alma Mater" remains a favorite. Although the words celebrate Illinois, the tune is Cornell University's *Amici Usque* (Friends all the way), which begins with the well-known "Far above Cayuga's waters."

To familiarize students with Illinois songs, Frederick Lawrence led some outdoor "sings" in the spring of 1902 and an indoor sing in the fall of 1903. Singing Illinois songs, said the *Illini*, would fill students "with a greater love for Illinois." About four hundred students attended the 1903 songfest. The favorites were popular items like "Bonnie" and "Goodnight Ladies."[14]

It is impossible to identify *the* University Hymn with any certainty. At one time or another the term was applied to Carnahan and Steele's "Illinois," to

Jones and Steele's "Dear Old Illinois," to Jones's "Illinois University Hymn," and to Rhoades's "The Watch on the Rhine." In any event, most of the songs of these years were eminently forgettable.

In addition to songs, the desire to arouse enthusiasm and unite the student body inspired a demand for yells with a distinctive University character. Considerable thought was given to the subject. The two things most essential for a University yell, one student explained, were facility for loud delivery and individuality. Not two or three yells were wanted, but one only, such that it would be recognized when heard.[15]

Charles M. Moss, professor of Greek, agreed that the University needed a yell that would "go" of its own gravity and be distinctly a yell for the University of Illinois. But to create such, one had to pay heed to the usefulness of the different vowel and diphthong sounds. The word *Illinois* somewhat handicapped one because it had two close vowel sounds in the first two syllables. "It seems, therefore, that this word can be used but once, and once it must be, and that at the end of the yell. The rest of the sounds must have in them the vowels *a* and *o*, chiefly; for *e*, *u* and *i* are in a further descending scale of openness, and so unsuitable for use. The diphthongs *ai* and *oi* are usable. Of course *a* must have the sound of *a* in father." Moss hoped that this matter would not be laid aside until the campus had a yell that by spontaneous assent of everyone would outrank and displace the current imperfect yells.[16]

In October 1895 the *Illini* published an account of three "University Yells." One was the zany 1888 classic that ended, "Ipsidi Iki, U. of I., Champaign." The second began "Hol-a-ba-loo! Hoorah! Hoorah!" repeated the "hoorahs," and ended "Wah-Hoo-Wah!" And the third one declared "Yah, yah, yah, ki! Yah, yah, yah, ki! Boom-a-langer! Boom-a-langer! U. of I.!"[17]

Cheering was considered appropriate for general University functions. But rooting and cheering were most appropriate at athletic contests. When football became the dominant college sport, guying initially met the need to arouse college spirit and support the team. A "guyer," a student especially gifted with a venomous tongue, ran along the sidelines making fun of or insulting and vilifying the opposition. But guying, or jollying the other fellows, was considered boorish and ineffective. Scattered spontaneous outbursts were good, but in May 1896 the *Illini* called for the appointment of leaders who could swell the noise at games. At an athletics mass meeting in October 1897, Rollin O. Everhart, '98, was appointed to take on the task. He selected two men from each class who were to be responsible for the noise made by members of the class.[18]

In the fall of 1901 the senior class chose three men to secure organized leadership in rooting; a year later the senior class perpetuated the custom.[19] At an October 1903 athletic mass meeting, R. C. "Red" Mathews was selected to take charge of the cheering. He named three section leaders. They took the names of students who agreed to yell more when the team was doing poorly than when it was winning. Shortly thereafter some 150 men signed up to report to Mathews on the bleachers for rooting practice. The guyer had become the cheerleader.[20]

## STUDENT PUBLICATIONS

Student publications were a common bond in the community. The most important of these was the campus newspaper, a monthly dating from 1871. In January 1874 the journal had taken a new and distinctive name, the *Illini*. In 1880 it began to appear every two weeks. The paper was a literary journal with some local news.

In 1894 the *Illini* became a weekly. The printing was moved from the old *Illini* office in the Mechanical Building and Drill Hall to The News Publishing Company in Champaign, with great typographical improvement. The circulation was one thousand, the subscription price was $2, and four hundred of the copies were sent to high schools and county superintendents throughout the state at the expense of the Board of Trustees. The subsidy made the paper an official publication of the University.[21]

In the five years that the paper was a weekly the editors were all excellent students. In practice the paper was a one-man operation reflecting the editor's interests. Yet it had a basic sameness from year to year. The page was about seven and a half by ten and a quarter inches, and each issue ran to sixteen pages plus six pages of advertisements. The editors tried to publish both a newspaper and a literary magazine, with different editors emphasizing one or the other. With weekly publication, local news was not newsworthy by the time it appeared in print. The editors did not use their office to promote any kind of reform.

In 1894–95 Edward L. Mann of Gilman, Illinois, a student in Literature and Arts and a member of the Adelphic Literary Society, was the editor. He resigned prematurely to be sure he would graduate. George H. Campbell of Edgewood, Illinois, a student in Literature and Arts and a member of the Philomathean and Blackstonian societies, filled out the year.

In May David H. Carnahan of Champaign, a student in Literature and Arts, an athlete, and a member of Sigma Chi, Shield and Trident, and Adelphic, took over. Appealing to a wide range of readers, he covered engineering and science as well as literature and published articles by the faculty and on the founding of famous colleges. He tried to lighten the tone of the paper, to improve the local department, and to establish an alumni department.

In 1896–97 Frederick W. (or F. Will) Schacht of Moline, a student in the College of Science who gained recognition in many campus activities, was editor. He urged students to take an interest in the paper; without the subsidy from the trustees the paper would have been in financial trouble. Schacht reported on athletic events extensively. He wrote few editorials and rarely expressed an opinion. His exchange column, with news of other colleges and universities, was popular.

In 1897–98 Arthur R. Crathorne, a native of Scarborough, England, who was a student in the College of Science, a Philomathean, a Phi Kappa Sigma, Hatchet Orator, and a captain in the University Regiment, was the editor. He reported regularly on the schools of pharmacy and medicine in Chicago. Although his editorials were weak and he largely ignored the Spanish-American War, Crathorne made the paper representative of the University by publishing items on math, on American authors, and on the history of the University.

The issue of 11 March 1898 was a *Women's Illini*, edited by Emma M. Rhoads of Ottawa, Illinois, a member of the Alethenai Literary Society and Kappa Kappa Gamma and president of the YWCA. Produced entirely by women, the issue contained articles about women in various academic disciplines. It was considered a great success.

In 1898–99 Horace A. Rhoads edited the paper. He published articles on the School of Music, the Astronomical Observatory, the Museum of Natural History, and on art and design. He invited women to produce another women's issue. Rhoads tried to make the journal a literary magazine. He published many rondeaus or rondels, a French lyric form.

In 1899–1900, under the editorship of William W. Smith, an African American from Homer, a student in Literature and Arts, and a member of his class football team, the rifle team, the YMCA, the student Republican Club, and the Philomathean Literary Society, the *Illini* became a student paper rather than the official organ of the University. It also became a triweekly, appearing on Monday, Wednesday, and Friday with a format of four pages, each of four columns, with the right column of the first page and other space given to advertisements. The subscription price was now $1.50 a year.

Smith aimed to make the *Illini* a mirror of campus life. He broke new ground with editorials that expressed opinions. He favored retention of a controversial football coach, for example, and contended that the University as an organization should not participate in politics.

In 1900–1 editor Franklin W. Scott of Centralia, a student in Literature and Arts, was the editor. He deplored the fact that the spirit of enthusiasm in all things pertaining to University life and work was weak. Under Draper the University had grown tremendously, Scott wrote, but it had not yet attained mature greatness. According to Scott, harsh treatment accorded students in Russian universities was not the concern of Illinois students.[22]

In 1901–2 Martin D. Brundage of Malta, Illinois, a student in Literature and Arts, succeeded Scott. He wrote editorials on current events and introduced both a humor column titled "Blots" and an exchange of letters between students. On 28 March he published another women's issue, the first since the paper became a triweekly. Ethel I. Dobbins, '02, headed the board of editors for this issue. It contained excellent material, including an essay by Lulu M. Lego, '03, on the history of women at Illinois, an article titled "The Social Life of Our Young Women," and a sketch, "The Varsity Girl."

In 1902 the *Illini* became a daily, although it did not change its name at this time, and was able to cover campus activities more completely than ever before. Irving M. Western of Dundee, class of 1902, who had been prominent in campus activities before entering law school, was editor. The paper followed the rhythm of the academic year, reporting on football in the fall, debates and social events in the winter, and baseball and musical events in the spring. Western introduced a cartoon on the first page, he encouraged students to exchange correspondence in the paper, and he expressed opinions in his editorials.

During 1903–4 editor Timothy O. Holcombe, apart from publishing a debate supplement, made no innovations. Several of his editorials noted the increasing stature of the University. Its real rapid growth began with Draper, Holcombe wrote, and "the time seems near at hand when the University of Illinois is to exceed in size any other university in the country." Ranking after Harvard, Columbia, Chicago, Michigan, and California, Illinois was the sixth largest American university.[23]

The college yearbook, founded in 1882 and sponsored by the sophomore class, was originally a literary production that did its best to promote the University's interest. In 1894, however, the publication was entrusted to the junior class and became known as the *Illio*.[24]

The yearbook was published in the spring of the year, with advertisements interspersed with the text or placed at the back of the volume. The editors aimed to provide an overview of campus life for the academic year. They ran biographies of trustees, officers (especially Draper), and faculty members. Draper contributed articles, and his photograph was often featured. *Illio 1904* was dedicated to him. Generally, the yearbook included accounts of each of the college classes, student clubs and organizations, the literary societies, fraternities, athletics, and the alumni. A literary section contained essays and poems, translations from Greek and Latin texts, and humor. Yearbooks identified students with the school by addressing some aspect of University history, and they incorporated material on the Chicago professional schools. Illustrations and art work, including full-page graphic designs, enlivened the production.

*Illini* editor Frank Scott had wished to free the college newspaper to concentrate on news by establishing a literary magazine. He was a member of the Fortnightly Club, a faculty–student group interested in all art forms. It sponsored the *'Varsity Fortnightly*, a journal of humor, art, and literature that first appeared in November 1900. The inaugural issue contained the text of "University Hymn," sketches from Paris by Professor Newton A. Wells, poetry, an essay on Thomas Hardy, and Draper's endorsement. The editors attributed the inspiration for the organ to Draper, "who has made Illinois the worthy house of the sturdiest and most progressive young men and women of the state and who seeks to send our sympathy back into the world."[25]

The 'Varsity Fortnightly furnished literary aspirants and artists a place where they might display their work. The second number printed a version of Draper's address, "University Freedom and Student Character," in which Draper elaborated the view that in education, character counted more than knowledge.[26] The 'Varsity Fortnightly led an uncertain and irregular life, and in May 1901 it expired.

As its successor the English Club, organized for the purpose of studying the writings of contemporary authors, sponsored The Illinois, a college monthly that first appeared in November 1902. In addition to essays on literary figures by students and faculty members, the editors published original fiction and poetry, articles on University life, and a good amount of material on football and other athletic activities, but nothing of a political nature. The Illinois appeared from October to May each year until 1907. After a break of eighteen months the periodical began again in November 1909 as the Illinois Magazine. Both Carl Van Doren and Allan Nevins were contributors. In 1906–7 Van Doren served as editor.

## RELIGION

Despite the constitutional principle of separation of church and state, the United States was still a Christian nation when the University of Illinois opened. The people of Illinois never doubted that religion should be perpetuated in their state university. When the school opened, no formal inducements were held out toward Christian life, but the whole tendency and spirit of the institution were favorable to that end.

Despite the Christian atmosphere, no courses in religion and few in philosophy were available. In this respect the University of Illinois differed significantly from the midwestern state universities founded prior to the Morrill Act of 1862. The universities of Wisconsin, Michigan, and Indiana had required students to take courses in natural theology, moral philosophy, and evidences of Christianity. A generation later these subjects were not part of the land-grant college offerings.

The University served the new industrial order by focusing on soluble technical problems. Although the curriculum included traditional liberal arts subjects, it was concerned with knowledge rather than faith and rarely dealt with imponderables. The course of study did not overtly undermine religious faith, but probably it silently encouraged secularism—the preoccupation with this world that ignores without necessarily denying spiritual concerns.

Attendance at daily chapel exercises was required when the University opened. In time, however, compulsory chapel became a focus of criticism. Serious chapel disorders contributed to the forced departure of the regent in 1891. The exercises had become stiff and formal, an object of ridicule. Doubts had arisen about compulsory chapel in a state university. Some felt that forced religious exercises did more harm than good. In March 1894 the faculty resolved to discontinue the requirement at the end of the year. The trustees agreed. Like the fabled one-hoss shay, chapel had simply worn out.[27]

At the time compulsory chapel was abolished, the churches ignored the state universities and University authorities assumed that a public institution could not offer courses in religion. Among the people the suspicion lingered that state universities were "godless." The University was solicitous about the religious welfare of students, nevertheless, and, as before, the spirit of the institution remained favorable to Christian life.

President Draper, who had previously belonged to both Congregational and Lutheran churches, was a Presbyterian while in Urbana. He thought that the different denominations should all agree, and he hoped to make the power of the University felt along religious lines more than it had been previously.[28] In his view the toleration of all religious opinion in a state university promoted a hearty and vigorous religious feeling. "There is no place," he wrote, with denominational colleges especially in mind, "where there is a more tolerant spirit, or freer discussion of religious questions, or a stronger, more unrestrained, and healthier religious life than in the State universities."[29]

Draper did all that could reasonably be done to encourage spiritual life. He made no sectarian faculty appointments, but application forms asked about church affiliation, and it counted favorably in the selection of faculty members. Draper believed that three-fourths or four-fifths of the instructional staff were church members, and he knew of no faculty member who was antagonistic to the churches.[30] An 1898 census showed thirty Congregationalists on the faculty, twenty-eight Presbyterians, twenty-five Methodists, nineteen Episcopalians, five Baptists, four Universalists, three Unitarians, two Christians, one Lutheran, and eight faculty without a church membership.[31]

Religion continued to find a place in the University. During his tenure, Draper delivered a baccalaureate address to the graduating seniors on the Sunday before commencement every year but one. He spoke on civic and moral topics, giving addresses with titles like "The College Graduate in Affairs" (1895), "The Worth of the Man" (1898), and "Factors of Success" (1903). Draper invited all local clergymen to attend commencement, at which one of them would give an invocation and a benediction.

Although the authorities promoted the faith along nonsectarian Protestant lines, students largely determined the religious and moral atmosphere of the campus. A majority of them came from mainstream Protestant families. Yet the student body was not as churchly as at other state universities. Francis W. Kelsey's figures for 1896–1897 show that an average of 57.5 percent of the students in seven midwestern state universities were church members. The figures credit Indiana with 63.8 percent; Iowa, 60.0; Wisconsin, 58.3; Michigan, 57.5; Minnesota, 57.0; Kansas 55.4; and Illinois, 50.6 percent.[32] A 1903–4 religious census published by the campus YMCA indicated that 56.4 percent of the Illinois men and 79.7 percent of the women claimed church membership.[33]

A census of students taken at registration in 1896 and another taken in 1898 offer data on members and adherents of various churches. The rank order was the same in both years. In 1898, when 1,046 students were enrolled and 633 students participated in the census, the results were as follows: Methodist, 188; Presbyterian, 126; Congregational, 48; Baptist, 44; Disciples of Christ, 32; Episcopal, 24; Lutheran, 11; Unitarian, 10; and Roman Catholic, 7, with the others divided among many different denominations.[34]

These relative proportions remained fairly constant for many years. Based on available data from 1898 to 1906, the leading church preferences were as follows (with percentages in rounded numbers): Methodist, 33; Presbyterian, 22; Congregationalist, 12; Baptist, 9; Disciples of Christ, 7; Episcopal, 5; Roman Catholic, 4; Lutheran, 3; and Unitarian, 2. This ordering closely resembled that at other state universities.[35]

Within the University the two Christian Associations were a force for righteousness. The Young Men's Christian Association, which dated from 3 February 1873, promoted interdenominationalism and conversion to the faith. Its strong presence helped offset the widespread notion that the school lacked religion. Authorities refused to allow men and women to combine in one Christian group, so in 1884 women organized the Young Women's Christian Association.

For some years after compulsory chapel ended and before the churches followed the students to campus, the distinctively religious work on the campus was left to the initiative of the two Christian Associations. The free religious atmosphere of a state university, together with the responsibility felt by individual Christian students to propagate his or her faith, "provided fertile soil for the growth of indigenous, student-initiated and controlled Christian Associations based on wide opportunity for interdenominational religious fellowship and expression."[36]

The Christian Associations embraced a significant proportion of the student body. In 1894–95, 61 of the 465 male students, or 13.1 percent, were members of the YMCA. Between 1896 and 1904 enrollment of men at the University increased a little over 280 percent, while in these same years membership in the YMCA increased over 400 percent. In 1903–4, 624 out of 1,892 male students, or 32.9 percent, were YMCA members. From 1894–95 to 1903–4 the average annual YMCA membership was 24.45 percent of the male student enrollment. The YWCA drew a larger proportion of eligible students than the YMCA. In 1900 YWCA membership was 165; by 1904 it had reached 370. Over these five years the YWCA annually enlisted an average 42 percent of all women students and 63.5 percent of women undergraduates.[37]

The organization of the YMCA included an advisory board, a cabinet, and a general secretary. Committees carried out the work of the association. The officers, committee chairmen, and faculty advisors had considerable authority. Student officers were transient. Faculty advisors gained influence through their age, moral stature, and length of service. For years Thomas J. Burrill, a botanist, Samuel W. Parr, a chemist, and Evarts B. Greene, a historian, played leading advisory roles.

The ultimate purpose of the YMCA was to lead individuals into the Christian life. It sought to convince men to devote their lives to Jesus Christ in both religious callings and secular pursuits. Its evangelical core principles served as a barrier to Unitarians and Universalists, and often to Episcopalians and Catholics as well. On 22 March 1898 the Council of Administration resolved that it would be wise for the Christian Associations to reorganize so as to admit to full rights of membership the member of any religious denomination.[38] Some antagonism existed between the Christian Associations and the Greek-letter societies. Joining a fraternity, it was understood, reduced religious commitment.

The program of the YMCA consisted of religious meetings, Bible study, missions, and service. Regular religious meetings included a prayer meeting, held at 9 a.m. on Sunday mornings, and a union meeting for prayer, held on Monday evening. In 1897–98, for example, the Sunday service, held in the chapel of the Preparatory School, attracted an average of sixty-eight souls. In 1903 the average attendance at regular devotional meetings was 217.[39]

Special religious meetings were revivalistic in character, reflecting the revivalism that was still prominent in American culture at the time. These meetings featured a visiting evangelist who spearheaded a moral crusade and generated intense excitement. In the spring of 1898 S. M. Sayford, for some years the state YMCA secretary of Massachusetts, visited the campus. As a result of his efforts, about 125 students took a stand for "truer manhood," and five accepted Christ. Students themselves were effective evangelists. In 1901–2 Y members converted fifteen men. A year later they won at least thirty "conversions or decisions for the higher life."[40]

In 1901 the YMCA brought John R. Mott to the campus. At a Sunday afternoon meeting in the chapel that was attended by at least seven hundred men—one of the largest religious meetings ever held in the chapel—Mott spoke for an hour on the temptations of men. These he divided into five classes, the first of which, the temptation to impurity, occupied all of his speaking time. As a remedy, Mott declared himself strongly in favor of athletics. At the conclusion of his talk he invited all who could to stay for a short time, during which he showed that the hope of relief from temptations lay in turning to Christ.[41]

The Bible study program sponsored by the YMCA occupied a large place in college life. It gave students access to subjects unavailable in the University curriculum proper, furnished a basis for personal evangelism, and provided practical training for careers in the ministry, as YMCA secretaries, or in cognate fields. At the heart of Bible study were classes led by students in students' rooms. Starting in 1898, the course curriculum was provided by the International Committee of the YMCA. The three courses regularly offered dealt in graduated order with the life of Christ, the apostolic age, and Old Testament characters. The course content reflected the liberal Protestant theology that was gaining ascendancy at the time. Classes, kept to about ten students each, met once a week for an hour, usually on Friday evenings. Every other Sunday a professor held a teachers' training class, and in 1902–3 a secretary was added to the staff to promote the study of scripture.[42]

As part of the program, faculty members gave lectures jointly with the YWCA. Dean Burrill gave a series of lectures titled "Creation by Evolution." Dean Kinley lectured on the idea of God as revealed in the Bible, and Dean Davenport lectured on Old Testament characters. Others spoke on the time of Christ, early apostolic history, modern religious teachers, Paul, and the Bible as literature.

In 1904 the YMCA introduced Bible study to a number of fraternities; at least three local chapters maintained classes during the larger part of the year. In 1908 thirteen classes were held in as many social fraternities, largely under the supervision of faculty men. The most satisfactory course that year was based on a book by Jeremiah W. Jenks, *The Political and Social Significance of the Life and Teachings of Jesus* (1906).

Bible Study Institutes were held periodically to train leaders and stimulate enrollment in the courses. In 1897, 1903, 1905, and twice in 1907, theologians from other institutions and YMCA staff members came to the campus for institutes lasting a few days each.

Enrollment in Bible study courses increased after courses provided by the Intercollegiate Department of the International Committee of the YMCA were introduced. In 1903–4 it rose to 475, and by 1905–6 to 640. In 1908–9

24 percent of the male students (710 men) were enrolled in Bible study classes. The course on the life of Christ drew the most students, the course on Old Testament characters the fewest.[43]

In 1905–6 the Illinois YMCA proudly noted that for three years it had led the collegiate institutions of North America in Bible study. Of 560 institutions conducting the work that year, Illinois, with 640 enrollments (560 different men) in 57 classes, was first. Iowa State, Toronto, Ohio State, Yale, Princeton, and Minnesota were among the top ten.[44]

Despite the pride in numbers, the program had many weaknesses. Student leaders were not well trained, courses were voluntary, much of the work was superficial, and men were distressingly irregular in their attendance. In 1904–5, for example, with 604 men enrolled, only 353 remained for two months or more. Dean Thomas Arkle Clark, who regularly taught Bible classes, described the students as "thoroughly careless in their study." He thought that it was impossible "to get together any group of men with fifty percent of them possessing the most elementary knowledge of the Bible."[45] Students themselves recognized the faults. In 1908 fully 150 men refused to enroll in Bible classes because of their experience the previous year.

The missionary program of the Y showed the influence of the Student Volunteer Movement for Foreign Missions (SVM). Inspired in 1886 by the revivalist Dwight L. Moody, the SVM was organized at Northfield, Massachusetts, two years later and was guided by its watchword, "The Evangelization of the World In This Generation." The SVM was closely affiliated with the Intercollegiate YMCA, which was led by John R. Mott. Thus the two organizations had a unified program. Mott mobilized a veritable army from the nation's colleges and universities on behalf of world evangelism.

Professor Evarts B. Greene, who was born and reared in Kobe, Japan, the son of a Congregational missionary, was the adviser of the Y's missionary program. One of its activities was missionary meetings designed to stimulate interest in domestic and foreign missions. Each year about six or eight such meetings were held, usually with outside speakers, many fresh from foreign fields. With one exception these meetings were for men only.

The study of foreign missions, which began in earnest in 1898, was an important part of the program. Under student leadership, classes dealing with the history of missionary work, its principles and problems, the lives and writings of individual missionaries, and their work in specific countries were held in conjunction with the YWCA. John R. Mott's *The Evangelization of the World in This Generation* (1900) was one of the texts used. In 1903–4 seventy students were enrolled in mission study.[46] To aid the work the YMCA maintained a missionary library with more than 200 books and pamphlets and a dozen missionary periodicals.

A Volunteer Band composed of those interested in foreign missions met weekly. In 1903–4 it boasted twenty-nine male and seventeen female members. Volunteers led young people's social meetings as well as evening services, and once a year they led a prayer meeting in churches in and around Urbana and Champaign. The Illinois Volunteers aimed at world evangelism, and they sailed to such distant places as China, Japan, Korea, India, Lebanon, Persia, Turkey, and Syria to advance the Kingdom of Christ. In the years from 1904 to 1906 Yale sent eighteen students to the mission field, Rochester Seminary sixteen, the University of Michigan fourteen, and Illinois twelve.[47] To support these Illinois missionaries the Y conducted a program of systematic giving.

Dwight Moody's summer Bible Schools, which began at Northfield in 1886, later became summer conferences lasting about two weeks. Later, additional conferences were held under the auspices of the Intercollegiate YMCA. The first of these was held at Lake Geneva, Wisconsin, in 1890, where national leaders such as John R. Mott, Wilbur Chapman, and Robert E. Speer and students discussed ways to make college life most meaningful. At the turn of the century delegates from the University attended the student conferences for the Midwest at Lake Geneva. YWCA conferences followed the men's conferences at the same location.[48]

In addition to their religious activities, the Christian Associations rendered valuable community services that brought the members into touch with almost every student and won warm approval from the authorities. One such effort was patterned after the experience of the British and American YMCA in helping young rural men adjust to urban life. Members of the University Y met every train at the start of the academic year to welcome new students, escorting them to the campus and helping them get settled. The YMCA arranged social events for the entering men, and with the YWCA it held an opening reception in the fall for faculty and students. Upperclassmen made friendly calls on all freshmen in their rooms, establishing cordial relations and laying a basis for further personal religious effort. The Y published a student handbook containing useful information on how to negotiate the perils of University life. It also maintained an employment bureau. In 1903–4 the Y assisted 140 male students in finding jobs.[49]

The Christian Associations fit the University like a hand in a glove. Above denominationalism, manifesting the features of an evangelical faith, and activist, they were the only religious agencies on the campus at the turn of the century. A common bond of union within the University community, these associations contributed significantly to the creation of a wholesome moral and religious atmosphere. Their strong presence dispelled the hoary notion that state universities were godless. Moreover, the associations prepared some students for careers as ministers, missionaries, YMCA or YWCA secretaries, or related religious work.

# NOTES

1. *Illini*, 1 November 1894.
2. Ibid., 11 October 1895, 11 October 1894, 6 November 1896 (quotation), 1 November 1894.
3. Ibid., 19 January 1900.
4. Ibid., 20 September, 11 October, 1 November 1894; 4/1/1, 3:265. See also Sheryl Kaczmarek, "It's Not Just Any Orange and Blue," *Illiniweek*, 5 February 1981, and "Hail to the Old Gold, Hail to the Black?" *Illiniweek*, 27 October 1983.
5. "College Song Books," *The Illinois*, 1 (December 1902), 53–54.
6. *Illini*, 7 February 1895.
7. Ibid., 18 October, 15 November 1894; 29 November 1895.
8. Ibid., 18 December 1895.
9. Ibid., 10 December 1897, 25 November 1898, 22 September 1899. In 1925 "Illinois" became the state song by act of the General Assembly. *Laws of Illinois. Fifty-Fourth General Assembly* (1925), 601. In 1897 Jones stated that he did not know who had written the lyrics. According to one source, the words were by Charles H. Chamberlain, the music by Archibald Johnston. Chamberlain, who had fought in the Civil War and later lived in Chicago, wrote the words sometime between 1890 and 1894 in connection with plans for securing for Chicago the World's Columbian Exposition. According to the same source, Johnston composed the music to the air of "Baby Mine," a popular song in the 1870s. Chamberlain's daughter said that "Illinois" as it was later known was first sung at a reunion of the Army of the Potomac in Chicago when McKinley was president, and immediately proved to be popular. Musically, Jones's song and the state song bear some resemblance but are not the same. The state song is pitched a full step lower and is less rhythmically complex; the music of Jones's song is introspective (*Blue Book of the State of Illinois, 1937–1938*, ed. Edward J. Hughes [Springfield, 1938], 322–24).
10. *Illini*, 24 April, 8 May 1901; *'Varsity Fortnightly*, 1 (May 1901), 151. I cannot find any reference to this book in the *Champaign Daily Gazette* for late April or May 1901. The University of Illinois Library contains a copy of sheet music by Jones titled *Illinois Song* that contains three versions of "By thy rivers gently flowing": one for male voices and another for mixed voices, both copyright 1901, and a third version for solo or unison chorus, copyright 1912. After leaving the University in 1901, Jones compiled and arranged *New Songs for Male Quartets* (New York: Hinds & Noble, 1903) and *Songs of the Flag and Nation* (New York: Hinds, Noble & Eldredge, 1904).
11. Bullard to Draper, 30 July, 23 December 1902, 2/4/1, B:1, F:Bullard. For this work, see *Illinois Songs: A Collection of the Songs of the University of Illinois*, comp. and ed. by Ethel C. S. Forbes and Ethel Dobbins under the auspices of the Watcheka League (New Haven: Thomas G. Shepard, 1903), 5–6 (0/1/804, Illinois Songs and Music, B:1).
12. *Illinois Songs*, 10–11.
13. David B. Chamberlain and Karl P. Harrington, comp. and ed., *Songs of All the Colleges* (New York: Hinds, Noble & Eldredge, 1901; the song appeared again in *The Most Popular College Songs* [New York: Hinds, Noble & Eldredge, 1904]); *ASCAP Biographical Dictionary*, 4th ed. (New York: R. R. Bowker Co., 1980), 431.

14. *Illini*, 13 October, 15 October 1903.

15. Ibid., 11 October 1895.

16. Ibid.

17. *Illini*, 4 October 1895.

18. S. Dix Harwood, ["History of the *Illini*"], 35, 26/1/20, B:11; *Illini*, 22 November 1894, 25 April 1895, 22 May 1896, 22 October 1897.

19. *Illini*, 4 October 1901, 30 September 1902.

20. Ibid., 5 October, 6 October, 1903.

21. Ibid., 6 June 1894.

22. Ibid., 27 March, 1 April, 24 April 1901.

23. Ibid., 5 October, 17 December 1903.

24. "The Sophograph," *Illini*, 28 January 1898.

25. *'Varsity Fortnightly*, 1 (November 1900), 15.

26. Ibid., 1 (December 10, 1900), 21; 1 (February 1901), 79.

27. 4/1/1, 3:238; Draper to the Rev. F. M. Bennett, 22 August 1898, Draper to R. H. Jesse (president of the University of Missouri), 15 January 1904, 2/4/3.

28. Lillie Heath (Draper's secretary) to the Rev. Franklin L. Graff, 23 November 1894, 2/4/3.

29. Andrew S. Draper, "State Universities of the Middle West," *Educational Review*, 13 (April 1897), 321.

30. Draper to Mrs. Marion Ells, 9 February 1899, 2/4/3.

31. Lillie Heath to Dr. J. Y. Shamel, 20 October 1898, 2/4/3.

32. Kelsey's figures are cited in Charles K. Adams, *The Duty of the Churches to the State University* (Madison, 1898), 5. See also Francis W. Kelsey, "State Universities and Church Colleges," *Atlantic Monthly*, 80 (December 1897), 826–32.

33. *Illini*, 27 January 1904.

34. Draper, "State Universities of the Middle West," 321; *Illini*, 7 October 1898. By 1905 the practice of taking a religious census at the time of registration had been dropped because someone had said it was no business of the University (Thomas J. Burrill to Edmund J. James, 11 July 1905, 2/5/6, B:2, F:A–D, 4/1/05–8/1/05).

35. This statement is based on scattered data, but see especially the *Illini*, 29 November 1899, 25 January 1906, and YMCA annual reports, 41/69/320, YMCA Publications, B:1. See also Kelsey, "State Universities and Church Colleges," 827.

36. *Illini*, 7 April 1899; Clarence P. Shedd, *Two Centuries of Student Christian Movements* (New York: Association Press, 1934), 104 (the quotation).

37. Membership figures are taken from the annual reports of the YMCA (41/69/320, YMCA Publications, B:1, Annual Reports); see also William A. Scott, "The Religious Situation in State Universities," *Biblical World*, 26 (July 1905), 23..

38. 3/1/1, 1:84.

39. *Christian Advocate*, 22 January 1903.

40. Thomas J. Burrill to the Rev. Harry Willard, 4 March 1903, 5/1/20, Thomas J. Burrill Papers, B:1.

41. *Illini*, 11 February 1901.

42. William H. Morgan, *Student Religion during Fifty Years: Programs and Policies of the Intercollegiate Y.M.C.A.* (New York: Association Press, 1935), 41–58.

43. Figures on enrollment in Bible study courses are taken from various issues of the *Illini*, annual reports of the YMCA, "Methodism and the University of Illinois"

(41/69/829, Wesley Foundation), and "The Bible in American Coleges," *Biblical World*, 26 (September 1905), 215–23.

44. YMCA Annual Report for 1906, 41/69/320, YMCA Publications.
45. Clark to Clayton S. Cooper, 19 November 1908, 41/2/2, Dean of Men Official Letterbooks.
46. YMCA Annual Report, 1903–4, 41/69/320, YMCA Publications, B:1, Annual Reports.
47. Wallace N. Stearns, "Religious Education in State Universities," *Biblical World*, 27 (June 1906), 443.
48. *Illini*, 7 April 1899; Morgan, *Student Religion during Fifty Years*, 20–23, 70–74.
49. *Christian Advocate*, 22 January 1903.

# CHAPTER 12

# THE CARE OF
# STUDENTS

Following English rather than Continental custom, American colleges assumed complete responsibility for their students. They aimed not only to develop the minds but also to promote the physical and moral welfare of their charges. The college stood in the place of the parents. The University of Illinois continued this tradition.

## ORGANIZATIONAL STRUCTURE

The Board of Trustees was the ultimate guardian of the physical and moral health of the student body. At its first annual organizational meeting after Draper became president, the board established as one of its standing committees a Committee on Students' Welfare. The members were Julia H. Smith, the chair, Lucy L. Flower, and Richard P. Morgan.

Because the president of the University was the board's agent in implementing its policies, responsibility for the welfare of students fell to Draper. He believed that the University's job was to preserve a moral atmosphere and to create conditions that allowed earnest students to do their work and the school to discharge its proper function. To aid him in discharging his duties he created a dean of women and a dean of men.

The University had first admitted women in 1870, but the curriculum was little adapted to their tastes. In the 1890s steps were taken to attract more women. Katharine Merrill, the lady principal, recommended establishing a department for women that would combine intellectual and practical education for women in domestic or sanitary science, especially nutrition, and require courses in physical culture to improve women's personal appearance and refine their manner and dress.[1]

Building on this foundation, President Draper found allies in trustees Julia Holmes Smith and Lucy Flower. These three felt their way forward on related fronts: a women's department with a dean, a woman's building, a lunchroom, and a department of domestic or household science. In December 1896 the trustees authorized Draper to search for a dean of women.[2]

Draper preferred someone educated in the East who was capable of adjusting to local conditions: a woman with strong scholarship (as evidenced by an M.A. and possibly a Ph.D.) who was a natural teacher (preferably of English literature), had well-balanced judgment, would be a creditable representative of the University on public occasions, and was able to work with others. He did not want someone "so possessed of the idea that the world has been doing women great wrongs through all the preceding centuries, that she is disposed to start issues upon controverted questions when there is no necessity for it."[3]

On 9 March 1897 Draper recommended creation of the Woman's Department headed by a dean who was to be the "representative, guide and friend" of women and to aid and advise them in their University work and in social life. The dean was to be a member of the Council of Administration. Her position was to be coupled with that of assistant professor of English.[4]

Draper secured Violet D. Jayne (b. 1867) to fill this vaguely defined position. A native of St. Charles, Minnesota, in 1887 Jayne had taken an A.B. at the University of Michigan. A year as assistant principal of the high school at Crookston, Minnesota, was followed by a year at Ann Arbor studying English literature. From 1889 to 1891 she was in charge of the English department at the Normal School in Oshkosh, Wisconsin; she then spent fourteen months abroad, studying and traveling. From 1893 to 1896 she taught at the Normal School in San Jose, California, receiving her master's degree from the University of Michigan in 1896 in absentia. Jayne accepted the offer at a salary of $1,500, with the position to be taken up on 1 September 1897. She was thirty at the time.[5]

Draper exercised ultimate responsibility for the welfare of men until he discovered Thomas Arkle Clark's gifts in this area. Clark was born Thomas Arkle Metcalf on 11 May 1862 in Minonk, a small town in central Illinois. His early years on an Illinois farm were decisive in shaping his character. His uncle and adoptive father, a Methodist, imposed a rigid discipline on the family. The family kept a strict Sabbath, walking to church when the animals needed rest and sanctifying the remainder of the day with rest and spiritual edification. Reading was permitted, but not of secular books. When Clark was fifteen his father died, and the lad assumed responsibility for the family. An older married brother who lived nearby helped, but he moved away before Clark turned seventeen. Farm work was hard for the slender stripling, but he could not ask for help, "for that would have been an open admission that I was not a man, and I scorned the weakness of such an admission." Clark viewed farm discipline as good experience; it taught self-reliance and manliness. In later life he celebrated the values instilled by rural, midwestern, Protestant culture.[6]

At the age of twenty-two Clark decided to attend college. A year later he sold off his stock and equipment, moved with his adoptive mother and an invalid brother to Urbana, and entered the Preparatory School. He became a freshman the following year and quickly made his mark in the University. A member of the Philomathean Literary Society, he edited the yearbook and the student newspaper and was both Junior and Senior Orator and Class Poet.

Graduating in 1890, Clark spent a year as principal of a school in Champaign before returning to the University to teach English and Latin in the Preparatory School.[7] Two years later he was put in charge of rhetoric in the University. During the summer of 1894 he attended the University of Chicago. During 1898–99 he took postgraduate studies at Harvard but fell short of degree requirements. Returning to Urbana, he became professor of rhetoric and published two small volumes on English and American literary figures. His highest degree was a bachelor of literature. By 1897, however, he had won Draper's favor and a reputation as the "Good Reformer."[8]

During 1900–1 Draper solicited his help in a disciplinary matter, and in rendering assistance Clark found his true calling. As the story goes, Draper had reached a heated impasse with a recalcitrant student who would neither go to class nor study. Draper refused to keep him unless his conduct changed. But the student was the son of a man whose influence on the University could not be ignored. So Draper turned him over to Clark. It was understood that whatever Clark did would meet Draper's approval. Clark redeemed the young man.[9]

"I suppose I was dean of men from that time on," wrote Clark of the salvage operation, "though I balked for a long time at the thought of taking the job over officially."[10] Confident that his protégé could relieve him of many unpleasant duties, on 11 June 1901 Draper named Clark dean of undergraduates and assistant to the president, which carried membership in the Council of Administration. Clark's salary was set at $2,250, a sum exceeded only by the four highest paid professors in the University. In addition, Draper amended the University Statutes, adding a section which said that the dean of undergraduates and assistant to the president "shall concern himself about the interests of individual students, shall see that the courses of undergraduate instruction are as well correlated as practicable[,] and shall render such assistance to the President as that officer may desire." For another ten years Clark also kept most of his work in the English department.[11]

## Promoting Student Welfare

The physical well-being of students was largely dependent on conditions over which authorities had little control. The school had neither a dormitory nor a dining hall. Students had to find room and board in the community. Boardinghouses sprang up to meet the need, but most of them left much to be desired. Living conditions were especially difficult for women.[12]

In March 1896 female faculty members and faculty wives formed the Woman's League of the University of Illinois. Its object was to further the interests and welfare of the women students and to establish friendly relations between them and the faculty ladies. The league did not last long.

When Violet Jayne arrived to take up her position as dean of women, she found among the women students—170 in the University proper and the 38 in the Preparatory School—"decided laxity in the matter of refined manner and behavior, of neat and suitable dress, and of the observance of ordinary standards of propriety in social life." Most of these women came from homes in which they received little or no culture, and the twenty or thirty who went into society at all went so frequently and kept such late hours that their health and scholarship suffered and the reputation of the University as a place for young women to study was injured. The great majority of the women had almost no opportunities for "social culture," and women had no esprit de corps. A feeling of antagonism existed between sorority and nonsorority women. "There had been almost no attempt on the part of all the women to do anything together, and thus the social training and character-molding which come from close contact with a large number of fellow students . . . were entirely lost."[13]

Jayne set about to improve conditions. She made the Woman's Parlor in University Hall an attractive meeting place, she counseled coeds, and she offered guidance in the discipline of women. She and the women students shared a growing desire to gain unity and strength through an organization. On 26 May 1898 all the women of the faculty and the student body assembled for the first time as a Woman's Department. Jayne informed those present that the object of the department was to increase the number of women students, to enlarge the facilities for their work, and to establish such conditions for their life as would develop "the best and the womanly side of them." One of the greatest obstacles to this development was the lack of suitable places for the young women to live. At Jayne's suggestion, the assembly unanimously adopted three resolutions on social usage: women students would insist upon a chaperon at all parties they attended, they would leave all parties at 12 a.m. except in the case of parties for which the Council of Administration had arranged a closing time, and they would attend dancing parties only on Friday and Saturday evenings. As a means of overcoming the "unfortunate conditions" in Champaign-Urbana, Jayne proposed a closer association of "all the University girls." Accordingly, on 10 October 1898, women students held a mass meeting at which they formed a league, later named Watcheka League ("Watcheka," as the story went, was the name of the woman who had saved the Illini from extermination by the Iroquois and caused the defeat of the latter; the name seemed the best feminine counterpart to "Illini"), whose aim was to facilitate united action on the part of women students in the University.[14]

Meanwhile, the campaign for a woman's building was making fitful progress. In 1897 the board included such a facility in its request for appropriations. Trustees Flower and Smith issued a circular asking alumnae to support the building, and the Illinois Federation of Women's Clubs sent a delegation to Springfield to lobby for women's interests. When the legislature denied the funds, the board endorsed Mary Turner Carriel's motion that the board approve the erection of such a building, which would cost $10,000 or more, by private enterprise.[15] In 1899 the legislature appropriated money for a woman's building, but Governor Tanner struck out the item, allegedly in order to humble its sponsor, Senator Dunlap.[16]

Lucy Flower and Julia Holmes Smith attributed the low enrollment of women to their difficulty in obtaining suitable board and room in the community. In April 1898 Draper informed the trustees that it was imperative to establish a self-supporting lunchroom. He linked the facility with a proposed department of domestic economy. The department might open a lunchroom; thus the University could doubly benefit. Carriel and Flower devoted considerable energy to launching these ventures. In the fall of 1900 a dining room for students and faculty was opened in the basement of University Hall.

Clark developed his style as dean of men under Draper's tutelage. Initially, the scope of his work was ill-defined. But as dean and assistant to the president he was able to make of his office what he pleased. In 1901 he began the practice of dispensing advice to the incoming freshmen: work hard, avoid discouragement, and support college organizations. College would be the happiest years in one's life.[17]

Clark assumed responsibility for many matters Draper had formerly handled, including monitoring class attendance and delinquent scholarship. Despite faculty resistance, Clark demanded cooperation. His authority was enhanced when he tended to presidential affairs from April to October 1902 while Draper was in New York recuperating after his carriage accident.

Clark's activities soon became more diverse. The handling of class attendance brought to his attention cases that enlisted his sympathy and aid in removing the causes for poor attendance. He visited sick students to see that they had proper care and medical attention, and assisted needy students in finding work or getting financial aid.

Clark's interest in moral welfare led him to keep a close watch on students. With "two thousand sinful undergraduates to look after," he spent his days and nights trying to make people good and get them out of trouble. He did not hesitate to reprove students for smoking, drinking, gambling, and immoral conduct. Paternalistic, he told students what to do while advising them to decide for themselves. But students knew that he cared about them, and they felt free to call on him for help.[18]

Two motives seem paramount in Clark's work as dean. One was a desire to aid students. Although Clark married in 1896, he and his wife had no children. His concern for young people was deep and genuine, although he was much more comfortable with men than with women.

A second motive was a craving for power. By personal inclination Clark favored discipline, order, and centralized authority. He kept a close watch on students and accumulated data that enabled him to know students as individuals. He knew, or claimed to know, intimate details about them, gaining facts from one student that he could use in dealing with another. For example, he informed Charles R. Rounds, a graduate student and instructor who had made many decisions without first consulting Clark, that he knew "things you tell at your boarding house."[19]

Besides the deans, two agencies arose to promote student well-being. In 1899 the Students' Hospital Fund Association came into being. All members of the University were eligible on payment of a fee of fifty cents a semester. By virtue of one office or another Jayne and Clark were active in the management of the association. The insurance scheme proved valuable. With one exception, until February 1903 the association paid in full all the hospital bills for seriously ill students.[20]

Another welfare agency was the Edward Snyder Department of Students' Aid. In March 1899, three years after resigning, Snyder, who had joined the faculty when the University opened, offered the University $12,000 to be used in the form of student loans. The money was to paid over gradually, with interest on the whole sum reserved to Snyder and his wife during their lifetimes.[21]

Under the rules devised for use of the Snyder Fund, the benefit was to be given to needy members of the upper classes, with $50 the maximum to be provided to a junior student and $150 the maximum for a senior or graduate student. The notes were to bear interest at 6 percent, with a maximum time limit of two years. Snyder's benevolence enabled many students to complete studies that might otherwise have been terminated.[22]

## THE DISCIPLINE OF STUDENTS

According to a prefatory statement in the 1893 *Rules for the Government of Students*, the rules were to be taken not as arbitrary regulations but as the normal law of the University, necessary to its organization and operation as an institution. University students neither lost the rights nor escaped the responsibilities of the citizen.[23]

Over time the rules grew with experience. The 1896 edition said that any or all of the rules might be temporarily suspended by vote of three-fourths of the members of the faculty present at any authorized meeting. In addition to the *Rules*, student conduct was governed by contemporary moral principles that were largely shaped by an evangelical Protestant culture. The prefatory statement, along with unwritten ethical standards, gave the authorities considerable discretion in student discipline.

Draper permitted students the largest freedom of individual action on the assumption that it would be within legitimate bounds.[24] The Council of Administration dealt with a wide variety of disciplinary cases: cheating, plagiarism, turning in the work of others, and conduct considered offensive. Dean Ricker once reported a student who "was unable to do the [class] work on account of disease contracted from lewd women." The man admitted that it was the fourth time this had occurred within the past two years. The council referred to the president an engineering student "reported for immorality" with women. According to Dean Clark, the University had the greatest interest in the moral welfare of students and took every precaution to see that their lives were what they should be. Clark usually knew "about what was going on" among his charges. He knew, for example, that a student from Argentina drank too much, gambled a little, and regularly had illegitimate relations with women, although not to the extent of overtaxing him physically. The Argentinean viewed all of these things as "ordinary events in the life of all men." Clark wanted the student removed from the University for the sake of "our own students." Clark informed the father of a student from Pontiac that his son's "irritable, nervous condition had been intensified by the fact that he has gratified his passions more than is physically good for him, not to speak of the moral effect." The young man should not be allowed to return after Christmas vacation to lie around his fraternity house; he was a bad influence on others.[25]

The most common "bad habits" involved drinking, betting, and gambling. Temperance groups had long sought to drive saloons from the Twin Cities. University officials joined in the effort. Yet in 1902–3 the combined city directory listed twenty-six saloons in Champaign and nine in Urbana.

Authorities took a strong stand against offenses involving drink. In September 1894 the Council of Administration suspended a student for a year for "drunkenness on the street car," and in 1897 it expelled a student brought up for drunkenness. That same year, the council declared that it looked with extreme disfavor upon the introduction of alcoholic beverages, a "moral and social taint," in fraternity life.[26] In March 1902, faced with the case of a student who had reportedly been intoxicated, the council voted that the rule decreeing the expulsion of students who visited saloons and became intoxicated, which was promulgated that year, be enforced against the student. But the council rescinded its action after friends testified that the student had not been intoxicated.[27]

Late in 1902, at the urging of the faculty Committee on Students' Welfare, a committee of the trustees wrote to Champaign city officials to express the board's desire that "much more" be done "to repress liquor selling, gambling, and vice in the city, and to guard more carefully the proper observance of Sunday."[28]

Drinking and betting in connection with football became a problem with the growing prominence of the sport. In November 1901, when the council learned of students who had visited a saloon when they went to Indiana for a game with Purdue, it declared that athletic success, however brilliant, was too dearly bought if it was the occasion for indulgence in drinking or betting. Draper made it clear that betting was forbidden. The council gave notice that it would summarily dismiss from the University any student who was guilty of betting, of frequenting saloons, or of becoming intoxicated.[29]

In May and early June 1902, six students were brought before the council for gambling, which the *Rules* then in force did not ban. All of them admitted that they had visited gambling houses that were located above saloons in downtown Champaign. Some had been there several times, one as often as nine times in two weeks. They had seen other students there as well as roulette tables and other gambling devices. Some had played a few times; one had wagered ten, fifteen, or twenty dollars. Questioned by the council as to the University's attitude toward gambling, one student said that he assumed it would be one of opposition. Another thought that gambling houses would hurt the University because parents would not send their sons. His own father would not object to the son's visits, only to gambling. The students refused to tell all they knew. "There is honor among thieves." When Dean Burrill wondered what would be necessary to make the student tell what he knew to help the University, the student replied, "I wonder." Asked whether it would be more honorable on the part of the University to require students to tell what they knew of "bad things" or to get this information by means of private detectives, the student said that the honorable course was the detectives. He had told the truth as to himself but would provide no information as to others. Told that the council had the right to compel witnesses to tell what they knew, the student responded that what the council wanted was personal names, and that giving names would not help to do away with the gambling houses.

After taking evidence and deliberating, on 5 June the council suspended the students until the opening of the fall semester. In effect, the penalty lacked force.[30]

## CLASS RIVALRY AND DISCIPLINE

The collegiate class system, which was perpetuated at Illinois, gave rise to class rivalry. Class rivalry was most intense between the two lower classes. It led to what Henry D. Sheldon called "numerous perversions."[31] These included the class rush or color rush, disruption of the annual freshman "sociable," and hazing.

Hazing was an American variation on the older European custom of initiating new students. In England the system under which a senior boy could compel a junior boy to perform vexatious tasks was called fagging. Hazing was the term employed to describe this rite of passage in America. The *Oxford English Dictionary* defines hazing as "a sound beating, a thrashing," and as "a species of brutal horseplay practiced on freshmen at some American Colleges." It records the *Harvard Magazine* in 1860 as the first to use the word to describe "the absurd and barbarous custom of hazing which has long prevailed in the college."[32]

In American colleges, hazing ran the gamut from practical jokes and tricks to serious and cold-blooded offenses. On average, Sheldon believed, not more than two or three such affairs occurred each year in a typical college, and probably not more than about 15 percent of any sophomore class engaged in hazing as described. The majority, however, exhibited only a passive opposition to the practice, and governing boards tried without success to extirpate this initiation rite. One reason was that students refused to inform on their classmates, but more important was students' own conservatism. "That freshmen had always been hazed seemed sufficient cause why hazing should be continued."[33]

Hazing was part of the intractable problem of student discipline in the nineteenth century. Because it shaded by degrees from the practical joke to the serious crime, it was difficult to manage. Neither an appeal to honor nor penalties proved successful in banishing the custom. By the end of the century such initiation rites were widespread.[34]

In 1871, hazing was an accepted form of conduct at the University of Michigan. In 1887, hazing was a serious problem at the University of Wisconsin, although "perhaps no worse . . . than elsewhere at the time." In the 1890s the hazing of unpopular or obstreperous individuals occurred at the University of Missouri, at Indiana University, and at the University of Iowa. Hazing was well entrenched at both the naval and the military academies.[35]

### Early Class Rivalry at Illinois

Shortly after the University opened, students began the practice of class rivalry. Normally the two lower classes were involved. Sophomores considered it their bound duty to spoil the annual freshman class social, and freshmen reciprocated with ingenious acts of aggression. In 1888 the clash over the freshman social was a riotous affair in which "eye water" (benzyl bromide), fists, and butcher knives were all employed.[36]

Class conflict was also manifested in the "rush," an organized struggle between freshmen and sophomores. In October 1891 the first color rush at Illinois took place when a freshman walked into the library with his class colors pinned to his coat and a number of sophomores jumped him in an effort to seize the colors. A melee ensued.[37]

Class rivalry led to repeated disruptions. In October 1893 freshmen again battled sophomores for possession of the sophomore colors. A month later the conflict erupted once more when a sophomore made his way to the top of an electric light pole to seize the freshman colors. The resulting battle lasted almost an hour. To avoid disruption of their social the next day, freshmen planned to gather quietly at the Wabash depot in Champaign and take the train to Bloomington for their big event. News of the ruse leaked out, and some sophomores went to the station and dispersed tear water in the waiting room and the railroad cars. After the Champaign police took the sophomores in hand, the freshmen proceeded to Bloomington unmolested.[38]

These affrays gave the University bad publicity. The Chicago *Inter Ocean* categorized the disorder as an example of hazing, which it called a vile British army custom that rested on a snobbish assumption of social superiority. Viewing hazing as brutal, cowardly, and un-American, the paper called on the faculty to deal severely with the offenders. The *Illini* saw nothing in the nature of hazing in either the freshman social or the color rush. "Both were merely spirited but good natured exhibitions of class rivalry—nothing more."[39]

## Class Rivalry and Hazing, 1894–1904

In 1894, class rivalry and hazing were well entrenched at Illinois. Officials and students alike approved of the color rush and the subjection of freshmen to initiation rites as long as they were not carried to extremes. But both customs held the potential for danger. Hazing afforded bullies an opportunity to humiliate and terrorize students whom they disliked, without regard to their class standing.

Sophomore intervention in the freshman social was objectionable, the *Illini* wrote, not because it excited a spirit of class animosity, but because class conflicts both gave the University an undesirable notoriety and contained an element of hazing. Disruption of the freshman social easily turned into hazing, and hazing was viewed with general disfavor.[40]

The sophomore class acknowledged the problem. It agreed to abandon the practice of interfering with the freshman social and instead to hold a welcoming reception. This decision was greeted as establishing a new precedent, one that meant the end of the annual color rush. Thus, the *Illini* wrote, there would no longer be any reason for newspapers of the state to call the students barbarians and the faculty weak-kneed. Rowdiness and class antagonism were not essential to the enjoyment of college life. Moreover, disorder generated by class rivalry had been an obstacle when the trustees asked the state for appropriations.

The reception for the freshmen was a great success. President Draper, who spoke to the four hundred guests, took a pledge from the freshmen that they would hold a similar reception the next year. The pledge effectively ended color rush, gushed the *Illini*. Class spirit had succumbed to University spirit.[41]

Tradition died hard, however, and on 23 February 1895, the day of the freshman social, a group of sophomores kidnapped three freshmen, including the class president, whom they bound and blindfolded and kept all day in a cold, deserted house. No one was hurt, and no one nursed hard feelings, but the Council of Administration suspended nine sophomores for the rest of the school year and gave five others, including a senior, three sophomores, and a Preparatory School student, first and second warnings (a third warning brought expulsion). Such action was necessary, Draper wrote, both to show students that rowdyism would not be tolerated and to placate public sentiment.

Suspension caused an uproar and made heroes of the "Naughty Nine." A delegation of local alumni protested the penalties, and people from Kewanee, the home town of four of the nine, threatened to descend on Urbana in a body. The council agreed to consider reducing the punishments if the students of the entire University gave explicit assurances that they would abandon this annual rite. Students then petitioned for reconsideration and for the greatest possible leniency for their classmates. When these appeals failed, both the freshman and the sophomore classes promised to cease engaging in a variety of disruptive practices. The agreements seemed to mark the end of hazing at Illinois. So the council terminated the suspension of the Naughty Nine at the beginning of the spring term.[42]

This episode became a matter of concern to the board. On 28 February, Trustee Napoleon B. Morrison urged Draper to "break down the spirit of lawless vandalism." On 12 March the full board commended the council for suspending students who engaged in kidnapping and promised to support whatever might be necessary to prevent any student conduct that interfered with the rights of individuals or reflected harmfully on the University. The trustees also expressed gratification at the moral courage and good sense of students in pledging themselves against hazing. On 5 March State Senator Thomas Hamer introduced a bill to punish hazing in state educational institutions. It passed the House by a vote of 27 to 10, but went no further.[43]

For a time peace and harmony prevailed. In 1895 and 1896 the sophomores sponsored a fall reception for freshmen that went well. Authorities and many students favored color rush as long as it was not carried to hurtful extremes. But some went to extremes. In early 1897 Draper offered to protect the freshmen while they held their social at the University. The freshman class spurned the offer and secretly scheduled the event off campus. Getting wind of the plans, a rude and boisterous mob of sophomores and others disrupted the assembly, breaking windows and dispersing a foul-smelling chemical. A freshman, Estella May Radenbaugh, of Champaign, received the noxious agent in her eyes and was blinded for two days. Although two students were arrested in the ensuing disorder, the police were unable to break up the crowd (the chief of police was not only drunk that evening but also in league with the mischief-makers). The mayor of Urbana ordered the fire department to disband the students by turning hoses on them.

The Council of Administration met the next morning to deal with the situation. Along with the state's attorney, it began an investigation that lasted ten days. The council immediately resolved that any student who had procured, given out, or thrown the chemical agent or was associated with others who did so, and any student who refused to name the student having the chemical, would be deemed a participant and deserving of expulsion. At a special convocation the authorities asked the offenders to admit their participation in order that there might be some excuse for leniency. None came forward.[44]

Early in its proceedings the council expelled Andrew Jackson Dougherty, Jr., of Mound City for complicity in throwing the chemical and for refusing on three separate occasions to provide information that he said he possessed. An unwritten honor code prevented students from informing on each other. Later, a citizen of Urbana and sundry students identified Dougherty as the guilty party. Soon after disciplining Dougherty, the council expelled another student for complicity in throwing the chemical and lying about the matter. After an extended investigation the council expelled six additional students—classmates celebrated them as the "Sinful Six"—and suspended one for their part in this affair. The disciplined students included five sophomores, two juniors, and two freshmen.[45]

This nasty disturbance brought reproach upon the University from all over the state. Newspaper accounts, although somewhat florid, were not far from the truth. A number of fathers, some assisted by a lawyer or a state legislator and one by Governor Altgeld, came before the council or wrote seeking reconsideration for their sons. Trustee Samuel A. Bullard, class of 1878, urged leniency. Draper replied that the affair was serious. Students who endangered persons, injured property, or interfered with the orderly progress of University life should be punished, even if the acts took place off University grounds. "Colleges should rid themselves of all vicious characters and of all who corrupt the student body, and they should have it understood that they will do so." Draper hinted, however, that the council would be willing to entertain applications for cancellation of the judgments against the expelled students the following year.[46]

Draper also insisted that the two lower classes agree to end the practice of hazing. He suggested that members of the freshman class draw up resolutions expressing regret for their part in the event and promising to abstain from ill treatment of lowerclassmen the following year, and he urged fathers to press their sons to sign the assurance. When all but three stubborn freshmen signed, Draper informed the fathers of the three holdouts that continued refusal would probably mean dismissal. The Council of Administration asked the sophomores to sign a document expressing disapproval of the assaults and pledging to use their influence to prevent such practices and to maintain good order in the future. All save half a dozen sophomores gave the desired assurances.[47]

This notorious incident may have briefly tempered the zeal for hazing. The freshmen who entered the University in 1897 had a quiet and peaceful social, and in 1899 ample police protection discouraged any attempt to interfere with the freshman social. In March 1901 about seventy-five couples attended the annual event without incident. Trouble had been expected, but it never arrived, perhaps because Draper was present for about an hour. From 1897 to 1899 the color rush took place without trouble. The *Illini* declared that this ritual had a good influence in stimulating class cohesiveness.

But the temptation to haze proved irresistible. For several weeks in the fall of 1901 the treatment of freshmen by sophomores went to unprecedented excesses. This wrongfulness lacked an element of malice, Draper thought, but in convocation he spoke against the practice. Appealing to the moral sense of students, he warned them to reform voluntarily or the faculty would step in. His remarks had no noticeable effect. Soon thereafter fifteen or twenty students, mainly sophomores, chased a young man and woman. When they took refuge in the home of a University professor, the mob tried to break in. The sophomores easily won color rush, after which several sophomores stripped some freshmen nearly or quite naked and left them to get home as best they could. Now ruffianism masqueraded as class spirit.[48]

Walter G. Diener, a sophomore from Chicago, was apparently the leader of some twenty-five to thirty students for whom hazing was a sport. Diener's Gang, as it was known, began their fun when school opened on Monday, 16 September 1901. That night, Diener and his buddies entered the room of Walter Parker, a freshman who lived in the same house as Diener, and asked him to play his mandolin. When Parker refused, the assailants took Parker to the Boneyard and threw him in with his clothes on. Parker resisted, so the gang gave him a second ducking.[49]

The potential for "innocent" hazing to get out of hand was made clear by a disturbance on Saturday, 21 September 1901. E. Clyde Conard, a freshman waiter, was informed by other waiters that by "sophomore law" his mustache had to come off before the end of the year. Conard replied that his mustache was his own business and that he would shoot anyone who tried to remove it. Such a threat was hot air, a fellow waiter responded. Conard, anticipating trouble, bought a pistol on Friday the 20th. On the following evening the headwaiter delayed Conard as he prepared to leave the Dining Hall about 6:30, allowing another waiter to leave first and alert others. When Conard went out, a group of about six men seized him. Someone brandished scissors. Conard threatened to shoot, and when ten or twelve men piled on, he fired. An assailant grabbed him and he fired again. The revolver was taken from Conard and the crowd scattered.[50]

The council did not consider Conard's case or other acts of hazing immediately, and meanwhile the campus was again disrupted. On Friday, 27 September, at the end of the second week of the school year, rowdies harassed freshmen the entire evening. Diener's Gang, the apparent agents of these misdeeds, went into five or six houses and found ten men. They made six of them sing, recite, run races, climb a pole, or some combination of these antics, and threw four others into the Boneyard. About 10:30 that evening the gang caught two students who were leaving a church social in Urbana, forcing one, a sophomore, to take his clothes off before they threw him into the Boneyard, and forcing the other, freshman J. H. Miner, who denied that he was a freshman, to climb a pole on Green Street and give the sophomore yell. The crowd then turned a hose on Miner, and then threw bricks and lime. The hapless Miner did not come down until 12:45 a.m.[51]

On 2 October the Council of Administration began gathering evidence on these commotions. Members pressed students not only to confess but also to inform on others. Called before the council, Diener, who claimed he had never heard of "Diener's Gang" except from Dean Thomas Arkle Clark, admitted that he had compelled ten boys to do things against their will. Some were made to run races, climb telephone poles, sing, or recite, and some were tossed in the Boneyard. The council voted to suspend Diener for the rest of the semester. The council expelled Fred E. Newton, a freshman law student, for assaulting Conard, and it dismissed three other waiters from the Dining Hall, two for hazing and Conard for carrying a gun on the campus.[52]

Two days later seven men rang the bell at a boardinghouse and inquired if any freshmen lived there. The visiting party then searched the house, entering the room of Manuel J. Jacobs. When they ordered Jacobs to play his clarinet, he drew his revolver and the men withdrew. At a brawl on Tuesday evening, 8 October, Dean Burrill reported hearing a student say, "I'll kill the first man that touches him."[53]

On 5 October the council adopted two resolutions designed to deal with such disruptions. One declared that entering the rooms of other students without authority or subjecting fellow students to indignities of any character were violations of University discipline that would be punished as soon as they were discovered. The second resolution declared that no conditions justified carrying pistols on University premises, and that the authorities would discipline any student found doing so. (Both resolutions were incorporated in the 1902 *Rules*.) The council urged a special convocation to deal with the matter, and on 8 October Draper condemned hazing as a pernicious activity that led to bitterness and threatened safety and discipline. "He spoke," reported the *Illini*, "as if there were behind him a great power which it is useless to oppose."[54]

Students continued to use weapons when they considered them necessary to their safety. Leroy Kershaw, a law student summoned before the council for an episode that occurred on Friday, 11 October, testified that he had owned a gun for five or six years and that he had brandished it on Friday, 28 September, when Diener and others entered his room with the intention of seizing his roommate. When the intruders saw his revolver, they left the roommate alone. On the 11th, Kershaw had carried his gun when he went to inquire about a friend who had reportedly been injured in color rush. Large crowds were out painting "04," the sophomore class numerals, on public and private property that evening, and a gang had seized Kershaw's hat. When they spotted Kershaw's revolver, they did not bother him further. Kershaw argued that because he had not attended convocation and had not heard that the University would punish students who carried weapons, he did not deserve punishment.[55] On 31 October, when recalled before the council, Conard pleaded that he was entitled to defend himself and therefore had not done wrong in carrying a revolver. After conferring with Dean Burrill, however, Conard acknowledged that his action was unwarranted and unwise, expressed regret, and promised not to repeat his offense. The council, lenient with the repentant, dropped the matter. Members agreed to issue a rule about hazing, warning against indulgence in it next year.[56]

Officials disliked the notoriety resulting from newspaper accounts of disturbances, and in the spring of 1902 the Council of Administration decreed that the freshmen could not hold a social, despite a petition by the class, and that there would be no more socials as long as the two lower classes showed animosity toward each other. The *Illini* acknowledged that the strong hand of authority could control the student body if need be. A few students carried hazing "a little too far," it said, but the great majority were disposed to have a little reasonable fun. The editor urged students to control themselves.[57]

In the fall, however, rogue elements broke the peace. A freshman threw a sophomore in the Boneyard, and later a gang of sophomores broke a locked door and a pane of glass in an attempt to seize some new students in a boardinghouse. Edward Wegenseil, a sophomore identified as one of the guilty parties, said he had been only an observer, not a participant, and declined to name those who were with him. He was expelled for his part in hazing. In a convocation address, Draper reminded students that hazing posed not only physical but also financial danger, since the University depended on public support. He demanded that the disorders cease. Accordingly, 150 sophomores, pleading for leniency to Wegenseil, signed a pledge to give up hazing and to discourage others from engaging in the rite. With these assurances, Draper prevailed on the council to rescind the expulsion of Wegenseil. The editor of the *Illini* hoped that the pledge would end the evil.[58]

Resolutions and pledges were unavailing. In the fall of 1903 hazing made the campus a veritable battlefield. Gangs of from twenty to fifty students roamed the streets on both weekday and weekend evenings, entering houses uninvited, seeking freshmen at random or (rarely) by design, and forcing them to do their bidding. The intruders sometimes pilfered items from rooms they entered, often "scalped" those they seized, and normally took as many as ten, twelve, or fifteen men at a time to the Boneyard, compelling them to get in or throwing them in. One student described the night as a "time of terror" for freshmen.[59]

Dean Thomas Arkle Clark complained that he had never known so much "deviltry" and had never seen information about evildoers so hard to obtain. Many students viewed these encounters as traditional collegiate sport. One participant, asked by the council what he thought of hazing and throwing strangers into the water, replied, "I do not think it a very serious matter, although it is not sanctioned." Some students refused to submit, however, and blows were struck. In early October the council "tried" eleven sophomores for assorted hazing practices. None admitted guilt, and most of them refused to incriminate others. In the end, the council dismissed two sophomores for the rest of the semester and four others—a freshman, a sophomore, and two special students—for the rest of the school year. The authorities ordered the *Illini* to publicize the suspensions.[60]

When some fifteen hundred students presented a petition on behalf of the men suspended stating that they would not take part in any more hazing and would do all in their power to prevent it, the council insisted that the different classes and the fraternities appoint committees to take effective measures to suppress hazing. These conditions met, the council reinstated the six suspended students. The *Illini* observed that the council would show little leniency in the future.[61]

In the spring of 1904 President Draper suddenly resigned his office and returned to Albany, New York, to take up his new job. He was experienced in dealing with all sorts of people, he had a reputation as an efficient and nononsense administrator, he was popular with students, and he valued order and decorum. But during his administration hazing became progressively worse. Class rivalry supplied the propulsive energy for hazing, which was an established tradition and difficult to eradicate. The student body not only tolerated but also enjoyed the activity. Granted student opinion, Draper and the administrative council were reluctant to punish those who engaged in what was done in frolic but often led to violence and bitterness. Officials hoped to redeem rather than condemn offenders. So hazing remained a serious problem.

## THE DEANS

As the first dean of women at the University, Violet Jayne inherited the difficult task of advancing the role of women on campus. Her report for 1902–3 indicates the remarkable progress made on behalf of women's affairs in the preceding five years.[62] In 1904, however, after years of being pulled in many ways by her duties, she resigned as dean of the Woman's Department and as associate professor of English to marry Edward C. Schmidt, a mechanical engineer who had joined the faculty in 1898. Dean David Kinley, commenting on her departure, observed that the position of dean of women was an exceedingly difficult one to fill because its duties were so vague and indefinite. Jayne had never really had a fair chance, he added, nor would anyone who took the place, without a careful definition of the scope, power, and authority of the office. "Indeed, it is doubtful whether a field of authority can well be marked out for the Dean of Women. The whole matter is mainly one of personal influence."[63]

Thomas Arkle Clark, generally regarded as the first dean of men in American higher education, demonstrated great personal influence. On 6 June 1904, when Draper, his patron, returned to wind up the academic year, he recommended raising Clark's salary from $2,750 to $3,000. The board demurred. The next day Clark asked to be relieved as dean. At a special meeting that same day, however, Trustee William B. McKinley, who gave his name to the Presbyterian church of which Clark was a member, moved to reconsider. Clark was appointed professor of rhetoric and dean of undergraduates at $3,000 a year.[64]

Clark then asked for and was granted a private office and a public reception room, his own secretary, and a messenger so that he could reach students readily.[65] His best years as dean were yet to come, but it would be well to note here his significance for the University. He upheld the old collegiate ideal at a time when the university was becoming the model in American higher education. For Clark, the purpose of college was character formation more than the advancement of knowledge. "College is really intended for moral development and for the acquiring of intellectual and moral ideas," he wrote. "One can not accomplish that end without getting some information, but it [college] is not intended for information primarily."[66] Thus it made little difference whether one studied "paleontology or physical training."[67]

Looking to the past, Clark became an object of derision to faculty members who looked to the future. He made his position in the University impregnable, however, and he was invulnerable to criticism. Clark served as dean until 1931, during which time his power on the campus and his national reputation steadily grew. He played an important role in instilling conservative values at the University. Clark became a legend in his own time, a legend that he helped create and then skillfully manipulated.

## NOTES

1. Mary Loise Filbey, "The Early History of the Deans of Women, University of Illinois," 41/20/38, Filbey Family Papers, B:2, F:Early History of the Deans of Women, 6–7; *17th Report* (1894), 79–81.
2. Draper to Flower, 22 May 1896, 2/4/3. Contemporary documents used *woman* and *women* interchangeably.
3. *19th Report* (1898), 46; Draper to President J. H. Taylor (Vassar College), 2 January 1897, 2/4/3.
4. *19th Report* (1898), 64–65.
5. On Jayne's appointment, see the correspondence in 2/4/2, B:2, F:Jayne, and *19th Report* (1898), 64–65.
6. Thomas Arkle Clark, "The Color of the Cup," *Zeta Beta Tau Quarterly*, 8 (March 1924), 87; idem, "What's the Matter with Our Young People?" *Rotarian*, 30 (May 1927), 6; idem, "Standing On One's Own Feet," *Rotarian*, 33 (March 1928), 15 (the quotation).
7. *Daily Illini*, 12 January 1927, 9.
8. Lillie Heath (President Draper's secretary) to T. A. Clark, 16 October 1897, 2/4/3 (the quotation).
9. The story of how Clark became dean has been told by Clark and others with many variations, but always after the fact. Reliable contemporary evidence on the matter is lacking, but the different versions all basically agree. Some accounts have Clark redeeming two hardcore delinquents during the year. Thomas Arkle Clark, "The Personal Touch," *Christian Education*, 5 (March 1922), 3–18; idem, "History and Development of the Office of Dean of Men," *School and Society*, 16 (15 July 1922), 66–67; A. R. Warnock (an assistant to Clark), "Origin and Development of Office of the Dean of Men in the University of Illinois," 26/1/20, B:11, F:M; Frank M. Chase, "Unusual Stories of Unusual Men: Thomas Arkle Clark— The Man of a Million Sympathies," *Rotarian*, 33 (March 1928), 29, 41–42. Clark won Draper's gratitude for his success in dealing with Draper's rebellious son, Edwin, with whom Clark became extremely close. See also Jo Ann Fley, "Thomas Arkle Clark: Patriarch and Dean from Illinois," *Journal of the National Association of Women Deans, Administrators and Counselors*, 41 (Spring 1978), 120–23.
10. Clark, "History and Development of the Office of Dean of Men," 67.
11. *21st Report* (1902), 79, 86.
12. Paula A. Treichler, "Alma Mater's Sorority: Women and the University of Illinois, 1890–1925," in *For Alma Mater: Theory and Practice in Feminine Scholarship*,

ed. Paula A. Treichler, Cheris Kramarae, and Beth Stafford (Urbana: University of Illinois Press, 1985), 5–61, treats the years covered in the present volume. Despite some valuable insights, this essay is a tendentious account written from a feminist perspective. It is often erroneous or misleading.

13. *Illini*, 13 March 1896; Jayne to Draper, 9 June 1899, 2/4/2, B:5, F:Jayne.

14. *Illini*, 8 June (the quotations), 14, 21 October 1898; Violet D. Jayne, "Leagues of College Women," *Illini*, 14 February 1899; Thomas J. Burrill to President James, 2 December 1904, 2/5/6, B:1, F:A–F.

15. Flower to Draper, 27 November 1896; Flower and Smith, "Alumnae of the University of Illinois," December 1896, 2/4/1, B:4, F:Flower, 1894–96; *19th Report* (1898), 53, 55, 197.

16. In 1903 the state finally appropriated funds for a woman's building.

17. See, for example, the *Illini*, 20 September 1901, 25 September 1902.

18. Clark to [Louis C.] Cornish, 30 October 1902, 41/2/20, Thomas A. Clark Papers, B:4, Personal Letterbook 1 (quotation); Clark to Mrs. P. T. Chapman, 11 June 1901, 41/2/2, Dean of Men, Official Letterbook.

19. Clark to C. R. Rounds, 30 June 1903, 41/2/2, Dean of Men, Official Letterbook.

20. *Illini*, 14 February, 3, 17 March, 5 May, 22 September 1899; 9 February, 8 October 1900; 1 October, 4 December 1902; 10 February 1903.

21. Ibid., 31 March 1899.

22. 3/1/1, 1:99, 101–5; *Illini*, 4 October 1899.

23. *Rules for the Government of Students* (1893), 25/7/801, Admissions and Records, Director's Office, Undergraduate Regulations, B:1.

24. Draper to C. W. Bardeen, 2 February 1897, 2/4/3 (published in the *School Bulletin*, 23 [March 1897], 117, and reprinted in *Educational Review*, 13 [April 1897], 412–24); see also the *Illini*, 2 November 1900.

25. Ricker to Draper, n.d. [about 5 February] 1895 (first quotation), 5 April 1895; 2/4/2, B:1, F:Ricker; 3/1/1, 1:37 (27 February 1895); Thomas A. Clark to George A. Powles, 9 January 1903; Clark to John S. Murphy, 17 December 1903; Clark to Mrs. Fred W. Isham, 22 October 1902; Clark to Dean E. Davenport, 26 November 1902; Clark to James H. Fitz Simon, 3 February 1903; Clark to Mrs. Frederick W. Isham, 9 February 1903, 22 February 1903; Clark to Rufus W. Stimson, 10 July 1903; all in 41/2/2, Dean of Men, Official Letterbooks.

26. 3/1/1, 1:4, 74, 68.

27. Ibid., 2:107–8, 110–11; *Rules for the Government of Students* (1902), 17.

28. 3/1/1, 3:6; Fred L. Hatch for the Board of Trustees to the Mayor and City Council of the City of Champaign, 11 December 1902, 2/4/4, B:1, F:Misc. Papers, 1902–3.

29. 3/1/1, 2:87–88, 90; *Illini*, 27 October, 27 November 1901.

30. 3/1/1, 2:124–28, 130, 132–33.

31. Henry D. Sheldon, *Student Life and Student Customs* (New York: D. Appleton & Co., 1901), 98.

32. *The Oxford English Dictionary*, 2d ed., prepared by J. A. Simpson and E. S. C. Weiner, 20 vols. (Oxford: Clarendon Press, 1989), s.v. *fagging* and *hazing*.

33. Sheldon, *Student Life and Student Customs*, 97–102 (quotations at 98, 100, 102); John S. Brubacher and Willis Rudy, *Higher Education in Transition: An American History: 1636–1956* (New York: Harper & Brothers, 1958), 46–47. See also [Lyman H. Bagg], *Four Years at Yale* (New Haven, 1871), 249–64.

34. Winton U. Solberg, "The University of Illinois and the Reform of Discipline in the Modern University, 1868–1891," *AAUP Bulletin*, 52 (September 1966), 305–14; David Starr Jordan, "College Discipline," *North American Review*, 165 (October 1897), 403–8; Hank Nuwer, *Broken Pledges: The Deadly Rite of Hazing* (Atlanta: Longstreet Press, 1990), 286–87.

35. Howard H. Peckham, *The Making of the University of Michigan, 1817–1967* (Ann Arbor: University of Michigan Press, 1967), 75–76; Merle Curti and Vernon Carstensen, *The University of Wisconsin: A History, 1848–1925*, 2 vols. (Madison: University of Wisconsin Press, 1949), 1:548–54; Jonas Viles et al., *The University of Missouri: A Centennial History* (Columbia: University of Missouri Press, 1939), 258; Thomas D. Clark, *Indiana University: Midwestern Pioneer*. Vol. II, *In Midpassage* (Bloomington: Indiana University Press, 1973), 140–47; Stow Persons, *The University of Iowa in the Twentieth Century: An Institutional History* (Iowa City: University of Iowa Press, 1990), 39; Cyrus T. Brady, "A Hazing Interregnum: Some Doings at Annapolis," *Lippincott's Magazine*, 67 (April 1901), 485–92; Julian Hawthorne, "The Crime of Hazing," *Munsey's Magazine*, 36 (March 1905), 809–12; Douglas MacArthur, *Reminiscences* (New York: McGraw-Hill, 1964), 25–26.

36. Charles A. Kiler, *On the Banks of the Boneyard* ([Urbana]: Illini Union Bookstore, 1942), 28–33.

37. Ibid., 46–47; S. Dix Harwood, ["History of the *Illini*"], 28, 26/1/20, B:11.

38. *Illini*, 12, 18 October, 29 November 1893; *Illio '95*, 42.

39. *Inter Ocean*, 25 November 1893 (editorial); "Make an End of Hazing," *Illini*, 29 November 1893.

40. *Illini*, 4 October 1894.

41. Ibid., 18, 25 October, 1, 8 November 1894.

42. Draper to (Trustee) Nelson W. Graham, 27 February 1895, 2/4/3; *Illini*, 7, 14 March 1895; 3/1/1, 1:37, 38; *Illio '97*, 244, 251.

43. Morrison to Draper, 28 February 1895, 2/4/1, B:10, F:Morrison; *Illini*, 14 March 1895; *18th Report* (1896), 74, 85; *Journal of the Senate of the Thirty-Ninth General Assembly of the State of Illinois* (Springfield, 1896), 246, 331, 393, 433; *Illini*, 18 April 1895.

44. Draper discusses this affair in his letter of 2 February 1897 to Bardeen; his letter to the state's attorney is printed along with this letter in the *School Bulletin* (see n. 24); 3/1/1, 1:62–63, 65–66. For his efforts to settle the matter, see Draper's letters of 10 and 15 February 1897, 2/4/3; *Illini*, 5 February 1897; *Illio '98*, 51; *19th Report* (1898), 66–69.

45. On the "Sinful Six," see the *Illio '98*, 81. On 27 January 1897 Dougherty wrote his parents an account of his involvement that stressed his refusal to name two students who had some chemicals, adding that he had the sympathy of the whole student body and a good many of the faculty. He joined the U.S. Army that fall, and on 19 April 1898 he wrote Draper from Jefferson Barracks, Missouri. "I did have chemicals & knew of them," he confessed, adding that he had not thrown the chemical and had not known who did. He bitterly regretted lying and prayed that someday he might once more be able to say, "I am a son of Illinois." He begged for Draper's forgiveness and that of the University he had wronged. Since his unit was leaving for "a possible fight," he wanted the ban of the University removed, "even tho I may never see her doors again" (Dougherty to Papa and Mama, 27 January 1897;

Dougherty to Draper, 19 April 1898, 2/4/1, B:3, F:Dougherty). During the Span-ish-American War Dougherty distinguished himself at El Caney and San Juan, which led to his appointment as a lieutenant in the 37th Regiment, U.S. Volun-teers. While en route to the Philippines his regiment was delayed at Honolulu, where he met Martha Ah Wong, the daughter of a wealthy Hawaiian, whom he married in Manila in 1901 (*Illini*, 27 February 1901).

46. Draper's efforts to deal with this disruption can be followed from 2 February to 27 February in 2/4/3. The quotation is from his 2 February letter to C. W. Bardeen (see n. 24).

47. The resolutions and correspondence with and regarding recalcitrant students are in 2/4/6, Freshman Social Affairs Expulsion File.

48. *Illini*, 6 March, 9 October 1896; 11, 14 October 1901; Draper to G. H. McKinley (president of the sophomore class), 16 October 1901, 2/4/3.

49. 3/1/1, 2:56, 67, 68.

50. Ibid., 2:56–57, 59–61, 63–65, 80–83.

51. Ibid., 2:66–67, 68, 69.

52. Ibid., 2:65, 67a, 70, 86.

53. Ibid., 2:63; Burrill to Draper, 9 October 1901, 2/4/2, B:8, F:Burrill.

54. 3/1/1, 2:67a, 71, 138; *Illini*, 11 October 1901.

55. 3/1/1, 2:72–73.

56. Ibid., 2:80–81, 82–83.

57. *Illini*, 21 March 1902.

58. 3/1/1, 3:7–8, 10; *Illini*, 10, 13 October 1902.

59. 3/1/1, 3:62–68.

60. Clark to Hugh J. Graham, 2 November 1903, 41/2/20, Thomas A. Clark Papers, B:5; 3/1/1, 3:62–68 (quotation at 66).

61. 3/1/1, 3:69–70; *Illini*, 21, 26 October 1903; *Illio 1904*, 73.

62. Jayne to President Draper, 1 May 1903, 2/4/4, B:2, F:Departmental Reports, 1903 (2).

63. Kinley to Mary Turner Carriel, 14 June 1904, 15/1/4.

64. Clark to Draper, 7 June 1904, 41/2/2, Dean of Men, Official Letterbook; *22nd Report* (1904), 292, 326.

65. Clark to Burrill, 18 July 1904, 41/2/2, Dean of Men, Official Letterbook.

66. Clark to Florence Butler, 23 April 1918, 41/2/1, Dean of Men, General Corre-spondence, B:14.

67. Clark to Charlotte Donders, 3 September 1901, 41/2/2, Dean of Men, Official Letterbook.

# CHAPTER 13

# THE INQUIRING MIND

Students obtained their formal education in a structured curriculum centered on classrooms and laboratories, but they also pursued learning by means of their own devising. The habit of forming voluntary associations to advance a common cause was deeply ingrained in the American character. By second nature, students were joiners.

## THE LITERARY SOCIETIES

Literary societies with names evoking memories of ancient Greece had long been a feature of American higher education. Most colleges had a pair of such organizations whose literary and declamatory exercises provided escape from the prescribed curriculum and an opportunity to discuss contemporary topics.[1]

At Urbana two literary societies for men, the Philomathean and the Adelphic, were organized in 1868, five days after the University opened. In 1871 women students formed the Alethenai Literary Society. About a third of all students belonged to one of these groups, which enlisted most of the seniors and the ablest, most prominent students. By 1894 the literary societies were well entrenched on campus.[2]

The heyday of the literary societies had already passed, however, and from 1894 to 1904 membership in these societies declined. Philomathean, the largest, had an annual average of 41 members during these years. Adelphic had an annual average of nearly 38; Alethenai had an annual average of 30. In 1904 the Iliola Literary Society emerged with 22 members. For the entire period under review, the four societies had an annual average of 111 members. Since undergraduate enrollment went from 750 in 1894–95 to 2,181 in 1903–4, membership in the literary societies declined from 15 percent to 9 percent of all students in these years.[3]

Even as their sun was setting, these groups played an important role on campus. The Philomathean and Adelphic societies were both designed to nourish the mind and to spur self-improvement by offering practice in oratory and debate. The Philomathean motto, "Come up Higher," captured the ethos of both societies. The clubs met on Friday evening in their own rooms in University Hall. Any student of good character was eligible to join, with new members elected by ballot. Programs, posted in advance, were open to the public. The *Illini* reported society activities in detail.[4]

Programs faithfully mirrored student interests. In addition to reciting famous set pieces and reading their own compositions, members enjoyed musical performances and spoke on current events, philosophical issues, the lives of famous people, and literature. Sometimes an entire evening was devoted to a theme. In November 1895 a Philo "darkey program" included such papers as "The Past, Present and Future of the Darkey," a paper on the life of Frederick Douglass, and a debate on setting aside an American state for Negroes. A Philomathean program on fortune telling included papers on astrology, phrenology, physiognomy, palmistry, and dreams.[5] The education provided by the literary societies paralleled and sometimes surpassed that offered in the classroom.

The men's societies featured debate, described by an Adelphic as "one of the best methods of obtaining a literary training."[6] The questions ranged from the frivolous to the philosophical. Religion was rarely considered. Most debates dealt with American foreign relations and contemporary political and social issues, such as the war with Spain, the direct election of senators, government control of railroads and telegraphs, anarchism, organized labor, free coinage of silver, the initiative and the referendum, women's suffrage, municipal socialism, and a federal income tax. Students also debated moving the capital of the United States to a point within twenty-five miles of the Mississippi River.

Each society elected a designated critic who was charged with the duty of evaluating the performance of the speakers. Although generous with praise for well-prepared talks that provided information and showed originality, critics could be harsh. One called an extempore dialogue "rather undignified and rambling." Another described a speaker as "very funny," but "something more intellectual and elevating could have been served. The main object of the society is moral, mental and intellectual improvement rather than social amusement.... Let us live up to our motto 'Come up Higher' and ... introduce some literary merit into our programs."[7] Critics opposed the use of slang, of words not found in *Webster's*, and mispronunciations.[8]

In addition to regular programs, the Philomathean Society scheduled an annual declamation contest, oratorical contest, and the Excelsior Program. The Excelsior Program was held on the Saturday nearest 21 March in commemoration of the placing of Lorado Taft's statue *Excelsior* in the club room. The program consisted of addresses and orations by officers of the club and a member of the faculty. The Adelphics held an annual David and Jonathan program and banquet. Members also presented an annual public concert of music, declamations, and readings.[9]

The men's societies each sent a delegate to the Students' Assembly, and a representative from both groups managed the Star Lecture Course, which brought speakers and artists to the campus. The two clubs engaged in intersociety debates, football games, and track meets, and they each entertained and in turn were entertained by the Alethenai. On 10 January 1902, in their first joint meeting, the Philomatheans entertained the Adelphics. The *Illini* viewed the event as evidence of a growing spirit in the University in favor of the literary organizations.[10]

The Alethenai's mission was mental and social elevation, reflecting an impulse toward literature and culture and providing a chance for women students to stand up and hear the sound of their own voices.[11] Its motto was "Live." Alethenai programs had their own distinctive character. The women scheduled debates, but not often, and they heard papers on and discussed such topics as imperialism, Cuba's struggle for freedom, and domestic politics. They also held an annual entertainment. At one such entertainment the program included musical selections and Molière's *L'Avare*, with a synopsis read in English, and a farce, *The Jack Trust*.[12]

From all outward appearances the literary societies seemed to be thriving, but in fact they were declining. An expanded curriculum was rendering their educational function less urgent than in the past, social fraternities were beginning to offer competition,[13] and students were turning to intercollegiate athletics. One sign of declension was absenteeism. During 1899–1900 an average of twelve Philomatheans—roughly a third of the group—were absent from nine of the regular Friday evening meetings. And on 29 September 1899 no program was held for lack of an audience.[14]

Another sign of declension was tardiness.[15] Perhaps more important was loss of a desire to "come up higher." In 1895 a Philomathean critic said, "if all our members spoke as well as this old member, we should have a society more alive than at present." Another critic reported a "lamentable lack of society spirit shown by members on the program." What the society needed was "good live meetings." Zeal for self-improvement was waning. In 1899 the Philomatheans agreed to amend their constitution so as to compel each member to deliver an oration during each year.[16]

## DEBATE AND ORATORY

Eloquence in public address has flourished wherever popular forms of government make free discussion of public questions essential. Politicians and lawyers deliver orations before legislative assemblies and courts to persuade others to a course of action. And since the Reformation the sermon has been an exalted art form. Public address had long been America's dominant rhetorical tradition. To succeed in life, students believed, they needed to develop skills in debate and oratory.

In the early years of the University, declamation, oratory, and debate had figured prominently on the campus. But student interest in these activities suddenly seemed to die. During 1892–93 the Illinois Intercollegiate Oratorical Association, of which the University was a member, perished, the literary societies dispensed with their usual declamation and oratorical contests for lack of participants, and the University's professor of rhetoric and oratory resigned his position.

The University nevertheless perpetuated a tradition of oratory in two rituals on Class Day, the day before commencement. One was the Senior Class Oration. In 1899, for example, Daniel C. Ketchum gave an address titled "Study to Be Useful." The other was the Hatchet Oration. In 1897 Louis D. Hall gave what was described as "the usual sarcastic address to the juniors" as he turned over a hatchet that symbolically marked the burying of rivalries between the two upper classes. Neal D. Reardon received the hatchet on behalf of the junior class.[17]

In the mid-1890s, however, a revival of interest in public speaking and debate occurred on American campuses. Repeated attacks on athletics stimulated in college men a desire for ideals of a somewhat different character, and intercollegiate debate enlisted those who were most strenuously opposed to the prominence of athletics.[18]

At Illinois, students seized the initiative in advancing the cause of public speaking. As the *Illini* contended, debate and oratory were more in harmony with the aims of the college than were football or baseball games, and since other universities were advancing these activities, Illinois had to keep pace. In addition, the argument went, the University's achievements in forensics should be on a par with those in athletics. Student editors praised the literary societies for emphasizing public speaking and for intersociety debates that trained students for intercollegiate competition while blaming both the societies and the student body for not taking sufficient interest in debate and oratory.[19]

In late 1895 the University of Chicago challenged the University of Illinois to a debate sometime the following March. Arrangements were made to enlist those desirous of entering the contest. A debating club led by Norman F. Marsh took over management of the project. Plans called for a preliminary debate, open to members of the three upper classes, followed by a prize debate, from which the three best contestants would be selected to represent the University.[20]

The scheduled encounter generated excitement on both campuses. President Draper presided over the prize debate, which drew a fair-sized audience. The winners were Norman F. Marsh, William H. Kiler, and Rollin O. Everhart, all juniors. Chicago submitted the topic, "Resolved, That the recent boundary dispute between Great Britain and Venezuela is not a legitimate cause for interference by the United States on the basis of the Monroe Doctrine," and Illinois chose the negative.

The debate was held at the Kent Theater on Friday evening, 13 March 1896, with William Jennings Bryan as presiding officer. The program began with a song by the Woodlawn Quartette. The Illinois men, in evening dress, were ushered to their places by Herbert C. Arms, class of '95. While the judges deliberated, Bryan spoke on the Monroe Doctrine and the silver question, amusing the audience. Illinois won, two to one.

An *Illini* editorial hailed the victory, asserting that it would build the reputation of the University along literary lines. At convocation on 18 March, Marsh, Kiler, and Everhart were given seats of honor on the platform. President Draper thanked the men on behalf of the University.[21]

Debate was regarded as the most practical branch of public speaking. Writing in the *Illini*, Professor Greene rehearsed the relation of public address to popular government and noted that the Lincoln–Douglas debates gave Illinois a tradition that the University should uphold. The University could hope "that the successes which have come to us in inter-collegiate athletics will come to us in equal or greater measure in these intellectual contests." So in 1896 the faculty decided to apply all of the $100 prize money for excellence in public speaking to debate—$50, $30, and $20 for the three winners.[22]

Either in the spring or autumn of 1896 a member of each of the men's literary societies together with a faculty member formed a committee whose purpose was to arrange debates with other schools and to devise plans to select students to represent the University in such encounters.

During 1897–98 the plan outlined by the committee was implemented. In January 1898 a newly formed University of Illinois Oratorical Association challenged the University of Wisconsin to a debate. A small but enthusiastic audience was present at the final contest to select the Illinois team. On 20 May the debate was held in the chapel of the University. This was the first intercollegiate debate ever held at the University. As anticipated, Illinois lost.[23]

Despite its reputation for bombast and show, oratory gained renewed prominence in these years. The committee had proposed an oratorical contest in which each of the three literary societies would be represented. Nothing came of the idea. The impetus for new activity in intercollegiate oratory came from a professor at Ohio Wesleyan who organized his school, Cornell, Indiana University, Ohio State, and the University of Illinois into the Central Oratorical League.

Students who wished to represent Illinois at its contests were initially judged by Professor Thomas A. Clark. William C. Lindley, class of '01, won with an oration, "James A. Garfield." He represented Illinois in the intercollegiate oratorical contest at Delaware, Ohio.[24]

By the fall of 1898 little progress had been made in the development of forensics. Sports had always received support, the editor of the *Illini* wrote, but "a reputation for athletical strength will not alone build up a university. That reputation must be supported by one for strength along lines of scholarship and learning." The University wanted students whose voices would someday be heard in the halls of Congress. If debating had one-fourth the student support of football, the University could produce an unbeatable team.[25]

During the academic year Professor Tooke chaired a faculty Committee on Debating and Oratory and the University engaged in two intercollegiate debates as well as one Central Oratorical League contest. On 21 April 1899 a University team debated the Wisconsin team at Madison on the question of adoption of a bill to replace existing U.S. Treasury notes with bank notes. Bruce A. Campbell, John W. Fisher, and Fred E. Newton, all class of '00, made up the University team; only Newton had experience as a debater. Another experienced Wisconsin team triumphed.[26]

On that same day another University team met the Indiana University team at the University on the question, "Resolved, That the American federal system is adapted to the government of the Philippine Islands." President Draper presided and the Military Band provided music. The *Illini* recounted the argument of each speaker in detail. The judges unanimously decided in favor of Illinois. "At the decision," the *Illini* gloated, "the chapel bell rang loudly with the University yell."[27]

At the contest to select a representative for the Central Oratorical League competition, President Draper presided and twenty students competed. The University Band, the Mandolin Club, and the University Quartet furnished music. Will C. Wait, a first-year law student, gained first place with an oration titled "The Reign of Queen Elizabeth." Professor Tooke went with Wait to Ithaca, New York, on 20 May 1899. Illinois was not among the top three of five competitors.[28]

The year 1899–1900 marked the beginning of more vigorous efforts in debate and oratory. Four agents contributed to this result. One was the Oratorical Association. In December 1899 this association emerged with a clear identity. Its purpose was to coordinate the University's participation in intercollegiate contests and to form a high-class debating club on the campus. Harlan H. Horner was the first president. This group made plans to hold interclass debates, two intercollegiate debates, and an intercollegiate declamation contest each year. At the close of the academic year the *Chicago Tribune* praised Illinois students for forming the association. "One direction in which the 'fresh water' colleges of the west excel, as a rule, the larger and more influential institutions of the east," it wrote, "is in the training of their students in public speaking."[29]

A second contributing agent was the Department of Rhetoric and Oratory. In 1899 William A. Adams joined the faculty as an instructor of rhetoric and public speaking. A Harvard A.B. (1898) who had taught a year in the Latin School in Brooklyn, New York, Adams introduced three courses to meet the long-felt need: Argumentative Composition, Oral Discussions, and Public Speaking.[30] When Adams left after two years, Charles R. Rounds, a University of Wisconsin A.B. (1901), replaced him in the classroom and as coach of the debate team.

A third contributing influence came from the School of Law, established in 1897. Students planning legal careers were eager to prepare themselves as effective speakers. A number of them competed for a place on the debate team.

Also important was the insistent drumbeat of the *Illini*. Over the years editors asserted the importance of debate and oratory at the University. Varsity debaters were equal in importance to varsity athletics, they contended. Illinois, they added, failed to keep pace with other universities in forensics. Students should show greater interest in these activities.

In 1899 the Oratorical Association laid plans for the University to participate in two intercollegiate debates each year from 1900 to 1903—one with Indiana in January and the second with Iowa in April. During 1899–1900 no intercollegiate debate was held on the campus, and only one away from home. The debate was held in Bloomington, Indiana, on the question of the conduct of the British government in the Transvaal controversy. Six hundred people paid an admission charge. An *Illini* headline trumpeted the Illinois victory.[31]

Meanwhile, Edna A. Rugg, class of '00, won the right to represent the University in the Central Oratorical League contest held on 25 May in Urbana. The chapel, which seated some 700, was only half full (previously, the league had drawn 1,500 with a fifty-cent admission charge at Ohio Wesleyan, and 2,000 at Cornell). In an oration titled "Radicalism," Rugg argued that true progress comes because radicals prepare the way for the work done by the great men of history. She placed second of the four entrants.[32]

Efforts to stimulate interest in debating led to the introduction of debates between the two lower classes. During 1900–1 thirteen freshmen and sophomores participated. These encounters served as a training ground for the intercollegiate debate team. That fall fifteen first-year law students organized a debating club, and another fifteen competed for a place on the University debating team. Illinois met Indiana to debate the question of immigration restriction, the first intercollegiate debate held on the campus in two years. Illinois lost.[33]

By 1901, then, leaders of the Oratorical Association had installed a program that featured interclass and intercollegiate debates and the Central Oratorical League contest. In addition to annual debates with Indiana, a committee from the Oratorical Association along with the faculty Committee on Oratory arranged for a series of three annual debates with the University of Iowa, and they contracted with the University of Missouri for a series of yearly debates.[34]

In 1902 the varsity met both Indiana and Missouri. The Indiana debate took place in Bloomington in February. Illinois lost. The *Illini* noted the radically different styles of the teams. Indiana followed "the eastern plan," with running fire and give-and-take, depending on pat replies, catchy phrases, and an occasional oratorical appeal to send the argument home. The Illinois strategy was plain and straightforward, relying on the sheer weight of the case, with no joking and no dramatic or oratorical effect. This event had become the highlight of the winter term.

Dean Scott presided at the Illinois–Missouri debate held in Urbana on 25 April. Missouri men had their speeches "committed," whereas Illinois men relied on extemporaneous rebuttal. Illinois lost.[35] A year later Illinois engaged in three intercollegiate debates. On 16 January 1903 Illinois went to Iowa City for the first of its debates with Iowa. Illinois won.[36]

In sum, the University failed to gain distinction in debate and oratory. The administration did little to encourage and support public speaking, and the student body demonstrated little zeal for such activity. Athletics excited more enthusiasm. A few devoted students shouldered the burden in this area. Their effort deserves credit.

## ACADEMICALLY ORIENTED STUDENT ORGANIZATIONS

As the University matured, acquiring the shape if not the spirit of a university, "clubs auxiliary to courses of study" proliferated. These student associations, which often included one or more faculty members, ranged in size from about twenty to as many as eighty members. The clubs complemented the course of study, honed professional skills, and provided opportunities for socialization. Student clubs with an academic orientation played an important part in the life of the University.[37]

These groups usually met at regular intervals, their programs varying according to the interests of the group. In most cases members heard and discussed papers or abstracts of the literature related to the nature of the club. Some of the clubs presented plays or other entertainments. A few examples afford a glimpse of the role these voluntary associations played in the life of the University.

In the College of Agriculture, the Agricultural Club was the sole student association. The College of Science was home to various sharply focused interest groups in natural history, chemistry (President Draper was a member), mathematics, and medicine.

The College of Engineering clubs—in civil engineering, mechanical engineering and electrical engineering, and architecture—were among the oldest of such groups on the campus.

The College of Literature and Arts produced a wide range of associations. The drama club flourished under various names. In November 1894 members presented a performance of Grace L. Furniss's *A Box of Monkeys* (1890), a popular farce in two acts, to an audience largely composed of residents of the Twin Cities.[38] In March 1901 the club secured costumes from Chicago and presented Richard Brinsley Sheridan's *The Rivals*. President Draper congratulated the performers for the best amateur performance he had ever seen. To take a standard play requiring deep study marked a decided advance in University affairs, he wrote, "but would it not have been just as good or a little better if the unnecessary 'damns' had been omitted?"[39] A year later the players put on Sheridan's *School for Scandal*, and in April 1904 the club offered a popular comedy in four acts by the English actor and playwright Jerome K. Jerome, *Miss Hobbs* (1899).[40]

In 1895 some students of Latin organized a Sodalitas Latina, whose object was to further the study of Latin, with special attention to acquiring facility in translation. The purpose was to enjoy the language as literature. The Latin Club met twice a month at the home of Professor Barton.[41]

During 1894–95 the Romance Language Club met every Monday morning to study current literature in the Romance languages.[42] Le Cercle Français, which originated about 1895, conducted its proceedings in French. During the fall of 1896 members planned to devote their attention to the Romantic movement.[43] In addition, the club presented a French play each year. The first of these was Molière's *L'Avare*. The second offering consisted of two short comedies by Eugène Labiche, and the third was Labiche's farcical comedy, *La Poudre aux Yeux* (1862).[44]

The annual French play became a fixed feature of the year. On 19 February 1898 members produced Molière's *Le Bourgeois Gentilhomme*. On 7 March 1899 Le Cercle followed with another Molière comedy, *Le Médicin Malgré Lui*. On 2 May 1900 members again performed Labiche's *La Poudre aux Yeux*, giving it a local setting with witty thrusts at faculty members.[45]

Der Deutsche Verein was formed on 28 February 1900 by Professor Rhoades. Like its francophone counterpart, it produced plays for local audiences. Its first one, on 23 May 1900, was *Einer Muss Heiraten*, a farce based on an incident supposed to have occurred in the lives of two German scholars, the brothers Jacob and Wilhelm Grimm. The second, on 13 March 1901, was a little farce, *Gunstige Vorzeichen,* for which Professor Rhoades and Dean Scott trained the five characters. The third, on 9 May 1902, was the well-known comedy by Lessing, *Minna von Barnhelm.* On 17 April 1903 the German Club gave a reception in the Music Hall at which the program consisted of German songs and instrumental works by German composers.[46]

The English Club came into being on 18 September 1895 to supplement the courses in the English department. Members gave their attention to contemporary poets and novelists. During 1897–98 the club studied William Morris, Dante Gabriel Rossetti, George du Maurier, Hamlin Garland, Rudyard Kipling, H. C. Bunner, and others. Members of the club founded the *'Varsity Fortnightly* and its successor, the *Illinois Magazine.* On 3 May 1904 they presented a performance of Shakespeare's *Twelfth Night.*[47]

The Political Science Club heard papers and sponsored debates on contemporary questions involving foreign and domestic issues. On one occasion women students debated the question of reform in politics.[48]

In addition to academically oriented clubs, new types of student organizations that encouraged intellectual distinction arose around 1900. One was the professional fraternity. It offered the advantages of fraternal affiliation as well as the benefits that came from association with those who had chosen the same profession for their life work. In the years from 1894 to 1904, the professional fraternities at Illinois, with one exception, were in law and health-related fields. The exception was Alpha Zeta, an agricultural fraternity whose Morrow chapter was formed at Illinois in 1900.[49]

A second innovation was the recognition society—an organization that acknowledged a high level of achievement in a field of study. In March 1899 Phi Lambda Upsilon, a national recognition society in chemistry for men, was established as an honor society at the University of Illinois. The founders were three seniors in chemistry, assisted by members of the chemistry faculty who continued for many years to lend their support. The aim of the fraternity was to promote high scholarship and original investigation in all branches of pure and applied chemistry. Male graduate students and seniors and juniors who majored in any branch of chemistry or chemical engineering were eligible for election to membership. The Alpha chapter at Illinois was well entrenched by 1906, when the society began to spread to other universities and colleges.

## NOTES

1. Frederick Rudolph, *The American College and University: A History* (New York: Alfred A. Knopf, 1962), 137–44.
2. Solberg, 193–97, 296–99.

3. Membership figures are from various editions of the *Illio* (which cannot be considered too reliable); enrollment data are from the reports of the Board of Trustees.
4. The following account is based primarily on records of the three societies and reports of their activities in the *Illini* and the *Illio*. Philomathean Society Records (41/75/23, 3 boxes) and Adelphic Literary Society Records (41/75/1, 3 boxes) contain the minutes and the comments of the critics. Alethenai Society Records (41/75/2, 1 box) contain nothing of value relating to the period covered in this book. The records of the men's societies are difficult to document. In the citations that follow, PSR indicates a Philomathean Society Record and ASR an Adelphic Society Record. Detailed citation would be more cumbersome than helpful.
5. *Illini*, 29 November 1895; PSR, "Minutes, 20 September 1895–26 September 1902," 90 (18 March 1898).
6. ASR, "Critics Book, 21 March 1890–23 April 1897," 381 (31 May 1895).
7. PSR, "Critics Book, 21 October 1892–1 November 1895," 232 (20 September 1895), 235 (4 October 1895), 244 (1 November 1895); PSR, "Critics Report, 22 November 1895–12 October 1900," 97 (17 December 1897).
8. PSR, "Critics Report, 22 November 1895–12 October 1900," 65 (12 March 1897); 129 (28 October 1898); PSR, "Critics Book, 21 October 1892–1 November 1895), 236 (11 October 1895); ASR, "Critics Book, 21 March 1890–23 April 1897," 317 (7 June 1897).
9. *Illini*, 5 May 1899, 15 November 1895.
10. Ibid., 13 January 1902.
11. *Illio '97*, 174.
12. *Illini*, 25 April 1895, 13 March 1896, 24 February, 10 March, 10 November 1899.
13. Ibid., 8 June 1898.
14. PSR, "Minutes of Philomathean, 20 September 1895–26 September 1902," 10 February 1899 to 2 February 1900.
15. PSR, "Critics Report, 22 November 1895–12 October 1900," Meetings of 30 September, 4, 11, 18, 25 October, 1 November 1895; 26 May 1899.
16. PSR, "Critics Book, 21 October 1892–1 November 1895," 23 (27 September 1895); PSR, "Critics Report, 22 November 1895–12 October 1900," 5 (7 December 1895); PSR, "Minutes, 20 September 1895–26 September 1902," 154 (14 April 1899), 166 (29 September 1899).
17. *Illini*, 21 June 1899.
18. Ralph C. Ringwalt, "Intercollegiate Debating," *Forum*, 22 (January 1897), 633–40.
19. *Illini*, 14 February, 28 March, 9 May 1895, 13 March 1896, 13 December 1899, 23 May 1900.
20. Ibid., 17 January 1896.
21. Ibid., 20 March 1896.
22. Ibid., 30 October 1896; Evarts B. Greene, "Debating at the University of Illinois," *Illini*, 30 October 1896.
23. *Illini*, 22 January, 11 February, 18 March, 20, 28 May 1898.
24. Ibid., 20 May 1898.
25. Ibid., 18 November 1898.
26. Ibid., 14 April 1899.
27. Ibid., 21, 28 April 1899.
28. Ibid., 2 December 1898, 3 March, 14 April, 19 May, 26 May 1899.

29. Ibid., 11 December 1899, 12 February, 6 June 1900 (quoting the *Chicago Tribune*); *Illio 1901*, 206.
30. David Kinley to T. A. Clark, 28 December 1898, 15/1/4; *Catalogue* (1898–1900), 245; *Catalog* (1899–1900), 258–59.
31. *Illini*, 27 November, 18 December 1899, 12 February 1900.
32. Ibid., 9 February, 5 March, 23 April, 28 May 1900.
33. Ibid., 16, 28 January 1901.
34. *Illio 1904*, 229; *Illini*, 6 May, 1 June 1901, 19 March 1902.
35. *Illini*, 13 December 1901, 3 February, 16, 28 April 1902.
36. Ibid., 19 January 1903.
37. *Catalogue* (1895–96), 225 (the quotation). University catalogs describe some of the clubs, and various editions of the *Illio* give membership figures and reproduce photographs of club members. The documentation in what follows is kept to a minimum; the text helps to direct readers to an appropriate source.
38. *Illini*, 22 November 1894.
39. Ibid., 29 March 1901.
40. Ibid., 23 May 1902, 6 April 1904.
41. Ibid., 6 December 1895; *Illio '97*, 147.
42. *Illio '95*, 83.
43. *Illini*, 30 October 1896.
44. Ibid., 18 December 1896.
45. Ibid., 25 February 1898, 17 March 1899, 4 May 1900.
46. Ibid., 25 May 1900, 15 March 1901, 12 May 1902, 16 April 1903.
47. *Illio '98*, 83; *Illio 1900*, 99; *Illini*, 4 May 1904.
48. *Illini*, 25 February, 20 May 1898.
49. *Baird's Manual of American College Fraternities*, 20th ed., ed. Jack L. Anson and Robert F. Marchesani, Jr. (Baird's Manual Foundation: Indianapolis, 1991), sect. 1:9.

# ALMA MATER.

Arranged by R. G. Mills, '03.

With compulsory chapel recently abolished and everyone in the University eager to find some visible symbols to provide a rallying point for expressing school spirit, efforts were made to generate songs that would belong distinctively to Illinois. One of the few from this period that survives is "Alma Mater," arranged by Ralph G. Mills, class of 1903. This illustration is from the *University of Illinois Song Book* (1908).

The class system of the older colleges was perpetuated for many years at the University. It gave rise to class rivalry, especially between the freshman and sophomores. Class conflict was manifested in the color rush, an organized struggle in which sophomores tried to fight their way to the top of a pole to seize the freshman colors, and in hazing. Courtesy of the University of Illinois Archives.

An entertainment arranged by Professors Charles M. Moss and Newton A. Wells, given on 11 November 1897, featured about a dozen tableaux representing principal scenes from Homer's *Iliad*. Against a black background, the faculty members, clad in white and illuminated by a pale blue light, looked like marble. In this scene Ajax and Teucer defend the ships of the Greeks. Courtesy of the University of Illinois Archives.

Some members of the Philomathean Literary Society employed their talents in designing programs for regular meetings of the society. This program, with the figures in color, was probably drawn by Alfred Fellheimer, an 1894 graduate in architecture. The program announced most likely occurred that year. Courtesy of the University of Illinois Archives.

The University Band began as the Cornet Band, with close ties to the military program, and in later years it retained this role and was known as the University Military Band. But the band also reflected contemporary cultural currents, and it became a concert ensemble playing orchestral works transcribed for the band medium. George W. Riley is seated behind the drum. This photograph was published in the *Illini*, 2 April 1897.

After the band the Glee Club was the oldest of the campus musical organizations. During the last quarter of the nineteenth century the mandolin came into use again and gained popularity. Many students were members of both the glee and the mandolin clubs. The Glee and Mandolin Club Association sponsored concert performances of the two groups at home and throughout the state. Walter Howe Jones, director of the School of Music and of this musical ensemble, is third from the right in the second row. This photograph was published in the *Illio '02*.

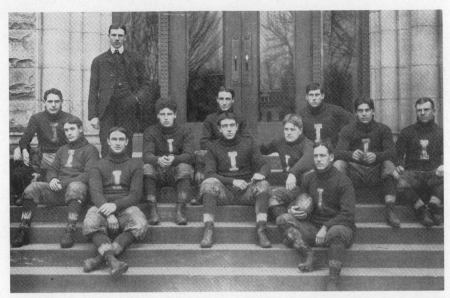

In 1900 the varsity football team was coached by Fred L. Smith, a former Princeton quarterback whose reappointment as Illinois coach that year caused considerable dissension. The team included Garland "Jake" Stahl, third from left, and Captain Arthur R. Hall, third from right. The team manager, George R. Carr, later a University trustee, is standing. Smith failed to redeem Illinois football. This photograph was published in the *Illio '02*.

Basketball was introduced to the University by women. The first intercollegiate basketball game at the University was played on 20 November 1896 by women's teams from Urbana and Illinois Wesleyan. Jennette E. Carpenter, director of the women's gymnasium, coached the team. She appears in the center of this group. This photograph was published in the *Illio '03*.

Several editions of the student yearbook contained a section titled "Roasts" in which students rendered humorous treatments of faculty members and other students. In this drawing the observatory in the background and Boneyard Creek are easily recognizable, but the sense of the jest has been lost with time. From left to right those depicted are Charles C. Pickett, professor of law, Dean Violet D. Jayne, Lester P. Breckenridge, professor of mechanical engineering, Dean Stephen A. Forbes, Samuel W. Shattuck, professor of mathematics, Dean David Kinley, Dean Nathan C. Ricker, Dean James B. Scott, Vice President Thomas J. Burrill, Dean Eugene Davenport, George A. Huff, director of physical education for men, and President Andrew S. Draper. This drawing was published in the *Illio '03*.

# CHAPTER 14

# THE MUSE OF MUSIC

The University began with a purpose far removed from anything musical except for the military band. Establishment of the School of Music in 1895 stimulated the musical life of the campus. Even so, music was slow to develop at the University. As the *Illini* observed in 1897, the musical education of a majority of the students at the University was nil. But development in this area depended largely on the tastes and inclinations of students. They provided the impetus for many of the campus music organizations, and many student performers were enrolled not in music but in technical subjects. At the turn of the century, for various good reasons, the musical culture of the University enjoyed steady upward growth.[1]

## THE UNIVERSITY BAND

The University Band, the oldest of the campus music organizations, began with close ties to the program in military training. Later, it reflected contemporary cultural currents. In nineteenth-century America bands were important social institutions. Professional bands, military bands, and amateur bands were among the most common of these musical organizations. The world of professional bands was dominated by two giants—Patrick S. Gilmore and John Philip Sousa. Gilmore made an important contribution in transcribing orchestral works for the band medium. Sousa, the March King, dazzled the world with the precision and style of his performances well into the twentieth century.

Amateur bands were far more numerous than professional bands, and of the amateur bands, town bands were by far the most common. The town band was a remarkably adaptable and democratic organism that introduced music to the people and provided cultural elevation. A band was essential to a community's self-respect and for many was a symbol of law and order. In 1889, according to one estimate, about ten thousand bands flourished in America. The golden age of the band extended down to 1920.[2]

The University Band (or the University Military Band) had been in existence almost as long as the University itself. When the Board of Trustees established a military department, it decreed that suitable music be provided for drill and ceremonies. The Cornet Band, as it was also known, was composed of students who were excused from drill while serving as members of the group. The University furnished the instruments and the music. The band played for military drill and other college functions. Led by students, the primitive ensemble played mostly marches.[3]

In the early 1890s the band gained a prominent place on the campus under student leaders. Following the path blazed by Gilmore and Sousa, the players ventured into concert music. On 3 May 1892 the ensemble presented its first concert at the Walker Opera House in Champaign. A month later the players gave a promenade concert on the Saturday before commencement. Both events were successful and became traditions.[4]

On 12 May 1893 the University Military Band in its second anniversary concert played a Sousa march, "High School Cadets," apparently its first rendition of a Sousa composition. A month later the band provided another promenade concert and music for both the senior ball and the graduation exercises.[5]

Two days later the University Band, thirty members strong, left for performances at the World's Fair in Chicago. Led by Charles A. Elder and Richard W. Sharpe, bandsmen played an engagement of two weeks, giving two daily concerts in the Illinois Building, one in the rotunda from 11 a.m. to 12 noon, the other on the main balcony from 3 to 4 p.m. Players were popular with women, one of whom said she liked the University Band better than Sousa's, which did not play loudly enough for her taste.[6]

Draper viewed the band as important in the life of the University, and he reoriented it. The services of seniors and juniors were necessary to the ensemble's efficiency, but these men, no longer subject to military duty, objected to continued service in the unit. Accordingly, in June 1895, the trustees resolved that all seniors and juniors who were members of the band should receive their term fees in return for faithful performance of their duties with the band throughout the year up to and including the day of the annual commencement.

In addition, Draper bestowed a musical scholarship on William L. Steele, an outstanding student and an excellent cornet player. Steele agreed to devote half of his time to music in return for a scholarship of $300 a year for the next two years.[7]

Under Steele, the band flourished. While providing music for battalion dress parades and football games, it made the concert hall its specialty. The program of its 1896 concert included overtures to *Dichter and Bauer* (Poet and Peasant), by Franz von Suppé, and to Rossini's *Guillaume Tell*, selections from Wagner's *Tannhäuser* and Verdi's *Il Trovatore*, characteristic Polish and Hungarian dances, medleys of popular airs, dance music, and marches. "No other university in the country can boast a band like ours," the *Illini* declared, "—a band whose specialty is concert music of the highest order."[8]

Steele's band was made up of thirty-two instruments. Six of these were cornets, which were prominent in the bands of the day, and three were drums. The band was "proud of its colored member, George W. Riley," who was "quite an artist on the snare drum."[9]

On 14 February 1896 the band gave its annual anniversary concert in Drill Hall.[10] The *Illini* praised the vigor, precision, and delicacy of the playing, describing Steele as "a born conductor" whose taste, genius, and careful work were evident. As a token of appreciation, the president of the band association presented Steele with an ivory baton inlaid with gold and mother-of-pearl.[11] Draper expressed great pleasure in the performance. "By common consent the band has never before been as thoroughly disciplined and efficient as now," he wrote. "Indeed it need not be fearful of comparison with the best professional military bands of the country."[12]

In 1896, Walter Howe Jones, professor of piano, became director of the band. He had no previous experience in this area, but he had a wide general knowledge of music and unbounded enthusiasm for the assignment. Many members of his band were excellent and experienced musicians. On 1 April 1897 Jones led the band in its anniversary concert. The program contained considerable music of high quality, along with the "University of Illinois Cadets' March," written by Jones, and a medley, "Musical Melange," that ended with "The Star Spangled Banner."[13]

In 1897–98 Jones had to rebuild the organization because approximately half of the previous year's members had not returned to the University to complete their studies. He assembled a fine group of musicians. The annual band concert on 24 February illustrates the range and diversity of the offerings. It included Sousa's "Stars and Stripes Forever," the overture to Wagner's *Rienzi*, a selection from Bizet's *Carmen*, the overture to Friedrich von Flotow's *Martha*, "Pickaninnies on Parade," by George D. Barnard, and Liszt's *Second Hungarian Rhapsody*. A year later the program included an air from Gluck's *Orfeo ed Euridice*, selections from Verdi's *La Traviata* and *Il Trovatore*, selections from Gounod's *Roméo et Juliette* and *Faust*, a song by Tchaikovsky, and waltzes from Sousa's *La Reine de la Mer*.[14]

Jones left the University in 1901. After a year in which the violin teacher also conducted the Military Band, Frederick L. Lawrence, head of the School of Music, took charge. But he soon turned over direction of the ensemble to Albert Austin Harding.

Born in Georgetown, Illinois, Harding had experienced a certain amount of family instability during his youth, going at the age of ten to live with a grandparent in Paris, Illinois. When he was fourteen he bought a cornet and a fingering chart and mastered the instrument, later teaching himself to play the fife and other instruments as well. After performing with various local ensembles, he became a member of the Paris Cornet Band. From 1899 to 1902 he worked full-time as a professional musician.

In 1902 the twenty-two-year-old Harding enrolled in the University to study mechanical engineering. He joined the band as a first cornet player, winning the attention of members when he gave a flawless performance of the famous piccolo obligato during a rehearsal of Sousa's "Stars and Stripes Forever." As a sophomore Harding occupied the second chair of the first cornet desk. A year later he held the solo position in that section. In the spring of 1905, near the end of his junior year, Harding accepted a position as part-time instructor in the School of Music effective that September. In the fall Lawrence assisted with the band auditions, but he never again conducted the band. Thereafter Harding carried full responsibility for the group, and on 17 October 1905 the trustees appointed him assistant director of the Military Band at a salary of $50 a year and "teacher of band instruments" in the School of Music at $200 a year. Still intending to complete his degree program, Harding cut back his engineering studies to half-time. But he glided into his career, and in 1916, long after he had become director of the band and a faculty member, Harding earned a bachelor of music degree.[15]

Highlights of the 1903 anniversary concert illustrate the ensemble's musical taste. The first half included the "Imperial Edward March" by Sousa; a selection from Gounod's *Faust*; the Largo (presumably from *Serse*) of Handel; and the March from *Scènes Pittoresques* by Massenet. The second half included a selection from Bizet's *Carmen*; the Intermezzo from the ballet *La Source, ou Naila* by the French composer Léo Delibes; the "Pilgrim Chorus" from Wagner's *Tannhäuser*; and a selection from *The Prince of Pilsen* (1902) by Gustav Luders, an American composer.[16]

## The University Orchestra

In the musical hierarchy, Gilmore insisted that bands deserved top billing. Sousa contended that military bands were not inferior to symphony orchestras—just different.[17] The existence of a military band that gave concert performances may have delayed the rise of a symphony orchestra. In any case, students furnished the impetus for orchestral music. Charles W. Foster, class of '74, had organized and led the first student orchestra in the 1870s. Reuben M. Hobbs, a student from 1891 to 1893, led a similar group. In 1894 President Draper appointed Foster, now back in Champaign and director of a music school, to supervise the University's musical work. One of his duties was to organize an orchestra. But Foster soon concluded that the administration did not support music as part of the regular course of study. At the end of the year he resigned.

In 1896–97, after a year of orchestral inactivity, Edwin H. Pierce of the music faculty took over an orchestral ensemble. The student newspaper described him as inefficient. In 1897 Walter Howe Jones assumed leadership of the group. He introduced a course in University orchestra and secured two-fifths credit for the year for all literary students who were members of the group. Under Jones, the *Illini* wrote, the orchestra would rank with the University's "pet" ensemble, the band.[18]

Within a year Jones had assembled an orchestra of twenty-five, but apparently the players were deemed inadequate to provide the music for the May Festival. The Jacobsohn Orchestra, an ad hoc group from Chicago, was imported for the occasion. In 1901 Lawrence replaced Jones as director of the group. The program for the orchestra's concert on 25 January 1902 included Schubert's Overture to *Rosamunde;* one of the arias for the Queen of the Night from Mozart's *Die Zauberflöte*, sung by Clara Gere, a student; and a march from the Swiss composer Joachim Raff's "Lenore" Symphony. The University String Quartet, composed of faculty members in music, then made its first appearance with the Andante from Tchaikovsky's String Quartet no. 11 and a Haydn quartet. Clara Gere sang the "Waltz Song" from Gounod's *Roméo et Juliette*. The musicians, wrote the *Illini*, made a splendid showing.[19]

## The Glee Clubs and the Mandolin Club

The Glee Club, after the band, was the oldest of the campus musical organizations. It dated from October 1891. Samuel W. Parr of the chemistry faculty was instrumental in organizing the group. As a student in the 1880s Parr had sung with the Philo Sextette. Now he carefully trained the new group, and on 28 March 1892 the Glee Club presented its first annual concert at the Walker Opera House.[20]

Under Parr for two years and then under Charles B. Burdick, a student, for another two years, the Glee Club built a fine reputation. On 27 January 1893 members gave their second annual concert in the opera house to a large and receptive audience. During the year the club also performed in Danville,

Mattoon, and Tuscola. In 1894 Norman F. Marsh, the student business manager, took the club on a weeklong trip to central and southern Illinois.

During the last quarter of the nineteenth century the mandolin, a small instrument of the lute family, came into use again. Its popularity spread to the United States. During 1891–92 Charles A. Elder, then the student leader of the University Band, organized a mandolin club. In 1893 it shared the annual anniversary concert with the band. Many students were members of both the glee and mandolin clubs. In the early 1890s the two groups formed the Glee and Mandolin Club Association for concert performances. In their rehearsal and preparation, however, the two organizations remained entirely separate.[21]

The Mandolin Club added guitars and was usually known as the Mandolin and Guitar Club. A Banjo Club was also organized with a student leader.[22] For two years Charles J. Butterfield, class of '94, led the University Mandolin, Banjo, and Guitar Club. Several men played in both groups; two guitar players were also Glee Club men. Following Butterfield, Jedidiah D. Morse took over the club and brought it to a high level of performance. In 1893 the Glee, Mandolin, and Banjo Club made a weeklong tour to nearby cities.

On 8 February 1895 the Glee and Mandolin Clubs gave their fourth annual home concert at the Walker Opera House. Mrs. Draper and other faculty wives were patronesses. The two clubs, with both separate and combined presentations as well as solos, presented a varied program. Along with Gianfranco Bellenghi's "Profumi Orientali" and "Ciao," described by a reporter as a beautiful Italian waltz by C. Graziani-Walter, the entertainment included "Girl Wanted," a comic song by Gus C. Weinburg, called the hit of the evening, "Hi Jenny, Ho Jenny Johnson," formerly a minstrel song, and "Private Tommy Atkins," from the light opera *A Gaiety Girl.* The evening closed with the varsity song "Illinois" by Frank G. Carnahan and William L. Steele.[23]

During that season Marsh arranged additional off-campus concerts. The men performed in Pekin, Peoria, Kewanee, Ottawa, Rockford, Aurora, Springfield, Alton, and Lincoln, scoring their greatest success at Springfield. Mrs. John P. Altgeld gave the musicians a reception at the Executive Mansion.[24]

In September 1895 Professor Walter Howe Jones took charge of the Glee Club and Horace C. Porter, class of '97, a student of chemistry who played violin in the orchestra, took over the Mandolin Club. Under new directors the two ensembles were reported as making rapid strides toward a higher plane of musical excellence.[25]

The music department and Norman Marsh threw their energies into making a success of the annual concert of the Glee and Mandolin Clubs on 6 December 1895. The entertainment was held in a University building for the first time. The *Illini*, which found "spots here and there where the knife ought to be applied somewhat vigorously," nevertheless congratulated the clubs on an auspicious beginning to their season. The full chorus numbers were the most popular, especially the rendition of "some real, genuine University of Illinois music." These included "Dear Old Illinois" and Jones's version of the University Hymn, which he dedicated to the Glee Club.[26]

In December 1895 the Glee Club and the Mandolin and Guitar Club gave their first concert in Chicago. The *Illini* reprinted accounts from the *Tribune* and the *News-Record* relating that the four hundred alumni in charge of the affair gave the singers a warm reception, and that of the two clubs, the Glee Club was superior in its work.[27] The Board of Trustees, in response to a request for aid, provided the Glee Club with $75.[28]

Glee and Mandolin Club performances garnered excellent press notices. The manager used these in a brochure to announce the availability of the clubs. During 1896–97 the clubs made two extensive trips. In December they presented concerts in Elgin, Aurora, Joliet, and again in Chicago. The appearance in Chicago, in the Central Music Hall, before an audience of nearly thirteen hundred, was a great success. A comic rendition of "Romeo and Juliet" was the hit of the evening. After the goodnight song, the clubs gave the "hulloo-ba-loo" yell, and the alumni responded with the "rah-hoo-rah" yell. According to the *Illini*, the success of the trip was largely due to the training of Jones and the arrangements made by manager Ralph S. Shepardson, class of '97.[29]

Enjoying a fine reputation, during 1897–98 the musicians made four trips that took them to twelve Illinois communities. At Carbondale they drew an audience of over five hundred. After the concert the clubs were entertained at the home of Judge and Mrs. Oliver A. Harker. The Glee and Mandolin Clubs spread the good name of the University far and wide while earning a few dollars for the members.[30]

Women formed their own vocal groups. A Ladies Glee Club made its first bow before a concert audience in May 1896, and during 1897–98 the women came under the leadership of Adeline W. Rowley. On 4 March 1898 the ensemble, which prepared only "high-class" music, presented a program at the Walker Opera House. When Rowley resigned in 1898, Alison M. Fernie of the music faculty took over. Her singers, seventeen in number, included scenes from Wagner's *Die fliegende Holländer* in their concert of 10 April 1899. The excellence of the group's home concerts caused a demand for performances in neighboring cities, so in March 1901 the club planned a tour lasting probably a week.[31] After Fernie left the University in 1903, May E. Breneman, a voice teacher, became the leader of a club that usually had from twenty to twenty-two members a year. The Ladies Quartet was made up of four of the best voices of the larger club. Around 1900 the University also had a Ladies Mandolin Club.

## CHORAL MUSIC

When Walter Howe Jones joined the faculty in 1895, the University had nothing to compare with the successful musical programs for which the University of Michigan was known. To deal with the situation, Jones quickly planned a series of musical events for 1895–96. A number of these were given by members of the music faculty or student musical organizations. Jones himself opened the season with a Chopin program. Later, Adeline W. Rowley offered a vocal recital, and Jones arranged a *soirée musicale*. During the year both the Glee Club and the Military Band presented programs, and Jones arranged for performances by three visiting groups. The most important of these was the Chicago Symphony Orchestra under the German-American conductor Theodore Thomas. The program included Beethoven's *Pastoral* Symphony, Liszt's Concerto no. 1 in E-Flat, with Jones at the piano, the overture to Carl Maria von Weber's *Oberon*, and the "Tournament March" from Wagner's *Tannhäuser*.

These programs went far to elevate the musical culture of the community. The chapel was filled to overflowing for Rowley's concert, and music lovers braved a rainstorm for the Thomas concert. Jones won acclaim for his solo with the Chicago Orchestra.[32] The Thomas concert left a deficit, however, so in May the music department presented a popular concert to remove it. The University Band, the Mandolin and Glee Club, the Ladies Glee Club, a quartet, and soloists, both vocal and instrumental, participated. Jones furnished two piano solos.[33]

During 1897–97 the School of Music arranged similar musical fare. In addition to recitals by Jones, Fernie, and other music faculty members, the visiting artists included the Spiering String Quartet. Founded in 1893 by Theodore Spiering, this quartet gave four hundred concerts over a period of twelve years.

Since arriving at the University, Jones had wished to organize a chorus similar to the University of Michigan Choral Union. This group was famous for its annual May Festival, the idea for which it had borrowed from Cincinnati. There, in 1873, Theodore Thomas had established the Cincinnati Biennial May Festival, which he developed into one of the New World's finest musical events.

On 8 October 1897 Jones proposed the formation of a society whose object was "to study classical music, and to promote the enjoyment and appreciation of the same." He invited students, faculty members, and townspeople to join. Students would receive a credit in music that counted toward graduation. Thus the Oratorio Society, interchangeably known as the Choral Union, came into being. Jones was the first president and Mrs. Andrew S. Draper was the vice president. For several years George T. Kemp, a physiologist who played a role in the formation of the society, served as president.[34]

On 7 April 1898 the Oratorio Society presented its first concert in the Music Hall (a room in University Hall). Fernie directed the seventy-five-member chorus. This performance, featuring choral numbers by Mendelssohn, was a decided success. On Baccalaureate Sunday, volunteers from the society sang several choruses from Handel's *Messiah*.

For the next five years the Oratorio Society and a series of Artists' Concerts provided the community with enriching music. During 1898–99 the Oratorio Society presented two concerts. The highlight of the first one, on 12 December, was selections from *Messiah* performed by a chorus of 125 and soloists from Chicago. Probably the first local performance of Handel's sacred oratorio, this was "one of the grandest and most successful musical events which the people of the twin cities have ever had the pleasure of attending." On 4–5 May the Oratorio Society introduced the May Festival to the University. The program included "Unfold the Portals" from Gounod's oratorio *The Redemption* (1882).[35]

During 1899–1900 the most distinguished of the visiting artists was Leopold Godowsky, a Polish-born American pianist who headed the piano department of the Chicago Conservatory from 1895 to 1900. The May Festival began with a popular concert featuring the "Bridal Chorus" from Wagner's *Lohengrin* and the "Soldier's Chorus" from Gounod's *Faust*. The popular concert was followed by a performance of Mendelssohn's *Elijah*, with the Jacobsohn Orchestra and four soloists. Some two thousand people attended the popular concert, and nearly three thousand attended *Elijah*. News reports described the orchestra as weak but praised the chorus of 157, which included faculty members and faculty wives.

A year later one of the visiting artists was the American David Bispham, the leading baritone of both the Covent Garden and Metropolitan operas. A concert by the Oratorio Society included Jules Massenet's *Narcissus* and Samuel Coleridge-Taylor's cantata, *Hiawatha's Wedding Feast*.

The May Festival that year was a musical banquet. The Boston Festival Orchestra, led by Emil Mollenhauer, and eight soloists were imported for the occasion. The first event, a popular evening concert, opened and closed with selections from Wagner's *Tannhäuser*. The Saturday matinee included Beethoven's *Leonore* Overture no. 3, Schubert's Symphony in B Minor (the "Unfinished"), and Tchaikovsky's "Slavonic March." The main offering was a concert performance of *Samson et Dalila*, an opera in three acts by Saint-Saëns. The Choral Society assumed a burden of at least $2,000 to mount the May Festival. Newspapers praised the promoters for providing the Twin Cities with music such as no other community in Illinois enjoyed.

Although Jones left the University in 1901, others carried on the work he had initiated. The 1902 May Festival illustrates the continuing effort to improve and expand musical taste. On Tuesday evening, 12 May, five visiting artists performed a concert arrangement of Gounod's *Faust* with a chorus of nearly two hundred. On Wednesday afternoon Mollenhauer's orchestra opened the program with the Prelude to Wagner's *Die Meistersinger.* It also played the symphonic poem *La Jeunesse d'Hercule* by Saint-Saëns and Liszt's Concerto no. 1 in E-flat for piano and orchestra.

On Wednesday evening the program included selections from Massenet's *Scènes Pittoresques,* played by the Boston Festival Orchestra, a string orchestra performing *Erotik,* arranged from a piano piece (op. 43, no. 5) by Norway's foremost composer, Edvard Grieg, and *Intermezzo* by Müller-Berghaus, along with several vocal selections by visiting artists. The high point of the concert was the performance of scenes from Samuel Coleridge-Taylor's *Hiawatha's Wedding Feast.* But attendance was disappointing. The year ended with a deficit of $200, which guarantors met.[36]

According to the *Champaign Daily News,* the Choral Society was an indispensable agent in advancing musical taste in a small provincial community. People had come to value the society and to appreciate the first-class artists on its programs. But further efforts were necessary to elevate the taste of Champaign-Urbana to the level of Ann Arbor or Madison. The Choral Society needed additional public support.[37]

In 1902–3 the society's sixth season went well enough. Rubin Goldmark, an American composer and teacher of composition, gave two lectures on Wagner, illustrating *Die Walküre* and *Siegfried* from the piano. The May Festival opened with the "Cockaigne" Overture (1901) by the English composer Edward Elgar, completed only the previous year, and *The Golden Legend* (1886), Longfellow's poem set to music by Sir Arthur Sullivan. The matinee concert featured the Boston Festival Orchestra. The oratorio was again Mendelssohn's *Elijah*.

At the end of the season the treasurer reported that attendance at the last two May Festivals had been less than needed to cover costs. Forced to abandon the original plan, the society gave up the Artists' Concerts. They had put the greatest strain on finances.[38]

Heeding what seemed to be a call for popular programs, the Choral Society and the University Orchestra, both conducted by Frederick Lawrence, gave a Christmas concert in the Armory in 1903. The performers opened with a festival overture on Martin Luther's "Ein feste Burg." The orchestra then played the first two movements of Beethoven's Symphony no. 1, later giving the first performance of a tone poem, *The Passing of Winter,* composed by Lawrence. Benjamin N. Breneman of the voice faculty sang a French Christmas solo, "Noël," and the chorus sang a number of selections, ending with the "Hallelujah Chorus" from *Messiah*. Eleven hundred people attended this concert.

In 1904 the May Festival began with five selections by the Boston Festival Orchestra conducted by Mollenhauer and Massenet's oratorio *Ève* with a chorus of two hundred conducted by Lawrence. The chorus, according to a newspaper account, "was much superior now to any time in its entire history." An evening performance of Handel's *Messiah* followed.[39]

## OPERA

Operatic productions require many varied artistic talents, and development of the School of Music made possible the introduction of opera, at least of the comic sort. Beginning in 1899, students staged five comic operas by William S. Gilbert and Sir Arthur Sullivan. On 1 May 1899 about fifty music students, outfitted in costumes imported from Chicago, performed *Patience* (1881) at the Walker Opera House. The production was a great hit. If the event could be made annual, the *Illini* urged, the musical standard of the student body would be greatly raised.[40]

A year later *The Mikado* (1885) was produced using exclusively local talent, with costumes from Chicago. Students sang the solo parts, Walter Howe Jones played the part of Ko-Ko, the Men's and the Ladies Glee Clubs served as the chorus, and the University Orchestra under the direction of Horace C. Porter furnished the instrumental accompaniment. The presentation, the *Illini* wrote, showed a healthy growth of the "better side of college life."[41]

In 1901 the glee clubs presented *The Pirates of Penzance* (1879), and a year later *Iolanthe* (1882). Reportedly it attracted about the largest audience that ever witnessed any University affair. Early in 1903 Benjamin W. Breneman, a voice teacher, organized the Opera Club. It took over the production of operas, limiting performance to students in the School of Music. On 8 April the club presented *H.M.S. Pinafore* (1878) at the Walker Opera House.[42]

Gilbert and Sullivan were certain crowd-pleasers, but on 12 April 1904 the glee clubs and the orchestra produced Edward Jakobowski's light opera *Erminie*.[43]

In sum, the story of the muse of music at Illinois is one of a steady effort to elevate musical taste in an inland university community and to put it on the road to becoming a capital of musical culture within the state of Illinois.

## NOTES

1. *Illini*, 12 November 1897. Also see the *Illio '96*, 40, and Ann L. Silverberg, *A Sympathy with Sounds: A Brief History of the University of Illinois School of Music to Celebrate Its Centennial* (Urbana: University of Illinois, School of Music, 1995).
2. Margaret H. Hazen and Robert M. Hazen, *The Music Men: An Illustrated History of Brass Bands in America, 1800–1920* (Washington, D.C.: Smithsonian Institution Press, 1987), passim.

3. Calvin E. Weber, "The Contribution of Albert Austin Harding and His Influence on the Development of School and College Bands" (Ph.D. diss., University of Illinois, 1963), 61–70.

4. *Illini*, 6 October 1891, 8 June 1892, 7 February, 29 May 1896.

5. Ibid., 23 May, 8 May [8 June] 1893, 7 February 1896.

6. Ibid., 7 February 1896; William L. Steele, "Those Band Boys of the '90s," *Illinois Alumni News*, 11 (June 1933), 319.

7. *Illini*, 7 February 1896; *18th Report* (1896), 95, 101, 107; see also 219, which explains that after one year Steele went on to other things.

8. Steele, "Those Band Boys of the '90s," 319; *Illini*, 7 February 1896. Programs for concerts of musical organizations often give only surnames of composers. Where possible, the given name of the composer is supplied in the text.

9. *Illini*, 7 February 1896.

10. The first concert was in 1892, the second in 1893, the third in 1894, and no concert was given in 1895. So the 1896 concert was the fourth. Later band programs assumed that the annual concerts began in 1891 and continued without a break. The program for 1906, for example, labels the annual concert as the sixteenth. See 12/9/802, University Band Concert Programs, B:1, F:1892–1914.

11. *Illini*, 21 February 1896, 2 April 1897.

12. Draper to Steele, 18 February 1896, 2/4/3.

13. *Illini*, 9 April, 9 June 1897.

14. For programs, see 12/9/802, University Band Concert Programs, B:1, F:1892–1914.

15. Weber, "The Contribution of Albert Austin Harding," 48–60.

16. *Illini*, 27 February 1903.

17. Hazen and Hazen, *Music Men*, 39–40.

18. *Illio '95*, 99; *Illio '98*, 73; *18th Report* (1896), 251; *19th Report* (1898), 147; *Illini*, 15 October, 22 October 1897.

19. *Illio '99*, 154; *Illini*, 24, 27 January 1902, 14 January 1903.

20. *Illini*, 7 March, 2 November 1891, 30 January, 15, 29 February, 28 March 1892; "The University of Illinois Glee Club," *Illini*, 6 December 1895.

21. *Illini*, 6 December 1895; but see also "The Mandolin and Guitar Club," *Illini*, 26 November 1897.

22. *Illini*, 14 March 1893.

23. For the program, see the *Illini*, 7 February 1895 (with many errors), and Glee, Mandolin, and Guitar Clubs, *Fourth Annual Home Concert, Feb. 8, 1895*, 41/6/840, Glee and Mandolin Club, B:14. For the review, see the *Illini*, 14 February 1895.

24. Glee, Mandolin, and Guitar Clubs, *Fourth Annual Home Concert, 8 Feb. 1895*, 41/6/840, Glee and Mandolin Club; *Illini*, 4 April, 6 December 1895.

25. "The University of Illinois Glee Club," *Illini*, 6 December 1895; "The Mandolin and Guitar Club," *Illini*, 26 November 1897.

26. *Illini*, 18 December 1895.

27. Ibid., 17 January 1896.

28. *18th Report* (1896), 215.

29. "University of Illinois, Glee, Mandolin Club Organization. 1896–1897," 41/6/840, Glee and Mandolin Club, B:14; *Illini*, 11 December 1896.

30. *Illini*, 19 November 1897, 28 January 1898, *Illio '99*, 149.

31. *Illini*, 8 May 1896, 17 December 1897, 25 February 1898, 14 April 1899, 22 January 1900, 6 March 1901.
32. Ibid., 4 October, 18 December 1895, 31 January, 14 February, 13 March, 24 April 1896.
33. Ibid., 8 May 1896.
34. Ibid., 15 October 1897, 28 April 1899; *Illio 1900*, 107–8. Kemp published "Historical Development of Oratorio" in the *Illini*, 15 October 1897. On his contribution in organizing and leading the society, see Kemp to E. J. Townsend, 19 November 1907, 15/1/3, B:9, F:Physiology (1).
35. The programs of the Choral Society along with newspaper clippings on the concerts for the period under review are in 41/65/9, University Choral and Orchestral Society Records, 1898–1913, B:1; Champaign *News*, 13 December 1899 (quotation); *Illio 1900*, 107–8.
36. *Illini*, 12 May, 14 May 1902.
37. *Champaign Daily News*, 11 April 1902, clipping in 41/65/9, University Choral and Oratorical Society Records, 1898–193, B:1.
38. The treasurer's report is in an issue of the *Champaign Daily News* during May 1903 in 41/65/9, University Choral and Orchestral Society Records, 1898–1913, B:1, F:1902–3.
39. The quotation is from the *Champaign Gazette*, 10 May 1904.
40. *Illini*, 28 April, 5 May 1899.
41. Ibid., 6 April 1900.
42. Ibid., 9 April, 15 December 1902, 10 April 1903.
43. Ibid., 10 April 1903, 13 April 1904.

# CHAPTER 15

# FRATERNITIES AND
# THE SOCIAL WHIRL

At Illinois as elsewhere, around 1900 the Greek-letter fraternity, a uniquely American institution, began to replace the literary society in prestige and importance. It offered students membership without regard to field of study, class year, or grade attainment above the minimum requirement. General fraternities were known as social fraternities. Originally, the "social" meant to socialize or promote the social development of members; later, the emphasis was on social activities. Fraternities for men and for women (the term "sorority" was rarely used in the early days of the movement) were mutually exclusive, self-perpetuating groups that provided an organized social life for members as part of their educational experience.

Phi Beta Kappa, the first American society bearing a Greek name, is the ancestor of all the later general fraternities. Established on 5 December 1776 at the College of William and Mary in Williamsburg, Virginia, for social and literary purposes, it had all the characteristics of its offspring—the mystery of secrecy, high idealism, a ritual, an oath of fidelity, a motto, a badge for external display, regular meetings, strong ties of friendship, and a desire to share its values by national expansion. Phi Beta Kappa later became and has since remained a scholarly honor society.

In the 1820s three Greek-letter fraternities bearing a close resemblance to Phi Beta Kappa in their external features emerged at Union College in Schenectady, New York: Kappa Alpha, Sigma Phi, and Delta Phi. The Union Triad spread over the eastern states and became the pattern for the American fraternity system. Between 1839 and 1855 Beta Theta Pi, Phi Delta Theta, and Sigma Chi were formed at Miami University in Oxford, Ohio. The Miami Triad furnished the pattern for colleges in the West and South.

The first general fraternities were inspired by lofty moral principles and ethical theories. They based their rituals on the wisdom of classical antiquity and on the Hebrew and Christian scriptures, and made intellectual pursuits central to their purposes. Yet the fledgling fraternities met suspicion and resistance. Their secrecy led to charges that they were subversive, a disruptive conspiracy against the established academic order.[1]

## FRATERNITY BEGINNINGS AT ILLINOIS

The Greek system planted roots at Illinois soon after the University opened. Early in 1872 the Upsilon Prime chapter of Delta Tau Delta was established. The first regent opposed secret societies on the grounds that they were undemocratic and corrupt, and the Delts gained control of the student government. On 7 June 1876 the trustees condemned secret societies in the University and urged students to disband them. The Delts were driven underground, and in 1879 their charter was withdrawn.[2]

During the 1880s Greeks made a spirited effort to replant the fraternity system. In 1881 a number of men formed a local chapter of Sigma Chi. When its existence became known, the Board of Trustees declared the organization and existence of fraternities "unwise, and detrimental to the best interests of the institution." They directed the regent to eliminate them. On 2 December the faculty decreed that after 1 January 1882 every matriculant be required to sign a pledge not to become a member of a secret society while at the University. Students petitioned the board to rescind the pledge, but the trustees refused.[3]

Sigma Chi mounted a vigorous campaign to gain recognition. The trustees considered the matter, but in 1886 they refused to lift the ban. The desire for fraternities persisted. Regent Selim H. Peabody's staunch opposition to Greek-letter societies contributed to his forced resignation in June 1891. As acting regent, Thomas J. Burrill welcomed fraternities. He may have been instrumental in persuading the trustees to change their minds.[4] In September the board dropped the "iron-clad pledge," and in December it ordered that antifraternity pledges held in the regent's office be destroyed and that this action be publicly announced. Thus, fraternities were given a green light. But under the rules for the government of students, no student society could be formed without express faculty permission.[5]

## Dawn of the Golden Age

Repeal of the iron-clad pledge inaugurated the golden age of fraternities at the University of Illinois. Students were eager to enjoy the advantages offered by secret societies, and in turn the University provided a great field of opportunity for the fraternity movement. From 1891 through 1904 eighteen chapters of national fraternities—thirteen for men and five for women—were formed at Illinois. This was the first wave of a flood. By 1928 the University had the largest number of Greek-letter secret societies of any university in the United States.[6]

Establishment of a chapter usually followed a set procedure. Students formed a local society and later applied to a national fraternity for a charter. The parent chapter or headquarters, safeguarding the organization's good name, often sent someone to evaluate the petitioners and the campus. The investigator's report went to a national convention of the fraternity, which was empowered to charter branches. Local chapters were installed in a dignified ceremony, followed by an elegant banquet.

### Fraternities for Men

Five chapters of national fraternities arose at Illinois soon after the lifting of the antifraternity ban. Kappa Sigma was the first. In September 1891 Robert A. Lackey, a Purdue football player, arrived in Urbana to coach the football team. A devoted Kappa Sig, Lackey petitioned the Worthy Grand Scribe for permission to form a chapter. On 15 October he pledged nine men, and on 17 November they were initiated. On 12 December, after the trustees had ordered the antifraternity pledges destroyed, the charter for Alpha Gamma chapter was issued.[7]

Meanwhile, Sigma Chi alumni had taken steps to revive their chapter. On 14 December 1891 the faculty voted approval, subject to certain conditions. On 22 December the chapter was revived.[8] John W. Arnold, Jr., was instrumental in organizing Phi Kappa Sigma on the campus. He and other members of the chapter at Northwestern University made an on-site investigation. Arnold applied for a charter. It was granted on 29 October 1892, and on that same day Arnold and others installed Rho chapter at the Columbian Hotel in Urbana. But in 1893 the chapter died out.[9]

Shortly after the antifraternity pledge was rescinded, Scott Williams, the student who introduced football at Illinois, and others informally applied to Phi Delta Theta for affiliation. A year later fifteen men organized a local society, Alpha Nu, with a view to securing a national charter. On 4 October 1893 the men applied to Phi Delta Theta. Fraternity officials visited Champaign and reported favorably. On 19 December the Grand Council granted a charter for

Illinois Eta chapter, and on 19 February 1894 two visiting Phi Delt officials conducted the installation exercises in Champaign.[10]

A chapter of Delta Tau Delta resulted from the efforts of George Jobst and others. Early in 1893 they formed a local fraternity with a view to securing a charter from one of the national organizations. Their application to Delta Tau Delta was successful, and on 7 April 1894 eighteen men were initiated by Chicago alumni in the library of the old Chicago Athletic Club in Chicago.[11]

When Draper became president he had no prior experience with fraternities and no special liking for them, but he cautiously endorsed the fraternity system. He did not see any objection "to persons who have a fancy for becoming affiliated with them." As a rule, he added, fraternities were composed of "very good students, that is young men who rank as well in their University work as others do and whose habits are above criticism." After further consideration, he found fraternities worthy of a place in college life and did his best to help them secure a footing.[12] Draper's son Edwin joined Phi Delta Theta, and his daughter Charlotte joined Alpha Chi Omega. No doubt Draper's views were also shaped by practical considerations. Fraternities helped solve the problem of providing room and board and they facilitated discipline. It was easier to control groups than masses of individuals. So fraternities sprouted like mushrooms after a spring rain.

Three local chapters of fraternities emerged in the early years of Draper's administration. Thomas Arkle Clark, a faculty member, helped organize Alpha Tau Omega at the University. He was the first person initiated when the Gamma Zeta chapter was installed on 16 March 1895 by three members of the Chicago Alumni Association of the society. Gamma Zeta took a leading position in the fraternity's affairs. Clark later became Worthy Grand Chief of Alpha Tau Omega. He publicly championed the fraternity system.[13]

Phi Gamma Delta gained a footing at the University on 15 October 1897 when the Chi Iota chapter was installed at the Hotel Beardsley. Members of the graduate chapter at Chicago and faculty members who had been Phi Gams during their college days had charge of the ceremonies. The initiates included Arthur H. Daniels, professor of philosophy. A reporter described the occasion: a "prettily draped" room, an orchestra, visitors—from Chicago and Wisconsin, Dean Kinley, Professors Burrill and Parr—a grand march into the banquet hall to the strains of "Die Wacht am Rhein," a sumptuous dinner, seven toasts and responses.[14]

George B. Worthen, an Illinois student who had first learned of Sigma Alpha Epsilon while a student at the University of the South, was instrumental in organizing the local chapter. In the fall of 1897 he formed the Red Ribbon Society, and its members subsequently applied for a charter. After a visiting province president reported favorably, the 1898 convention approved the request. On 28 January 1899 eighteen men were initiated into Illinois Beta.

That evening members celebrated with a banquet at the Beardsley. "The chapter from the first," the Sigma Alpha Epsilon historian wrote, "has been as strong and progressive as any chapter ever enrolled."[15]

In 1902 three new secret societies were chartered. Beta Theta Pi experienced labor pains in emerging. On five occasions since 1879 the national organization had rejected petitions for a chapter at Illinois. Success came when three graduate students organized the local fraternity Sigma Delta for the express purpose of securing a Beta Theta Pi chapter. They petitioned the national convention of 1901. Their application, referred to a mail vote, won the necessary majority. On 28 February 1902 a committee of nine visiting fraternity officials installed the Sigma Rho chapter of Beta Theta Pi.[16]

On three occasions over a period of seven years different groups at Illinois had attempted to secure a charter from Sigma Nu. The fraternity denied the requests. In the fall of 1901 students and two faculty members petitioned for a charter. A division inspector disapproved certain members of the group. In January 1902 Vice Regent George M. Cook and other fraternity officials visited Urbana. Approving some but not all of the fellows, they rejected the entire group. Cook then recruited ten worthy men, who petitioned for and received a charter. On 7 June the chapter was secretly installed on the third floor of the home of Professor Ira O. Baker. His sons Cecil F. and Ira W. were among the ten charter members. On 19 September a public announcement of the matter was made, and the Gamma Mu chapter joined the fraternity circle at the University.[17]

On 20 December 1901, some of those present at the annual banquet of the Wisconsin chapter of Phi Kappa Sigma discussed their interest in reviving the chapter of their fraternity at Illinois. Members from Wisconsin, Northwestern, and the Armour Institute of Technology, working in connection with the Grand Chapter, reestablished Rho chapter on 6 December 1902.[18]

Another wave of three fraternities soon followed. In 1903 a local society was converted into Illinois Alpha of Sigma Phi Epsilon. The Illinois chapter of Phi Kappa Psi had a long period of gestation. In the spring of 1893 some fellows petitioned the fraternity for a charter. The petition was denied. Later, Dan G. Swanell, a Champaign man who attended the University for one year and then transferred to Michigan, where he became a Phi Psi, determined to introduce his fraternity at Illinois when the time was ripe. In the fall of 1900 he and other Phi Psis who were enrolled in the University agitated for a chapter at Illinois. Meeting no success, they decided to disband. Three years later Swannell resumed his efforts, and in April 1904 he and other Phi Psis studying at the University appealed to the Grand Arch Council meeting in Indianapolis. The Executive Council agreed to grant a charter as soon as a suitable number of petitioners of satisfactory character had been secured. Swanell and others then pledged eight men. On 28 May members of the Executive Council visited the Twin Cities and wrote a strong recommendation. But the council postponed the granting of the charter until the autumn. At that time the new president of the University, Edmund J. James, a Phi Psi, aided their cause, and on 24 October 1904 a charter was granted to Illinois Delta of Phi Kappa Psi.[19]

On 17 November 1904 a local social group became affiliated with Delta Kappa Epsilon as the Delta Pi chapter at Illinois.[20]

In the period from 1894–95 through 1903–4, fraternities for men had relatively few members. According to data from 1897, 17 percent of the Illinois student body belonged to a fraternity, compared to 80 percent at Amherst College, 48 percent at Virginia, 33 percent at Cornell, 29 percent at Ann Arbor, 24 percent at Chicago, and 22 percent at Wisconsin.[21] Data in the college yearbooks reveal the number of undergraduates in the local chapters, from which we get an idea of the relative size of the groups. In the years previously noted both Sigma Chi and Phi Delta Theta had 228 members, an annual average of 22.8. Sigma Alpha Epsilon in five years at Illinois had a total of 106 members, a yearly average of 21.2. Phi Gamma Delta in six years had 138 members, an annual average of 19.6. Delta Tau Delta in nine years had 169 members, a yearly average of 18.7. Beta Theta Pi in two years had 35 undergrads, an annual average of 17.5. Kappa Sigma, with 169 members in ten years, had an annual average of 16.9. Alpha Tau Omega in eight years had 131 members, an annual average of 16.3. Sigma Nu in its one year had 18 members. Phi Kappa Psi and Delta Kappa Epsilon, chartered in the fall of 1904, are not included in this assessment.

Some local men's fraternities were also part of the campus scene. The K. K. Club, which was founded in 1902, approved by the Council of Administration on 14 December 1903, and claimed 26 members in 1904–5, later became a chapter of Delta Upsilon. The Sphinx, also founded in 1902, over a six-year period averaged about 13 members annually, including students and faculty members who were affiliated with general fraternities. Pi Theta, organized as a local in February 1903, had 18 members in 1904–5. Others were class societies. The Shield and Trident, organized in 1893 for senior men, was a local with 117 members from 1894–95 to 1902–3, or an annual average of 13. Most of its members also belonged to a fraternity. Alpha Delta Sigma, which was organized at Illinois on 15 November 1895, was a junior-class fraternity.

Theta Nu Epsilon was a special case. Founded in 1870 at Wesleyan University in Connecticut, primarily as a fraternity for sophomores, the society accepted members of other Greek-letter groups. Theta Nu Epsilon was loosely governed nationally. In many institutions the behavior of its members was so egregious that the organization fell into disrepute. Most national organizations prohibited their members from joining the society. At Illinois, however, the Alpha Phi chapter of Theta Nu Epsilon flourished. Membership may have ranged from sixteen to twenty-three, plus honorary members (we cannot be sure because the society cloaked itself in secrecy). The *Illio* did not print names or photographs of members. But it named members of other fraternities who were also members of Theta Nu Epsilon. In *Illio 1900*, for example, Sigma Chi had four members in this organization; Kappa Sigma, seven; Alpha Tau Omega, six; Phi Delta Theta; five, and Delta Tau Delta, one. Later, Theta Nu Epsilon fell into such disrepute that Dean Clark penetrated its secrecy and rooted it out.

## Fraternities for Women

Women were entering higher education in greater numbers as the fraternity movement advanced, and women formed their own fraternities to secure a social position for themselves in university life, for mutual improvement, and for congenial companionship. They modeled their Greek-letter groups after the men's secret societies.

In the fall of 1892 some young women applied to the faculty for permission to organize a Greek-letter society. Nothing came of the matter.[22] From 1894–95 through 1903–4 the number of women in the student body rose from 16.5 percent to 26 percent. By the spring of 1895 the time was ripe for the women to proceed. One group of women petitioned Kappa Alpha Theta for a charter, and another petitioned Pi Beta Phi.

Kappa Alpha Theta antedated Pi Beta Phi by a few days. In early October the national convention of the society approved the transfer of the charter of the Alpha chapter at Illinois Wesleyan to the University. On 9 November the deed was done. Renamed, the Delta chapter was installed at the home of Judge Francis M. Wright in Urbana.[23] On 26 October 1895 Grace Lass, grand president of Pi Phi, installed the Illinois Zeta chapter of Pi Beta Phi in a private home on South Neil Street in Champaign, following which the hostess provided the women a delicious banquet.[24]

Four years elapsed before the demand for sisterhood led to additional societies. Katharine L. Sharp, the head librarian and the director of the Library School at Illinois, and her colleague Frances Simpson had both been members of Kappa Kappa Gamma at Northwestern. They received permission from the grand officers to establish a chapter at Illinois. On 28 April 1899 the grand secretary, assisted by the Epsilon Chapter of Illinois Wesleyan, installed the Beta Lambda Chapter at the University.[25]

Alpha Chi Omega was a social rather than a professional fraternity. Designed to advance the art of music, it was not a strictly musical organization. Alpha Chi Omega expanded as a general fraternity with musical traditions. On 8 December 1899 five delegates from the Alpha (or mother) chapter at DePauw University installed the Iota chapter at Illinois. On the night before the installation President Draper, whose daughter Charlotte was one of the charter members, held a reception for the visiting delegates.[26]

The fifth sorority at Illinois was Chi Omega. On 13 June 1900 the Omicron chapter was installed at Illinois.[27] In the fall of 1900 Phi Mu Epsilon fraternity sent two young women from its chapter at DePauw University in Greencastle, Indiana, to organize a chapter at Illinois. They secured six potential charter members and then asked the authorities for permission to proceed. Without explaining, the Council of Administration denied the request.[28]

The fraternities for women flourished at Illinois. Most of them had several patronesses, including Mrs. Draper and other prominent local women. Pi Beta Phi was the largest. The others in order of size were Kappa Alpha Theta, Kappa Kappa Gamma, Chi Omega, and Alpha Chi Omega.

## GREEKS AND BARBARIANS

The advent of Greek-letter societies changed the character of the University. The fraternity movement had started on a wave of idealism. The founders aimed at promoting not only deeper fraternal bonds but also the intellectual, moral, and social development of members. Their rituals appealed to the young. At first the new secret societies were much like the older literary societies. Members met weekly in their own club room, devoting themselves to literature and oratory and socializing. Under these conditions fraternity members were not visibly different from the rest of the student body.

By the turn of the century, however, fraternities had changed. Their original idealism had dissipated, social activities had become increasingly important, and greater material resources had enabled members to branch out in new directions. After being chartered, fraternities secured their own rooms, often in downtown Champaign, and soon thereafter they acquired their own houses near the campus.

The fraternity house was a turning point in the evolution of the Greek-letter system. On the one hand, the house fostered pride in an organization, developed social discipline, afforded a field for mutual helpfulness, and encouraged close friendships. The house also held out the promise of benefits in later life. Members might well find a spouse at a fraternity function or someone who would be helpful in advancing one's career. The house was a magnet for fraternity alumni.

On the other hand, the house promoted social exclusiveness. It narrowed members, who basked in the reputation of the chapter. It also increased the expenses of college and shifted attention from intellectual to social pursuits. And because the chapters competed with each other for preeminence, jealousy and antagonism were common among the fraternities.[29]

Above all, the fraternity system aggravated an old problem in higher education—the division of the student body into "college students" and "outsiders." These groups represented different sets of values, which were often based on socioeconomic distinctions. "College students" were prominent and prestigious in campus life; "outsiders" existed on the periphery. The fraternity system institutionalized this division. "College students" were the fraternity members, or Greeks; "outsiders" were the Independents or "barbarians." The division led to a mutual antagonism that only increased over time.[30]

## THE SOCIAL WHIRL

In 1894 the pace of social life on the campus suddenly seemed to quicken. The Christian Associations took an active part in this area. The YMCA and the YWCA opened the social season by tendering a reception for new students at the beginning of the college year. Addresses of welcome by President Draper and the presidents of the two groups, a program of music, and light refreshments made up the evening's entertainment. In some years these affairs attracted over five hundred students.[31]

The Students' Assembly was designed to cultivate a better social life for students. It was composed of those student organizations which chose to become members. The executive committee included one delegate from each affiliated student group. The assembly was of, by, and for students, but those who were not members of student organizations were not represented.

For a number of years the Students' Assembly filled a social void. The executive committee tried to hold at least one meeting each term. One or more rooms were decorated for the occasion. The evening consisted of conversation, a music program, games and other amusements, the singing of college songs, and dancing, all in an atmosphere of freedom and informality. Refreshments were served. Some faculty members and wives attended. The *Illini* called the first of these, held in 1894, a "grand success" and "an epoch in the social history of our University."[32] A year later the paper described the assemblies as "the mainspring of University social life," a bond that united and fostered college spirit.[33]

By the spring of 1901, however, the Students' Assembly had outlived its usefulness. The bills incurred earlier had not yet been paid, and the student body had grown so large as to render the organization neither practicable nor pleasurable.[34]

Women were a minority in the student body, with their own social needs. One recognition of this reality was the "at home" which Mrs. Draper held on Saturday, 23 May 1896, for the young women of the University. "All the

University girls were present," it was reported, along with some women faculty and faculty wives. President Draper made an appearance to welcome the guests. To see how "his girls" would look as a group, he had their picture taken on the porch of the president's house.[35]

Class functions enjoyed a prominent place on the social calendar. The freshman sociable, the sophomore cotillion, the junior promenade, and the senior ball, all followed a similar format. After 13 January 1896, when the authorities ruled that all University social gatherings held in University buildings were to terminate not later than 11:30 p.m. except for the senior ball, which was to close not later than 2 a.m.,[36] these affairs were held in a hotel or hall in Champaign or Urbana. The *Illini* reported these affairs in glowing terms. The junior prom was described as "the greatest social event in the history of a man's college life until he reaches his senior year."[37]

Students paid to attend class functions, and any balance after expenses accrued to the managers. To prevent profiteering, on 10 March 1898 the Council of Administration ruled that no organization connected with the University would be permitted to hold any entertainment with a view to raising money to be divided among its members. All funds received from entertainments given by University organizations were to be used for the benefit of the organization as a whole.[38]

During commencement week the senior class enjoyed many special events: President Draper's reception, the Promenade Concert, a baccalaureate service, and Class Day. The morning program for Class Day included an address by the class president, the class history, the Motto Oration, the class poem, the Hatchet Oration, the class prophecy, and a valedictory, all interspersed with music. The Motto Oration was based on the class motto, chosen four years earlier. In the Hatchet Oration—a vestige of the class rivalry that had long characterized the American college—a senior made sarcastic remarks to the junior class and a junior wittily replied in kind.

In the afternoon the University Band gave a concert in front of the Main Building. Then seniors visited the sites and buildings in which they had spent their college years, and a member of the class closely identified with the place bade it farewell for the entire class. After this the class formed a circle in front of the library for the ritual burning of thesis papers—a throwback to a time when students symbolically freed themselves from hated texts at the end of the academic year. In the evening came the senior ball.[39]

Dancing was a favorite pastime, perhaps because it enabled students to embrace members of the opposite sex. The Christian Associations held no dances. The Students' Assembly scheduled both games and dancing. Some objected to these gatherings. Francis E. King, a member of the YMCA, prepared a petition on the subject that was signed by ninety-six male and thirty-three female students. They wanted provision made for the entertainment of "the large number who neither dance nor play cards, together with not a few who do not approve the public dance."[40]

But most students were eager to dance. Passion for the activity gave rise to a sophomore hop, a sophomore-freshman hop, a junior class dance, a series of informal cadet hops, and the annual Military Ball. The first of these, in April 1896, was limited to members of the battalion and their guests. "That the affair was a success," the *Illini* wrote, "is putting it very mildly." But some complained about its exclusive nature.[41]

Several dancing clubs arose to satisfy demand for the pastime. The first of these was the Students' Dancing Club (SDC), which fraternity men dominated.[42] From January through early April each year the SDC sponsored at two-week intervals a series of five to seven dances open to all students for a fee. In January 1897 twenty-five couples attended the first of a series at Imperial Hall. Dance programs alternated between the waltz and the two-step.[43]

In 1902 rivals began to challenge the SDC as a sponsor of dances. On 10 January both the Orange and Blue Dancing Club, most of whose members seemed to be Independents, and the SDC opened the winter social season with dance programs. On or about the same day members of Alpha Tau Omega, Sigma Chi, Beta Theta Pi, and Phi Gamma Delta withdrew from the SDC and established the Illinois Club. Explaining these rifts, the *Illini* wrote that "politics seems to have been the cause for the opening of hostilities which give promise of lasting for some time." On 17 January the Illinois Club held its opening program in Illinois Hall. Soon thereafter the Varsity Dancing Club, made up mainly of engineering students and Independents, sponsored dances.[44]

In social life, the line dividing Greeks from barbarians was highly visible. Leaders of local society showered attention on the secret societies, and the college newspaper reported fraternity activities in loving detail. Among sororities, the affairs of Kappa Alpha Theta and Pi Beta Phi received the most press coverage. The women served their male friends oyster suppers, entertained them at receptions and dances, and together with their escorts enjoyed a picnic at the casino in West End Park in Champaign. The program included selection and crowning of a May Queen, a Maypole dance, and dancing.[45]

On 3 February 1898 Kappa Alpha Theta received over four hundred friends at the home of Mrs. J. R. Trevett on West University Avenue in Champaign. The patronesses, Mmes. A. S. Draper, F. M. Wright, and J. R. Trevett, assisted in entertaining the guests. Snyder's Orchestra provided music.[46]

For sororities the main social event of the year was a formal party. In 1900 the Pi Phis held theirs on a Friday evening in March in Miebach's Hall. Each of the other sororities was represented among the guests. Thirty-five couples attended; the grand march began at 9 p.m. A month later Alpha Chi Omega entertained forty at a musical reception. On 18 January 1902 the local chapter of Kappa Kappa Gamma held its first annual party in Illinois Hall. A banquet of seven courses, a grand march, seventeen dance numbers, and four extras established for the sorority "an enviable reputation as entertainers."[47]

Arbiters of local society often entertained fraternity men. On 17 January 1896, for example, Mr. and Mrs. R. D. Burnham gave a waltz party for Sigma Chi. A mandolin orchestra furnished music for twenty dances, and a caterer provided "elegant refreshments." In March 1901 Mrs. John L. Ray, assisted by Mrs. Draper and four other matrons, received Sigma Alpha Epsilon from 3 to 10 p.m. at 711 West University Avenue in Champaign.[48]

Fraternities for men enjoyed their own social activities. These included a card party, a smoker, and a "term party," which offered dancing and "elegant refreshments" to twenty-five men and twenty-one women. On a Monday night in 1895 Sigma Chi gave a party in favor of their new members. After a short reception in the fraternity rooms, everyone adjourned to the Walker Opera House for refreshments and dancing.

For men's fraternities the highlight of the year was the celebration of the anniversary of the installation of the local chapter. Such affairs were impressive, as a few examples will demonstrate. On 5 March 1896 Sigma Chi tendered a reception and banquet for the grand consul of the fraternity, General Benjamin P. Runkle. Among the guests were President and Mrs. Draper, Vice President and Mrs. Burrill, and alumnus W. A. Heath and his wife. Around 10 a mandolin orchestra summoned those present into the banquet hall. A little after midnight the nine toasts began. At times the toasts were interrupted by the fraternity songs and yells, together with the University yell. General Runkle, one of the founders of the fraternity, spoke last. At 2 a.m. the banquet ended with the singing of the Sigma Chi national hymn, and "soon the greatest event in the history of the local chapter of Sigma Chi was over."[49]

On 2–3 April 1898 the annual convention of the western division of Delta Tau Delta was held in Champaign with the Beta Upsilon chapter. On Saturday evening the menu of the dinner at the Beardsley included oysters, green turtle soup, planked shad, tenderloin of beef, veal sweetbreads, and roast squab, washed down by claret and champagne punch. Seven toasts were made. The dinner concluded with "the time-honored Choctaw walk-around."[50]

## THE CHALLENGE OF THE FRATERNITIES

On 6 April 1900, at the celebration of the founding of Beta Upsilon chapter of Delta Tau Delta, President Draper said that there was a large place in every university for fraternities, "and that they represented nothing foreign to the democratic idea of a great school." They fostered brotherhood and helped one another. The University would never reach its "symmetrical development until every Greek letter society should have its own fraternity house looking across the Illinois campus."[51]

Draper's declaration was both muddled and fatuous. In fact, Greek-letter societies presented a novel challenge. Presumably Draper recognized this shortly after his banquet remarks. In March 1901 he asked each of the fraternities on the campus to send three representatives to meet with him to discuss their common interests and to obtain a clearer understanding of the attitude of the University toward fraternities. A general discussion ensued. Nothing specific came of this meeting, but Draper reaffirmed the policy of encouraging the Greeks and stated that the interests of the University and the societies were common and mutual.[52]

Actually, fraternities introduced an antidemocratic element into the student body. Dean Violet Jayne underscored this point when she commented on the antagonism between sorority and nonsorority girls. Moreover, fraternities distorted the main purpose of the University by carrying social pursuits to excess. For example, a number of Greek-letter groups held social events during the week. On 17 February 1902, when the Council of Administration learned that Kappa Sigma was preparing to hold its annual celebration on a Thursday evening despite the fact that members must have known that authorities opposed the practice, the council said that the chapter deserved censure. But since the council had not hitherto explicitly declared itself on the subject, it would take no further notice of the matter. Nevertheless, the authorities added, the holding of annuals or informals on other than Friday or Saturday evenings contravened the purposes of the University and constituted an infraction of University discipline.[53]

In 1902 a revision of the *Rules for the Government of Students* incorporated this prohibition. In May 1903, however, Sigma Chi tried to circumvent the rule by holding an informal dance party on a Wednesday evening because it had been impossible to schedule it on a Friday or Saturday. When members applied for permission for the Wednesday date, Dean Clark refused them by President Draper's express direction. As a result, the alumni of the fraternity gave the dance in their name, with the active members thinking that in this way they could get around the letter of the law. So the council wrote a reprimand to the fraternity, published it in the college newspaper, and sent a copy to the officers of the national fraternity.[54]

As Dean Jayne observed, some women went into society so much that their scholarship suffered. The sororities recognized the problem. In a mock Declaration of Independence signed by all of the women's societies, members declared that it had become necessary to dispense with the pleasurable company of their gentlemen friends "and to secure the regulation amount of rest to which the laws of Nature and Nature's God entitle[d] them." Thus all social calls had to be terminated at 10 p.m., and the men were to be discouraged from making more than three calls per week.[55]

As a segment of society, fraternities reflected the larger culture, and as early as 1895 the Greeks had earned a reputation for drinking. Writing Draper, the mother of a student reported hearing that fraternities "result most frequently in drunkenness and card playing, etc."[56] Contemporary records do not indicate that alcohol was a problem. But the young men did drink. In 1897, the Council of Administration warned against the practice.

Dean Clark, who always saw the best in the Greek system, viewed the problems arising from fraternity life as faults common to all college men. He wanted fraternity growth encouraged under the supervision of the administration. Under that policy the Greek-letter societies were to flourish at Illinois.

## NOTES

1. *Baird's Manual of American College Fraternities*, 20th ed., ed. Jack L. Anson and Robert F. Marchesani, Jr. (Indianapolis: Baird's Manual Foundation, 1991), 1–5, 10–24.
2. *8th Report* (1877), 185; W. A. Heath, "The Mythology of Illinois," *Illinois Magazine*, 3 (May 1912), 411.
3. Joseph C. Nate, *The History of Sigma Chi Fraternity, 1855–1925*, 4 vols. ([Chicago]: The Fraternity, [1925]), 3:173–84; *11th Report* (1882), 191, 192, 206–7, 220, 228; *12th Report* (1884), 191–92; 4/1/1, vol. 2, 29 November, 2 December 1881 (the text of the pledge is in the minutes for 9 December 1881).
4. According to Stewart Howe, "The Early Fraternity History at the University of Illinois," *Banta's Greek Exchange*, 16 (October 1928), 302, Burrill distrusted fraternities, believing that they "indulged in all manner of deviltry" and could represent a "terror to university discipline." Howe offers no evidence for his statement. In 1881 Burrill, along with Peabody and Ricker, had been a member of the committee that recommended the antifraternity pledge, but Burrill's actions as acting regent belie Howe's interpretation.
5. *16th Report* (1892), 151, 195, 193.
6. Howe, "Early Fraternity History," 300.
7. Ibid., 302–3; Finis K. Farr, *Kappa Sigma: A History, 1869–1929* (Denver: The Fraternity, 1929), 153; *Illini*, 11 April, 25 April, 21 September 1892. The following account draws on *Baird's Manual* without citing page references.
8. Heath, "Mythology of Illinois," 415; 4/1/1, 3:109–10, 121; Nate, *History of Sigma Chi*, 3:184; *Illini*, 12 March, 25 April, 22 May, 21 September 1892.
9. *Illini*, 15 November 1892; David E. van der Werff, Phi Kappa Sigma Educational Consultant, to author, [c. 20 August 1998].
10. *Illini*, 14 March 1893; Walter B. Palmer, *The History of Phi Delta Theta Fraternity* (Menasha, Wisc.: George Banta Publishing Co., 1906), 588–89, 842.
11. *Illini*, 14 March 1893; Howe, "Early Fraternity History," 303.
12. Draper to Mrs. E. J. Chacy, 2 October 1895, 2/4/3; *Illini*, 9 April 1900.

13. Claude T. Reno, *The ATΩ Story: The First Fifty Years* (Champaign, Ill.: Alpha Tau Omega Fraternity, 1962), 143–44, 193–94. Clark's publications include *The Fraternity and the College* (Menasha, Wisc.: George Banta Publishing Co., 1915; new ed., 1931), and *The Fraternity and the Undergraduate* (Menasha, Wisc.: George Banta Publishing Co., 1917; new ed., 1923).

14. *Illini*, 22 October 1897.

15. William C. Levere, *The History of the Sigma Alpha Epsilon Fraternity*, 3 vols. (Chicago: The Fraternity, 1911), 2:439–43 (quotation at 442).

16. *Illini*, 28 February 1902; Francis W. Shepardson, *The Beta Book: The Story and Manual of Beta Theta Pi*, 3d ed., rev. (Menasha, Wisc.: Collegiate Press, George Banta Publishing Co., 1935), 100, 105, 107, 133–34, 135, 415. Shepardson writes that thirteen members were initiated at the installation.

17. 3/1/1, 3:4 (19 September 1902); *Illini*, 23 September 1902; John C. Scott, *The Story of Sigma Nu: A Narrative History of the Fraternity, 1869–1926* (Indianapolis: The Fraternity, 1927), 412–25.

18. *Illini*, 23 January 1903.

19. Charles L. Van Cleve, *The History of the Phi Kappa Psi Fraternity: From Its Foundation in 1852 to Its Fiftieth Anniversary* (Philadelphia: Franklin Printing Co., 1902); Harry S. Gorgas and J. Duncan Campbell, *The Centennial History of the Phi Kappa Psi Fraternity, 1852–1952*, vol. 2 ([Binghamton, N.Y.]: Phi Kappa Psi Fraternity, 1952), 65–66, 77–80.

20. *General Catalog: Delta Kappa Epsilon* ([New York], Council of Delta Kappa Epsilon, 1926), 519.

21. *Illini*, 8 October 1897.

22. 4/1/1, 3:159 (3 October 1892).

23. *Illini*, 11 October, 15 November 1895; Estelle R. Dodge, *Sixty Years in Kappa Alpha Theta, 1870–1929* (Menasha, Wisc.: George Banta Publishing Co., 1930), 129; Carol G. Wilson, *We Who Wear Kites: The Story of Kappa Alpha Theta, 1870–1956* (Menasha, Wisc.: George Banta Publishing Co., 1956), 8–9. The *Illini* reports that the charter was granted on 5 October and that the installation occurred on 11 November.

24. *Illini*, 1 November 1895, 4 March 1901; Emma Jane Sheppherd Ittner, "History of Illinois Zeta Chapter of Pi Beta Phi, 1895–1938," 41/72/38, Pi Beta Phi Records, 1895–1995; Fran Becque, Director of Academics, Pi Beta Phi, to author, 28 July, 22 August 1998.

25. Florence Burton-Roth and May C. Whiting-Westermann, *The History of Kappa Kappa Gamma Fraternity, 1870–1930* ([Columbus, Ohio]: The Fraternity, 1932), 369–71.

26. Esther B. Wilson, *History of Alpha Chi Omega Fraternity (1885–1928)*, 4th (rev.) ed. ([Menasha, Wisc.]: George Banta Publishing Co., 1929]), 7–12, 18, 24–25, 38–39, 201.

27. Christelle Ferguson, et al., *A History of Chi Omega*, 3 vols. (Menasha, Wisc.: George Banta Publishing Co., 1928), 1:82.

28. *Illini*, 5 November 1900; 3/1/1, 2:11 (6 November 1900).

29. "Origins and Evolution of the College Fraternity," in *Baird's Manual*, 1:14.

30. Helen L. Horowitz, *Campus Life: Undergraduate Cultures from the End of the Eighteenth Century to the Present* (New York: Alfred A. Knopf, 1987), 11–22, 56–66; *Illini*, 21 September 1892, 7 March 1895, 9 April 1900.

31. *Illini*, 25 April, 20 September 1895, 12 November 1897, 23 September 1898, 14 May 1900.
32. Ibid., 22 November 1896.
33. Ibid., 11 October 1895, 7 February, 8 May 1896.
34. Ibid., 25 April 1895, 29 May 1901.
35. Ibid., 8 November 1895, 14 February, 29 May 1896.
36. 3/1/1, 1:52.
37. *Illini*, 3 December 1897.
38. 3/1/1, 1:83.
39. For examples of Class Day, see the *Illini*, 13 June 1895, 10 June 1896 Supplement, 9 June 1897, and 8 June 1898.
40. Frank E. King to President Draper, [undated, but most likely 1895], 2/4/1, B:10, F:KI.
41. *Illini*, 20 March, 1 May 1896.
42. *Illio '95*, 81; *Illio '99*, 202; *Illio 1901*, 230.
43. *Illini*, 17 January 1895, 29 January, 12 February 1897.
44. Ibid., 10, 13, 20 January 1902; *Illio 1905*, 158, 259, 260, 262.
45. *Illini*, 5 March 1897, 8 May 1896.
46. Ibid., 11 February 1898.
47. Ibid., 12 March, 20 April 1900, 20 January 1902.
48. Ibid., 24 January, 8 May 1896, 25 March 1901.
49. Ibid., 13 March 1896.
50. Ibid., 9 April 1897.
51. Ibid., 9 April 1900.
52. Ibid., 29 March, 1 April 1901.
53. 3/1/1/, 2:103.
54. Ibid., 3:49–50; *Illini*, 2 June 1903.
55. *Illio 1904*, 350.
56. Mrs. E. J. Chacy to Draper, 30 September 1895, 2/4/1, B:2, F:Cha; 3/1/1, 1:68 (19 April 1897).

# CHAPTER 16

# THE RISE OF INTERCOLLEGIATE ATHLETICS

Athletics are a response to a natural impulse, as George Santayana wrote, and exist only as an end in themselves. They have a necessary relation to youth but no necessary relation to higher education. In America, however, colleges and universities became prime centers of athletic activity. By about 1850 students had overcome faculty opposition and raised athletics to a leading place on the American college campus. For years, rowing, baseball, and track were the favorite activities, but in the 1890s football assumed undisputed supremacy as *the* college sport.

Students had long engaged in athletics as a health-promoting pastime and for the sheer joy of it. But later they adopted a characteristically American attitude toward sports—a fierce determination to win at any cost; at the same time, universities came to view athletic victories as the quickest route to institutional recognition. These attitudes led to professionalism and commercialism in collegiate athletics.

The radical transformation of collegiate athletics in the late nineteenth century raised new and important questions. Perhaps most important was the impact of intercollegiate athletics on academic ideals. Athletics generated irrational enthusiasm and demonstrated a capacity to undermine, even to corrupt, academic values.[1]

## EARLY ATHLETIC DEVELOPMENT

When the University opened, in 1868, athletics had no part in the life of the campus. Students soon organized baseball teams, however, and for some time baseball was favored. In the 1870s football made its appearance: the English game of rugby was transformed, with many changes, into an American game of speed, dexterity, and body contact. With momentum mass plays, which were one or another kind of formation in which the ends, pulled back from the line of scrimmage, joined the backs to form a wedge that drove the ball forward over the center, football became a tough, rough, brutal sport.[2]

In 1876 Ethan Philbrick and other students engaged in the first football game ever played at Illinois.[3] Two years later Samuel C. Stanton brought over a football from England and started teaching the game to some fellow students. The faculty abruptly stopped the activity, considering it "too brutal."[4] For a time interest waned, but in 1880 the student newspaper asked, "Can not foot-ball be revived among us? There is a woful [sic] need of some such game to call forth the energy and enthusiasm of all the students."[5]

Sometime in the 1880s students had "an occasional game of drive, kick-about, or a class rush, or a rough-and-tumble game that bore a slight resemblance to the Canadian game [rugby]." In 1888 the so-called "first game of football" at Illinois took place between the freshman and sophomore classes. A contemporary description indicates that this event was actually rugby.[6]

A year later Scott Williams, who had previously played and liked a game, probably rugby, tried to organize a football team at Illinois. The boys played "a few minutes in a funny kind of way." They liked it and agreed to come out again. Most people viewed football as a "brutal Indian game," but Williams gave fair warning that there would be football the following year.[7]

In 1890 Williams organized the first "regular" football team. He was the manager, coach, and captain. The Athletic Association, a student organization, gave the players permission to represent the University at the Intercollegiate Oratorical Contest. On 2 October 1890 the University lost its first intercollegiate football game to Illinois Wesleyan, 16–0.[8]

The president of Purdue then challenged Illinois to play at Lafayette, Indiana. An experienced Purdue eleven quickly took possession of the field. The Illinois men, knowing nothing about football, could not even understand their own signals. Purdue won, 62–0. To close the season, the University played Illinois Wesleyan again on Thanksgiving Day at the Champaign County fairgrounds. The University employed tricks learned from Purdue. When several players were hurt, some of the crowd of nearly three hundred were pressed into action. Illinois won, 12–6.[9]

Thus football had made its appearance, joining baseball and track as intercollegiate sports. Attitudes toward sports were then divided. Regent

Selim H. Peabody strongly opposed organized athletics. The faculty was large-ly indifferent on the subject. The student newspaper cautioned against em-phasizing athletics. But some students, faculty, and alumni were passionate about sports. The growing importance of athletics led the Athletic Associa-tion, formed by students in 1883, to incorporate on 21 February 1890 as a nonprofit organization under the laws of Illinois. Unwilling to leave athletics entirely to student direction, on 20 April 1891 Peabody appointed a faculty Committee on Athletics.[10]

Peabody's antagonism toward athletics contributed to his forced departure on 10 June 1891. When he left, students seized the initiative in promoting football. No local coach was available, so Scott Williams invited Robert A. Lackey of Purdue, recognized as one of the best football players in the Mid-west, to take over. Lackey accepted out of a desire to form a chapter of the Kappa Sigma fraternity in Urbana. To preserve his amateur standing so that he could again play at Purdue, Lackey matriculated as a student and took no pay for his services.

On arrival Lackey was dismayed to find that the University had no football team and no scheduled games. He suggested moving into a better class of competition. So the student manager arranged a game with Lake Forest Uni-versity, reputed to have the best football team in the state. The Illinois men practiced less than a week and lost, 8–0. Thereafter the team improved. The University easily won its six other games that year in a league that included four small private colleges.[11]

The Athletic Association was instrumental in obtaining a new athletic field for sports. The Board of Trustees, responding to a petition of the Athletic Association, granted permission and provided $350 to develop part of the north campus for this purpose. The Athletic Association raised the balance of the money needed. On 15 May 1892 Athletic Park was inaugurated. In 1896 it was renamed Illinois Field.[12]

In June 1892 the University appointed Edward K. Hall as instructor in athletics and director of the gymnasium at a salary of $1,200. An excellent ath-lete who had just graduated from Dartmouth (eastern colleges were then viewed as the best in athletics), Hall was the first director of athletics and the first full-time professional coach at the University. He systematized both phys-ical training and team sports.

Hall improved the quality of Illinois football. In 1892 the team played twelve opponents—a high school, colleges, athletic clubs, and universities—winning seven games, losing three, and tying two. On a grueling trip to Mis-souri, Kansas, and Nebraska, the varsity played six games in eight days. A year later the eleven won three, lost two, and tied three. Rules were loose, the game was rough, and on occasion Hall himself played.

An evangelist of athletics, Hall, who also coached baseball and track,[13] was familiar with the eastern schools' custom of recruiting college athletes from secondary schools. In 1893 he initiated the first interscholastic meet to be held in the Midwest. Hall used this annual competition, which brought high school track teams from throughout Illinois to Urbana, to recruit. By 1898 over fifty high schools were members of the association.[14]

## ATHLETICS ADVERTISES THE UNIVERSITY

In 1893 the editor of the *Illini* boasted that athletics advertised the University and had doubled the number of students. As a result, he wrote, everyone now classed Illinois with the greatest of the western colleges. The Athletic Association had done more to make the institution great and respected than all the other departments of the University combined.[15]

The new University of Chicago, which opened on 1 October 1892, provided grounds for this type of thinking. William Rainey Harper, the young and aggressive president, was determined to make the University of Chicago a leading American university. He felt it imperative to win a national reputation for his school, and within two or three years after its opening he had an adequate if not a great university functioning.[16]

Athletics, Harper believed, offered a great promotional opportunity. To head the athletic program at Chicago Harper appointed his former student, Amos Alonzo Stagg. The two men had formed a close attachment. A gifted Yale athlete, Stagg had been named to the first All-American football team. After a year in divinity school he had abandoned the ministry and become a director of athletic programs and a football coach.[17]

Stagg's appointment as associate professor and director of the Department of Physical Culture and Athletics was a double precedent in American higher education. It was the first tenured academic appointment of a physical education department head and of a coach of intercollegiate athletic teams. His appointment began the professionalization of college coaching in America.[18]

Harper supported athletics warmly and uncritically. "The University of Chicago believes in football," he said. "We shall encourage it here." He viewed the cost of limbs broken and lives lost in the game as nothing compared to the "vigorous and unsullied manhood," "moral purity," and "human self-restraint" outdoor athletics developed. He wanted Stagg "to develop teams which we can send around the country and knock out all the colleges. We will give them a palace car and a vacation too." Stagg was pleased to have such support because he loved outdoor athletics, believed that sports could "create a strong college spirit," and saw athletics as giving him "a fine chance to do Christian work among the boys who are sure to have the most influence" in college life.[19]

Stagg established an intercollegiate football program at Chicago without delay. During the 1892 season, Stagg was both coach and player. In 1893 a Thanksgiving Day game with Michigan in Chicago established an instant tradition and attracted a following from the city. A year later the Chicago team played nineteen games and attracted widespread attention from the press. Another Thanksgiving Day game with Michigan proved that the city of Chicago was the best entertainment marketplace in the Midwest. The most significant event that year was the team's 6,200-mile trip to the Pacific Coast in December and January. The western swing and its attendant publicity demonstrated the enormous possibilities of the intercollegiate game.[20]

By 1894, football had become the great American college sport. Draper, who became president that year, had no prior experience with athletics. But he expressed the popular notion that football was "a manly and inspiring game." With compulsory chapel only recently abolished, he believed that football served "to stimulate University spirit and hold the whole crowd together."[21] And with a mandate from the trustees to put Illinois on the map, he endorsed the view that athletics advertised the University and won it public favor.

## GOVERNING THE UNGOVERNABLE

In the 1890s many evils beset intercollegiate athletics. Rules were loose, games were badly managed, and teams broke up contests they were about to lose. Professionalism and betting were widespread. Worst of all was the unnecessary roughness. Coaches taught their teams to disable the best man on the opposing squad in the first minutes of play.

In 1894 these problems were evident at Illinois. The Athletic Association engaged Louis D. ("Bucky") Vail, a former football player at the University of Pennsylvania, as coach through the end of November. Only a few men turned out for the team. Vail scheduled games with Wabash College, Lake Forest University, Northwestern, Purdue, the University of Chicago, the Indianapolis Light Artillery, and the Pastime Athletic Club of St. Louis. In the match with Chicago the Illinois quarterback was injured and Vail went in. Play resumed, but when Illinois took the lead, the Chicago captain refused to play further. Vail offered to withdraw, but Chicago still refused to play. So the umpire awarded the game to Illinois.[22]

Trustee Francis M. McKay warned that the ensuing dispute might harm the University. He thought that football was becoming "a disgrace to college athletics." Draper replied that the game was "a healthful one and calculated to inspire manliness in the student body." In any event football was fashionable, "and we 'might as well be out of the world as out of the fashion.'" The problem was that Chicago was in imminent danger of being beaten, and "the thought of being beaten by the team from this University made them hysterical." So they broke up the game.[23]

In November President James H. Smart of Purdue suggested that the presidents of leading midwestern colleges deal with the problem. Draper agreed, and on 11 January 1895, the presidents of seven universities—Chicago, Illinois, Michigan, Minnesota, Northwestern, Purdue, and Wisconsin—met in Chicago and adopted a set of rules for the regulation of athletics.[24]

The presidents called on each university to appoint a faculty committee to supervise athletics. In addition, under the rules, only bona fide students in residence for six months could participate in any athletic sport; no one could receive any gift or pay for services on a college team; students in graduate or professional school were permitted to play for the minimum number of years required to complete their course; coaches were forbidden to play and professionals were banned; students could not play under an assumed name; all players must be doing satisfactory academic work; all games were to be played under control of the colleges and under student management; the election of managers and team captains was subject to approval of the faculty committee on athletics; and college teams were to play only with other college teams.[25]

These rules, which became known as the Presidents' Rules, were adopted, with only Draper dissenting. He dissented because of many loopholes in the rules, especially those related to time limits and amateur standing.[26]

On 4 February 1895 the Illinois faculty adopted the new rules while noting their deficiencies. According to the faculty, the aim of college athletics should be the physical development and growth of a manly spirit among all the students. The faculty encouraged sport for its own sake. The faculty felt that the presidents had set too low a standard for an amateur and had placed no time limit on eligibility for college teams.[27]

Football nevertheless continued to gain favor. In 1895 George A. Huff was the coach. Born in 1872 on a dairy farm near Champaign, Huff had attended high school in Champaign and in Englewood, Illinois, and entered the University in 1888. Described as "a good natured fat boy," Huff was an average student but an excellent athlete. In 1891–92 he dropped out of school. When he returned, Hall was the coach. Huff played guard and made a reputation as a football player. The next spring he was captain and manager of the baseball team. Hall advised Huff to make a career of athletics. So in 1893 "G" went to Dartmouth, Hall's alma mater. He demonstrated unusual ability in football—at 240 pounds he played guard—and as captain of the baseball team. In the spring of 1895 Huff returned to Urbana. He guided the baseball team to ten victories in fourteen games. On 11 June 1895 Draper named Huff assistant director of the gymnasium and coach of the athletic teams at a salary of $1,000, half to be paid by the University and half by the Athletic Association.[28]

Ben Donnelly, Huff's assistant, had earned a reputation on the championship Princeton team of 1889 and had coached the Purdue team. The 1895 varsity player averaged just over 21 years, 153 pounds, and 5 feet 10.5 inches. This squad played seven games, trouncing three colleges and Northwestern, tying Wisconsin, and bowing to the Chicago Athletic Club (8–0) and Purdue (6–2). President Draper and the faculty held a post-season reception and banquet for the players. After dinner Draper made "a strong manly speech in favor of clean football."[29]

On 6 January 1896 the Illinois faculty created an Athletic Advisory Board. It was the executive committee of the Athletic Association, membership in which was open to any faculty member or student on payment of the annual dues. The board was to consist of three faculty members, three nonfaculty alumni, and the captains of the baseball, football, and track teams. The president of the University appointed the faculty members and the Athletic Association elected the alumni members, all to three-year terms. Thus students had six seats. The board elected its own officers, supervised all University athletic exercises, and controlled all funds entrusted to it for athletic purposes. In 1898, the president of the Athletic Association became a member of Athletic Advisory Board and the board was renamed the Board of Control.[30]

On 3 February 1896 the University adopted its own athletic rules. Although similar to the Presidents' Rules, Illinois's rules set a higher standard. One limited participation in intercollegiate contests to four years and required students to spend a full term at Illinois and pass the term examinations before being eligible to play. Another decreed that failure to adhere strictly to the rules would lead to forfeiture of the contest. In addition, the faculty defined an amateur athlete so as to prevent a student from membership on any team if he had taken money for participating in or teaching athletics as a livelihood. A student could have received expenses incurred in representing an organization.[31]

On 8 February a faculty representative from each of the Big Seven institutions represented at the presidents' conference met in Chicago. Those present endorsed the spirit of the Presidents' Rules but criticized them in detail. The rule on professionalism was drastically altered. One revision said that no student was to participate in any intercollegiate contest who had ever used or was using his knowledge of athletics or his athletic skill for gain. It was made operative after 1 October 1896. Another said that no one who received any compensation from a university for instructional services could play on any team. It was to take effect on 1 December 1896.[32]

This Intercollegiate Conference of Faculty Representatives added two new rules. One directed athletic committees to require each candidate for a varsity team to subscribe to a statement that he was eligible under the letter and spirit of the rules. The other, designed to eliminate the "tramp athlete," decreed that no student could participate in any intercollegiate contest who had not been in residence at least six months of the preceding year of the course. In addition, athletic association accounts were to be audited by a university committee, and intercollegiate athletic contests were to be kept within such bounds as would make them "the incidental and not the principal features of university and intercollegiate life."[33]

The Intercollegiate Conference transmitted the modified rules to the institutions represented for their consideration. Illinois, Minnesota, Purdue, and Wisconsin adopted the rules without alteration. According to *Harper's Weekly*, Illinois was the only one of the lot to have shown any appreciation of the importance of the question.[34]

Three universities endorsed the rules with amendments. Northwestern adopted all but the six months' residence rule. Chicago took exception to this rule and interpreted another rule so that acknowledged professionals would be legally permitted to play indefinitely. Michigan did not accept the six months' residence rule, and it changed the rule forbidding those who had coached for money to play after 1 October 1896 so as to permit men then in the University to play even if they had coached.[35]

The Intercollegiate Conference of Faculty Representatives, commonly known as the Intercollegiate Conference, the Western Conference, or the Western Intercollegiate Conference, was the rule-making body of the Big Seven. The faculty representatives met once a year, after the football season. The rules left the control of athletics mainly with student managers. On 1 December 1899 Indiana University and the University of Iowa were admitted to membership and the organization became the Big Nine, the precursor to the Big Ten.

Failure to obey conference rules troubled many. The conduct of Northwestern and Wisconsin destroyed the agreements, President Smart of Purdue informed Draper as the 1896 season began, and those who played Wisconsin consented to abrogation of the code. The athletic situation was bad, Draper agreed, and the fact that authorities in other colleges were either ignorant of affairs, too weak to control them, or deliberately abetted the wrong was most discouraging. Most of the teams Illinois met used hired players. It was very well to say that Illinois should not play with such colleges, "but we must play with some one or stop match games altogether." Illinois had signed contracts for games with both Chicago and Northwestern, and if Illinois protested they would say that Illinois knew when the games were arranged that they had never adopted the six-months' rule. "Moreover, our team is dependent upon the receipts of those games for expenses." To relieve the situation, Draper suggested another conference of presidents of *state* university presidents to deal with general matters, including athletics. Thus we would "eliminate at least one of the institutions [meaning Chicago] which is doing more to demoralize athletics in the west than all other agencies combined." As Draper revealed, money was a powerful engine that helped drive intercollegiate athletics.[36]

In 1896 Huff was the football coach, and the Athletic Board of Control appointed as assistants W. J. Randall, who had played with Huff at Dartmouth, and J. C. Fairchild, who had been a fullback at Harvard, from which he had just graduated. Illinois prided itself on the purity of its athletics, and early in the season its commitment to the Western Conference code was severely tested. When several students with long experience playing football in other colleges enrolled in the University, the faculty was requested to suspend the residence rule, "so far at least as to permit them to play in contests with colleges which do not observe said rule." No exceptions to the rule should be made, the faculty decreed, and the University should use its influence to secure adoption of this rule by competing colleges as "indispensable to the permanent maintenance of a high standard of amateur athletics." The faculty authorized its Committee on Athletics to write both Northwestern and Wisconsin protesting their violation of rules adopted in February 1896.[37]

Robert J. Hotchkiss presented another test case. A Peoria lad, his first association with athletics at the University was at the 1893 interscholastic meet arranged by Hall. That fall Hotchkiss entered Dartmouth and played halfback on the team with Huff. In 1895, as a sophomore, Hotchkiss was captain of the football team. As the 1896 season opened he was regarded as perhaps Illinois's best player. Needing money, he had engaged to coach the Eureka College team for $35 a week and expenses. He went there, found things so discouraging that he remained only two weeks, and was paid $10. So the question of his eligibility to play football was put to the Council of Administration. Members declared him ineligible because he had elected to become a professional when he made an agreement with Eureka. It was "a very close case," said Draper, but the council decided to be on the safe side and not to have to explain.[38]

Illinois met seven opponents in a fairly uneventful season. The *Illini* provided a play-by-play account of each game. The varsity readily dispatched four opponents, lost to Chicago and Northwestern, and tied Purdue. The game with Chicago led to bitter recriminations. Illinois was vastly superior, wrote a reporter, "but Stagg's much advertised aggregation of hirelings managed to win 12 to 0." The umpire made many "shady decisions," and in the second half Stagg trotted out his professional star, Fred D. Nichols, whose studies were in the nature of a farce. Nichols had been in athletics at Chicago since the institution opened, the *Illini* wrote, and it was an open secret that for years he had played for money. But he was fresh when he entered the game. Then Chicago scored. "The rotten state of athletics at Chicago is well known and her name has become synonymous for corruption in that branch of college life."[39]

Football was gaining favor, but enthusiasm for it was not irrational. All the midwestern universities except Illinois violated the athletic rules, opined the *Illini*, and refusal to abide by Western Conference rules made the question of purity a matter of vital importance. When the commercial spirit entered university life, athletics became merely a specialized part of the university for training professional athletes, and amateur sport died. Athletics exerted a powerful influence in unifying divergent campus elements and crystallizing a sentiment of loyalty to alma mater, the *Illini* added. But once admit professionalism and a death blow was struck at amateur athletics, "the strongest unifying force in the university life of today."[40]

In 1897 Huff, the head football coach, had two assistants—Fred L. Smith, Princeton '97, a reputed Tigerback,[41] and Harry W. Baum, Illinois '95, an all-around athlete. With few returning players, prospects were gloomy. The manager arranged games in increasing order of difficulty. The highlight of the season was a game with the Carlisle Indians. Draper and Captain R. H. Pratt, superintendent of the U.S. Indian Industrial School in Carlisle, Pennsylvania, made the arrangements. Draper suggested a game in Chicago on the Saturday before Thanksgiving because other teams played on the holiday, and Chicago was a large market. Pratt suggested that the Carlisle Indians play Chicago, Northwestern, or Illinois, or the winner of them, in Chicago, but not on the Saturday before Thanksgiving. Carlisle was to play the University of Chicago that day. The Carlisle Indians were a powerful eastern team. Chicago, both men realized, meant big receipts.[42]

Both Chicago and Northwestern had refused to adopt the Western Conference rules because, Draper remarked, if they did they would lose several members from their teams. So Draper asked Pratt to impose the condition that the teams be made up as provided by the rules. If this were done, he was confident that Illinois would be the one to meet Carlisle. "By common consent our teams are cleaner than the teams of other western institutions, and our playing is on a higher plain [*sic*], and notwithstanding that, we have won more than our share of games."[43]

The game was played on Saturday night, 20 November, in the Coliseum. Illinois played extremely well during the first half, leading 6–5. Then the tide turned. Bemus Pierce, the Carlisle captain, repeatedly led his warriors down the field in mass momentum plays, and "the superior endurance of the aborigines told." Carlisle won 23–6.

The following Tuesday a special convocation was held for Pratt and the Carlisle Indians. The band played and Draper and Pratt both spoke, as did Bemus Pierce and other Carlisle players. The game had enriched each of the schools by $4,000, Professor Kinley reported. The Business Men's Association of Urbana then fêted the players at the Columbian Hotel. Draper and Pratt led the banquet march, the faculty followed, and next came the teams, led by their captains. In a speech concluding the toasts, Kinley raised the pressing question, "Should Foot-ball be Abolished?"[44]

Before the game with Carlisle, the Athletic Association had been in debt about $1,500 and the Advisory Board's finance committee had appealed to alumni to help remove the debt. Many contributors included a letter endorsing athletics, but one respondent urged that football be prohibited. When a

Champaign newspaper reported that if Frederick W. von Oven were elected captain of the football team he would be offered a fellowship to the University, Draper replied, "when the University awards fellowships upon such a basis, it had better close its doors and let down its fires."[45] Even so, Draper wanted to play Carlisle again. "I have no doubt," he wrote Pratt, "there is some added glory and considerable money in it for both of us."[46]

In the spring of 1898 a controversy over the amateur status of two Wisconsin athletes prompted Illinois, Michigan, and Chicago to withdraw from the Western Intercollegiate Athletic Association track meet that year. When the executive committee of the WIAA upheld the amateur standing of the two, the "Big Three" seceded from the WIAA and held their own meet the next day. The WIAA then expelled the three universities from the association and suspended all their teams from the games it sponsored. In the fall the rupture was healed. The WIAA reinstated the dissidents and admitted the inadequacy of its rules on professionalism, and Wisconsin's athletic council declared the two "amateurs" ineligible.[47]

Throughout these controversies Draper battled somewhat naively to uphold amateurism and purity in collegiate athletics. He complained about the difficulties Illinois had with other universities over professionals and other abuses. Rules, he complained, were made "to be paraded before the public in fair weather and tossed to the winds in a storm." And heads of colleges were unwilling to believe that the alumni and town crowd who surrounded their institutions practiced so much chicanery. Moreover, athletic managers were "artists of the first magnitude" in deceiving faculty committees. Stagg, the worst offender, was trying to demoralize and separate his rivals, who were natural allies of each other. Accordingly, in 1898 Illinois refused to schedule games with Chicago. Draper also complained to President Charles K. Adams about Wisconsin's athletic relations with Chicago. Draper wanted an alliance between Illinois, Michigan, and Wisconsin to exclude Chicago from competition.[48]

The 1898 football season unfolded against this background. Three weeks after he arrived, Coach Smith had to abandon the season's work, reportedly because he was taken ill with malaria. The average weight of the varsity members was just over 170 pounds. The best college teams were reluctant to play a weak opponent, so the football manager was able to schedule only two conference games. After mixed results with various teams, including the Illinois Alumni, on 12 November Illinois played Michigan in Detroit on a muddy field, losing 12–5. A week later the Carlisle Indians beat Illinois 11–0 in a clean, well-played battle in Chicago. The contest was not the financial success Draper and Pratt had hoped for. The match with Minnesota on Thanksgiving Day—which the Athletic Advisory Board moved at the last minute from Urbana to Minneapolis, a larger market—went to Illinois, 11–10.[49]

The Athletic Association ended the season with a debt of about $1,800. President Draper asked students to show their school spirit by supporting athletics and liquidating the debt. At his urging a representative from every student group planned an Athletic Association benefit concert, which cleared $872.[50]

During the winter of 1899 Draper and Albert H. Pattengill, professor of Greek and a member of the Board of Control of Athletics at Michigan, devised plans for an alliance to curb Chicago. Draper attributed the discouraging abuses in athletics to the narrow vision of managers and athletics committees that sacrificed long-term goals for momentary success. He could not raise the subject with other university presidents, he felt, without their becoming defensive. He wanted Illinois, Michigan, and Wisconsin to stand together athletically, with the heads of these institutions taking the initiative.[51]

Pattengill identified the problem as Stagg and the Chicago Board of Athletics. They believed that Chicago was the center of the world and that because they furnished the audience, they had the largest claim on receipts. The time would soon come, he feared, when Chicago would insist that the big games with Chicago should all be played in Chicago, and Chicago would offer visitors such a percentage of receipts as they thought others might be worth. Pattengill insisted on absolute equality.[52]

His analysis was essentially accurate. With Harper's support, Stagg controlled the University of Chicago athletic program. The city of Chicago was an entertainment marketplace. Football was a commercial enterprise that produced a financial surplus. In 1902 all of the University of Chicago's football games were at home. From 1903 to 1905 Stagg scheduled twenty-eight home games and only five away.[53]

Pattengill would prefer Michigan to act independently, but he agreed that it was well to have an understanding regarding Chicago. Thus the three presidents arranged for their athletic managers—Huff of Illinois, Charles Baird of Michigan, and John L. Fisher of Wisconsin—to meet in Chicago to discuss matters. No alliance was contemplated. But if the managers found that their universities shared common ground, each could take its own course. The same action by all three would force the hand of Chicago.[54]

Draper told Pattengill that it was the policy of Illinois never to play for anything but equal division of game receipts. For this reason Illinois was not playing Chicago in 1899. Draper was willing to attend another conference on rules, but he was not disposed to discuss rules with coaches. The reputation of athletics depended on higher university authorities enforcing a uniform set of athletic rules.[55]

Negotiations to cement the triple alliance resumed in the fall during a football season that proved to be disastrous. Huff was again in charge of football. Neilson Poe, a Princeton fullback (class of '97), was the imported coach, with graduate players as assistants. The schedule included some presumably easy opponents (Illinois Wesleyan, Knox College, and alumni teams from both Illinois and St. Louis University), plus university foes (Iowa, Indiana, Purdue, Michigan, and Wisconsin). Games with the latter two were the first in a proposed series of championship matches between Illinois, Michigan, and Wisconsin. The varsity barely eked out victories over Wesleyan (6–0) and Knox (5–0) and lost to Indiana (5–0). Illinois lost to Purdue, 5–0. In the only big home game Michigan won, 5–0. Huff and Poe agreed about that contest: Illinois played "rotten ball." With two games still scheduled, Poe left to resume his law studies at the University of Maryland. Seventeen players made the trip to Milwaukee, where Wisconsin defeated Illinois 23–0. The season ended in a meeting with Iowa before 6,000 in Rockford. Iowa won 58–0, delivering the most crushing defeat an Illinois team had yet received.[56]

During the season Draper and Pattengill tried to cement the Illinois-Michigan-Wisconsin alliance and to prevent Stagg from dominating midwestern football. Scant evidence along with the guarded language of the negotiators makes it difficult to determine with certainty what occurred. But the main outlines seem clear. Chicago had a game with Wisconsin in 1899 because of a pre-existing contract. But at some time that year Illinois, Michigan, and Wisconsin agreed to sever relations with Chicago in all branches of athletics. Because the 1899 Thanksgiving Day game was between Michigan and Wisconsin, Pattengill thought that Stagg, an "athletic dictator" aided in his effort to make Chicago the center of midwestern football by alumni of various universities living in Chicago, would begin to feel the pressure exerted by the alliance.

But the attempt to boycott Chicago failed. While Draper and Pattengill remained steady, Wisconsin broke ranks. Fisher, the Wisconsin manager, apparently violated the understanding that he, Baird, and Huff had reached the previous March. Fisher agreed that Wisconsin would play Chicago the following year and later lied about his conduct, knowing that the disputed contract between the parties to the triple alliance could not be used to refute him because he had spirited it away. President Charles K. Adams, an uncritical supporter of athletics, supported Fisher, explaining that Wisconsin acted unilaterally because it suspected Michigan of doing so. So nothing came of the alliance, and thereafter each of the three schools charted its own course in football.[57]

## COACH SMITH'S REAPPOINTMENT: A CAUSE CÉLÈBRE

By the fall of 1899 Illinois had had two years of dismal football and the Athletic Association was burdened with a $2,600 debt. Illinois had to produce winning teams or be relegated to second rank, the Athletic Association concluded.

So Huff went east to recruit a coach. He visited Harvard, Yale, Princeton, Brown, Cornell, and Pennsylvania, returning about 20 December with an option on several good men, especially one whom he would not identify.[58]

The man was Fred L. Smith, the Tiger quarterback who had coached Illinois in 1897 and 1898. On 2 January Vice President Burrill, one of a few people who soon learned Smith's identity, protested to President Draper. "His [Smith's] history here was enough to condemn him for all time," wrote Burrill. "To win on the athletic field by such a compromise with immorality would be worse than a thousand failures in honorable contest."[59]

Arthur H. Daniels, chairman of the faculty Committee on Students' Welfare, discussed the matter with Draper. On 5 January Draper informed both Barton and Huff that it would be inadvisable for the Athletic Advisory Board to employ Smith. "While I have not myself felt that there was any insuperable objection to his employment I think that we are bound to respect the feelings of our colleagues who differ with me in opinion."[60]

On 10 January 1900 the *Illini* reported that Smith would be brought back. Athletic authorities would neither confirm nor deny the report. Draper informed one trustee that Smith "was probably the most efficient coach we have ever had." Students concerned with athletics were eager to get him back. Criticism surrounding his appointment stemmed from his "alleged habits" when at the University. Draper professed to a neutral stand, communicating criticism he had heard so that it might be considered.[61]

Daniels's repeated conferences on the subject with members of the athletic board proved fruitless. So on 22 January he presented to the faculty a report from his committee opposing the appointment on the grounds that Smith was "alleged to have a reputation that in the judgment of many would reflect upon the good name of this University," and that his appointment would be "detrimental to the welfare of the students." The committee hoped to secure an expression of faculty opinion before the contract with Smith was approved. Draper vigorously criticized Daniels's report. Barton, the chairman of the athletic board, vehemently attacked it and moved to table it. His motion lost by a vote of 22 to 14. Then Parr, a member of the athletic board, having assured the faculty that the board would take no precipitate action, moved adjournment. The faculty adjourned with the report pending. Within a few hours thereafter the athletic board approved the contract.[62]

On 26 January Dean Forbes informed Draper that the Council of Administration should consider the matter at issue before it became more complicated. The faculty would accept a decision agreed upon by the council, he thought, but he did not know whether the Athletic Advisory Board would do the same.[63]

A day later the council discussed the case. Members requested Draper to write to Smith, "stating the allegations made against him and inquiring as to the facts." Draper wrote to President Francis L. Patton of Princeton, asking for information on Smith's habits and character. He enclosed a letter for Smith which said that a faculty committee had objected to Smith's appointment on the grounds of immoral character, specifically, while at Illinois Smith had been "incapacitated from work by reason of disease contracted by immoral practices." Because these charges were hearsay, Draper offered Smith a chance to respond.[64]

Within a few hours after the faculty meeting of 22 January the athletic board approved Smith's contract. On 27 January, the day the council met, Huff publicly announced that Smith would be the head coach. He linked the appointment with a statement that the Athletic Association was $2,600 in debt and that Champaign businessmen had pledged $750 for athletics provided the student body raised a similar amount.[65]

The contract with Smith indicated an intention on the part of the athletic board to proceed without regard to any judgment by the faculty. The issue raised, said Forbes, was "one of *judgment* on a question of *good morals* affecting the welfare of our students and the good name of the University." So Forbes took the unusual step of carrying the matter to the trustees. He prepared a petition which the other three deans approved and a number of faculty members signed. The petition was directed only against the Athletic Advisory Board. Forbes reasoned that quite possibly Draper would take steps to arrest the action of the athletic board. If so, he could stop the communication to the trustees in his office and avoid unnecessary publicity. If the affair had gone "technically" beyond Draper's control, he might let the document go to the trustees for what it was worth.[66]

Responding to Forbes, Draper said that he was incensed that Daniels had presented the matter to the faculty, which had no jurisdiction over scandals. Moreover, he did not believe that the athletic board was precluded by the facts from taking the action it had taken. Members of the athletic board intended no wrong, they had some things on their side, and "the boys" did not think the opposition to Smith was without prejudice. Aside from all this, there was no occasion for excitement because the administration had the power to do whatever needed to be done. The petition had caused Draper pain and humiliation. If it had gone to the trustees, the implication would have been that there were differences within the University that could not be reconciled. Draper went on to assert his authority, experience, and intention to do the right thing. He thought it needless to add that he did not impose his will upon his associates.[67]

In the end Draper approved the appointment. The Chicago papers had made the subject common property, the *Illini* wrote, and a majority of students, vocal alumni, the Athletic Advisory Board, and local businessmen all favored Smith. On 14 February the senior class declared that Smith should be retained "in the interests of our athletics." Two days later the *Illini* printed a supplement with letters supporting Smith. The writers, mainly former athletes, advanced these arguments: the University needed a winning football team because football was the best means of advertising the University, without victories the University would have no place in midwestern football, the Athletic Association had to avoid bankruptcy, and a winning team required a good coach. Protest had been raised because Smith had committed what one called "a single breach of moral fortitude." A good disciplinarian, Smith would be a good moral influence: "His morals, so far as I have been informed, are such as to be unobjectionable as a coach." Moreover, Smith's opponents took no interest in athletics. The contract with Smith was binding. If it were broken it would be impossible to get another coach. J. M. Kaufman, one of the businessmen who had agreed to raise funds for the next year's team, wrote that "unless the team is to be coached by a man competent to make it a credit to the University, and worthy of our support, our support cannot be depended upon."[68] In all likelihood, in approving Smith's appointment Draper bowed to public opinion.

Later, the Council of Administration described Smith's appointment as "hazardous and unwise," but it did not feel called on to prevent the fulfillment of the contract made by the Athletic Advisory Board. To guard against such a mistake being repeated, the council recommended that thereafter its approval was to be obtained before the athletic board entered into a contract.[69]

Smith's appointment was like a shot of adrenalin. In the spring of 1900 a canvas brought the Athletic Association $1,500. Draper and some faculty members contributed. Businessmen more than made good their pledge. Membership in the Athletic Association dramatically increased. In 1897 250 out of 930 students had belonged; now 575 students joined. By the fall the Athletic Association had over 700 members, including 25 women. In September the trustees appropriated $100 for the Athletic Association. By early 1901, however, the Athletic Association still had a debt. Many pledges had not been paid.[70]

## FOOTBALL, 1900–1904

In 1900 Fred L. Smith returned as football coach. The season began with spring training, perhaps the first of its type. For the first time the team captain rather than the team manager had the prerogative of choosing the players.[71] Members of the varsity averaged 166 pounds and 5 feet 9 inches, and at first glance their record looks good. Illinois won seven, lost three, and tied two, scoring a total of 184 points to 67. But six of the games were with small colleges or weak teams. In the Western Conference, Illinois beat Purdue, tied both Indiana and Northwestern, and lost to Michigan (12–0), Minnesota (23–0), and Wisconsin (27–0). Smith had failed to redeem Illinois football.

Accordingly, on 30 March 1901 the Council of Administration expressed its opposition to western universities hiring high-priced coaches from schools in the East. The council offered many reasons for its stand. The practice destroyed university self-dependence, it encouraged extravagant expenditure and invited professionalism, it made the game a battle between rival coaches, and it resulted in overtraining. Overtraining was hurtful to the players physically and unfit them for regular university work. The council urged conference universities to agree that, after 1901, teams would be coached by none but regular instructors on the staff and former players. The council communicated this decision to the faculty.[72]

Football fans were determined to win. In 1901 W. A. Kiler, a graduate player, conducted spring practice. Edgar G. Holt, Princeton '00, was brought in as coach. Huff, Arthur R. Hall, a former student player, and George Mattis, a Princeton graduate who lived in Champaign, assisted. Physically, the team resembled the previous year's, and again the record looks good at first glance. Illinois won eight games and lost two, scoring 243 points to 41 for its foes. But three games were with weak opponents, including one or two high school teams. Illinois won three of six games with Western Conference teams. The varsity beat Chicago 24–0 before a crowd of 7,000, including 2,000 who went by rail from Champaign.

Over the years Draper's enthusiasm for football waned. He considered it advantageous to scholarship, but it was too dangerous and exerted unwholesome influences. It unsettled the morals of the student body and led to "irrational conviviality." Nevertheless, Draper would keep the game. No one university could cast it out, he admitted, and it was worth fighting for.[73]

In 1902 Holt again coached football, assisted by Arthur R. Hall. Garland "Jake" Stahl, a baseball star, was captain of the varsity squad, whose members averaged 168 pounds and 5 feet 9 inches. Only three men had more than a year of experience in college football. Huff refused to arrange baseball games with schools that would not also play Illinois in football. The varsity engaged two high schools and four other assorted teams, winning easily. In contests with schools then or later in the Western Conference, Illinois defeated Purdue, Indiana, Northwestern, and Iowa, tied Ohio, and lost to Chicago and Minnesota. In the game with Chicago, the Chicago Maroons injured Stahl on the first play by an "unusual tackle." Huff later described Holt as the best coach Illinois ever had. But dissension allegedly impaired the team, and fans clamored for a new coach.[74]

Early in its history football earned a national reputation as a brutal sport. In February 1903 David J. Underwood of McLeansboro introduced in the General Assembly a bill to ban football in Illinois. The bill died in committee. Two months later Professor Edwin G. Dexter published an article in which he contended that the public press had exaggerated the roughness of football.

Based on a survey, Dexter reported that the number of college football play-ers who were permanently injured or who died from the effects of the game was so small as to be practically negligible. And he found that when college of-ficers weighed the game in terms of enrollments, they favored it by roughly seventeen to one.[75]

In 1903, pursuit of a winner led to the hiring of George W. Woodruff as coach. Woodruff had played football at Yale with Stagg. He had coached at the University of Pennsylvania, where he developed new plays that were suc-cessful but heightened the violence. Woodruff was strong in scholarship (he later became attorney general of Pennsylvania); the *Illini* hoped he would urge his players to lead in their classes. Student liberality enabled Woodruff to take thirty-eight players to Spring Lake, Michigan, for two weeks of preseason practice. In seven pre-conference games Illinois easily humbled Englewood High School, Lombard and Knox colleges, and teams from three medical schools and one dental school. Then, after shutting out Purdue 24–0, Illinois suffered six successive defeats. It went scoreless against Indiana, Minnesota, Iowa, and Nebraska, which together racked up a total of seventy-seven points. In a blistering letter, Draper criticized the referee of the Northwestern game for a "manifestly erroneous ruling." The referee described Draper's complaint as "puerile."[76]

Although Draper valued football as a "clean, manly sport" that would advertise the University, the football record during his tenure was at best mediocre. Following Woodruff's disastrous season, the athletic board aban-doned the practice of employing coaches from eastern schools and adopted the alumni coaching system. In 1904 Arthur R. Hall was named head coach, assisted by three former players. The system of graduate coaches lasted until 1912, when the athletic board hired Robert Zuppke as football coach.

## SUMMARY AND CONCLUSION

The rise of intercollegiate athletics was highly significant for both American higher education and American culture. Students had the sporting spirit, ath-letes were determined to win, universities viewed athletic success as a means of gaining institutional recognition, an increasingly urban society looked to col-lege athletics for entertainment, and the press featured sports in order to sell newspapers. These diverse streams fed a rising torrent.

No human agency, individual or collective, could master this mighty new force. Like war, athletics demanded organization for the sake of victory. Stu-dents alone could not manage the monster. Authorities assumed internal con-trol. Then schools combined to formulate rules designed to preserve ama-teurism and purity in intercollegiate athletics. But to gain advantage, schools continually broke the rules, and the coming of professional coaches changed the nature of collegiate athletics.

Many praised football as the greatest of college sports and a power for good. A major reason for endorsement was the belief that it bred manliness, an indefinable, highly prized attribute. The notion gained greater currency when Teddy Roosevelt, the Rough Rider, was president.[77] Football, like war, displayed the dramatic essence of physical combat. Americans valued the clash of bodies and good-natured roughness for instilling discipline and self-control. Football allegedly built character. Gridiron heroes were held up as exemplary.

Football was also valued because it inspired "college spirit" and united the University community. Compulsory chapel no longer performed this function, and universities were becoming larger and more diverse. Fans maintained that football toned the morals of the student body and afforded a safe outlet for surplus energy. Nevertheless, college athletics had a darker side, and the corrupting influence of football was all too obvious. Aspects of American culture were accurately reflected, perhaps intensified, in the college game. Greed for material gain had its counterpart in a determination to win, for example, and in the mad chase after victories universities employed dishonest and demoralizing methods. By 1905 condemnation of football was so widespread that President Roosevelt summoned the presidents of Harvard, Yale, and Princeton to the White House to discuss abolishing or reforming the game. One argument against football was its brutality: necessary roughness led to unnecessary roughness. Players were seriously injured or killed. Another argument was the lack of ethics. The win-at-all-costs attitude led to uncontrollable abuses. Efforts to keep within conference rules made more liars and hypocrites than amateurs, said George Huff. The strongest argument against football, opined President Eliot of Harvard, was not death and injuries but the fact that the cheating and brutality it bred were profitable. And the idea that football was the test of excellence of a university and the proper means of advertising it was absurd. Although abuses led a few universities to abolish football, the game was saved on the understanding that it would be reformed.[78]

The University of Illinois prided itself on its purity in intercollegiate athletics. But it judged itself comparatively. Athletic programs were expensive. The need for revenue led those responsible in this area to compromise principle. George Huff admitted that to win games, he had recruited athletes the best way he could on meager resources. But having seen few college athletes of any ability who were willing to study and do honest work to sustain themselves in college after a position on the team had been assured, he reportedly gave up the practice.

Nevertheless, academic ideals were prostituted in pursuit of athletic prestige. Although the faculty opposed the recruitment of students for their athletic ability, in 1905 two students brought to the University to play football were dismissed because the faculty concluded they were not capable of doing the academic work. In sum, the irrational passion for football threatened to permeate the campus and to exert a profound and reciprocal influence on the American character.[79]

## NOTES

1. George Santayana, "Philosophy on the Bleachers," (1894), in *George Santayana's America: Essays on Literature and Culture*, ed. James Ballowe (Urbana: University of Illinois Press, 1967), 121–30; and Ronald A. Smith, *Sports and Freedom: The Rise of Big-Time College Athletics* (New York: Oxford University Press, 1988).
2. David Riesman and Reuel Denny, "Football in America: A Study in Culture Diffusion," *American Quarterly*, 3 (Winter 1951), 309–25; Allison Danzig, *The History of American Football* (Englewood Cliffs, N.J.: Prentice-Hall, 1956), 3–29.
3. *Illinois Alumni News*, 8 (October 1929), 17.
4. Ibid., 20 (January 5, 1942), 6.
5. *Illini*, 20 October 1880.
6. Athlete '88, "Athletics in the Early Stages," *Illio '97*, 81; "Early Foot Ball at the University of Illinois," ibid., 248–49.
7. O. S. Storm (city editor of the Sterling, Illinois, *Gazette*) interview with Scott Williams, n.d. (about 1915?), in 26/1/20, B:8, F:Athletics, History; see also Carol F. Pullen, "A History of Intercollegiate Football at the University of Illinois" (master's thesis, University of Illinois, 1957).
8. *Illini*, 11 October 1890. Some sources give the score as 20–0.
9. Storm interview with Scott Williams, 5–7; *Illini*, 6 December 1890.
10. 4/2/1, 7:65–66 (3 December 1923); 4/1/1, 3:72, 93, 134.
11. *Illinois Alumni News*, 6 (January 1928), 167.
12. *16th Report* (1892), 39, 48, 67, 69–70, 88; *18th Report* (1896), 235; *Illini*, 4 April, 18 April, 16 May 1891.
13. Space limitations preclude a history of sports other than football, which overshadowed other intercollegiate athletics in the years from 1894 to 1904. Illinois took part in track and field meets under several different coaches during this period. But the record was poor. In 1904 Harry Gill became the track coach and the team began to improve. Gill was to have a distinguished career at Illinois.

   Basketball was introduced in the 1890s—by women. The first intercollegiate basketball game at the University was played on 20 November 1896 by women's teams from Urbana and Illinois Wesleyan. Men did not play intercollegiate basketball at Illinois until 1906.

   Illinois excelled in baseball. George Huff was devoted to the game. In 1891, as a student, George Huff was captain and manager of a team that won the state intercollegiate baseball championship. After joining the faculty, Huff as baseball coach compiled an enviable record. In 1897 Illinois defeated Michigan on the diamond—the first time that Illinois had beaten Michigan in any athletic contest. In 1898 Illinois downed Michigan twice in baseball. In 1902 the team captured a second conference championship in three years. The players then set out on a tour of baseball strongholds in the East. Losing only to Harvard, Illinois beat

Princeton, Army, Yale, and Pennsylvania. A cartoon by McCutcheon in the Chicago *Record-American* celebrated the triumph of a team called the "champions of the United States." On 9 May 1903, Garland "Jake" Stahl hit ten home runs in a game with Michigan. In 1904 Illinois again won the conference championship in baseball. Huff coached many players who went on to the major leagues.

14. *Illini*, 1 April 1898.
15. Ibid., 8 May 1893.
16. Paul Shorey, "Harper, William Rainey," in *Dictionary of American Biography*, ed. Allen Johnson and Dumas Malone, 20 vols. (New York: Charles Scribner's Sons, 1928–36), 8:289; Richard J. Storr, *A History of the University of Chicago: Harper's University. The Beginnings* (Chicago: University of Chicago Press, 1966).
17. Storr, *Harper's University*, 178–81; Robin Lester, *Stagg's University: The Rise, Decline, and Fall of Big-Time Football at Chicago* (Urbana: University of Illinois Press, 1995), 1–13.
18. Lester, *Stagg's University*, 17.
19. As quoted in ibid., 18, 19.
20. Ibid., 22–31.
21. Draper to Fred Englehard, 21 November 1898, 2/4/3.
22. *Illini*, 4, 11 October, 29 November 1894. Illinois records and L. H. Baker, *Football: Facts and Figures* (New York: Farrar & Rinehart, 1945), 367, claim victory, 6–0, but Lester, *Stagg's University*, 200, gives Chicago 10, Illinois 6.
23. McKay to Draper, 27 November 1894, 2/4/1, B:12, F:McKay; Draper to McKay, 28 November 1894, 2/4/3. Lester, *Stagg's University*, shows that Stagg often played with his team.
24. Smart to Draper, 19 November 1894, 2/4/1, B:16, F:Smart; *Proceedings: The Intercollegiate Conference of Faculty Representatives of the Athletic Committees or Boards of Control of [Nine] Universities* (Minneapolis: University Press, 1901), 3–4; Carl D. Voltmer, *A Brief History of the Intercollegiate Conference of Faculty Representatives* (New York: Western Intercollegiate Conference, 1935), 4–5. According to Voltmer, the Presidents' Conference included Lake Forest but not Michigan.
25. *Proceedings: The Intercollegiate Conference*, 3–4.
26. Draper to Caspar W. Whitney, 21 May 1896, 2/4/3; *Illini*, 23 October 1896; Herbert J. Barton, "The College Conference of the Middle West," *Educational Review*, 27 (January 1904), 46–48.
27. 4/1/1, 3:272–74.
28. *18th Report* (1896), 95; William J. Barber, Jr., "George Huff: A Short Biography" (master's thesis, University of Illinois, 1951), 3–13 (quotation at 5); John H. Bartlett and John P. Gifford, *Dartmouth Athletics* (Concord, N.H., 1893), 243, 251.
29. *Illini*, 18 December 1895.
30. 4/1/1, 3:299, 301–4. The Advisory Board's constitution is also in the *Illini*, 24 January 1896. On the relation between the Athletic Association and the Board of Control, see S. W. Parr in the *Illini*, 21 May 1897. University of Illinois, *Regulations for the Government of Athletics* (Urbana, 1896), 28/1/801, Athletic Association Director, Constitution and Bylaws, B:1, contains the constitution of the Athletic Association along with other athletic rules. The revised Athletic Association constitution is in the *Illini*, 16 December 1898.
31. 4/1/1, 3:306–8.
32. *Proceedings: The Intercollegiate Conference*, 5–9.

33. Ibid.; Barton, "The College Conference of the Middle West," 48–49; *Illini*, 23 October 1896.

34. 4/1/1, 3:318–19, 315; *Harper's Weekly*, 40 (23 May 1896), 525; University of Illinois, *Regulations for the Government of Athletics* (Urbana, 1896).

35. *Illini*, 23 October 1896; Barton, "The College Conference of the Middle West," 49.

36. Smart to Draper, 20 October 1896, 2/4/1, B:16, F:Smart; Draper to Smart, 22 October 1896, 2/4/3.

37. Draper to Herman S. Piatt, 29 October 1896, 2/4/3; 4/1/1, 3:328–29.

38. Hotchkiss to L. M. Tobin, 20 August 1937, 26/1/20, B:8, F:History, Athletic; Bartlett and Gifford, *Dartmouth Athletics*, 243–63 passim; 3/1/1, 1:59 (20 October 1896); Draper to Smart, 22 October 1896, 2/4/3. Hotchkiss, who never graduated from the University, became an architect in Peoria.

39. *Illini*, 6 November, 23 October 1896.

40. Ibid., 16, 23, 30 October 1896.

41. Frank Presbrey and James H. Moffat, eds., *Athletics at Princeton: A History* (New York: Frank Presbrey Co., 1901), 241, 364, 375. Apparently Smith never graduated from Princeton. He is not listed in the *General Catalogue of Princeton University: 1746–1906* (Princeton: Princeton University Press, 1908).

42. Draper to Pratt, 21 January 1897, 2/4/3; Pratt to Draper, 1, 8, 19 February, 30 October 1897, 2/4/1, B:15, F:Pratt. Carlisle dropped its proposed game with Chicago in order to play the University of Cincinnati on Thanksgiving Day.

43. Draper to Pratt, 5 February 1897, 2/4/3.

44. *Illini*, 26 November 1897.

45. David Kinley to John Frederickson, 19 October 1897, 15/1/4; *Illini*, 3 December 1897; Draper to the *Gazette*, 10 December 1897, 2/4/3.

46. Draper to Pratt, 10 December 1897, 2/4/3.

47. *Illini*, 8 June 1898.

48. Draper to Charles K. Adams, 29 April, 18 June 1898 (the quotations); Draper to Charles R. Van Hise (then a professor at the University of Wisconsin), 31 October 1898, 2/4/3.

49. *Illini*, 23, 30 September, 7, 14, 21, 28 October, 18, 25 November, 2 December 1898.

50. Ibid., 2 December 1898, 3 February, 10 March, 7 April 1899.

51. Draper to Pattengill, 29 February 1899, 2/4/3.

52. Pattengill to Draper, 4 March 1899, 2/4/1, B:14, F:Pattengill.

53. Lester, *Stagg's University*, 17, 39–40.

54. Pattengill to Draper, 4 March 1899, 2/4/1, B:14, F:Pattengill. Baird received both an A.B. and an LL.B. from Michigan in 1895. I infer that Fisher, whose given name is not in the documents consulted, is the John L. Fisher who received a law degree from Wisconsin in 1899.

55. Draper to Pattengill, 6 March 1899, 2/4/3.

56. *Illio 1901*, 242; *Illini*, 20 September to 4 December 1899, passim.

57. Pattengill to Draper, nine letters from 18 February 1898 (actually 1899) to 21 December 1899, 2/4/1, B:14, F:Pattengill; Draper to Pattengill, 21 February, 6 March, 22, 28 November, 11, 23 December, 2/4/3. Charles K. Adams's letters to Draper are not in the University of Illinois Archives, but see Draper to Adams, 6 December 1899, 2/4/3. Draper and Harper of Chicago rarely corresponded on athletic

matters, but see Wilfred Shaw, *The University of Michigan* (New York: Harcourt, Brace & Howe, 1920), 252–54, and Merle Curti and Vernon Carstensen, *The University of Wisconsin, A History, 1848–1925*, 2 vols. (Madison: University of Wisconsin Press, 1949), 1:710.

58. *Illini*, 10, 29 January, 16 February 1900 (Special Supplement, Briggs letter), 22 December 1899.

59. Burrill to Draper, 2 January 1900, 2/4/2, B:6, F:Burrill (the same letter went to Herbert J. Barton and Jacob K. Shell, 15/4/1, Botany Departmental Correspondence, B:1, vol. 3).

60. Draper to Barton, Draper to Huff, 5 January 1900, 2/4/3.

61. Draper to Carriel, 18 January 1900, 2/4/3.

62. 4/1/1, 3:397–98; Forbes to Draper, 3 February 1900, 2/4/2, B:6, F:Forbes.

63. Forbes to Draper, 26 January 1900, 2/4/2, B:6, F:Forbes.

64. Draper to Patton, Draper to Smith, 29 January 1900, 2/4/3. Patton forwarded Draper's letter to Profesor Henry B. Fine, chairman of the Faculty Committee on Outdoor Sports, who informed Draper that he knew of nothing discreditable in Smith's career at Princeton. Fine had no reason to think that Smith's influence as one of the coaches of the Princeton football team was in any way bad. Patton to Draper, 1 February 1900, Seeley G. Mudd Manuscript Library, Princeton University Archives; Fine to Draper, 5 February 1900, 2/4/1, B:4, F:FI 1897–1904.

65. *Illini*, 10, 29 January 1900.

66. Forbes to Draper, 3 February 1900, 2/4/2, B:6, F:Forbes.

67. Draper to Forbes, 6 February 1900, 2/4/3.

68. *Illini*, 16 February 1900.

69. 3/1/1, 1:118 (16 March 1900).

70. *Illini*, 29 October 1897; 4 June, 19 September 1900; 6 March 1901; *21st Report* (1902), 6.

71. *Illini*, 29 January 1900.

72. 3/1/1, 2:34–35; 4/1/1, 3:430.

73. Draper to Joseph Swain, 4 November 1901, Draper to Thwing, 23 December 1901, 2/4/3.

74. *Illini*, 8 October 1902; George A. Huff, "The Present Athletic Status of Illinois," *Alumni Quarterly*, 1 (January 1907), 13; C. E. Stone, "Football Review," *Illio 1904*, 299–300.

75. State of Illinois, *Journal of the House of Representatives of the 43d General Assembly of the State of Illinois* (Springfield, 1903), 173; Edwin G. Dexter, "Some Accidents from College Football," *Educational Review*, 25 (April 1903), 415–28.

76. *Illini*, 4 March 1903; Lester, *Stagg's University*, 10, 73; W. A. McKnight, "Football Review," *Illio 1905*, 298–99; Draper to J. F. Darby, 2 November 1903, Darby to Draper, 30 March 1904, 2/4/1, B:3, F:Dar–Day.

77. See E. Anthony Rotunda, *American Manhood: Transformations in American Masculinity from the Revolution to the Modern Era* ([New York]: Basic Books, 1993), 243–44.

78. Smith, *Sports and Freedom*, 191–208; Edward S. Jordan, "Buying Football Victories," *Colliers*, 36 (11 November 1905), 19.

79. Jordan, "Buying Football Victories," 19–20, 23; 3/1/1, 3:190.

# PART IV

# POISED FOR TAKE-OFF

# CHAPTER 17

# THE TURMOIL OF DRAPER'S DEPARTURE

By the spring of 1904 Draper had been president of the University for nearly ten years. The Illinois offer had come at a time when his work in Cleveland was done and nothing suitable was available in New York. He had accepted the appointment in the hope that after serving five to eight years he would be able to return to Albany.

Draper served at the pleasure of the Board of Trustees. When he was hired, nothing was said about the duration of his appointment. Consequently, every other March from 1897 to 1903, the trustees reelected him for the ensuing biennium. In 1898 Draper announced that, although he had repeatedly refused to permit the use of his name, he had been elected superintendent of schools of the city of New York. When he refused the offer, the trustees praised his decision to remain at Illinois "and lead to still higher ground and a more triumphant future the grand advance which has already been made under his wise and efficient leadership."[1]

As president, Draper devoted his full energy to the welfare of the University. A national figure, he made the institution known through his many publications and public addresses to a wide range of audiences, and was quick to take umbrage at anything that he perceived as a slight to the University. A strong proponent of centralized administration, Draper was gruff and abrasive and had a lawyer's knack for putting others on the defensive. Though well regarded by trustees and students, Draper antagonized deans and faculty members, creating deep bitterness.

Draper was quick to criticize those who violated his strict standards regarding appointments and resignations, and he insisted on early notice if faculty members intended to leave for other employment. Yet his own resignation flagrantly departed from the conduct he demanded of others. On 10 March 1903 the trustees had reelected him president for the next biennium; at the time his salary was $7,000 a year.[2] On 26 January 1904 the board held a regular meeting at which Draper said nothing about leaving Illinois, but the next day the *Chicago Daily Tribune* reported that Draper would accept the position of Commissioner of Education of the state of New York that was about to be created.

The state had long had two bodies that dealt with public education. The Board of Regents of the University of the State of New York had oversight of the colleges and academies of the state, whereas the Superintendent of Public Instruction had supervisory authority over all common schools. Draper had once held the latter office. Conflict in jurisdiction between these two departments had led to a plan to combine them in the office of the Commissioner of Education, and Draper was prominently mentioned for the new position.

The *Tribune*'s report came as a total surprise to Frederic L. Hatch, president of the Board of Trustees. "Is there truth in the article in todays Chicago papers that you are to leave the University for a position in New York State?" Hatch inquired. "I can hardly believe that you would not mention so important a matter to the board yesterday. Hoping that this is a false alarm." A few days later Bullard, who was also present at the board meeting, asked, "Is there really any fire where all this smoke is coming from about your accepting some position in New York? . . . You have said nothing hence I suppose there is little to it all." Bullard hoped that Draper would stay another five years.[3]

Draper replied that he had said nothing to the board about the New York matter because there was nothing to say. Though his name had been mentioned for the job, which carried salary of $9,000, no one had made any proposition to him, and if he received a call his response would turn on what was presented and all the circumstances. A call from New York state would mean much to him, but he also had opportunities at Illinois, and everyone there had been considerate to him. Yet some things of "a rather radical nature" needed to be done if the University were to mount higher, and he might meet opposition if he advanced them. He sometimes thought that a different kind of man was needed for the job. To Trustee Augustus F. Nightingale Draper confided that one member of the board—he meant Bullard—seemed to think that Draper had wholly lost his senses because he was ready to act as he thought best in the matter.[4]

Word of Draper's prospects spread,[5] and in light of the turmoil it generated, Draper's appraisal of conditions in the University on the eve of his resignation becomes important. In early February, explaining why he could not attend an alumni event in St. Louis, Draper glowingly described the University. All matters were going well, he wrote. "Better than all else, we are working together in harmony. . . . Not only is there entire concord among those who must bear the responsibility of administration, but there is good fellowship between teachers and students. There are not many severe strains on the ship."[6] As events soon revealed, either Draper was dispensing taffy or he did not know his own University.

On 9 March Draper delivered his formal resignation, to take effect 1 April. The trustees accepted it to take final effect 1 July and granted Draper a leave of absence without salary from 1 April to 1 July with the understanding that he would return to serve as president in closing out the academic year. The board also directed that the board's president appoint two committees, one to draft a resolution expressing the regret the trustees felt in severing relations "which for ten years had been so pleasant, and so profitable," the other to find and recommend a suitable person to be the next president of the University.[7]

The day after Draper announced his resignation Dean David Kinley wrote a friend, "We are all here breathing 'Gott sei Dank'!" But Draper had not gone yet, and Kinley did not know what he might do before he went.[8] On 1 April Draper took up his new duties in Albany. Burrill stepped easily into the work, with Harlan H. Horner, Draper's assistant, handling routine affairs until 1 May, when he joined Draper in Albany.

Draper's departure reopened a problem that had persisted during his entire administration: the power to determine policy within the University. After Draper announced his resignation, the deans at Urbana conferred among themselves on the situation, and on 21 March they sent a letter to the governing board calling attention to certain features in the conduct of affairs that deserved attention before a new president was appointed.

Noting the advantage to the interests represented by the existence of standing committees of the board (on Agriculture, the College of Engineering, the School of Pharmacy, and the College of Medicine), the deans wanted the colleges of Science, Literature and Arts, and Law each represented by a standing committee that would look out for the interests of those in charge of these units. A dean should be at liberty to confer with the chairman of the appropriate committee touching the affairs of his college. As the letter related, the former practice of the deans' transmitting their reports to members of the board had been discontinued, except under conditions that made their transmission uncertain, so the colleges not represented by committees found themselves at an increasing disadvantage. These reports should be transmitted to the trustees as formerly, for the purpose of laying before that body the fullest information.

"This is not a movement of the deans to secure more power during an interregnum;" the deans wrote, "but it is a frank statement of a desire to have adequate representation before your body, which determines policies." The affairs of the University were so diverse and its needs so complex that the time had come when their full and equal presentation could not reach the board through the medium of any one man alone, no matter what his opportunities for securing information and no matter how free he might be from personal bias.

Regarding the succession to the presidency, the deans expressed their deepest conviction that the person finally chosen should be "a man of broad and substantial scholarship, qualified by temperament and experience to comprehend and appreciate university standards, and to deal justly and intelligently with university men." In addition, he should have had "actual and successful experience with university administration under conditions not far different from those existing here, to the end that his policies regarding internal interests may be foretold with reasonable certainty." [9]

This letter is a strong indictment of the Board of Trustees for selecting and continuing to support Draper for ten years, and an even stronger criticism of Draper—a man limited by training, experience, and temperament to preside over a university.

On 28 April Forbes went to Chicago at the request of the deans for a conversation with President Hatch after a meeting of the Board of Trustees, and at Hatch's request Forbes had a long talk with trustees Bullard, Nightingale, and McLean. He gave them a paper—presumably it dealt with the organization of the University—that had been approved by the deans. According to the deans, the time was favorable and the necessity great for adopting a fundamental law of the University that should control all University authorities and not be subject to easy amendment. Older universities had traditions and precedents that made written constitutions unnecessary, but at Illinois "we have suffered greatly from sudden and serious changes of policy and from imperfect limitation and definition of powers and responsibilities throughout our whole organization." The deans wished to organize from the department up, not from the president's office down, and to lodge with each subordinate agency of the University all the functions that it could perform best and most intelligently, with the residue passed up to the next higher agency. By this process the president's office would finally be left "with those functions of general administration and coordination for which a president is necessary, and which, when fully performed, will make a great work for a great man, leaving the more special and less comprehensive duties to men more especially fitted by experience, training, and university association to discharge them easily and intelligently."[10]

In early June Draper returned to Urbana to end the school year—he met with the Board of Trustees over two days—and to preside over commencement week. On 7 June the trustees reversed their earlier decision and agreed to pay Draper his salary for the period from 1 April to 1 July. The board also voted that after 1 July Thomas J. Burrill should be acting president.[11]

On 10 June Draper responded to the deans in a letter to Burrill that Burrill showed the deans. No copy can be located, but the deans responded to Burrill fifteen days later, and we can infer the contents of Draper's letter from the deans' response.[12] Draper charged that the deans had expressed the view that the president should be merely the presiding officer and executive of the faculty, without executive independence or general authority essential to the University's organic unity. The deans had been unwilling to meet him in free conference on University affairs, and particularly on the choice of his successor. The deans had recently gone to the trustees, without notice to Draper, asking them to overturn the existing form of University government and complaining that the deans had been ignored or snubbed by Draper. They had failed to make to Draper on his departure from the University any expression, either personal or official, of respect, sympathy, or regard, and they had used their influence to stifle such expression from the faculty. They had availed themselves of the impending change in the presidency to belittle his office and to endeavor to enlarge their own functions and prerogatives as deans. They had "worn his life" unjustly and unnecessarily and had been angered when he had not followed their advice. They had conferred secretly together to embarrass his administration and "to send him to 'the martyr's realm' as had been done to his two predecessors."

In replying to Burrill, the deans explained that they wrote not for his own information but for such use as he might find desirable and expedient. In fact, they were writing for the benefit of Draper and the trustees.

Although not in the order described, the deans addressed many of the charges levied against them. As for the charges relating to Draper's presidency, the deans denied any intention "to minify" his services to the University or to the state, and they expressed full agreement with the resolution passed by the University Senate on 11 April. (That statement—composed by deans Forbes and Davenport; Charles M. Moss, professor of Greek, who had recommended Draper for the presidency; Lester P. Breckenridge, professor of mechanical engineering and a personal friend of Draper; and William M. Drew, professor of law—described advances made within the University during Draper's administration, carefully adding that in all this "progressive and constructive movement" the president had had "a large and influential share." By his dealings with the public, with neighboring colleges and universities, and with the public schools, the authors added, "Draper has impressed himself strongly on the life of this University and on the educational institutions of Illinois.")[13] The deans described Draper's statement of their position with reference to the functions of the president as "radically erroneous." They had never held or even discussed any such view as the one he imputed to them.

As for the charge of "conferring secretly together to embarrass President Draper's administration," the deans replied that they had never held conferences of any description until after his resignation, and the conferences held since had been directed solely toward bettering conditions after his resignation became effective. Burrill had participated in all these conferences and had been in full accord with the acts and conclusions of the deans.

On Draper's complaint that the college deans had lately withheld their confidence from him, they stated that they had stood, personally and as a body, "loyally by an administration in many of whose methods we did not believe, simply because it was the administration of the University, and because it seemed to us that its methods were the best possible under President Draper's leadership."

The implication that previous presidents had been sent to "the martyr's realm" by the faculty was quite contrary to the known facts. "We are not aware that any president of this University except Dr. Draper has had any serious or continued disagreement with the University Faculty."

In their letter the deans emphasized organization. They had no wish to overturn the existing system of University government but had merely proposed to certain trustees that its organization be made more complete and self-consistent and that its essential principles be formulated in a way to establish them securely as a University constitution. They differed from Draper with respect to the location of the primary emphasis in University work. He would place it in the administration; they would place it in the departments of instruction. "He would subordinate everything to 'smooth administration;' we would subordinate everything to effective educational work." Draper would concentrate all initiative and executive power in the person of the president, they would distribute it so that each University function should be performed by the agency with the fullest intelligence and the most experienced judgment concerning it. The deans restated the conviction that the University should be organized from the department up, but "this University has been organized from the President's office down, with the general idea that only those duties should be transmitted to other agencies which could not conveniently be performed by the President or any of his immediate aids."

Draper's statement that the essential principles of the University's existing system of administration had prevailed wherever a university had grown strong and great in this country was wholly unsupported by the facts. "Some of the greatest universities are democratic to the extreme in their organization and policy, and we doubt if another institution of the first importance can be found whose system of government is so despotic as our own." The University's system was more nearly that normal to a small college or high school than to a great and complex university.

The deans viewed the method of making up the budget of the University as "extremely crude and very unsatisfactory." In the absence of all knowledge of the funds available or the demands made by others on the common resources, estimates submitted by department heads and deans were sometimes far beyond what was possible or short of what was necessary, "varying according to the temperament of those making them, and according to their belief in their standing with the administration." The deans wanted a system of conferences on finances and needs of the various units such as found at Wisconsin and Michigan.

The deans added that their relations with Draper's office had been seriously affected by the fact that at a board meeting on 8 June 1903, Draper, without the knowledge of the deans or notice to them, officially charged them, in their absence, with putting into their reports matters with which they had no business, and with assuming to report to the trustees and to the public, whereas their reports were due to the president only. This charge of presumption and insubordination was wholly without foundation, said the deans. "It was deeply resented by us at the time, and finally destroyed our confidence in [Draper's] fairness and candor as a university officer."

Concluding, the deans expressed great regret that they had been compelled to take issue with the retiring president on matters of importance, and particularly that any element of personal feeling should have appeared in a discussion of what was, in substance, a difference of aims and ideals in the organization and conduct of the institution. The deans had acted in this matter carefully and conscientiously, uninfluenced by personal considerations, and controlled only by their regard for the future of a University to which they had given their best abilities "and which we believe to have just escaped a most serious danger, due to errors whose repetition or continuance we are bound to do our best in every way to prevent."[14]

In the deans Draper had more than met his match, and events raised the subject of university organization for discussion among the faculty. During the summer Forbes sought information from seven universities about their systems of organization and administration, and in later years the demand for a constitution for the University drew on this body of evidence.[15]

By late June 1904 Draper was gone but not forgotten. In December 1904, when a former student asked Kinley to request that Draper write on her behalf, he declined. "My relations with him are not such as to make it possible for me to write him a letter on any subject." And comparing Draper with his successor as president, Kinley said, "one does not feel, upon entering his office, that he must put himself on guard against insults."[16]

The new president, Edmund J. James, was installed in October 1905, and Draper was invited to speak on the subject of the University presidency at a conference of college and university trustees held at the time. Anticipating this event, and writing in confidence to Charles F. Mills of Springfield, Davenport said, "We all know substantially what he will say. He is an autocrat of autocrats, and so considered by educators over the country in general." Draper believed that all authority proceeded from the president's office and that nothing should be entrusted to others except as it was assigned to them. "This radical view is bitterly opposed by University people generally, not only here but elsewhere." People would assume that Draper spoke for the University in this matter, "which assumption would be entirely erroneous and must not go unchallenged." Faculty members would take some hand in the discussion if obliged to do so, but they preferred that it should be handled by outside parties. A Mr. Skiff, who was known to agree with the Illinois faculty on the point at issue, would receive an invitation to take part in this discussion, and if Mills would urge Skiff to accept he would render a great service.[17]

Samuel A. Bullard presided over the conference of trustees, and Draper opened the proceedings with his address.[18] In an article on this event published in the Boston *Transcript*, James P. Monroe, president of the Massachusetts Reform Club, described Draper's dictatorship at Illinois as an example of the successful work of an autocratic president. In reply, Kinley stated that the facts were to the contrary. The tremendous growth of the University began under the acting presidency of Burrill, and some important features of the University's development were carried through in spite of Draper. This was particularly true of the agricultural development. The University owed the establishment of the College of Law to Governor Altgeld, and Draper had done nothing to aid in establishing the University's courses in business training. Kinley need not mention other matters to illustrate the point. "Moreover, it is a pertinent question whether an administration can be looked upon as successful, when the man responsible for it leaves the institution with the dozen men who have been most closely associated with him in his work for ten years so alienated from him that they refuse to offer him the ordinary tribute of regret at his departure. Such was the case here."[19]

A month after Draper spoke at the installation, Kinley received an invitation to attend the second annual dinner of the University of Illinois Club of New York City. "It is not worth while for me to consider whether I could come," he replied, "as I see that on your program you have Dr. A. S. Draper, Commissioner of Education of New York. I will not appear on any program with Dr. Draper, anywhere. It would be embarrassing to him and to me, as well as to the rest of you, if we were to appear at the same dinner table."[20]

## THE AFTERMATH

The battle over power between Draper and the deans dealt with a matter of fundamental importance. Unfortunately, the dispute led to bitter personal relations that clouded the issue. Draper's insistence that communications to the governing board go through the president's office established a point essential to the welfare of the University. But the practical problem was not simple or clear-cut. The deans differed with Draper on policy. They concluded that educational advances at Illinois had to be carried out despite Draper's ignorance and over his opposition, and they did not trust him to relay their concerns fully and accurately to the trustees. To discharge their responsibilities they thought it essential to be able to transmit their reports to members of the board. To what extent the deans desired access to the trustees because of Draper's educational views as opposed to his autocratic methods is impossible to determine. Perhaps the two motives were so intermixed they cannot be disentangled.

Although the deans acknowledged that the president should be finally charged with matters of general university concern, they wanted the University organized from the departments up, not from the president's office downward. This was the heart of the matter. During the summer of 1904 Forbes and others drafted a constitution for the University, and on 12 August they informed Burrill what they wished to have incorporated into the University Statutes. They asked that the trustees maintain a standing committee for each college and that typewritten copies of the deans' reports dealing with matters that needed trustee action be forwarded in advance of board meetings to the members of such committees. Presumably the reports were to be forwarded by the office of the president, but the president could not deny the deans access to the trustees.[21]

This controversy surfaced during the administration of President James. At the 4 June 1907 meeting of the Board of Trustees, James noted that there might be some misunderstanding among members concerning transmission of certain reports from the dean to trustees in advance of meetings. He reminded the board of what had occurred during Draper's tenure: the 1899 policy of sending copies of the reports of the deans from the office of the president five days before quarterly meetings, and the 1903 reversal of that decision so as to allow the president to use his discretion in sending such reports to the board in advance of meetings. James described the policy of 1903 as "eminently proper," and declared that he would follow it.[22]

Draper, who followed events at the University closely, was glad that James had taken such a positive attitude about the matter. "The fact was," he wrote, "that the deans were trying to reduce the office of president to that of an unimportant way station on the road between themselves and the Board of Trustees."[23]

The conflict between Draper and the deans touched on vital matters. Draper was correct in insisting that communications to the governing board must go through the president's office, and the deans were correct in wanting fair and unbiased treatment for their colleges and in their conviction that such was impossible under Draper. Lacking an understanding of the nature of a university, Draper was the wrong man for the job. The situation had reached an impasse, and Draper's departure augured well for the future of the University.

## NOTES

1. *19th Report* (1898), 230–31, 235.
2. *22nd Report* (1904), 42. For his salary, see the "General University Warrants" starting on p. 340 in this volume.
3. Hatch to Draper, 27 January 1904, Bullard to Draper, 2 February 1904, 2/4/1, B:6, F:Hatch, B:1, F:Bullard.
4. Draper to Hatch, 29 January 1904, Draper to Bullard, 3 February 1904, Draper to Nightingale, 15 February 1904, 2/4/3.
5. Forbes to W. T. Sedgwick, 8 April 1904, 15/1/2.
6. Draper to J. A. Ockerson, 2 February 1904, 2/4/3.
7. *22nd Report* (1904), 262–64, 274–75.
8. Kinley to A. P. Winston, 10 March 1904, 15/1/4.
9. The deans to the Trustees of the University of Illinois, 21 March 1904, 2/5/6, B:1, F:University Organization and Administration, 1900–4.
10. Forbes to Kerrick, 30 April 1904, 15/1/2.
11. *22nd Report* (1904), 312–13, 325–26.
12. Draper was in Urbana until at least 14 June. His letterbook contains copies of letters he wrote on 9 and 11 June, but not the 10 June letter. An unsigned draft of the deans' letter to Burrill, dated 20 June 1904, is in 2/5/6, B:1, F:University Organization and Administration, 1900–4. See also Kinley to Ricker, 27 June 1904, 15/1/4.
13. 4/2/1, 1:76–77. On 14 June Draper received a note from Professor Arthur H. Daniels transmitting the resolution. Draper to Daniels, 18 June 1904, 2/6/1, President [Kinley's] General Correspondence, B:129, F:Historical Letters.
14. Forbes, Kinley, Davenport, and Ricker to Burrill, 25 June 1904, 15/1/2.
15. Forbes to Charles W. Woodworth (University of California); same to persons in Minnesota, Wisconsin, Michigan, Ohio State, Cornell, and Missouri, 18 June 1904, 15/1/2.
16. Kinley to Lucile A. Booker, 16 December 1904, Kinley to H. G. Paul, 21 December 1904, 15/1/4.
17. Davenport to Mills, 4 October 1905, 8/1/21.
18. Draper, "The University Presidency," in *Installation of Edmund Janes James . . . as President of the University of Illinois, October 15–21, 190[5]* (Urbana, 1906), 8–20 (published in the *Atlantic Monthly*, 97 [January 1906], 34–43).

19. Kinley to James P. Monroe, 17 November 1905, 15/1/4. But Draper was awarded an honorary LL.D.
20. Kinley to S. T. Henry, 17 November 1905, 15/1/4.
21. Forbes, Ricker, Kinley, Davenport, and Harker to Burrill, 12 August 1904, 2/5/6, B:1, F:University Organization and Administration, 1900–4.
22. *24th Report* (1908), 108.
23. Draper to James, 17 June 1907, 2/5/3, B:5, F:Draper, 1906–8.

# CHAPTER 18

# STRUCTURE
# WITHOUT SPIRIT

The University of Illinois was significantly transformed at the turn of the century. In 1890, after years of hardscrabble but productive endeavor, the institution was predominantly an engineering school, one that was neither well known nor highly regarded by the people of the state.

In the early 1890s, however, the Board of Trustees boldly resolved to chart a new course. Pursuing this goal, they began a search for a person to lead the way, wanting someone with both executive ability and a national reputation. In due time they selected Andrew S. Draper. John P. Altgeld, elected governor of Illinois in 1892, lent personal support to the board's determination to improve the University. A man of the people and the first Democrat to serve in the executive office since the University opened, Altgeld was determined to create a complete university and to make it the distinguished capstone of the public system of education in Illinois.

These converging forces enabled the University to acquire the structure of a modern university. The school's measurable growth in academic programs, buildings, enrollment, and financial resources was impressive. The School of Music, the School of Library Science, the Graduate School, the College of Law, the School of Pharmacy, the College of Medicine, and the School of Dentistry were all established in the decade between 1894 and 1904. The Library School was the fourth such school in the nation and the only one in the Midwest. The University was similarly a pioneer in offering courses in comparative literature, programs in chemical engineering and architectural

STRUCTURE WITHOUT SPIRIT ... 393

engineering, and a sabbatical leave policy. The University also pioneered in establishing the office of the dean of men and honor societies in chemistry and in both the law and medical schools. During the same decade the University established the Biological Experiment Station, the Water Survey, and the Engineering Experiment Station. Research at Illinois led to the development of hybrid corn and methods to increase soil fertility.

The property grew to accommodate the maturing enterprise. In 1896 the University consisted of six main buildings. During the next decade several buildings were acquired or rebuilt: Machinery Hall, the Mechanical and Electrical Engineering Laboratory, the Wood Shop and Foundry Building, the Laboratory of Applied Mechanics (the latter two replacing the Mechanical Building and Drill Hall, which had been destroyed by fire), and the Chemical Laboratory, a new building completed in 1903 and equipped over time. Among the more notable of the newly erected structures were the Library, the Agricultural Building, the Observatory, the Men's Gymnasium, and the President's House. Illinois Field was also carved out of the north campus and dedicated to the pursuit of physical culture. In Chicago, the University owned properties occupied by its schools of pharmacy and dentistry and the College of Medicine.

Enrollments pushed the physical expansion. In 1894–95 the student body at Urbana was 751, including 627 men and 124 women; by 1903–4 it was 2,181, representing 1,610 men and 571 women. In a decade's time the total enrollment had increased by 290 percent and the number of women enrolled had increased by 460 percent. In addition, the medical center enrolled 1,042 students—185 in pharmacy, 694 in medicine, and 163 in dentistry. The Urbana faculty had quadrupled—from 80 in 1894–95 to 351 in 1903–4.[1]

Growing financial resources helped fuel these dramatic advances. For the biennium 1895–97, the first in which Draper had a hand, the state appropriation yielded the University a total of $427,000. For the biennium 1903–5 the appropriation was $1,152,400, representing an increase of nearly 270 percent.

Such striking development was part of a nationwide phenomenon: Americans were beginning to realize the value of higher education and were sending their sons and daughters to college in ever increasing number. In 1894–95 Illinois was the fourteenth largest collegiate enterprise in the nation; in 1903–4 it ranked seventh nationally in undergraduate enrollment.[2]

Besides, Illinois was becoming increasingly attractive to women students. In 1894–95 women constituted 13 percent of the undergraduates at Urbana, whereas by 1903–4 they made up 28 percent of the undergraduates. In the latter year the proportion of women undergraduates in ten public universities with which Illinois compared itself ranged from 42 percent at California to 15 percent at Ohio State. Illinois ranked eighth in this group of eleven.[3]

A graduate school and research were distinguishing features of the emerging order in higher education, and the number of resident graduates is an index to the evolution of an institution as a complete university. By 1903–4 Illinois was eighth out of the eleven public universities in the sample. This ranking registered the fact that Illinois lagged in developing a commitment to research. It would be difficult to make up lost ground.[4]

A well-stocked library is essential to a worthy graduate program, and by 1903–4 Illinois was in the middle of the sample group of peer institutions.[5]

American universities, unlike those elsewhere in the world, were becoming more than merely academic institutions at the turn of the century. Among the features that made American schools unique were the conspicuous places of secret societies and intercollegiate athletics in collegiate culture. Draper believed that a university had to go with the flow, and during his tenure both fraternities and football became prominent at Illinois. The atmosphere of the University, a public institution, was conducive to religious faith. In the number of students engaged in Bible study the Illinois YMCA led the collegiate institutions of North America.

These transformations gave the institution the shape of a university. How do we account for such remarkable changes? Draper and his partisans were eager to magnify his role in the achievement, but much of the reconstruction was the product of intellectual, cultural, and socioeconomic forces at work in the nation. With the university replacing the college as the characteristic form of American higher education, more young people were continuing their education beyond high school, and the specialization of knowledge was giving rise to graduate education and professional schools. Governor Altgeld deserves considerable credit for the advances made.

Although Draper presided over the University during a period of tremendous growth, Dean Kinley, who had been with the University since 1893, accurately noted that the growth of the University began under the acting presidency of Burrill from 1891 to 1894, and that some important features of the University's development were carried through in spite of Draper.[6]

After Draper resigned, the University Senate placed on record its appreciation of the "distinguished service" he had rendered to the University and to the state during the period of his administration. Admitting that Draper's tenure had been "a time of unbroken prosperity and rapid growth," the resolution described the creation of new buildings, the establishment of new schools and departments, the increase in the number of students and instructors, and a remarkable enlargement in the state appropriation to the University. "In all this progressive and constructive movement," the authors added, choosing their words carefully, "the President of the University has had a large and influential share."

The resolution testified to Draper's personal qualities—his "manly public addresses," his knowledge of public affairs and his acquaintance with public men, his courageous temper in meeting all issues, and the cordial relations he had sustained with neighboring colleges and universities and with the public schools.[7]

Draper was an able man with many splendid qualities. In the prime of life while at Illinois, he had an imposing physical presence and was supremely self-confident. He wrote and spoke with facility and was effective in dealing with the state's General Assembly. As a university president, however, he had serious limitations. He had no experience in university administration when he took office, and he disparaged disinterested research and made no significant contribution to its development on the campus. He was not the prime mover in the establishment of the professional schools in law and the medical sciences. He opposed the rebirth of the College of Agriculture, he did nothing to aid in establishing the University's courses in business training, and he did little to develop the liberal arts. Aggravating matters, Draper believed that all authority should be concentrated in his office, and he ruled with an autocratic hand. He had a running battle with his deans over the power to determine policy within the University, and resolution of this problem could not have long been deferred.

Draper's presidency needs to be seen in perspective. He was the agent of the Board of Trustees, a body that wanted as president a man with a national reputation and executive ability and got a schoolman, an administrator with the ability to impress others. Trustees could not have known in advance how effective Draper would be in office. After Draper took over, however, the board continued to support him. Although they did not allow Draper to prevent the rebirth of the College of Agriculture, they followed his lead in dealing with the problem of authority within the University. And despite repeated requests, the board neither formulated a policy on research nor directed Draper to do so.

Granted, the lack of funds conditioned every policy choice. But Draper did not operate openly and fairly in distributing the available resources. The board allowed him to play favorites, notably in advancing Thomas Arkle Clark. And it approved his quixotic proposal to spend $250 to domesticate squirrels on the campus. Shortly after Draper left, the Committee on Instruction reported that it "found the [faculty] salary list extending over a series of years full of incongruities and inconsistencies."[8]

Draper always put the best possible face on things. He had access to board members, and he was skillful in giving them his version of events. In all likelihood the board was not aware of the internal bitterness that existed well before Draper announced his resignation.

In fairness, it must be noted that the Board of Trustees was the agent of the people of Illinois. The state had been settled by people from the Southeast who had little or no tradition of public support for education. Illinois was late among the states in establishing publicly supported common schools, a normal school, and a university. The unwillingness to pay for a state system of public education persisted. In the 1890s, however, the Board of Trustees began to ask for more state support for the University. Even though Draper and the trustees did comparatively well in obtaining appropriations, the state still did not adequately support the University. As Thomas J. Burrill often said, the people of Illinois, the empire state of the West, had the resources to do whatever they wished. But a leader who could mobilize the state to provide the resources to develop a leading national university had not yet emerged.

By the spring of 1904 the University had the structure if not the spirit of a modern university. The foundations had been laid. The University was poised for take-off. Under a new leader, a native son of Illinois who thoroughly understood the nature of the modern university, the University of Illinois would soon become a leading American university.

## NOTES

1. Enrollment figures for Urbana are compiled from the records of the Board of Trustees; the figures for the medical center are from Edwin E. Slosson, *Great American Universities* (New York: MacMillan, 1910), 311. Data on the faculty are from the *Alumni Record*, lxxxi.
2. House of Representatives, 58th Cong., 3d sess., doc. 5, *Report of the Commissioner of Education* [for the fiscal year ended 30 June 1904], 2 vols. (Washington: GPO, 1905), 2:1472–88. On Illinois enrollment, I cite the figures in the minutes of the board. The schools larger than Illinois in rank order were Harvard, Wisconsin, California, Yale, Michigan, and Minnesota.
3. Ibid. The U.S. Commissioner of Education reported women as 26 percent of the undergraduates. For the comparable universities, see the next note.
4. *Report of the Commissioner of Education*, 2:1472–88. In rank order California, Iowa, Nebraska, Minnesota, Michigan, Wisconsin, and Indiana surpassed Illinois in number of resident graduates. Kansas, Missouri, and Ohio State trailed.
5. Ibid., 2:1508–24. Libraries at Michigan, California, Minnesota, and Wisconsin outranked Illinois. Missouri, Nebraska, Iowa, Ohio, Indiana, and Kansas followed.
6. Kinley to S. T. Henry, 17 November 1905, 15/1/4.
7. 4/2/1, 11 April 1904.
8. *21st Report* (1902), 107; *23rd Report* (1906), 39.

# INDEX